Discourse Theory in European Politics

*Also by David Howarth*

South African Transition Discourse

*Also by Jacob Torfing*

Politics, Regulation and the Modern Welfare State (1998)

New Theories of Discourse (1999)

# Discourse Theory in European Politics

## Identity, Policy and Governance

Edited by

David Howarth

*Lecturer in Political Theory, University of Essex, UK*

and

Jacob Torfing

*Professor of Politics and Institutions, Roskilde University, Denmark*

palgrave
macmillan

First published 2005 by
PALGRAVE MACMILLAN
Houndmills, Basingstoke, Hampshire RG21 6XS and
175 Fifth Avenue, New York, N.Y. 10010
Companies and representatives throughout the world

PALGRAVE MACMILLAN is the global academic imprint of the Palgrave Macmillan division of St. Martin's Press, LLC and of Palgrave Macmillan Ltd. Macmillan® is a registered trademark in the United States, United Kingdom and other countries. Palgrave is a registered trademark in the European Union and other countries.

ISBN 0–333–96843–3 hardback
ISBN 1–4039–1719–1 paperback

This book is printed on paper suitable for recycling and made from fully managed and sustained forest sources.

A catalogue record for this book is available from the British Library.

Library of Congress Cataloging-in-Publication Data
Discourse theory in European politics : identity, policy and governance / edited by David Howarth and Jacob Torfing.
p. cm.
Includes bibliographical references and index.
ISBN 0–333–96843–3 — ISBN 1–4039–1719–1 (pbk.)
1. Europe—Politics and government—1989– 2. Discourse analysis—Political aspects. I. Howarth, David R. II. Torfing, Jacob.

JN8.D57 2005
320.94′01—dc22

2004051403

10 9 8 7 6 5 4 3 2 1
14 13 12 11 10 09 08 07 06 05

Printed and bound in Great Britain by
Antony Rowe Ltd, Chippenham and Eastbourne

*In memory of our mothers*

*'So you want another story?'*

*'Uhh . . . perhaps in English. In Japanese a story would have an element of* invention *in it. We don't want any invention. We want the "straight facts", as you say in English.'*

*'Isn't telling about something – using words, English or Japanese – already something of an invention? Isn't just looking upon this world already something of an invention?'*

*'Uhh . . .'*

*'The world isn't just the way it is. It is how we understand it, no? And in understanding something, we bring something to it, no? Doesn't that make life a story?'*

(Yann Martel, *Life of Pi*)

# Contents

# Notes on Contributors

**Niels Åkerstrøm Andersen** is a professor at Copenhagen Business School, Denmark. He is currently working on system theory and discourse analysis in relation to public governance and administration. He has published several books on theoretical, methodological, and empirical aspects of discourse analysis.

**Steven Bastow** is a senior lecturer in Politics at Kingston University, London. He has published a number of articles and book chapters on Déat and the contemporary French extreme right. He is currently working on Third Way discourse in inter-war France and on the contemporary French radical right.

**Lilie Chouliariaki** is Associate Professor at the Copenhagen Business School, Denmark, and co-ordinator of the CBS Media Hub. She has published widely on pedagogic discourse, as well as media discourse and national identity. Her books include *Discourse in Late Modernity: Rethinking Critical Discourse Analysis* (co-authored with Norman Fairclough).

**Anthony M. Clohesy** teaches Politics at the University of Essex. His current research concerns Third Way politics and Irish nationalism from a discourse theory perspective, and he has published a series of papers and chapters on these issues.

**Steven Griggs** is a lecturer in Public Policy at Birmingham University in the UK. He has published articles on developments in French health policy and politics, and is currently studying the mobilization and decision-making process surrounding direct action campaigns in the UK. He is the co-author of *French Politics: Debates and Controversies* (2000).

**Maarten A. Hajer** is Professor of Public Policy and Political Science in the Department of Political Studies of the University of Amsterdam. His previous publications include *The Politics of Environmental Discourse* (1995); *Living with Nature* (1999) edited with Frank Fischer; *In Search of the New Public Domain* (with Arnold Reijndorp, 2001); and *Deliberative Policy Analysis* (2003, co-edited with Hendrik Wagenaar).

**Allan Dreyer Hansen** is an associate professor in Public Administration, at Roskilde University. His research interests include discourse theory, democratic theory, and local political participation and institutions. He is a co-founder of the Danish Centre for Discourse Theory, and he has published several articles and books of discourse theory and social constructivism.

**David Howarth** is a lecturer in Political Theory in the Department of Government at the University of Essex, where he is currently Director of the Doctoral Programme in Ideology and Discourse Analysis. His publications include *Discourse* (2000); *South Africa in Transition: New Theoretical Perspectives* (1998); and *Discourse Theory and Political Analysis: Identities, Hegemonies and Social Change* (2000). He has also published numerous articles and chapters on theories on discourse, post-Marxist political theory and its application to empirical cases, most notably South African politics and new environmental movements.

**James Martin** is a senior lecturer in Politics at Goldsmiths College, University of London. He is author of *Gramsci's Political Analysis: a Critical Introduction* (1998) and co-author of *Contemporary Social and Political Theory: an Introduction* (1999). He has published on Gramsci in various journals and is currently working on theories of civil society. In addition to interests in Italian politics and political theory, he edits the Newsletter of the PSA specialist group for Post-Structuralism and Radical Politics.

**Véronique Mottier** is a FNS Research Professor at the University of Lausanne and a Fellow of Jesus College, Cambridge. Her books include *Politics of Sexuality: Identity, Gender, Citizenship* (1998), edited with T. Carver; *Genre et politique: débats et perspectives* (2000), co-edited with T.-H. Ballmer-Cao and L. Sgier; and *French Social Theory: From Merleau-Ponty to Bourdieu* (forthcoming).

**Oscar Reyes** is currently completing his PhD in the Department of Government at the University of Essex. He has published articles and chapters on different aspects of British politics.

**Eva Sørensen** is a professor in Public Administration at Roskilde University, Denmark. She is currently working on governance theory, local democracy, and transformation of political identity. She has published extensively in this area and is director of a major research project on the changing identities of politicians and bureaucrats in the face of new forms of governance.

**Yannis Stavrakakis** is Visiting Research Fellow in the Department of Government at the University of Essex. He is author of *Lacan and the Political* (1999) and co-editor of *Discourse Theory and Political Analysis* (2000) and *Lacan & Science* (2002).

**Jacob Torfing** is a professor in Politics and Institutions, at Roskilde University, Denmark. He is currently working on discourse theory, welfare reform and the democratic implications of new forms of governance. His books include *New Theories of Discourse* (1999) and *Politics, Regulation, and the Modern Welfare State* (1995). He is co-founder of the Danish Centre for Discourse Theory and director of the Centre for Democratic Network Governance. He has published several articles and books on discourse theory and its use in political science.

**Patrick de Vos** has completed his doctorate at the Belgian Ghent University where he was a teaching and research assistant in political science. He has previously published articles on right-wing extremism, social democracy, post-feminism, discourse analysis, and labour relations. His current research interests include globalization and the welfare state, social democratic neo-revisionism, populism, and discourse theoretical approaches to political analysis.

**Ole Wæver** is Professor in International Politics at the University of Copenhagen, Denmark. He is a co-founder of the Copenhagen School in Security Politics and he is currently working on international politics, security theory, and EU integration. He is a board member of several international journals and he has written extensively on post-structuralism and international politics. His books include *Identity, Migration and the New Security Agenda in Europe* (1993) and *Security: a New Framework for Analysis* (1998).

# Acknowledgements

This volume is the product of a collaborative intellectual adventure that began many years ago when the editors studied together in the Ideology and Discourse Theory Programme in the Department of Government at the University of Essex. This programme, which was founded and directed by the inspirational figure of Professor Ernesto Laclau, has provided the editors of this book, and a number of its contributors, with a rich set of intellectual tools to conduct social and political analysis. This volume extends this research programme by bringing together and engaging with a number of different approaches to discourse theory and analysis, with a view to disclosing commonalities, divergences, and future directions.

As the contributors will themselves attest, the book itself crystallizes a series of ongoing conversations, discussions, and exchanges that began some three years ago. Many of the contributors participated in two specifically convened workshops at the universities of Essex and Roskilde, respectively, in order to discuss and comment on the chapters included in the volume. In between, there have been innumerable communications between editors and contributors about the arguments presented below. As editors, we should like to thank the contributors for their cheery patience in dealing with our many queries, comments, and urgings.

In this regard, we should particularly like to thank Louise Piel Christensen for organizing the Danish workshop, as well as the Department of Social Sciences at Roskilde University for hosting it, and the Danish Social Science Research Council for providing the necessary funding. The editors would also like to acknowledge the support of the Department of Government at the University of Essex, which has again gone beyond the call of duty to support this project. The editors would also like to thank David Traynier for his excellent reading of the entire text and Peter Andrews for his copy-editing.

# Discourse Theory: Achievements, Arguments, and Challenges

*Jacob Torfing*

## Introduction

During the last decade there has been mounting interest in various kinds of discourse theory and discourse analysis within what we can broadly define as the social sciences. This is evidenced by the growing number of publications, workshops, conference panels, university courses, and dissertations that draw on the intellectual resources of discourse theory. Some countries and subdisciplines have been more susceptible than others to the influence of the new theories of discourse. In some places, discourse theory has almost become the dominant paradigm, while in other places it has remained marginal. However, very few areas of research have been able to withstand the impact of its new ideas.

Discourse theory emerged in the late 1970s as an intellectual response to the problematization of mainstream theory in the wake of May 1968, the critique of the structuralist theories of language, culture and society, and the crisis of Marxism in the face of the emerging neoliberal and neoconservative hegemony. Discourse theory did not, however, attempt to provide a new theoretical apparatus, consisting of a set of core assumptions, some clearly defined concepts and taxonomies, and a series of ready-made arguments disclosing the mechanisms of a rapidly changing society. Instead, it offered a new analytical perspective which focused on the rules and meanings that condition the construction of social, political, and cultural identity. The analytical tools, in terms of concepts, arguments, and ideas, were developed in specific theoretical and empirical contexts and their general validity was limited and conditional upon endless adjustments and reinterpretations. The open, contingent, and theoretically polyvalent character of the new theories of discourse attracted a great number of scholars who, in discourse theory, found an undogmatic framework for exploring new intellectual avenues based on post-structuralist and postmodernist insights.

Over the years, many excellent books have been published, which aim to develop different theoretical and philosophical aspects of discourse theory.

The scholarly texts on discourse theory are abundant, and during the last couple of years we have even seen the publication of text books trying to explain the concepts and arguments of discourse theory to a larger audience (see Howarth, 2000; Torfing, 1999). There has also been a growing number of empirical studies of discourse (Howarth, Norval, and Stavrakakis, 2000; Dyrberg, Hansen, and Torfing, 2000). However, there is still a dearth of books in the social sciences that systematically deploy a connected body of theory and methods in empirical studies of mainstream topics. Many books are either theoretical or empirical, and those that aim to connect theoretical and empirical studies often fail to reflect on methodological issues. This is a serious problem since the lack of exemplary studies showing how to conduct a discourse analysis prevents a more widespread application of discourse theory amongst social scientists and hinders dialogue with people from other theoretical quarters who want to assess the validity of the results of discourse analytical studies.

This volume aims to tackle this problem by drawing together a number of original empirical case studies conducted by a group of young but distinguished discourse theorists from four different European countries. The book focuses on political science in the broad sense of the term. As such, it covers a wide set of mainstream topics, including administrative reforms and policy analysis, eugenics, mass media debate, constitutional law, and security politics. Each author will briefly explain the theoretical point of departure for their problem-oriented study of an empirical case, and reflect on the methodological aspects of their discourse analysis.

The book is intended to summarize and take stock of the present state of discourse theory in relation to politics and political developments in Europe. It addresses a wide audience that includes theoreticians and empiricists, discourse enthusiasts and sympathetic critics, and established researchers and advanced graduate students. Our hope is that the book will stimulate both theoretical and empirical studies and help to develop critical reflection about methodology and the conduct of theoretically informed empirical studies of social, political, and cultural discourses.

## Achievements

Fifteen years ago, discourse theorists were few and far between. They constituted a small exotic sect with a strong group identity that was fed by the daily dose of scorn and ridicule from their colleagues. This picture has dramatically changed. Today discourse theory is highly popular among academics and graduate students and constitutes a well-recognized branch of social and political science. For example, discourse theory now has its own summer school programme within the European Consortium of Political Research (ECPR), and it runs its own stream of panels at many of the big political science conferences. This was unthinkable only a decade ago.

Discourse theory comes in many shapes and colours reflecting different traditions, disciplines, and ontologies. This book focuses on the post-structuralist version of discourse theory which has been the dominant version within political science. Post-structuralist discourse theory provides a serious challenge to mainstream theory, but its support amongst political scientists is unevenly distributed. In countries such as Britain and Denmark post-structuralist discourse theory is one of the predominant intellectual currents and has a strong organizational support. In other countries such as the Netherlands, Germany, Greece, and Austria discourse theory is also strong and well represented amongst political scientists. France has its own peculiar tradition for discourse theory, which is much stronger within philosophy and sociology than in political science. Countries like Italy and Spain appear to be less inclined towards discourse theory, although exceptions to this rule exist.

If we look outside of Europe we must recognize the impact of the large number of students from the PhD-programme at the University of Essex, who return either to South Africa or to countries in Latin America, where they make hard efforts to spur interest in post-structuralist discourse theory. The USA constitutes a special case. Many North American academics like Judith Butler (1990), William Connolly (1991), and Mark Poster (1990) were captured by French post-structuralism and developed a strong interest in theoretical and ontological questions. However, in the USA, a large group of political sociologists fashioned a discourse theoretical approach that combined post-structuralist ideas with basic methodological insights from the highly influential currents of symbolic interactionism and ethnomethodology (see Eliasoph, 1998; Gumbrium and Holstein, 1997; Reinarman, 1987).

Post-structuralist discourse theory has transformed itself from an intellectual curiosity to a well-established political science research programme. However, we should remember that increasing support is by no means the same as academic and scholarly achievement. The scornful critics of yesterday will no doubt still be prepared to accuse discourse theory of being a trendy jargon that fails to deliver new plausible insights and undermines scientific beliefs in truth and reality. The more sympathetic critics will buy large parts of the argument of discourse theory, but point out a number of gaps theoretically and, empirically, areas of benign neglect. We shall return to the response to the first type of critique in a short while. To the second and more friendly accusation we shall plead guilty. Post-structuralist discourse theory is a young, open, and unfinished research programme and there is still a lot of work to be done before it can claim to constitute a fully fledged paradigm with a distinctive set of theoretical concepts, research strategies, and methods. However, in at least three different ways, discourse theory has already had a significant impact on the social sciences in general and political science in particular.

First of all, it has produced a range of rather sophisticated concepts and arguments that help us to transcend the objectivistic, reductionist, and rationalistic bias of modern social science theory and radicalize hermeneutic alternatives by emphasizing the role of discourse and politics in shaping social, political, and cultural interpretations. If the concepts and arguments of discourse theory have notoriously failed to meet the modernist quest for conceptual clarity and rigour, it is because they are not derived from axiomatic higher order assumptions, but are developed in and through a contextual engagement with preexisting discourses of both academics and lay people. Another reason is that they try to conceptualize phenomena which are just as *necessary* as they are *impossible* (Laclau, 2000). Meaning itself is necessary since without the ability to confer meaning on social phenomena and political events we would not be able to orient ourselves and act upon our orientations. However, at the same time, meaning is also impossible because it is constructed within relational ensembles that are subject to endless displacements and constant disruptions. To conceptualize the shaping and reshaping of social and political meanings is, therefore, a hard task that often precludes clear definitions and self-explanatory categories.

Secondly, discourse theory has contributed to the critical renewal of many different disciplines, including IR-theory, EU-studies, public administration, mass media analysis, cultural geography, and urban studies. Many of these fields of study have suffered from the use of overly simplistic models of human action and functionalist explanations of structural changes, in both cases often backed by a purely quantitative analysis. Where, occasionally, hermeneutic approaches have aimed to provide a sound alternative to mainstream theory, the problem has often been that the qualitative studies of the actors' interpretations of their context and interests have lapsed into an impressionistic descriptivism that lacks a solid theoretical underpinning. In both cases discourse theory has something to offer, and in many disciplines and subdisciplines discourse theory has resulted in an analytical reorganization around theoretically informed analyses of discursively constructed identities and structures.

Thirdly, discourse theory has persuaded many mainstream theorists to pay attention to new issues such as knowledge paradigms, identity formation, and the discursive construction of sedimented norms, values, and symbols. Hence, policy analysts tend to recognize the importance of paradigmatic frameworks of knowledge for the identification and solution of policy problems. Organization theorists tend to acknowledge the importance of the symbolic construction of identity of organizational actors in their assessment of their interests and preferences. Finally, students of political change pay increasing attention to the path-dependence that is produced by sedimented meaning structures that define what it is appropriate to do in a certain situation. In other words, what we see today is not a sharp division between positivistic behaviourists and radical constructivists, but rather an open discussion about the impact of discursive forms of knowledge, identity, and rule-following. In this ongoing debate there are no strict dividing lines, as the theoretical positions are scattered along a continuum stretching from rational choice institutionalism to post-structuralist discourse theory. Although discourse theory is not solely responsible for the fruitful softening of the sharp frontiers in political science, it has no doubt exerted a huge influence on mainstream theory. It might be the case that some professors from the 'old school' are only flirting with the notion of discourse. It signals a new openness, however, and we should bear in mind that new notions permit new thing to happen.

In sum, post-structuralist discourse theory has had a significant impact, despite its lack of paradigmatic completion. Its impact should not be exaggerated and some of the results are precarious and subject to counter-strategies on the part of the social and political science establishment. However, post-structuralist discourse theory has gained a self-perpetuating momentum. It is here to stay.

## Three generations of discourse theory

Discourse theory emerged as a cross-disciplinary attempt to integrate central insights from linguistics and hermeneutics with key ideas from social and political science. This endeavour was prompted by the growing recognition of the intertwining of language and politics in the process of societal transformation. Social and political events change our vocabulary, and linguistic ambiguities and rhetorical innovations facilitate the advancement of new political strategies and projects.

This important insight was a result of a mixture of empirical and analytical developments in the 1970s and early 1980s. The events following in the wake of May 1968 aimed to liberate subjugated knowledges from the repressive grip of the dominant ideology and challenged the traditional understanding of politics in terms of the activities of elected politicians and their administrative advisers. The critique of structuralist theories revealed the mutual interaction of, on the one hand, social, economic, and linguistic structures and, on the other hand, social and political agency. Finally, the neoliberal and neoconservative hegemony of Margaret Thatcher and Ronald Reagan exposed the inherent problems of Marxism, in terms of its economic determinism and class reductionism, and called for a renewed focus on the political and moral-intellectual struggles for the hearts and minds of the population. All these developments added up to the basic understanding that 'discourse matters' and 'politics matter', and discourse theory emerged exactly in order to flesh out the analytical consequences of this understanding.

A quick look at the burgeoning literature on discourse theory and discourse analysis shows that there are many kinds of discourse theory, which vary both according to their understanding of discourse and their understanding of the imbrication of language and political power struggles (see Torfing, 2004).

Generally speaking, it is possible to identify at least three different generations or traditions.

The *first generation* of discourse theory defines discourse in the narrow linguistic sense of a textual unit that is larger than a sentence, and focuses on the semantic aspects of spoken or written text. In this early generation of discourse theory we find theories focusing on the individual speakers' actual use of language. *Socio-linguistics* (Downes, 1984) analyses the relation between the speakers' socioeconomic status and their vocabulary, while *content analysis* (Holsti, 1969) analyses their usage of particular words, word classes, and word combinations. We also find various forms of *conversation analysis* (Schegloff and Sacks, 1993; Sinclair and Coulthards, 1975; Atkinson and Heritage, 1984) that draw on the sociological method of ethnomethodology in their analysis of the organization of linguistic interaction, for instance, the rules governing initiation and conclusion of conversations, turn taking, choice and change of topics, and the sequence of sentences.

*Discourse psychology* (Labov and Franchel, 1977; Potter and Wetherell, 1987) also analyses formal and informal dialogues. Inspired by the speech-act theory developed within analytical philosophy (Austin, 1975), however, it shifts the focus from the organizational features of conversations to the strategies of the speakers. The speakers want to achieve something in and through the conversation, and they aim to realize their intentions by changing the framing and style of the dialogue. Whereas discourse psychology confines itself to the analysis of spoken language, the *critical linguists* at the University of East Anglia (Fowler et al., 1979) broaden the semantic analysis of discourse to include both spoken and written language. They share with the French ideology theorist Michel Pêcheux (1982) an interest in how discourse, through the choice and combination of linguistic expressions and styles, produces a particular representation of reality, and they aim to show that processes of representation often result in ideological misrepresentation of reality.

The linguistic bias of the first generation means that there is no attempt within sociolinguistics, content analysis, and conversation analysis to link the analysis of discourse with the analysis of politics and power struggles. However, the focus on the strategies of the speakers in discourse psychology and the focus on ideological distortion in critical linguistics makes it possible to analyse the repressive effects of different forms of discourse. Unfortunately, both of these early discourse theories are trapped in a purely linguistic analysis of the semantic aspects of discourse, and the notions of ideology and power remain undertheorized.

The *second generation* of discourse theory defines discourse in a broader way than the first generation. Discourse is not restricted to spoken and written language, but is extended to a wider set of social practices. *Critical Discourse Analysis* (CDA), which is developed most consistently by Norman Fairclough (1992, 1995), is inspired by Michel Foucault's analysis of the discursive practices that form subjects and objects, but explicitly rejects his quasi-transcendental conception of discourse (Fairclough, 1992, pp. 38–9). Discourse is defined as an empirical collection of practices that qualify as discursive in so far as they contain a semiotic element. Hence, discourse is reduced to a subset of a broader range of social practices. It includes all kinds of linguistically mediated practices in terms of speech, writing, images, and gestures that social actors draw upon in their production and interpretation of meaning. Discursive practices are said to be ideological in so far as they contribute to the naturalization of contingently constructed meanings. Social classes and ethnic groups produce ideological discourses in order to maintain their hegemonic power, or establish a counter-hegemony. Hence, ideological discourse contributes not only to the reproduction of social and political order but also to its transformation. In this way CDA clearly demonstrates the power effects of discourse. However, CDA is unclear about how to understand the relation between discourse and its non-discursive contexts. Its reliance on critical realism (Bhaskar, 1978; Sayer, 1984) tends to reduce discourse to a linguistic mediation of the events that are produced by the causal powers and mechanisms embedded in the independently existing structure of society. This significantly reduces the explanatory power of discourse analysis.

*Michel Foucault* also defines discourse in terms of a wide set of social practices. But instead of focusing on the actual form and content of linguistic statements and semiotic practices, Foucault (1985) takes one step back and focuses on the rules governing the production of such statements and practices. He is concerned neither with the truth nor the meaning of actual statements, but with their discursive conditions of possibility. Hence, he draws our attention to the 'rules of formation' that regulate what can be said, how it can be said, who can speak and in which name, and what kind of strategies that can be realized at the level of discourse. In contrast to CDA, Foucault maintains that all practices are discursive in the sense that they are shaped by discursive rules of formation that vary in time and space. However, influenced by the Marxist legacy, Foucault insists, in his early, *archaeological writings*, that the discursive rules of formation are conditioned by non-discursive relations. However, the criteria for distinguishing the discursive real from the non-discursive, and the exact nature of the conditioning of the former by the latter, remain unclear.

Foucault is less concerned with the distinction between the discursive and the non-discursive in his *genealogical writings* (Foucault, 1986a, 1986c, 1986d). In these later writings, he attempts to distance himself from the quasi-structuralist account of discourse, found in his early, archaeological writings, by paying more attention to the power struggles that shape and reshape particular discursive formations. Foucault's power analytics replaces the classical notion of sovereign power, which basically conceives power as dominance and repression, with a new notion of discursive power that emphasizes the productive aspects of power (Foucault, 1990). Power is neither a relation of dominance, nor a capacity to act, but the 'conduct of conduct' which refers to the ways in which discourse regulates actions by means of shaping the identities, capacities, and relations of subordination of the social actors. Hence, power and discourse are mutually constitutive and we cannot have one without the other. This makes Foucault the antidote to Jürgen Habermas (1987, 1990, 1992), who also tends to label his work discourse theory. Whereas Habermas wants to eliminate power in order to realize his ideal of a communicative rationality, Foucault claims that both communication and rationality is constituted in and through discursive power struggles.

The *third generation* of discourse theory further extends the notion of discourse so that it now covers all social phenomena. These are discursive because their meaning depends upon a decentred system of contingently constructed rules and differences. Discourse no longer refers to a particular part of the overall social system, but is taken to be coterminous with the social. This view is, for example, found in the works of *Jacques Derrida*. Hence, Derrida (1978) claims that the consequence of giving up the metaphysical idea of a transcendental centre that structures the entire structure while itself escaping structuration is that everything becomes discourse. Hence, when we discard the idea of an underlying essence that is given in and by itself, the social identities are no longer fixed once and for all with reference to a determining centre. As a result the play of meaning extends infinitely, and an endless displacement of limited and provisional centres begins. In short: social meaning becomes partially fixed in and through discourse.

Other *post-structuralist writers* share the basic view of social identity as constructed in and through decentred discursive systems. Hence, despite their differences, people like Roland Barthes, Julia Kristeva, and Jacques Lacan all subscribe to a broad understanding of discourse as a relational system of signifying practices that is produced through historical and ultimately political interventions and provides a contingent horizon for the construction of any meaningful object. Whereas the post-structuralist thinkers have arrived at this broad notion of discourse through a deconstruction of the traditional concept of structure as a closed and centred totality, other distinguished philosophers have developed similar notions by following other deconstructive paths. As such, the notion of 'language games' in the postanalytical philosophy of Ludwig Wittgenstein (1953) and the assertion of 'the contingency of language, communities and selves' found in the neopragmatist philosophy of Richard Rorty (1989) points in the same direction. In some respects the notion of communication in the systems theory of Niklas Luhman (1995) has clear affinities with the post-structuralist notion of discourse. Even in the open and undogmatic Marxism of Antonio Gramsci (1971) we find concepts and arguments that come close to, or at least tend to imply, a broad notion of discourse.

The British-based political theorists *Ernesto Laclau and Chantal Mouffe* (1982, 1985, 1987) have aimed to draw together all these different theories that belong to the third generation of discourse theory in order to develop a synthetic post-Marxist, post-structuralist, and postmodern political theory. They have engaged in critical but constructive debates with all the major scholars and theories in the field and have attempted to translate the different theoretical insights into a coherent framework that can serve as a starting point of social and political analysis.

Laclau and Mouffe have elaborated a synthetic third generation theory which is both a development of and a departure from the second generation. Hence, they agree with Foucault's insistence on the internal relation between power and discourse, and they define discourse in the quasi-transcendental terms of the historically variable conditions of possibility of what we say, think, imagine, and do. However, they take issue with, and ultimately abandon, the unsustainable distinction between the discursive and the non-discursive. They argue that the seemingly non-discursive phenomena like technology, institutions, and economic processes are ultimately constructed in and through discursive systems of difference and from that they draw the conclusion that discourse is co-extensive with the social (Laclau and Mouffe, 1985).

As for their relation to Fairclough and his Critical Discourse Analysis there is not much to say. Laclau and Mouffe reject the naturalist ontology implicit in the idea that discourse is somehow determined by extra-discursive powers at the level of the economy or the state, and they have strong reservations about the emphasis that Fairclough, inspired by the theory of structuration by Anthony Giddens (1984), puts on the actions and reflexivity of human agents in reproducing and transforming the social world. However, when it comes to the actual analysis of social and political discourse, the differences between Fairclough and Laclau and Mouffe are small. Many of Fairclough's analytical notions and categories for analysing concrete discourse and distinguishing between different types and genres of discourse can be used in conjunction with concepts from post-structuralist discourse theory.

In sum, as we pass through the three generations of discourse theory we clearly see a gradual development towards a more inclusive and quasi-transcendental notion of discourse and towards a broader constructivist notion of power. This development is not governed by an inherent telos, and is not the end of history. Rather, it is a result of contingent intellectual articulations that open a variety of future paths of development.

## The genealogy of post-structuralist discourse theory

The post-structuralist notion of discourse in Foucault, Derrida, and Laclau and Mouffe has its distant root in the classical transcendental philosophy of Immanuel Kant (Laclau, 1993). Against the sceptical empiricism of David Hume, Kant argued that perception and experience of empirical phenomena are made possible by some pregiven categories in the human mind. Discourse theory agrees that we should focus on the conditions of possibility for our perceptions, utterances, and actions, rather than on the factual immediacy or hidden meaning of the social world. Hence, in the analysis of the NATO-intervention in Kosovo it is not enough to study the factual evidence of the crisis, the political decision to intervene, and the effects of the military campaign. Neither is it enough to study whether the intervention should really be seen as a humanitarian intervention as suggested by NATO. Discourse theory must take one step further and analyse the shifting historical conditions for constructing a military campaign as a humanitarian intervention. Hence, discourse analysis must study the reversal of the discursively inscribed hierarchy between the respect for national sovereignty and the respect for human rights. In Kampuchea, the Pol Pot regime was allowed to slaughter millions of people out of respect for national sovereignty, while in Kosovo NATO intervened in order to protect the human rights of the Kosovan Albanians.

However, as the example seems to indicate, there are two important differences between classical transcendentalism and post-structuralist discourse theory. First, the conditions of possibility are not invariable and ahistorical as Kant suggests, but subject to political struggles and historical transformation. As such, discourse theory adopts a quasi-transcendental view of the conditions of possibility. Second, discourse theory does not see the conditions of possibility as an inherent feature of the human mind, but takes them to be a structural feature of contingently constructed discourses. Discourse theory focuses neither on observable facts nor on deep meanings, but on the historical formation of the discursive conditions of social being.

The blossoming of discourse theory within social and political science from the late 1970s and onwards is influenced by the intellectual currents of British post-Marxism, French post-structuralism and Anglo-American debates about postmodernity and postmodernism. In Britain and other European countries the neo-Gramscian wave in the 1980s helped to solve the inherent problems of class reductionism and economic determinism. These problems were found both in the classical Marxist texts and in the structuralist reinterpretation of Marxism advanced by Louis Althusser (1965) and his associates. However, close and vigorous studies of Gramsci's works (Gramsci, 1971) helped many Marxists to leave the problematic dogmas of the Marxist legacy behind, while holding on to the basic theoretical problematic of Marxism. Gramsci opposes the Marxist attempt to identify the subjects of political actions with social classes that are organized around a paradigmatic set of interests that are determined by their structural position at the level of production. Instead he talked about collective wills that are produced through an intellectual and moral reform which breaks up the ideological terrain and rearticulates the ideological elements in order to create a new political project with a national-popular character.

Gramsci also opposed what he saw as the iron determinism of Marxism. Marxism tends to view the state and the political class struggles that are fought out at the level of the political and ideological superstructure as being determined by the inner movements of the economic infrastructure. When, finally, the productive forces are fully developed, the proletarian revolution will render the political superstructure of state and class struggle obsolete. This clearly reveals the paradoxical tendency towards the disappearance of politics in Marxism. By contrast, we should see the political as a constitutive force of society. According to Gramsci, politics in the modern mass society takes the form of a struggle for hegemony in terms of the establishment of a political and moral-intellectual leadership. The highest moment in the struggle for hegemony is when the hegemonic force becomes a state, in Gramsci's integral sense of the term defined as political society plus civil society. As such, the institutionalization of a hegemonic project in an organic coupling of state and civil society is more important than taking control with the means of production. However, Gramsci is not content with simply reversing the hierarchy between the privileged and non-political realm of the economy and the epiphenomenal level of the state. He aims to inscribe the institutional forms of state, economy, and civil society as relational moments in what he defines as a historical bloc. The uneven articulation of a historical bloc is, according to Gramsci, a result of hegemonic struggles. In this way Gramsci opens up for an assertion of the primacy of politics. Politics is not determined by non-political socio-economic infrastructures. Politics is a constitutive force that constructs the intra-societal forms and relations of state, economy, and civil society in a context of social strife and antagonisms. From here, it only takes a deconstruction of Gramsci's essentialist assumption that only the fundamental classes can exercise hegemony to arrive at the notion of discourse advanced by Laclau and Mouffe.

Gramsci's attempt to transcend the economic determinism of Marxism can, in this reading, be seen as an anticipation of post-structuralist deconstructivism, which is another major source of inspiration for discourse theory. Derrida (1978, 1981, 1982) deconstructs the binary hierarchies found in the structural linguistics of Ferdinand de Saussure (1974). He also makes deconstructive readings of other structuralist thinkers, such as Claude Lévi-Strauss (1969, 1972). These deconstructions are a part of a general attack on the binary oppositions that pervade Western thought. Derrida argues that Western thinking tends to organize the world in terms of binary hierarchies between the privileged essential inside and an excluded, inferior, and accidental outside (see Howarth, 2000). He shows that the outside is not merely posing a corruptive and ruinous threat to the inside, but is actually required for the definition of the inside. The inside is marked by a constitutive lack that the outside helps to fill. The outside is, therefore, just as necessary as the inside. In fact, since the outside is required for the inside to be what it is, the outside in a sense becomes more important than the inside, thus paving the way for a reversal of the binary hierarchy. However, this reversal only goes to show that, ultimately, it is impossible to maintain a stable hierarchy between the essential and the accidental, the original and the supplement, the present and the absent, the reasonable and the unreasonable, etc. Although the world appears to be organized in terms of an endless series of binary hierarchies, the deconstructive destabilization of these hierarchies reveals an ultimate undecidability. The social world is founded upon an undecidable oscillation between different poles that cannot be arrested by rational calculation or any other totalizing gesture, but requires an ethico-political decision, which inscribes a contingent decidability that privileges some options, meanings, or identities over others. The deconstructive argument provides an important understanding of the relation between political decisions and the discursive structures of the social world. Political decisions are facilitated by the deconstruction of the stable, naturalized hierarchies that surround us, but politics is also the force that constructs these hierarchies. Because politics takes place in an undecidable terrain of non-totalizable openness it will always involve both inclusion and exclusion of meanings and identities. In other words, politics involves the exercise of power.

In the late 1980s and the early 1990s it became increasingly fashionable to talk about postmodernity. The debates about postmodernity were highly confusing, as everything new under the sun was seen as a part of an epoch of postmodernity, which allegedly abandoned or reversed the ideas of modernity. Basically, there are two problems with this idea of a new postmodern era (Laclau, 1989). First, the idea of postmodernity as a new epoch merely continues the modern account of history as consisting of a progressive series of clearly defined epochs. Second, the conception of postmodernity as a negation of modernity tends to affirm the possibility of the full presence of all these things of modernity that are supposed to be abandoned or turned upside down. A solution to these problems is to view postmodernity as an expression of an increasing awareness of the limits of modernity. Postmodernity is not a celebration of irrationality, schizophrenia, fluidity, or chaos. Rather, it involves a recognition of the flaws and limits of the modernist belief in the reconciling force of reason, the nomadic account of the individual, the quest for self-determined meanings and identities, and the emancipation from power through a rational reorganization of the social order. The problematization of hopes and aspirations of modernity began with Friedrich Nietzsche and Martin Heidegger and has continued until today; and, instead of surrendering to gloom and dispair, we should take advantage of the new possibilities opened by the weakening of modernist ontology and epistemology. This is precisely the challenge, which discourse theory accepts and aims to respond to, and, in this way, discourse theory can be seen as an attempt to fashion a postmodern social and political theory.

Post-Marxism, post-structuralism and postmodernity are the key sources of inspiration in the development of third generation discourse theory. However, it also draws upon other intellectual sources, such as postpositivism, rhetorics, neopragmatism, and postanalytical philosophy. Some theorists belonging to the third generation have been inspired by crucial insights from

Freudean and Lacanian psychoanalysis, which have recently been reinterpreted and elaborated by Slavoj Žižek (1989, 1990, 1991), who offers a peculiar, Hegelian reading of Freud and Lacan. Psychoanalysis can help us to further our understanding of important issues such as the disruption and unification of discourse, the working and effects of ideological concealment, and the construction of identity through acts of identification. As we shall see in a short while, Laclau and Mouffe draw on Lacanian psychoanalysis in order to go beyond the post-structuralist conception of the subject as a relatively unified ensemble of discursively constructed identities (see Laclau, 1990). This quasi-structuralist understanding of subjectivity as a dispersion of subject positions fails to account for the drives and mechanisms that govern the attempt of human beings to construct a fully achieved identity. Lacanian psychoanalysis goes a little deeper in its attempt to theorize the subject before its subjectivation. As such, it claims that identification is triggered by the ultimate failure of the subject to constitute itself as a locus of a positively defined identity.

## Post-structuralist discourse theory in a nutshell

Having traced its main sources of influence, it is now time to have a closer look at the key arguments of post-structuralist discourse theory. In order to establish its basic characteristics we might begin with an assertion of its *anti-essentialist ontology* and its *anti-foundationalist epistemology*. As such, discourse theory argues, with Derrida, that there is no pregiven, self-determining essence that is capable of determining and ultimately fixing all other identities within a stable and totalizing structure. There have been many attempts in the history of Western thought to explain the course of history, the structure of society, and the identities of subjects and objects by reference to an underlying essence which is given in a full presence and plenitude and not implicated in any historical processes of structuration. God, Reason, Humanity, Nature, and the Iron Laws of Capitalism are some of the celebrated candidates for this transcendental determining centre. As Derrida (1978, p. 279) remarks, the longing for such a centre reflects our desire to master the anxiety that accompanies a certain mode of being implicated in contingent processes of structuration. Discourse theory aims to draw out the consequences of giving up the idea of a transcendental centre. The result is not total chaos and flux, but playful determination of social meanings and identities within a relational system which is provisionally anchored in nodal points that are capable of partially fixing a series of floating signifiers.

Likewise, discourse theory agrees with Rorty (1989) that, while the world exists out there, truth does not. Truth is not a feature of externally existing reality, but a feature of language. Hence, there is no extra-discursive instance, in terms of empirical facts, methodological rules, or privileged scientific criteria, which can safeguard either Truth or Science. Truth is always local and flexible, as it is conditioned by a discursive truth regime which specifies the criteria for judging something to be true or false. Within a certain vocabulary we can assess the truth claim of different discursive statements in relation to the different states of affairs that we perceive. However, reality does not determine the kind of vocabulary and truth regime that we will construct.

We can develop the characterization of discourse theory by highlighting its *relationalist, contextual,* and ultimately *historicist* view of identity formation. As such, discourse theory holds that identity is shaped in and through its relation to other meanings. This means that we can only understand the term 'socialism' in relation to 'liberalism', 'conservatism', and 'fascism'. This line of reasoning also suggests that singular meanings or identities should always be analysed in specific discursive contexts that condition how they are constructed and interpreted. Finally, it is asserted that the formative order of discourse is not a stable self-reproducing structure, but a precarious system, which is constantly subjected to political attempts to undermine and/or restructure the discursive context in the course of history.

In order to come to grips with the analytical potentials of post-structuralist discourse theory we shall briefly summarize the five key arguments of Laclau and Mouffe (see Torfing, 1999). These arguments can, in varying degrees, be found in the works of other post-structuralist writers who will tend to use a slightly different vocabulary, invoke productive disagreements and elaborations, and infer slightly different analytical consequences. The first argument is that all forms of social practice take place against a background of historically specific *discourses*, which can be broadly defined as relational systems of signification. Whatever we say, think, or do is conditioned by a more or less sedimented discourse which is constantly modified and transformed by what we are saying, thinking, and doing. At an abstract level, discourse can be defined as a relational ensemble of signifying sequences that weaves together semantic aspects of language and pragmatic aspects of action. Within discourse, meaning is constructed either in terms of difference or equivalence (metonymical or metaphorical). In some situations, the logic of difference predominates, in others, the logic of equivalence prevails. Most often, meaning is constructed both through the assertion of difference and the articulation of chains of equivalence. There is no ultimate centre that is capable of invoking a totalizing discursive closure, but tendentially empty signifiers will tend to function as nodal points for the partial fixation of meaning. At a more concrete level, discourse can be analysed as an ensemble of cognitive schemes, conceptual articulations, rhetorical strategies, pictures and images, symbolic actions (rituals), and structures (architectures), enunciative modalities, and narrative flows and rythms. All these things should be analysed both in terms of their ability to shape and reshape meaning and in terms of their ultimate failure to provide a homogenous space of representation.

The second argument is that discourse is constructed in and through *hegemonic struggles* that aim to establish a political and moral-intellectual leadership through the articulation of meaning and identity. This argument merely asserts that discourse is neither determined by structural pressures emanating from socioeconomic infrastructures nor a result of the dialectical unfolding of reason. Because of the ultimate undecidability of the social world, discourse is a result of political decisions. We are not talking here about conscious decisions taken by some central decision makers on the basis of rational calculation, but rather about an endless series of de facto decisions, which result from a myriad of decentred strategic actions undertaken by political agents aiming to forge a hegemonic discourse. A discourse is forged and expanded by means of articulation, which is defined as a practice that establishes a relation among discursive elements that invokes a mutual modification of their identity. Articulations that manage to provide a credible principle upon which to read past, present, and future events, and capture people's hearts and minds, become hegemonic. Hegemonic practices of articulation that unify a discursive space around a particular set of nodal points always involve an element of ideological totalization (Laclau, 1996b). However, ideology can no longer be defined as a distorted representation of an objectively given social reality, since reality is always-already a discursive construction. However, ideology can still be defined in terms of distortion, not of how things really are, but of the undecidability of all social identity. As such, ideology constructs reality as a part of a totalizing horizon of meaning that denies the contingent, precarious, and paradoxical character of social identity. The construction of naturalizing and universalizing myths and imaginaries is a central part of the hegemonic drive towards ideological totalization.

The third argument is that the hegemonic articulation of meaning and identity is intrinsically linked to the construction of *social antagonism*, which involves the exclusion of a threatening Otherness that stabilizes the discursive system while, at the same time, preventing its ultimate closure. This argument concerns the construction of the limits and unity of a discursive system. Foucault convincingly demonstrated that the limits and unity of discourse cannot be constructed by reference to an inner essence, in terms of a particular theme, style, conceptual framework, etc. Alternatively, we have to look for something outside the discourse in order to account for its limits. If the outside is simply different from the discursive moments in the same way as these moments are different from each other, however, the outside will be reduced to one more difference within the discursive system. So, what we are looking for is a constitutive outside which has no common measure with the discourse in question. Such an outside is constructed in and through social antagonism. Social antagonism involves the exclusion of a series of identities and meanings that are articulated as part of a chain of equivalence, which emphasize the 'sameness' of the excluded elements.

As the chain of equivalence is extended to include still more elements it becomes clear that the excluded elements can only have one thing in common: they pose a threat to the discursive system. Hence, social antagonism involves the construction of a threatening otherness that is incommensurable with the discursive system and therefore constructs its unity and limits. In this sense, the process of 'othering' helps to stabilize the discursive system, However, the price for this stabilization is the introduction of a radical other that threatens and problematizes the discursive system and prevents it from achieving a full closure.

In a concrete analysis of discourse, social antagonism shows itself through the production of political frontiers, which often invoke stereotyped pictures of friends and enemies. However, the line separating the friendly inside from the threatening outside is not completely fixed. The struggle over what and who are included and excluded from the hegemonic discourse is a central part of politics. There are also political attempts to make antagonistic identities coexist within the same discursive space. Hence, the political construction of democratic 'rules of the game' makes it possible for political actors to agree on institutionalized norms about respect and responsiveness while disagreeing on the interpretation of such norms as well as on more substantial issues.

The fourth argument is that a stable hegemonic discourse becomes *dislocated* when it is confronted by new events that it cannot explain, represent, or in other ways domesticate. Most discourses are flexible and capable of integrating a lot of new events into their symbolic order. But all discourses are finite and they will eventually confront events that they fail to integrate. The failure to domesticate new events will disrupt the discursive system. This will open a terrain for hegemonic struggles about how to heal the rift in the social order. There will be political struggles about how to define and solve the problem at hand. The political struggles lead to the articulation of a new hegemonic discourse, which is sustained through the construction of a new set of political frontiers. Dislocation shows itself through a structural, or organic, crisis in which there is a proliferation of floating signifiers. The hegemonic struggles that are made possible by the dislocation of the social order will aim to fix the floating signifiers by articulating them with a new set of nodal points. These will, for a large part, take the form of empty universals – in the sense of appeals to vaguely defined notions such as Revolution, Modernization, the Nation, or the People – that aim to signify the lack of a fully achieved community, which is revealed by the dislocation of the social order.

The final argument is that the dislocation of the discursive structure means that the subject always emerges as a *split subject* that might attempt to reconstruct a full identity through acts of identification. This argument is inspired by psychoanalysis and challenges the post-structuralist assertion that the subject can be reduced to an ensemble of subject positions, which are stamped upon the subject by the discursive structure in which it is located. When it comes to the theory of the subject, post-structuralism has retained a rather structuralist view that threatens to reduce the subject to an objective location within the discursive structure, or, as Louis Althusser phrased it: to a 'mere bearer of the structure'. The idea that the subject simultaneously occupies the position of being a worker, a woman, an environmentalist, and so on, might help us to combat class reductionism, but provides an inadequate understanding of the processes that lead to the formation of multiple selves. Here, the notion of dislocation provides a fruitful starting point. The recurrent dislocations of the discursive system mean that the subject cannot be conceived in terms of a collection of structurally given positions. The discursive structure is disrupted and this prevents it from fully determining the identity of the subject. This does not mean that we have to reintroduce an ahistorical subjectivity that is given outside the structure. The subject is internal to the structure, but it has neither a complete structural identity nor a complete lack of structural identity. Rather it has a failed structural identity (Laclau, 1990). Because of dislocation, the subject emerges as a split subject, which is traumatized by its lack of fullness. The split subject might either disintegrate or try to recapture the illusion of a full identity by means of identifying itself with the promise of fullness offered by different political projects. Hence, a dislocated Russian party functionary might aim to reconstitute a full identity by identifying with the promise of Russian nationalism, neoliberalism, social democracy, or some religious movement. The split subject might identify with many different things at the same time. In this situation the hegemonic struggles will have to offer ways of articulating the different points of identification into a relatively coherent discourse. Social antagonism will play a crucial role for the attempt to unify dissimilar points of identification. The construction of a constitutive outside facilitates the displacement of responsibility for the split subject's lack onto an enemy, which is held responsible for all evil. The externalization of the subject's lack to an enemy is likely to fuel political action that will be driven by an illusionary promise: that the elimination of the other will remove the subject's original lack.

These five basic arguments underpin each of the chapters which follow. Either with reference to Laclau and Mouffe or other theorists, and through a variety of empirical contexts, they are the threads which bind this book.

## Common concerns responding

The many different versions of post-structuralist discourse theory have been met by fierce criticism from a number of quarters. Some of these criticisms are helpful in pointing out significant differences between discourse theory and other theoretical approaches. Others are completely ill-founded and based on clear misunderstandings or a failure to engage with the literature on discourse theory. Between these extremes there are some recurrent criticisms from people who seem to be interested in the argument, but tend to think that discourse theory has significant problems. These people seem concerned about the consequences of adopting a discourse theoretical position. Let us look at some of the most common concerns and see how they can be eased through a closer inspection of what discourse theory actually says.

The first misgiving is that discourse theory leads to idealism. Many people seem to think that the assertion of the discursive character of all social meanings and identities leads to a denial of the independent existence of reality. However, discourse theory does not dispute in any way the realist assertion that matter exists independently of our consciousness, thoughts, and language. The contention is merely that nothing follows from the bare existence of matter. Matter does not carry the means of its own representation. In fact, the social forms that render matter intelligible are neither passive reflections of an immanent essence of the experienced objects nor are they constituted by the omnipotence of the experiencing subject that reduces the object to a thought object. Rather, intelligible social forms are constructed in and through different discourses. Hence, a particular piece of land can be constructed as habitat for an endangered species by a group of biologists, a recreational facility by the urban population, fertile farm land by the local farmers, or a business opportunity by urban developers. This example allows us to make three remarks that qualify the ontological position of discourse theory further. First, the discursive construction of matter in and through processes of discursive signification also tends to produce or at least reinforce particular subjectivities. Hence, the construction of the land as a 'business opportunity' constructs certain people as urban developers. Second, matter does not merely await a particular signification that is stamped upon it by discourse. Discursive forms play an active role in constructing that which they signify. Hence, the referent in terms of 'a particular piece of land' is retroactively constructed by the discursive form which carves out a particular piece of brute matter to be signified. Third, the discourses that construct matter as a meaningful object are constantly disrupted by dislocation and social antagonism. The dream of constructing a final vocabulary that captures the world as it really is must be abandonned because there is always an unrepresentable kernel that prevents the symbolic order of a discursive system from fixing social meaning in a way that completely absorbs matter. Hence, discourse theory subscribes not only to the realist idea of independently existing matter but also to the materialist insistence on an irreducible distance between form and matter.

The second common objection to discourse theory is that it is adrift in relativist gloom. According to this, sometimes rather crudely expressed accusation (Geras, 1987; Howard, 1989), discourse theory entails nihilistic relativism. The argument is that since there are no bedrock foundations and everything is discursive, it is impossible to defend any particular set of claims about what is true, right, or good. The premise of this argument is correct, since discourse theory maintains that there is no such thing as an extra-discursive truth, morality, or ethics (Rorty, 1989; Mouffe, 1996). However, the conclusion is wrong, since we never find ourselves in a situation where we are prepared to contend that all claims are equally valid. We are always part of a particular discourse that provides us with a set of relatively determinate values, standards, and criteria for judging something to be true or false, right or wrong, good or bad. God is the only entity capable of rising above the historically contingent discourses and viewing all the competing truth regimes and ethical standards as equally valid. We mortals are tied to a particular discursive framework within which we define and negotiate our criteria for accepting something as true, right, or good. Now, if we were trapped within a set of completely unified, closed, and self-reproducing discourses, the possibility of an agonistic dialogue between people with different, discursively conditioned truth claims would be impossible. However, the different cultures, traditions, and contexts that condition our truth claims are constantly dis-articulated and re-articulated through processes of mutual learning, political struggles, or violent conflicts. No discourse can be protected from contestation and contamination as their boundaries are continuously breached and redrawn.

The third perceived problem concerns the status of discourse theory as an explanatory theory. Some critics doubt that discourse theory can do more than describe the articulatory practices within and between various discourses; that it can understand but not explain social, political, and culture life. However, one should be careful not to see understanding and explanation as readily opposed alternatives (Howarth, 2000). Peter Winch (1990) argues that explanation always requires some initial understanding of what one tries to explain and that explanation is an attempt to complete our initial and somewhat fragmented understanding of a particular state of affairs. In keeping with Winch's blurring of the lines separating explanation and understanding, we might ask how discourse theory attempts to explain things. Discourse theory opposes the causal explanations of social phenomena, which harness empirical events to the yoke of universal laws. It does not accept that the task of the social scientist should be to establish a covering law (Hempel, 1966) or to reveal the intrinsic causal properties of social objects (Bhaskar, 1988). Instead discourse theory aims to describe, understand, and explain how and why particular discursive formations were constructed, stabilized, and transformed. In order to reveal the necessary and sufficient conditions for discourse to be shaped and reshaped in a particular way, discourse theory employs a contextualized conceptual tool kit that includes important concepts like dislocation, hegemony, social antagonism etc. In other words, invoking Aristotle's distinction between different scientific rationalities, we might conclude that discourse theory is a phronetic rather than epistemic theory. It aspires to both understand and explain social phenomena, through contextualized studies of the historical conditions in which discourses emerge and take effect.

A fourth canard is that discourse theory must give up the ambition of criticizing the discourses that it is analysing. The farewell to the emancipatory project of the Enlightenment, the celebration of an unrestricted diversity, and the absence of unquestionable values that can serve as yardsticks of critique effectively prevents discourse theory from launching any kind of critique. The problem here is that neither the premises nor the conclusion are correct. First, discourse theory does not discard the emancipatory values of the Enlightenment. We are thrown into a political culture pregnant with emancipatory hopes that we do not want to abandon. However, the problem is that emancipation is both necessary and impossible. We might want to produce a radical break with the existing structure of capitalist domination and extend liberty and equality to all spheres of society but we soon realize that there can be no such thing as a radical refoundation of society and that the idea of freeing ourselves from power is absurd. Power has no deep foundation and resistance to power entails only the substitution of one power configuration for another, which, on pragmatic grounds, we judge more agreeable. Second, discourse theory does not support an unrestrained proliferation of difference, which legitimizes all political projects in the name of diversity. Certainly, we should, both analytically and in the kind of politics we pursue, try to avoid reducing difference to identity and the alterity of the other to our domesticated image of the other. However, the idea of a limitless diversity is self-defeating, since diversity can only exist to the extent that we are willing to repress those forces that seek to eliminate diversity. Intolerance towards the intolerant is the condition of possibility for tolerance. Finally, while it is true that all ethical and normative claims can be deconstructed, this does not mean that critique is impossible. We just have to rethink the very idea of critique. Critique should not consist of measuring a current state of affairs against some preestablished yardstick, defining once and for all what is right and good. It should rather take the form of an attempt to deconstruct the closure invoked by ethical, normative, political, cultural, economic, and other discourses. Deconstruction is a kind of internal critique that turns the text against itself by showing that the binary hierarchies are not consistently sustained, but rather problematized in the name of a non-totalizable openness. The conceptual and pragmatic undecidables that are revealed through deconstruction escape definition and institutionalization, but are captured by the promise of something yet to come and always endlessly deferred. As such, we can criticize the emminently deconstructable law in the face of the indeconstructable justice, which is always a justice to come. We can do that by confronting the totalizing closure it produces with the aporias it fails to eliminate and which point towards an unrealized sense of justice.

The fifth worry concerns what is generally known as the 'liar's paradox'. Discourse theory claims to be anti-essentialist, but in claiming that there is no essence it makes an essentialist stipulation about the world as having no essence. In other words, discourse theory is caught in a performative contradiction as it does what it clearly says it must not do. If we accept that the claim about the absence of a deep essence of the social world is a decontextualized and thus truly universal statement, there is no logical escape from the performative contraction. However, a closer analysis of the semantics reveals the paradox as a being based on a fallacy of equivocation. The essence ends up meaning two different things in the claim 'there is no essence' and the claim that 'the stipulation of the absence of essences is an essentialist stipulation'. Hence, when discourse theorists claim that there is no essence they take issue with the metaphysical idea of a positively defined essence that is given in and by itself and from which it is possible to derive a whole series of determinate effects. Now, for the claim that there is no such essence to be an essentialist stipulation it requires that the affirmation of the absence of a deep ground of social identities produces a series of determinate effects. This requirement is exactly what is not fulfilled. Whereas it is possible to derive a whole series of effects from a positively defined ground, nothing follows from the affirmation on an abyss of pure negativity. An economic structure is logically speaking capable of determining the structure of society, but nothing follows by logical implication from the dislocation of the economic structure. In other words, the rejection of an essentialist grounding of the social world cannot fulfil the role of a new essentialist ground.

## The added value of discourse theory

In the 1970s, the social sciences underwent a 'linguistic turn' and, building on that, we may speak today of an emerging 'discursive turn'. In all the major social science disciplines there is an increasing recognition of the need to study discourse. In sociology it is widely recognized that social integration and system integration is problematized by individualization and globalization processes, with the result that social action can no longer rely on a given set of generally accepted norms, rules, and values that socialize human actors. In this situation, social agency is forced to construct the ground of its own actions. The active construction of a contingent ground on which to base one's actions takes place at the level of discourse, and this prompts an increasing number of sociologists to focus their analysis on discourse. Economics has been conquered by neoclassical formalism and mathematization. In Europe, however, a growing number of bolder economists insists that economic transactions have a social character and are conditioned by institutionalized rules, norms, and paradigms. Hence, in the various forms of institutional economics that discuss the economic modes of regulation, path-dependent learning processes, and varieties of capitalism, we find mounting appreciation of the role of historically contingent discourses in structuring economic processes. Finally, as is currently signalled by the attempt to transform political science in political studies, the individualistic and rationalistic models of political action have been questioned by people who insist that preferences, interests, and information are endogenous to social institutions and political processes, and that rationality is merely one logic of appropriate action among many others (March and Olsen, 1985). Hence, rationalistic exchange theories have been replaced by institutionalist theories with a hermeneutic and constructivist approach to political analysis, which tends to draw nearer to the approach of post-structuralist discourse analysis.

The 'discursive turn' is evident beyond the traditional social science disciplines, as an increasing number of cross-disciplinary studies is heavily influenced by the new theories of discourse. People from different disciplines will often be able to come together in a study of the discourses that construct the object of analysis, as well as the social, cultural, and economic relations that it engenders.

The reaction of mainstream political theory to the emerging 'discursive turn' has shifted from down-right rejection to grudging tolerance and, latterly, critical dialogue. This means that discourse theorists are, to an increasing extent, asked what value the discourse approach adds to the study of politics. The first response to this question is that discourse theory *poses other kinds of research questions* than those generated by behaviourist, institutionalist, and rational choice perspectives. Discourse theory has no intention of developing a general theory of voting, nation building, or welfare state reform. Rather, it is problem driven, in the sense that it seeks to identify specific empirical, analytical, or societal puzzles. It then employs its analytical tool kit, often refashioned by the integration of new problem-relevant theories, to shed light on the problem and flesh out the wider implications for the future analysis of similar problems.

Another response to this objection is that discourse theory draws attention to the *contingent formation* of social phenomena. It refuses to take pregiven social structures or subjective interests as the privileged starting points of social and political analysis. It insists that the contingent political processes leading to the formation of particular structures and institutions and particular accounts of the preferences and interests of the social actors are a central part of the analysis. Hence, before we analyse the realization of the interests of the working class we must first account for the formation of the proletariat into a class and analyse the overdetermined construction of a particular class interest. Likewise, instead of taking the globalized capitalist economy as a given starting point for the analysis of political responses in terms of political regulation of the financial markets, discourse theory will analyse how the discourse on globalization constructs different accounts of globalization and its likely effects.

The emphasis on the *semantic, pragmatic, and rhetorical aspects* in the construction of social structures and identities is a third distinctive feature of discourse theory. Few, if any, theories in mainstream political science pay attention to language and the interweaving of language and action. By contrast, discourse theory makes a point of analysing the overlap and mutual influence between different language games that are seen as constitutive of social structures and identities. It analyses the semantic aspects of language in terms of the production of more or less fixed and sedimented meanings. It analyses the pragmatic aspects in terms of the construction of enunciative modalities and the rhetorical aspects in terms of attempts to link social meanings and close the gaps of the discourse through the deployment of figurative language.

A fourth example of the added value of discourse theory is its *emphasis on both continuity and change*. Discourse theory does not see history as a result of the dialectical unfolding of a basic contradiction, or the progressive realization of a certain telos. Rather, history is marked by radical discontinuity, where one discursive formation is dislocated and breaks down and a new discursive formation is constructed through intense political struggle that reorganizes the social order around an external hegemonic principle. However, in most cases the dislocation of the social order only scratches the surface and this means that the hegemonic attempts to restructure the social order must achieve credibility as a solution to the dislocation that is broadly consonant with the established order. As such, discourse theory pays attention to both discontinuity and continuity and always seeks to unravel the interplay between discursive path-shaping and discursive path-dependency.

The fifth response is that discourse theory *puts power and power struggles at the top of the agenda*. Power is not analysed in terms of a resource or capacity one can possess, store, or retrieve, or as a relation of domination. Power is conceived in terms of the political acts of inclusion and exclusion that shape social meanings and identities and condition the construction of social antagonisms and political frontiers. The construction of discourse always involves both inclusion and exclusion of identity and this means that discourse and power are intrinsically linked with each other.

A final response to the question of what discourse theory brings to the table is to stress its interest in *the driving forces behind the formation and cohesion* of political alliances, governance networks, political communities, social groups, and so on. Discourse theory criticizes both the liberal notion of an unencumbered self and the neoclassical model of 'economic man'. It subscribes to the view that individual identity is formed within larger communities, but it refuses to take these communities for granted. It is a crucial task for political studies to analyse the formation of political communities, and discourse theory offers a three-step argument to facilitate this. First, it claims that the formation of communities is often a response to dislocations. Common experiences of negation, frustration, and hope for future improvement are expressed by tendentially empty signifiers that function as a catalyst for the formation of communities. Second, communities are often held together by common identities, vocabularies and narratives, and the analysis of these holds the key to understanding the inclusions within, and exclusions from, various communities. Third, the discursive meanings and identities that bind together individual or collective actors in a community often have a totalizing, imaginary, or even fantasmatic dimension, as they brandish the promise of a fully achieved identity in a land of idle happiness. Hence, ideological myths are a key feature of political community.

Now, it would be foolish to claim that discourse theory is the only theory that aims to do these things. Many theories attempt to walk down the same roads as post-structuralist discourse theory. However, where discourse theory distinguishes itself from most theories within political science, and where its added value can most clearly be seen, is in the fact that it defines and measures itself in terms of its ability to deliver on all the criteria described above.

## Challenges to discourse theory

The growing popularity of discourse theory should be welcomed. It is good to see people discard objectivist and rationalist theories in favour of more constructivist approaches that help to account for the historicity of social being. In addition, it saves discourse theorists from the exhausting task of constantly having to justify what they are doing in the face of sceptical or bewildered colleagues. However, increasing popularity also carries the risk of trivialization and reabsorption into mainstream theory. Hence, some people tend merely to pick up a few concepts and arguments and thereby produce a kind of 'discourse theory light'. While a particular research problem might sometimes call for or legitimize such an approach, the problem is that the argument of discourse theory is watered down and disconnected from the basic ontological assumptions, or even eclectically combined with theories with different ontologies. Equally problematic is when the concepts and arguments of discourse theory are absorbed into mainstream theory by people who, for example, see discursive articulations as a conscious means deployed by rational actors to further their own interests, by manipulating the perception that other people have of the problems, solutions, and premises at hand in political decision-making processes. The only weapon against these two problems that follow in the wake of the increasing success of discourse theory is to insist that concrete discourse analyses are embedded within a theoretical and philosophical framework, which ensures a vigorous and consistent argument. We are not calling for a dogmatic assertion of some fundamental assumptions of discourse theory, but rather on a continued anchoring of discourse analysis in theoretical and philosophical debates, which can help to keep discourse theory sharp and alive.

Discourse has gained increasing prominence within social and political science, but it has not become a new mainstream. There is still a lot of unrealized potential. In order to develop this potential, discourse theory must respond to three important challenges:

1. *It must demonstrate the analytical value of discourse theory in empirical studies that take us beyond the mere illustration of the arguments and concepts.* Thus, in order to avoid lapsing into a self-indulgent theoreticism, discourse theory must prove its ability to produce new insights through problem-driven studies of specific discourses that permit the analytical categories and the empirical analysis of texts (in a wide sense of the term) to hegemonize each other.
2. *It must address the core topics and areas within social and political science and not be content with specializing in allegedly 'soft' topics such as gender, ethnicity, and social movements.* Discourse theory has made many significant contributions in these fields of study, but it has been too easy for mainstream theorists to establish a rigid division of labour, according to which the new theories of discourse are used in studies of the various forms of identity politics, whereas conventional objectivist and rationalist theories continue to deal with the traditional core topics, such as public administration, policy analysis, security politics etc. This kind of 'repressive tolerance' must be counteracted by deliberate attempts to colonize what is considered to be the mainstream of political science. Such a colonization will inevitably result in a re-articulation of the basic research questions and a deconstruction of the hierarchy between 'hard' and 'soft issues' within political science.
3. *It must critically reflect upon the questions of method and research strategy.* In order to justify the validity of the insights generated through empirical discourse analyses of the central topics in political science, discourse theorists must address questions about the choice and design of research strategies, methodological problems relating to the collection and interpretation of data, and technical issues about the use of different methods of text analysis. We should not surrender to the positivist obsession with method that is founded on the belief that the observation of a set of methodological rules somehow guarantees the truth of the research results. However, we need to reflect, openly and critically, upon the many methodological choices that we make in the analysis of specific discursive formations. That will not only help us to improve the quality of our discourse analysis, but also help to justify the validity of our research results, because other researchers will see what, how, and why we are doing what we do.

The founders of discourse theory are, with a few exceptions, not very interested in these issues. This is why we call for the formation of a new generation of discourse theorists who will respond to these challenges. We take a first step in this book, but we have no illusions of finishing the job. There is much work ahead.

## Some initial responses

The initial response of discourse theory to the challenge of demonstrating its analytical value in empirical studies is to admit that many discourse theorists have been more inclined towards theoretical and philosophical work than towards empirical analysis. This is a natural consequence of discourse theory's attempt to break with traditional theories and establish its own distinctive ontology. This endeavour could not be undertaken without hard theoretical and philosophical labour. Some discourse theorists continue to work theoretically, but many have begun to do empirical work as well. Hence, in the last couple of years at the time of writing there have been a growing number of empirical studies. However, some of these studies merely try to illustrate a preestablished theoretical argument and do not attempt to learn from the empirical analysis. The challenge is to go beyond illustrative analysis and conduct discourse analysis in order to produce new, unexpected insights and sharpen the theoretical categories and arguments. In fact, this is something most discourse theorists aim to accomplish, but the heavy theoretical and philosophical inclination still stands in the way of a genuine integration of theoretical and empirical analysis.

The initial response to the bias in the choice of topics is that, while it is true that discourse theory has not addressed many of the topics cultivated by mainstream theory, discourse theorists are today making significant inroads into the traditional issues of political science. Discourse theory has, from the beginning, focused more on the formation of new political identities, the basis of gender, ethnicity, nationality, and other postmaterialist issues. Not only were these issues relatively easy to analyse in terms of discursive identity construction, they were also glossed over and marginalized by mainstream theory, and studying them helps to sustain the oppositional self-image and the feeling of breaking new ground. Discourse theory often did a very good job in analysing and highlighting the new forms of identity politics, and it was easy for mainstream theorists to give discourse theory credit for this kind of study as long it kept its hands off the core issues of conventional political science. However, discourse theory also has a lot to offer in the study of these mainstream issues and its future expansion depends on its ability to realize its huge potential in the traditional fields of study, where rather simplistic theories have reigned far too long.

The challenge for discourse theory to reflect more on methodological issues is the most demanding, and it requires a more lengthy response. The initial reply of discourse theory to this challenge will be to point to the fact that there are actually very few social science theories that provide any detailed methodological accounts of what they do in their empirical work. Quantitative studies based on surveys or register studies usually carry long accounts of technical problems and solutions, and that is generally as far as it goes. Concrete methodological accounts of the role of the researcher, the choice of research strategy, the procedures for collection, analysis, and interpretation of different kinds of data etc. are often neglected in social and political studies. There are many general books on method and methodology, but the discussions in these books are most often divorced from discussions of the theoretical approaches. Very few theories discuss the methodological implications of the particular approach they are advocating. Naturally, none of this frees discourse theory from the challenge of offering a much more detailed account of the methodological aspects of discourse analysis.

The next response to this challenge would be to explain the reluctance of discourse theory to deal with methodological issues by referring to its anti-epistemological stance. Discourse theory adopts and even radicalizes the postpositivist critique of epistemology. Hence, it claims that there are no extra-discursive facts, rules of method, or criteria for establishing that can guarantee the production of true knowledge. There is no such thing as brute facts, but only theoretically informed and culturally shaped descriptions of a discursively constructed reality. Methodological rules are always formulated within particular scientific paradigms, and there are no clear and privileged criteria for determining when to abandon a scientific paradigm in favour of a new one.

The anti-epistemological stance of discourse theory rests on solid argumentative ground, but one of its unfortunate consequences has been been the dismissal, as a positivist obsession, of questions of method and methodology. In other words, discourse theory has thrown the methodological baby out with the epistomological bath water. This reveals the huge size of the methodological gap to be filled.

A last response to this challenge is to problematize the idea of an all-purpose method with the character of a 'complete user's guide to discourse analysis', and to question the very idea of 'applying a rule'. Discourse theory should not aim to develop a general set of methodological rules that can and should be used in all kinds of discourse analysis. The aspiration for a rigid decontextualized method is absurd, as a problem-driven analysis of discourse will require a constant invention and adjustment of particular methodological rules. In fact, the very idea of following a rule in a concrete analysis can be questioned. As Ludwig Wittgenstein (1953) demonstrates, the content of a rule is always an instance of its usage. We never really know how to follow a rule, and we need another rule to show us how, which in turn requires another rule etc. To halt this infinite regress we have to step in and make a constitutive, pragmatic, and context-bound interpretation of the rule in and through its usage. However, whereas there is no doubt that the idea of a universal method consisting of rigid and inflexible rules is problematic, this does not prevent us from addressing methodological questions that arise as a part of particular problem-driven research projects.

In sum, none of these defensive responses to the methodological challenge justifies a systematic lack of critical reflection with regard to method and methodology within post-structuralist discourse theory. In order to improve the quality of empirical discourse analysis and facilitate dialogue with other theoretical approaches, discourse theory must become much more explicit in its reflections about the many methodological choices involved in concrete analysis. Surely, we must cease trying to produce a decontextualized intersubjective knowledge that is validated by the application of a pregiven method, but there is an urgent need for critical, explicit and context-bound discussion of what we do in discourse analysis, why we do it, and what the consequences are.

## Plan of the book

This book is a first attempt to respond to the three above-mentioned challenges. In the next 12 chapters we present a broad range of empirical discourse analyses that focus on central aspects of European politics. The authors come from different European countries and are all experts in their field. They draw on different versions of discourse theory in order to study the crucial aspects of the kind of political identities, policies, and forms of governance that are emerging in Europe today. Each chapter defines its own problematic, provides an original empirical analysis, and reflects on the methodological questions raised by their investigations.

The volume begins with some general reflections about *the character of European politics*. In the first chapter Ole Wæver draws on post-structuralist discourse theory in order to show how major European powers like Germany and France construct different forms of 'we'-identity by integrating certain notions of 'state', 'nation', and 'Europe' in their self-defining narratives. These narratives inform the European strategies of Germany and France and thus have an important impact on European integration and security. From a different perspective, Yannis Stavrakakis supplements discourse theory with insights from Lacanian theory to explore the contemporary paradoxes and dilemmas surrounding the construction of a European identity. He employs this novel theoretical synthesis to account for the current obstacles and pathologies evident in the construction of European identity as a collectively appealing object of identification, and he proposes a theoretical model which can redirect the debate around this issue in an uncharted but promising direction.

Having examined the logics of state politics and identity construction on a global level, the next four chapters examine particular instances of *governance and administration* in Europe. In Chapter 3, Allan Dreyer Hansen and Eva Sørensen analyse the discursive construction and effects of local governance and institutional reform in contemporary Europe. The analysis draws on the discourse theory of Laclau and Mouffe and focuses on local policy processes in a small, provincial town in Denmark. In Chapter 4, Steven Griggs employs discourse theory to explain the formation of discourse coalitions in public health care systems. Focusing upon a group of public hospital directors in France during the 1970s and 1980s, Griggs challenges orthodox rational choice and interest-based approaches by stressing the way in which the group constructed a common political identity to advance their interests. In so doing, he emphasizes the role of empty signifiers and individuals in the articulation of group identities. In Chapter 5, Niels Åkerstrøm Andersen draws on the Luhmanian systems theory in his analysis of the emergence, construction, and function of the distinction between politics and administration within the political system. The focus is on Danish public administrative reforms, and in particular the recent reforms inspired by the doctrine of New Public Management. Anthony Clohesy explores the growing impact of European integration on constitutional arrangements in the United Kingdom in Chapter 6. More specifically, he shows how discourse theory can explain why a Labour government in the UK, traditionally sceptical about the value of rights-based approaches to politics, introduced the Human Rights Act into the British constitution. He then goes on to explore the political and ethical consequences of the Act's introduction.

The next three chapters concentrate on the *character, articulation, and effects of new political ideologies* in contemporary Europe. In Chapter 7, Patrick de Vos engages with mainstream explanations of the electoral growth of the xenophobic and separatist Flemish far-right party Vlaams Blok since the late 1980s. Drawing on discourse theory, especially Chantal Mouffe's critique of Third Way politics, he argues that mainstream frames of thinking fail to grasp that the rise of an ultra-nationalist and authoritarian-populist party in Flanders, as elsewhere in Europe, has to be understood in relation to the establishment of a hegemonic consensus around the political centre. This is because the resultant ideological convergence between the established political parties has been accompanied by the disappearance and repression of political antagonism, thus opening the space for a new radicalism of the right. Chapter 8 of the volume continues the exploration of Third Way politics, as Steven Bastow and James Martin use discourse theory to investigate the specificity of Third Way politics today. Criticizing approaches that evaluate Third Way politics by reference to an 'objective' or 'external' referent, they examine the way the discourse constructs its own objectivity and then poses itself as a response to these objective circumstances that other ideological positions have 'failed' to grasp. In so doing, they outline the generic discursive 'repertoire' from which a variety of Third Way ideologies have drawn in the course of the twentieth century, which enables them to contextualize the social democratic Third Way in a wider theoretical and ideological context. In Chapter 9, Oscar Reyes engages further with Third Way politics by examining New Labour ideology in the United Kingdom. He argues that the 'hard-working family' has emerged as the principal subject posited by New Labour discourse, and he sheds light on how the contradictions of New Labour's approach to work and the family, and its conflicting liberal and authoritarian commitments, are reconciled at the level of popular discourse.

The last set of chapters shows how discourse analysis can be used in the study of *policy-making and public opinion*. In Chapter 10, Véronique Mottier studies the role of eugenic expert discourses for the construction of the Swiss welfare state. Her study draws on Foucauldian discourse analysis in order to analyse the effects of the eugenicist practices of inclusion and exclusion on the formation of social policy and national identity in pre-war Switzerland. In Chapter 11, Lillie Chouliaraki combines Fairclough's Critical Discourse Analysis and Laclau's theory of discourse in a study of the politics of truth in a public debate on the journalistic practices of celebrity magazines that was staged and broadcast by national Danish television. In Chapter 12, Maarten A. Hajer takes issue with the dominant rationalistic approach to policy analysis in his study of the role of metaphor, narratives, and story-lines in shaping and advancing strong and successful discourse coalitions. The analysis draws upon new insights from the so-called deliberative policy analysis and focuses on the environmental discourse in Britain.

In the concluding chapter David Howarth reflects on the role and character of method in discourse theory. Although each of the previous chapters reflects and contributes its own distinctive conception of this issue, while employing a variety of methods to explain particular aspects of European politics, this last chapter seeks to condense these discussions around a particular problem confronting the use of discourse theory in conducting empirical research. This is the problem of applying the abstract and formal theoretical logics and concepts of discourse to concrete cases. In so doing, Howarth draws on a variety of post-structuralist and hermeneutical themes to elaborate a problem-driven method of articulatory practice. The principles underlying this method are then used to inform a series of more concrete ideas about appropriate research strategies and techniques.

## Bibliography

Althusser, Louis (1965), *For Marx*. London: Verso Press.

Atkinson, Maxwell, and John Heritage (1984), *Structures of Social Action: Studies in Conversation Analysis*. Cambridge: Cambridge University Press.

Austin, John L. (1975), *How to Do Things with Words*. Oxford: Oxford University Press.

Bhaskar, Roy (1978), *A Realist Theory of Science*, 2nd edn. Brighton: Harvester.

Butler, Judith (1990), *Gender Trouble: Feminism and the Subversion of Identity*. New York: Routledge.

Connolly, William E. (1991), *Identity/Difference: Democratic Negotiations of Political Paradox*. Ithaca, NY: Cornell University Press.

Derrida, Jacques (1978), *Writing and Difference*. London: Routledge and Kegan Paul.

Derrida, Jacques (1981), *Positions*. London: The Athlone Press.
Derrida, Jacques (1982), *Margins of Philosophy*. Brighton: Harvester Press.
Downes, William (1984), *Language and Society*. London: Fontana.
Dyrberg, Torben Bech, Allan Dreyer Hansen, and Jacob Torfing (2000), *Diskursteoren på arbejde*. Roskilde: Samfundslitteratur.
Eliasoph, Nina (1998), *Avoiding Politics: How Americans Produce Apathy in Their Everyday Life*. Cambridge: Cambridge University Press.
Fairclough, Norman (1992), *Discourse and Social Change*. Cambridge: Polity Press.
Fairclough, Norman (1995), *Critical Discourse Analysis*. London: Longman.
Foucault, Michel (1985), *The Archaeology of Knowledge*. London: Tavistock.
Foucault, Michel (1886a), *Power/Knowledge*. Brighton: Harvester.
Foucault, Michel (1986b), 'Nietzsche, Genealogy, History', in Paul Rabinow (ed.), *The Foucault Reader*. Harmondsworth: Penguin Books, pp. 32–75.
Foucault, Michel (1986c), 'Power and the Subject', in Herbert L. Dreyfus and Paul Rabinow (eds), *Michel Foucault: Beyond Structuralism and Hermeneutics*. Brighton: Harvester Press, pp. 208–26.
Foucault, Michel (1986d), *Discipline and Punish*. Harmondsworth: Penguin Books.
Foucault, Michel (1990), *History of Sexuality*. Harmondsworth: Penguin Books.
Fowler, Roger et al. (1979), *Language and Control*. London: Routledge and Kegan Paul.
Geras, Norman (1987), 'Post-Marxism?', *New Left Review*, 163, pp. 40–82.
Giddens, Anthony (1984), *The Constitution of Society: Outline of a Theory of Structuration*. Cambridge: Polity Press.
Gramsci, Antonio (1971), *Selections from Prison Notebooks*. London: Lawrence & Wishart.
Gubrium, Jaber F., and James A. Holstein (1997), *The New Language of Qualitative Method*. Oxford: Oxford University Press.
Habermas, Jürgen (1987), *The Theory of Communicative Action: vols I–II*. Cambridge: Polity Press.
Habermas, Jürgen (1990), *The Philosophical Discourse of Modernity: Twelve Lectures*. Cambridge: Polity Press.
Habermas, Jürgen (1992), *Faktizität und Geltung: beiträge zur diskurstheorie des rechts und des demokratischen rechtsstaats*. Frankfurt am Main: Suhrkamp Verlag.
Hempel, Carl G. (1966), *Philosophy of Natural Science*. Englewood Cliffs: Prentice Hall.
Holsti, Ole R. (1969), *Content Analysis for the Social Sciences and the Humanities*. Reading: Addisson-Wesley.
Howard, Dick (1987), *Defining the Political*. London: Macmillan.
Howarth, David (2000), *Discourse*. Buckingham: Open University Press.
Howarth, David, Aletta J. Norval, and Yannis Stavrakakis (2000), *Discourse Theory and Political Analysis*. Manchester: Manchester University Press.
Labov, William, and David Franchel (1977), *Therapeutic Discourse: Psychotherapy as Conversation*. New York: Academic Press.
Laclau, Ernesto (1989), 'Politics and the Limits of Modernity', in Andrew Ross (ed.), *Universal Abandon*? Mineapolis: University of Minnesota Press, pp. 63–82.
Laclau, Ernesto (1990), *New Reflections of the Revolution of Our Time*. London: Verso Press.
Laclau, Ernesto (1993), 'Discourse', in Robert E. Gooding and Philip Pettit (eds), *The Blackwell Companion to Contemporary Political Philosophy*. Oxford: Blackwell, pp. 431–7.
Laclau, Ernesto (1996a), 'The Death and Resurrection of Ideology', *Journal of Political Ideologies*, vol. 1, no. 3, pp. 201–20.

Laclau, Ernesto (1996b), *Emancipations*. London: Verso Press.
Laclau, Ernesto (2000), 'Identity and Hegemony', 'Structure, History and the Political', and 'Constructing Universality', in Judith Butler, Ernesto Laclau, and Slavoj Žižek, *Contingency, Hegemony, Universality*. London: Verso Press, pp. 44–89, 182–212, 281–308.
Laclau, Ernesto, and Chantal Mouffe (1982), 'Recasting Marxism: Hegemony and New Political Movements', *Socialist Review*, 12, November, pp. 91–113.
Laclau, Ernesto, and Chantal Mouffe (1985), *Hegemony and Socialist Strategy*. London: Verso Press.
Laclau, Ernesto, and Chantal Mouffe (1987), 'Post-Marxism without Apologies', *New Left Review*, no. 166, pp. 79–106.
Lévi-Strauss, Claude (1969), *Totemism*. London: Fontana.
Lévi-Strauss, Claude (1972), *The Savage Mind*. Oxford: Oxford University Press.
Luhmann, Niklas (1995), *Social Systems*. Stanford: Stanford University Press.
March, James G., and Johan P. Olsen (1989), *Rediscovering Institutions: the Organizational Basis of Politics*. New York: The Free Press.
Mouffe, Chantal (ed.) (1996), *Deconstruction and Pragmatism*. New York: Routledge.
Pêcheux, Michel (1982), *Language, Semantics and Ideology*. London: Macmillan.
Poster, Mark (1990), *The Mode of Information: Poststructuralism and Social Context*. Chicago: University of Chicago Press.
Potter, Jonathan, and Margaret Wetherell (1987), *Discourse and Social Psychology*. London: Sage.
Reinarman, Craig (1987), *American States of Mind*. New Haven: Yale University Press.
Rorty, Richard (1989), *Contingency, Irony, and Solidarity*. Cambridge: Cambridge University Press.
Saussure, Ferdinand de (1974), *Course in General Linguistics*. Suffolk: Fontana.
Sayer, Andrew (1984), *Method in Social Science: a Realist Approach*. London: Hutchinson.
Schegloff, Emanuel A., and Harvey Sacks (1973), 'Opening Up Closings', *Semiotica*, vol. 8, no. 4, pp. 289–327.
Sinclair, John M., and Malcolm Coulthard (1975), *Towards an Analysis of Discourse*. Oxford: Oxford University Press.
Torfing, Jacob (1999), *New Theories of Discourse*. Oxford: Blackwell.
Torfing, Jacob (2004), *Det stille sporskifte i Velfœrdsstaten*. Aarhus: Aarhus Universitetsforlag.
Winch, Peter (1990), *The Idea of Social Science and Its Relation to Philosophy*, 2nd edn. London: Routledge.
Wittgenstein, Ludwig (1953), *Philosophical Investigations*. Oxford: Basil Blackwell.
Žižek, Slavoj (1989), *The Sublime Object of Ideology*. London: Verso Press.
Žižek, Slavoj (1990), 'Beyond Discourse Analysis', in E. Laclau (ed.), *New Reflections on the Revolution of Our Time*. London: Verso Press, pp. 249–60.
Žižek, Slavoj (1991), *For They Know Not What They Do: Enjoyment as a Political Factor*. London: Verso Press.

# 1

# European Integration and Security: Analysing French and German Discourses on State, Nation, and Europe

*Ole Wæver*

> [Security] is not a mechanical problem...[A]n exact balance is impossible...because while powers may appear to outsiders as factors in a security arrangement, they appear domestically as expressions of a historical existence. No power will submit to a settlement, however well-balanced and however 'secure', which seems totally to deny its vision of itself.
>
> (Henry A. Kissinger, 1957, p. 146)

An analysis of domestic discourses regarding 'we'concepts, like state, nation, and Europe in the major European states can explain and, up to a point, predict developments in their over-all policies on security and Europe. Therefore, it explains big patterns (but not details) in European integration.

Although the European nation-states remain powerful, their identities have been transformed by including 'Europe' as concept, vision, and project within their self-defining narratives. This is what gives European security its current (relative) stability – although a precarious one, because the dominant narrative is vulnerable, especially in France. Should France turn dramatically less European, Germany will also pursue more old-fashioned, narrowly defined self-interest. A major aim of European security policy must therefore be to ensure a reasonable degree of success for French aims and ideas.

## Discourse analysis as a theory of foreign policy

Whereas much post-structuralism in International Relations (IR) has focused on the general, systemic construction – in policy and theory – of 'the international' around concepts like inside/outside, war/peace, and realism/idealism, this chapter presents discourse analysis as a *foreign policy theory*. In other words, it focuses on the individual state and tries to explain its options and actions. The application of discourse analysis at this level might surprise some people: can post-structuralists deal with problematic and 'outdated' concepts like state and foreign policy? In contrast, it is in line with post-structuralism and other forms of radical constructivism to study how worlds are constructed from within as well as from without. Radical constructivists must address how actors each have to struggle to make their own worlds (Onuf, 1989; Ringmar, 1997; Wæver, 1998b).

### Identity and foreign policy

Identity and foreign policy has become a popular subject in recent years. One motivation for this was the arrival of post-structuralism and some forms of constructivism, with their tendency generally to frame questions in terms of identity (in order to show how constructions are contingent and that the starting points that are usually taken for granted have to be explored in terms of how and why anything is or tries to be something and not something else). Writers from these backgrounds have, with great sophistication, explored many of the links between identity and foreign policy, but mainly *from* foreign policy *to* identity: how foreign policy serves to reproduce a certain identity. The other motivation behind the popularity of identity and foreign policy was empirical: the increasing importance of nationalism and other forms of 'identity politics' after the Cold War. The superficial inclusion of identity as a 'factor' in theories that were unconcerned about the self-referential implications of identity questions led to either culturalist truisms (whatever the Serbs do is caused by their culture), or unacceptable ad-hocism, where some countries are explained by culture (the others, those who are very ethnic, such as East Europeans), while other countries (we) are explained by more 'rational' factors. Thus, there is still a need for a systematically identity-based theory to explain foreign policy and thereby explore the meaning of identity for regional (European) security.

### High politics

The *theme* of this analysis is the foreign, Europe, and security policy of major European powers. This suits the method because Europe and state/nation are mutually constitutive for these countries. The major powers project a conception of Europe as part of their national vision of where they are going and who they are: their identity. France and Germany are indispensable to European integration and, therefore, the relationship becomes nicely circular. Europe has, de facto, to take a shape and, not least, a direction that enables political leaders in each country to uphold narratives (not necessarily identical or even similar to each other) of the future of France/Europe and Germany/Europe that are compatible with each nation's traditional political speech. If not compatible, these powers are so crucial to European integration that they always retain the option of blocking it. A Europe without integration is a policy option for them. 'Europe' (as idea, concept, and vision) is necessary to any political vision (and thus any stable government) in these countries, while compatibility with their national traditions is necessary for 'Europe' (as political process) to continue.[1]

Thus, the theory simultaneously explains foreign policy and European integration. The aspiration is not to explain the detailed policy in an EU context, for example, on the colour of feta cheese. Since the unifying dynamic is that of 'making sense' and projecting oneself into the future, this mode of analysis is most relevant for over-arching questions: what kind of Europe? What kind of security order?

## Discourse and structure

### Methodologically, discourses are the source for understanding . . . discourses

Discourse analysis works on public texts. It does not try to get to the thoughts or motives of the actors, their hidden intentions or secret plans. Especially for the study of foreign policy where much *is* hidden, it becomes a huge methodological advantage to stay at the level of discourse. A central feature of the theory is to be conscious of this, and not slide between talking discourse and perceptions, speech, and thought.[2]

What is often presented as a weakness of discourse analysis – 'how do you find out if they really *mean* it?', 'what if it is only rhetoric?' – can be turned into a methodological strength, as soon as one is scrupulous about sticking to discourse as discourse. Such questions or critiques derive from a confusion of discourse analysis with psychological or cognitive approaches, or it just assumes commonsensically that 'real' motives *must be* what everybody is interested in, with texts only a means to get to this. Not so: structures within discourse condition possible policies.

In particular, *overall* policy must hold a definite relationship to discursive structures, because it is always necessary for policy makers to be able to argue where 'this takes us'. Models of political structures are therefore built from concepts of state and nation, because an overall foreign policy line has to be able to articulate a country's 'vision of itself' and include the most profound 'we' categories.

Public, discursive activity constitutes a realm with its own coherence, logic, and meaningful tensions. Foreign policy discourse conditions future moves. The customary image of political speech, as haphazard and offhand, is replaced with a view of politics as a constant and relatively tight loop; where political argumentation about a specific issue is, on the one hand, strongly dependent on the basic conceptual logic available in a society and, on the other hand, reproduces or modifies this conceptual code, thereby setting the conditions for the next political struggle (cf. Pedersen, 1970).

Discourses organise knowledge systematically, and thus delimit what can and cannot be meaningfully said (Foucault, 1972; Dreyfus and Rabinow, 1982; Bartelson, 1995). Discourse is seen as a system, and some elements, and not least their constellation, are central to this system. Therefore, much of the actual textual work is about tracing the development of a few key concepts, their historical origins, their transformations, and not least their constitutive relationship to other concepts (cf. Koselleck, 1979).

**Layered structures**

Structures are layered. Depth-levels are a central feature of the current approach. An external reason for this is the aspiration for a parallel to the international structure suggested by the prominent IR theorist Kenneth Waltz (1979), a structure of successive depth-levels (Ruggie, 1983). A reason internal to discourse analysis is the problem of change.

With a Foucauldian concept of discourse, change appears in the form of incomprehensible jumps between synchronic and structural orders. From one order (episteme/discourse/structure), everything is suddenly different and we are in another constellation of mutual conditioning. Foucauldian discourse analysis studies logical spaces; how meaning is governed by specific rules, and thus how a number of seemingly contradictory and opposed enunciations can be seen as regulated by some system defining possible, meaningful speech. One of the advantages of the concept of a *layered* structure is that it can specify change within continuity.

Change is not an either–or question, because we are not operating at one level only. The concept of a 'dominant' discourse becomes relative, too. That something is in 'opposition' or even 'marginalised' means only that it is 'outside' and 'different' at the level of manifest politics, while it probably *shares* codes at the next (deeper) level of abstraction. The 'dominant' political line and the main opposition most often share a lot (except *the* question on the agenda), and the more marginalised opposition shares less, but still some, basic codes. This follows from the fact that political opponents relate to each other, and therefore almost always deal with some of the same issues and use related concepts and images while struggling to reformulate and conquer other key terms (Laclau and Mouffe, 1985, Chs 3 and 4).

This is not a complete solution. Since we do not make Lévi-Strauss's assumption of an over-arching structural logic, including rules of transformation, our systems are all contingent, and it is – and *should* be – possible to imagine a change beyond the system. In case of such change, we can say very little about how things would look. We have not solved the logical problem that discourse analysis, qua structural analysis of logical spaces, inevitably orders its material into synchronic patterns. We have only placed Foucauldian boxes within each other, which, up to a point, enables a dynamic analysis.

The depth-levels do not imply that the deeper is truer or that the surface is caught eternally by some structures that are perpetual 'winners' (classical structuralism). Rather it refers to *degrees* of sedimentation: the deeper structures are more solidly sedimented and more difficult to politicise and change, partly because they are more abstract and thereby logically implied across a wide spectrum. But, principally, change is always possible since all these structures are socially constituted (Laclau, 1990, pp. 33–6; Bertramsen, Thomsen, and Torfing, 1991: pp. 30–1).[3]

When pressure builds up in a system and discourse does not easily handle a problem anymore ('dislocation'), it is possible first to make 'surface changes' which keep all the deeper levels intact. This can become increasingly uncomfortable and unstable, however, and at some point a deeper change might happen.

Every new layer adds specifications and variations on the deeper one, but one cannot take a gradual change at, for instance, the third layer and say that it weighs more heavily than the second.[4] Either one is still inside the frame set by the prior 'choice' at the first and second level, and then the changes at level 3 are variations on this basic premise, *or* pressure becomes sufficiently great to generate a change at the first or second level, and then the change will be to a radically new agenda at the higher level. The system makes a 'jump' and tendencies, therefore, cannot be extrapolated – they can lead to a rupture, and then a new creative act rebuilds compatibility in a place, which is probably 'surprising' when seen in relation to 'tendencies', but logical in relation to the possibilities defined by the deep structure.

In line with post-structuralist decentring of structure, the suggested hierarchy rests on impossible closure and constant destabilisation. The tree-like structure corresponds to Laclau and Mouffe's emphasis on internal connections in politics. In contrast to classical Marxism, political opponents are not totally external and contrasted – they struggle to conquer shared nodal points, they integrate in hegemonic projects some integrative schemes that inevitably enter into their own conceptions, and thus rivals become partly divergent articulations of shared components.[5]

Obviously, it remains controversial whether the different constellations over a longer time span stay within such a tree-shaped set of options or whether change invalidates even such non-essentialist structures.

## National and European identity

Much reflection on European security and integration is hampered by the problem of working out the relationship between the European level and that of the nation-states. Due to the presumption of sovereignty and state-centrism in IR theory, 'state or EU' is mostly treated as having necessarily one level as dominant. Either the states ultimately decide and the EU is just another international organisation, *or* the EU is becoming a polity in its own right and the states are consequently fading into a subordinate status.

This either–or form is most acute in discussions on 'European identity'. It is argued that there is no European identity for which people are willing to make the ultimate sacrifice. This is a false either–or: European identity will not be important and relevant only if it wins out against national identities. 'Europe' *is* important for the way national identities have been reshaped. Identity questions too often get translated into anthropological questions about how people *are* or *live* (and then Danes and Italians allegedly are too different) but, as it is argued by most of the contemporary literature on nationalism, political identity is a discursive and symbolic construction (notably Anderson, 1983). It is furthermore a second-order concept, where a nation means to identify with *the idea* of being French, and to assume that others do so – not concretely to feel that one is 'identical' to other (concrete) French (Gellner, 1983, pp. 175–6; Žižek, 1992, p. 196; Wæver, 1997, pp. 329–31). Because an identity is discursive, it should not be studied primarily in relation to its concrete people but in relation to other identities – not only the famous 'Other' of arguments obsessed with self–other relations, but more importantly other 'we's: because all people construct their self with the help of a complex constellation of collective identifications, these have to be articulated with each other. For instance, *national* identity often depends on how the identification with nation works synergistically with an identification as *man* ('just warrior') or *woman* (the defended 'beautiful soul') (Elshtain, 1987). The motor in the present theory is therefore the eternal problematique to articulate the primary political we-concepts in a given area with *each other* in a viable form.

Hereby, the question of regional stability can be addressed as well. Power has not been 'transferred' to supra-national institutions; the main decisions are still made in national capitals. But Europe is not a purely external or dependent matter. 'Europe' is a central component of the 'we' for which decisions are made. It is no longer possible to talk about the future of France or Germany without Europe entering this vision. In other words, the relationship between nation/state and Europe is internal. Stability – regional security – consequently depends crucially on the domestic articulation in each major power of a project for Europe with long-held concepts of state and nation.

## Method

### How does one construct the models?

This question can be subdivided into two further questions: what should be the different layers of the layered structure? And, how does one get to the precise content in a specific case?

The first layer is a *state-nation core concept*: the basic idea of what 'state' and 'nation' refers to and not least whether the two are closely connected (France) or separately constituted (Germany). The second layer is made up of *the relational position vis-à-vis Europe*. In the German case, where the twin concepts of power state and romantic nation are constitutive but not fused (as in the French concept), the second level also includes the combination of yes/no in relation to each of the two concepts. At the second level Europe is only relationally constituted: does it have an internal, external, or no relationship to ideas of state and nation? At the third layer we find the content of Europe: *what kind of Europe is promoted*? Confederation or federation, Western Europe or All-Europe?

The reason for selecting state, nation, and Europe (and in some other cases 'people' and, for example, 'Norden') as central categories is that these are the forms the 'we' takes. Thus, the claim for pre-eminence of state/nation over, say, conceptions of international relations or concepts of security is that the most important categories are the identity-related ones. Not simply 'who' we are, but the *way(s)* one thinks the 'we'. We (French) are conceived as nation and as state, but Europe is also emerging as a 'we' category and, therefore, the relationship between state/nation and Europe is one of different layers of identity in complex constellations of competition and mutual definition.[6]

When working on a specific case, how does one find these concepts? There is no formalised way to generate the model, such as computer-based methods of getting from a text to structure (cf. Alker, 1996). One gets the clues from reading texts, but the structure is generated more as is suggested by Waltz (or Marx or Popper): creatively! One has to come up with some good ideas – and then try them out; either with strict tests (Popper, 1963), or by elaborating deductively a large story, which convinces through its rationalised reconstruction of complex reality when it finally reaches 'the surface' (Marx, 1956 [1867]).

The use of *national* discourses is only one way to construct models. One could instead focus on different socio-economic/integrationist visions for Europe, and then possibly look at the different balances between these in different European countries (Diez, 1999). The stress here on national settings is motivated not only by the familiar IR argument that the most important decisions are still made on behalf of nation-states, but equally by the importance for discourse analysis of language, and of traditions of political thought: therefore it is structured by language areas and major political units (two things that in the present cases largely overlap).[7]

## Reading what?

This kind of discourse analysis has a synchronic and a diachronic component, each with its characteristic way of using texts. The first establishes a model by fitting material from different contexts, actors, and years into a 'structure';

the second moves through time with differentiated actors and sees how the structure shapes action and how the structure is in turn reproduced and modified. In the first part, the task is to clarify the logic with powerful examples from diverse contexts (and thus fragments are fitted together as a puzzle without much attention to their origins). In the second, there is much more attention to context and interactions: who tries to do what and how they either draw on the structure or run up against it and therefore try to modify it (cf. Skinner, 2002).

The former treats actors as *instances* of discourse, an *internal* relationship between structure and agent. In the latter, the relationship is *external*, and structures and agents *interact*.

- For the construction of the synchronic model, the key factor is leading politicians acting in their official capacity (cf. Pedersen, 1970), but others contribute to shaping public discourse. Often intellectuals, even researchers, present a logic more explicitly. It can then be checked whether the same mechanism is more implicitly at play with politicians. When reading politicians, it is fruitful to select 'difficult situations': not negotiated, blurred statements like party platforms, but interventions in heated debates (for instance, in Parliament). Here they need to mobilise rhetorical power and therefore draw on those semiotic structures that generate most meaning for their purpose.[8]
- For the explanatory, diachronic, part the task is to show how these structures constrained or suggested arguments and positions. Therefore, one must trace both how actors performed linguistic actions to modify discursive structures when needed, and when they carried out counter-intuitive foreign policy acts, which can be explained by the restraints imposed by discursive structures. Thus, this part of the analysis must follow political processes and actors in a more traditional way, while using, as an analytical instrument, the structures created in the first part of the analysis.[9]

Particularly for the synchronic part, a typical question is: how many and which texts should I read? The flippant, but not wholly incorrect, answer is: any text, as long as you read for long enough! The rationale is this: if discursive structures operate in a political space, they will show up in any text. If you analyse it deeply enough, you will find the most abstract and general forces in it. In practice, however, as well as for theoretical reasons having to do with the post-structuralist critique of structuralism, this is not the way it works. Rather, one has to establish a general sense of the country and its politics, read an awful lot, gradually recognise recurring patterns, and stumble across puzzling formulations – often details – that afterwards reveal important general insights. Thus, one has to pursue a kind of knowledge characteristic of the humanities (for example, someone studying French or German culture). This is one of the reasons why this method is not always received with enthusiasm in political science. You can only deal with a rather limited number of countries because you have to know the language, the history of the country, and a rather broad spectrum of its culture and politics. Political science is of course much more 'efficient' when it can take statistical data from lots of countries (of which one does not speak the language) and manipulate them with a computer.

**Reading how?**

The strategy is basically to look for key concepts and their mutual relationship. One asks *how* the text argues, not *what* it says. For instance, in a debate on Bosnia in the German parliament, the interesting question is not who takes what position regarding what intervention, but *how* they argue their case. What are the powerful categories on which the argument rests, how are they related, are some concepts presented as, by necessity, companions (for example, 'us', Europe, Germans, civilisation), are some presented as self-evident opposites (for example, Balkan and peace or nationalism and Europe)? More interesting than the arguments made are the assumptions not stated, but necessary for the argument to be meaningful, the structural arrangements of key concepts, and chains of equivalence and oppositions. There can be many of these, but one tries to boil them down to the most general and recurrent axes of valorisation, which enable the text to generate meaning.

**'Explaining', 'predicting'? Is this really possible?**

Does this theory *explain* European developments? It does not offer ultimate causes for explanation.[10] Often, the causes of change stem from outside the theory (as in Waltzianism), but it explains where we are more or less likely to arrive if the situation changes, as well as essential elements of how this new situation would operate. When simultaneously analysing two or more countries, the combined *negative predictions* encircle a limited number of European possibilities.

Ideally, one should combine the layered international structure (Waltz, à la Ruggie) with the layered structures of the domestic discourses within major regional actors to produce a dynamic model of structure and change in a regional setting. Whenever an actor is unable to fulfil the dual criteria of compatibility with both structures, it will have to try to modify the one that is least rigid (cf. Kissinger, 1957; Wæver, 1994). This leads occasionally to quite drastic reorientations of policy, when the dual structural squeeze makes a policy unsustainable.

'Change' does not, therefore, entail the question whether it is possible or not to change something, but instead how much pressure is necessary and what the ratio is of (political) costs tolerated per depth of change on either side. Ultimately, anything is possible – some changes are just very unlikely, or entail very dramatic changes of many other issues. With a stable system, one can make predictions based upon one's understanding of the sources of meaning. However, if the system is under pressure, one cannot take the specific system, as such, as a premise, but only move one level down and ask what other combinations are possible on the basis of the deeper elements. And if the crisis is severe, then move down one more level. In the latter case, the theory does not make specific predictions about future policy, but points to certain possible directions of change. Several possible policies can therefore be presented as possible, although they are, at the surface level (concrete issues), quite far from each other; what they share is being logically possible constructions on the basis of the basic discourse elements. The model makes 'negative predictions'; it describes what is impossible given a certain structure (and what level of structural change would be necessary to make such a change possible).

## France, Germany, and Europe

Since concepts of state and nation are strong organising ideas for foreign policy, a consistent European definition of these can be the social anchor for regional stability. In the central narration of what 'Germany' is and where it is heading, 'Europe'/EU is essential. If integration collapsed, the meaning of Germany would have to be radically rearticulated. Identity is narrative (Ricoeur, 1995; Brunner, 1991), and only so many basic stories can be told defining what Germany is about.

The interweaving of state, nation, and Europe is most easy to see in the case of Germany, which has systematically tried to act only 'in Europe's name' (Ash, 1993). But also for France it has become difficult to imagine a policy, which projects an attractive and realistic France, without implicating a European project. This is no guarantee for a specific 'pro-EU' line, but in order to 'act French', one has to be able to construct a vision for Europe. It can be one based on French alliance policy against Germany, or integration with Germany, but the set of 'we's from which a future is constructed has grown from state, nation, *patrie*, *Volk* to include also 'Europe'.

Especially for a major power, the overall foreign policy must explain where this leaves 'us': what kind of future for 'France'/'Germany'/'Russia' in what kind of Europe. This is not a static challenge in the sense that there is one fixed idea of, say, France. A few basic core meanings (the state-nation) can be related to Europe in a limited number of ways, and thus one can construct several different Europe policies that are meaningful in a French political context – but not just *any* Europe policy. Several policies that would seem perfectly logical from a Finnish perspective – or from the perspective of some abstract theory of 'state interests' – can be very difficult to present in the French political language.

Henry Kissinger introduced the important concept of a power's *vision of itself*:

> [Security] is not a mechanical problem... [A]n exact balance is impossible... because while powers may appear to outsiders as factors in a security

> arrangement, they appear domestically as expressions of a historical existence. No power will submit to a settlement, however well-balanced and however 'secure', which seems totally to deny its vision of itself. (Kissinger, 1957, p. 146)

An international order should not be judged in relation to abstract, universal criteria but in [illegible] each nation views it on the basis of basic categories and conceptions about what it means to be 'France'/'Germany'/ and so on.[11] Sections 4.1 and 4.2 present the discursive structure for France and Germany respectively, as it has developed over the centuries until the 1980s. Section 4.3 focuses upon the transformations following the end of the Cold War and looks more dynamically at moves and manoeuvring. In 4.4, the current situation is analysed in terms of current competitors and overall stability.

### France

The French model starts from a very specific and historically grounded concept of the 'state-nation'. The idea of a centralised state predates the French Revolution and was stimulated by its poor fit with reality, that is, the existence of very strong regions. A concept of nation defined in relation to the state and a simultaneous grounding of state legitimacy in the nation was born with the French Revolution.

The first layer of the structure consists of this basic state-nation idea (Fig. 1.1), the fusion of state and nation. Two more elements are constitutive of the general model of the state-nation principally: the necessity of *some* external role for the state, and the necessity of a foundation for the nation in *patrie*.[12]

For the French, political thinking has to be about the state, about an actor, coherence, and will. In most variants of French thinking the state is centralised, demarcated by clear borders and endowed with a certain mission. If Europe is to become a political reality, it will have to take on these qualities.

In the time of de Gaulle, the slogan (though not actually his expression) was *L'Europe des patries*, respecting the full sovereignty of the *état-nation*. This seemed to be an enactment of the tradition: the state-nation was the only foundation on which the new Europe could be built. In 1983–84 came a dramatic shift in French European policy. France started to press for the European Community to exercise a state-like role in as many areas as possible – to operate as a political actor. Had France experienced a volte-face?

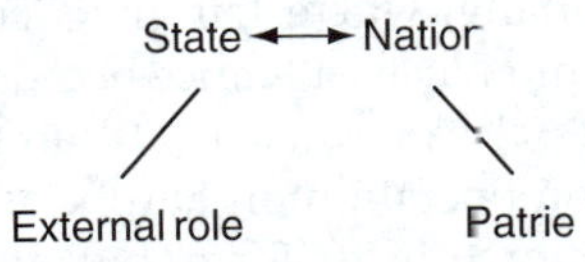


*Figure 1.1* Model of the state-nation

On the contrary, the political thinking was the same – just one level up. Now Europe had to be what France had always wanted to be. France had become too small, and its mission must be taken over by 'Europe'. Thus the French concept of the state was repeated at the level of Europe, and the apparent turn-around of 1983–84 was actually based on continuity at the level of political thinking.

This seems incomprehensible to Danes and probably to the British, who think more in zero-sum terms: what is given to Brussels is lost to Copenhagen or London – what is won back to the nation is taken away from a federalising Europe. Not in France, where Mitterrand could say: 'The more Europe there will be, the more France.' The explanation lies in French thinking about the state-nation, which implies that the nation has a mission and that it *has* to act and be recognised by others. The French idea of France is not that the French are superior in principle; but that the values France represents are *universal* values: human rights, political rights, and the idea of the state-nation. The French have, through the French Revolution, a particularly intimate relationship with these values. It is this logic that made it possible for de Gaulle to state in his New Year's speech in 1967: 'Our action is directed toward goals which are connected and which, because they are French, reflect the desire of all men' (Grosser, 1980 [1978], p. 184). In this way an inner link is forged between France and Europe. The Europe created must necessarily have a heart that beats in French. To be *political*, Europe must have a pulse that only France is capable of supplying. This ensures for France, when transferring its ambitions to Europe, that the European project is worthwhile; that it is sufficiently French. We are not talking of *control* by France, nor French influence as such, but about Europe being constituted and acting *in a way* that is French.

This reveals the *logic* of the French Europe (of the last two decades), but *where* precisely is it? The German one is located at the centre of the continent, within complex networks, and de Gaulle's was 'Atlantic to the Urals'. The new French Europe, of necessity, has been the European Union (EU). This follows from the tasks Europe is called upon to fulfil. Only Western Europe, or more precisely the EU, can attain state-like qualities and become coherent enough to act decisively. Thus it is unacceptable to the French to have a Europe with an unclear border or uncertain membership (in the 1980s the Germans were often suspected of wanting a Europe that just 'faded out' somewhere to the East, un-statelike, and unable to act in unity).

More systematically (Fig. 1.2), this state-nation can relate to Europe in three ways. First, externally with Europe as the scene on which France acts. Secondly, through a doubling, where Europe is created as a larger France which takes on the tasks and ideals of France because France has become too small to project its universal values itself (Mitterrand). Thirdly, to execute the full French state-nation operation on Europe as such, in other words, to create a Europe that is French in its form, but not with a distinct France

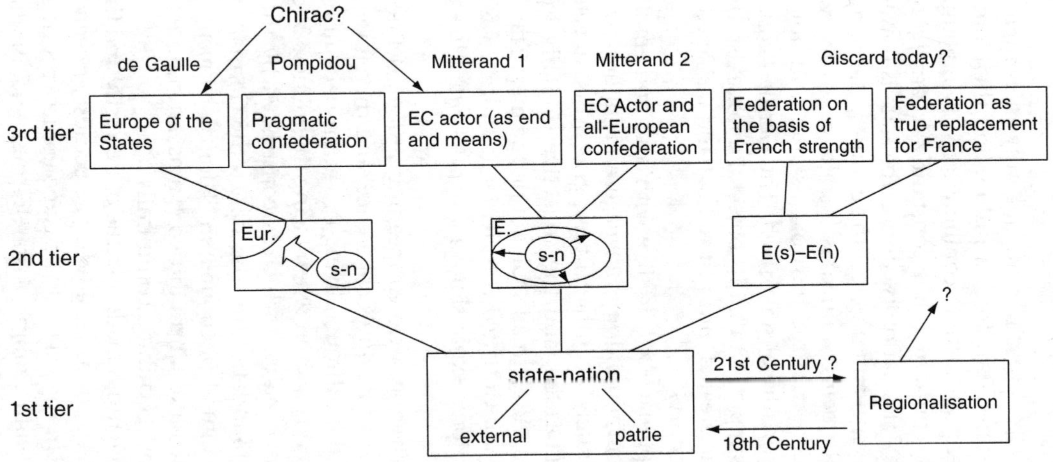


*Figure 1.2* French concepts of state, nation, and Europe

in it.[13] The second layer is purely relational: where is France in relation to Europe? It does not include the content/form of Europe. The third is: exactly what Europe do we deal with, Western Europe or all-Europe, Federation or Confederation?[14]

**Germany**

The German model is very different, not only in content but also in its architecture. It does not start from a fusion, and therefore it becomes less elegant, more a menu of possible combinations. Two guiding ideas can be combined, negated, contrasted, but constantly recur: the romantic nation and the power state – the nation is culture, the state is power.

During the eighteenth and nineteenth centuries, Germany was shaped by its experience of not being unified as a state, at a time when important neighbours formed centralised territorial states, and not approximating a state-nation when nationalism arrived. The German concept of the state was shaped by the simple fact that its object did not exist; the German state was something to be created, not just refined and reshaped with new ideas of nation and modernity.

One important approach was to 'live with' this and emphasise *the nation* as directly grounded in community, language, and culture – without a German state. From the mid-eighteenth century, the inner development of the individual was emphasised, and the collective similarly internalised. The Nation exists deep in the German soul, not on the map. The 'inventor' of the modern nation, Johann Gottfried von Herder, definitely was not a supporter of the state, of a nation's expression in a nation-*state*. He was interested in culture and people.

A culture is conceived as a closed meaning system, defined by its unique traits, exhibiting an organic inner coherence, and therefore only possible to understand from within, through living it. The abstract, universal principles of enlightenment come up short when facing the fullness of concrete life. In contrast to the French nation, which is constituted by the state – and is simultaneously the foundation for the state – the German nation exists in itself as an ethno-cultural phenomenon. Thomas Nipperdey (1986, p. 32) summarises romantic nationalism in two claims: all culture is national, and a nation is defined by its cultural community.[15]

For a while, the romantics made a virtue of necessity and the impossibility of German unity was seen as an advantage because a deeper, truer nation could be cultivated. In the wake of the Napoleonic wars (which taught the Germans about the vulnerability of statelessness and stimulated a general European nationalism) the state moved to centre stage.

The state was also conceived in a particular way, now shaped by both romanticism and German idealism and, not least, the 'power school' among German historians. German idealism was a thinking of strong concepts, and it developed a strong concept of the state.[16] Historian Heinrich von

Treitschke offered the famous definition according to which 'the nature of the state is first power, then secondly power, and thirdly again power'. International politics had for some centuries increasingly been about states, but this was in a much more concrete manner where ruler, state, and interests were connected in confusing ways. Only with German idealism (to which the discipline of International Relations therefore owes much more than it likes to think [Wæver 1996, 1998a]) did international politics become steered by an *abstract* state, by the state as absolute notion. The state ranks above the individual, and history is ultimately its struggle for power and self-expression. State, power, meaning, and history are all tied together in intense logical connections. The power state as idea is created in Germany. Compared to elsewhere, the state in German is more abstract, more absolute, and defined by power Fig. 1.3).

German post-war thinking about state, nation, and Europe builds on this German set of ideas. Seen superficially, it could seem that the West Germans were 're-educated' and turned into 'normal Western' democrats, but one does not understand the German way of thinking politics if one misses how they reach such positions from their own starting point. The power state is negated, but not forgotten. The state is still at the centre, and it is still about power. But the state as condensation of power is no longer the aim, measure, and meaning of everything; but rather the big, structuring *problem*.[17] Internally, this thinking led to a constitutional system counteracting any concentration of power (by ruling out referenda, for instance). In foreign policy Germany was binding itself in almost every imaginable international organisation.

In 1945, *the nation* was at least as problematic a concept as the state. Germanness was darkened by the shadow of Auschwitz. Thus, one could hardly retreat from the state to celebrate the nation. A part of the solution (especially for the hegemonic centre-left from the 1960s onwards) became what Bernhard Giesen (1993) has called the 'Holocaust nation'. Nazi-Germany's unspeakable crimes must be acknowledged and taken-upon-oneself by Germans. The community they join – based on the fight against

| | late 18th Century | 19th Century–1945 | 1945–80 | 1980–90 | 1990– |
|---|---|---|---|---|---|
| Romantic Nation | + | + | 0 or – | + | + or 0 |
| Power State | 0 | + | – | – | Emerging Battle |

\+ = functioning  – = negated  0 = not active

*Figure 1.3* History of German concepts of nation and state

political nationalism – is a truly German one, because it is based on a unique event, which cannot be communicated, compared, or in any other way relativised. Thus, the intellectuals created a kind of paradoxical German identity in line with romantic nationalism in its form – even if allegedly taking the opposite view. The misdeeds of the Nazi period are the definite argument. All discussions are, in the last instance, settled in one point: Auschwitz. The only way to relate responsibly to being German is by fighting nationalism, war, and power politics, and especially in preventing the re-emergence of a strong and heroised German state. The dominant conception of the state, the anti-power-state, had been given a support pillar: the Holocaust nation.

In the 1980s, the romantic nation reappeared in the original sense of existence in the absence of political structures. Both *Germany* and *Mitteleuropa* took this shape. An important part of the 'German Europe' was, especially in the 1980s, the *lowering in importance of borders*: lessening their dividing force and creating dynamic non-state processes across formal borders (between states and, before 1989, borders between different political systems). Social democratic 'Germany policy' became a vision for a relationship with East Germany, where human, cultural, economic, and, in some sense, even political Germany could heal, while the country stayed formally divided in two. Other projects were about letting 'natural spaces' – such as *Mitteleuropa* – reappear without challenging the borders of the nation-states. In the years around unification, the relationship to former German areas in Poland and the Czech Republic were conceived in such cultural, non-state terms as well. Germany should not move borders but strive for a Europe where borders mean less – thereby letting historical ties return.

Germany supports the institution-building EU-project for several reasons. One follows directly from the state-nation conception: to divide power on as many levels as possible and thereby avoid a fusion of state and power. Another is that EU shapes Europe as not state-to-state driven, and thereby not the balance-of-power Europe that goes together with a German power state. Thirdly, formal institutions produce confidence and stability which makes otherwise suspicious neighbours accept a certain German dominance at the heart of the Continent through networks of German firms, nostalgia tourists, regionalist policies, and much else.

At this point one should look carefully at the two lower levels in the model (Fig. 1.4), because the model is updated to the present day and therefore much of level 3 can only be understood in relation to developments after German unification – the more basic options were already clear before this.

## Adjustments in 1989–90 – reacting to the fall of the Berlin Wall

French reactions to events in Germany in 1989–90 were, understandably, somewhat confused. Such developments brought the basic dilemmas of French foreign policy into the open. The changes in Eastern Europe had to

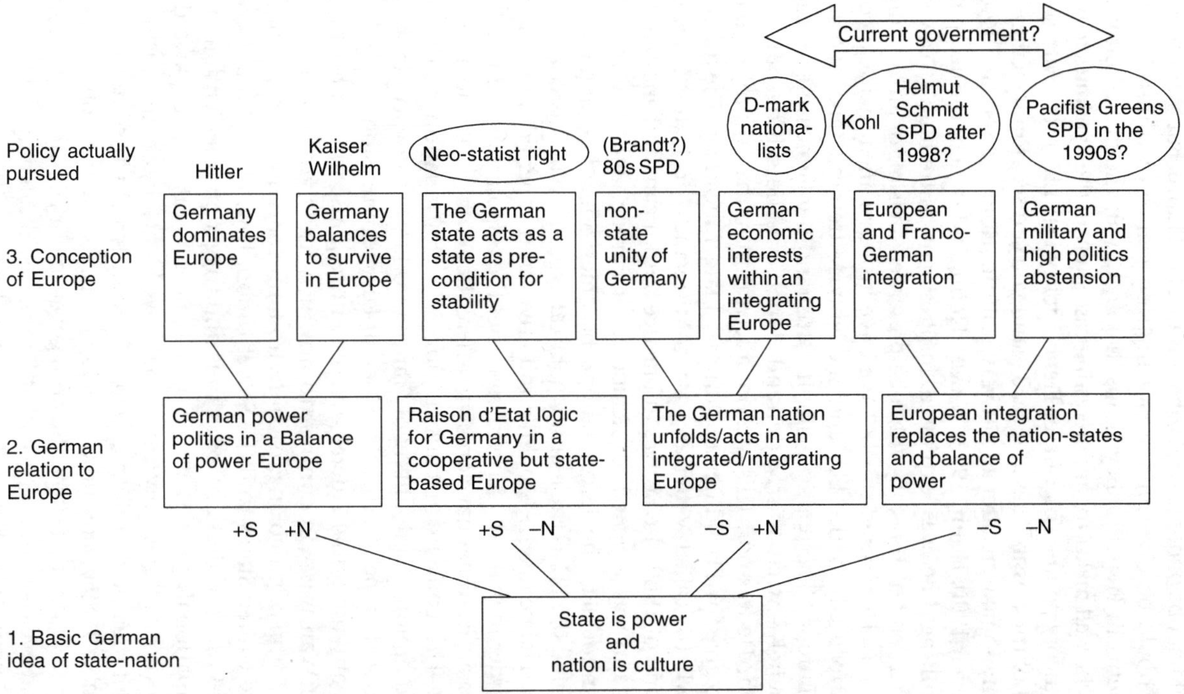


*Figure 1.4* German concepts of state, nation, and Europe

be welcomed since they represented French Revolutionary democratic values (Mitterrand pointed out that these events were continuations of the impulse from the French Revolution). Freedom, democracy, and a nation becoming whole could not be opposed while one was loyal to France. But that the nation to unify should be *Germany* was not high on France's wishlist. To follow developments in French policy almost day by day in the first months after the fall of the wall makes for an interesting case study of the dynamics to which discourse theory points. You can see French policy experimenting with several (if not all) of the possibilities at level 3 – and you can see from reactions and debates why some were after all not very realistic (Holm, Larsen, and Wæver, 1990; Wæver, 1990; Holm, 1992; Wæver, Holm, and Larsen, forthcoming).

The resulting line was expressed in President Mitterrand's New Year speech at the end of 1989, in which he presented a vision of an 'all Europe' confederation. How could this be? We have just explained that France was decidedly focused on the EU, and suddenly Mitterrand talks about 'the whole of Europe'! The political elite in Paris (and the French press) reacted with disbelief – what was Mitterrand doing, was he selling out on EU integration? He was not. This was not a retreat from the EU project, but an attempt to give the EU a different purpose, a larger meaning. The difference between what is called Mitterrand-1 and Mitterand-2 in Figure 1.2 is that, until the end of 1989, the EU was in practice both means and end but, from 1989, the aim was widened to include all of Europe. But since this wider Europe cannot act, the larger Europe becomes one more argument for strengthening the EU as the realistic political expression of this vision. More concretely, France takes 'Ostpolitik' initiatives in this period (EBRD, and so forth) in order to make the Eastern countries the responsibility of the EU, in contrast to an informal development where they would fall under German influence. The conceptual construction is a continuation of the basic Mitterrand option of a doubling of France into EU, but now equipped also with a double Europe of EU and a wider all-European mission.

In Germany the initial federal government response to the breaching of the Berlin Wall was – in contrast to how it is usually presented today – cautious; fearful of provoking reactions from the four Allied powers, Britain, France, the United States, and the Soviet Union. It was feared that German time would run ahead of European time and trigger an intervention by the four occupational powers, which would be a giant leap backward for Germans who had gradually conquered sovereignty by marginalising the relevance of their peculiar formal status. So Kohl actually tried in November and December 1989 to slow down developments, so as to stave off four-power intervention. In this first stage, the Kohl government tried to keep the speed of German development down so that Europe could catch up.

From February 1990, however, it became clear that West Germany could not control developments. The East Germans decided – partly with their feet, partly by the election – to join with the West Germans. But this 'loss of control' for Bonn was actually a diplomatic *victory*. In this way, all potential four-power vetoes were circumvented. How do you veto a collapse? East Germany seemed to cave in and stream under the door to the Federal Republic. Bonn, seemingly, could not be blamed (Wæver, 1990).

That unification would come, and rather sooner than expected, became clear in early February 1990 when Kohl and Genscher in Moscow obtained Soviet endorsement of unification. From now on German policy became much more focused on European developments. The dilemma of German and European time remained: German developments could not be slowed down, European developments had to take on German speed. *This did not mean a Europe on German terms; on the contrary, it meant German speed and Franco-Russian form.* Germany approached the EU along French lines (which became the treaty of Maastricht), and the German foreign ministry came up with ideas for all-European security structures, fulfilling Soviet wishes, but hardly articulated in Moscow (*Der Spiegel*, 12 February 1990, p. 23). In the terminology of 'three competing Europes' (Wæver, 1990), *from February 1990 German diplomacy became very active in building the French and the Russian Europe.* Why? Because the Germans were getting their own Europe – one with room for national unity and economic expansion in central Europe (the high cost of German unification had yet to be realised). In order to keep the overall process stable it was necessary to keep a balance between all three major Europes.

France and Russia have been accommodated largely because they could most easily impede the German process of unification. This is not because they hold the strongest cards, but on the contrary because they hold the weakest. German unity affects them directly as their status had been defined in relation to Germany. French identity in the post-war world rested largely on its *difference* from Germany, France being fully sovereign and independent, one of the four occupying powers, and possessing nuclear weapons. Now that Germany became a 'normal' state, France was correspondingly reduced in stature. Nuclear weapons seemed generally to lose symbolic value, while economics gained importance. As Dominique Moïsi put it: 'the balance between the Mark and the Bomb is sliding to the advantage of the former' (*Die Zeit*, 9 December 1988). Furthermore, the French mission involved in 'transcending Yalta' is lost when Yalta is actually overcome. For many Russians, the control of eastern Germany was the ultimate symbol of victory in the Second World War and the guarantee against its repetition. Letting go of the main prize of victory was criticised as an offence to millions of Russian war dead.

The UK is not on a par with France and Russia, first because the UK is not affected to the same degree by developments in Germany. There is no identity crisis over German unification. Secondly, Britain has not really joined in the competition for the formation of the image of Europe. British reticence over Europe has meant that she is not part of that game.

The US, with more justice, could be included as a major European power. US policy has played an active and constructive role in the German-European unification process (the US being the most pro-unification of the four), and furthermore succeeded in securing at the time a surprisingly strong position for NATO.

Good statesmanship will try to find ways to articulate the nation-state through Europe policies that also leave room for the other major nation-states (and their Europes). Immediately after the fall of the Berlin Wall, Germany – who had potentially much to win, but also a lot to lose if others turned against it – was especially active in building the French and Russian Europe (and the Americans by playing along with and not against unification secured a place for the Atlantic Europe). Thus emerged the relatively successful 'grand bargain' of 1990 (Wæver, 1990). Europe to the French meant the strengthening of a France-like EU; to the Russians it meant securing an all-European framework that defined Russia as within Europe; and to the Germans Europe meant allowing interactions, societies, and economies to reconnect across old divisions.

In 1990 it was possible to give Europe a direction of development where all of the Europe projects could unfold simultaneously. They are competitors, but not incompatible – and thereby all major powers were able to imagine themselves in the Europe promised.

**Status 2004: risks and recommendations**

The European post-wall order was stable because it fulfilled the dual criteria of two kinds of compatibility (Fig. 1.5). First, each of the major countries construct a narrative of state, nation, and Europe that makes sense in relation to the national tradition of political thought. Secondly, when we in this way get Europe in the plural, these different Europes are politically compatible – it is possible for a French integration project, German border-penetrating networks, and Russian all-European structures to unfold at the same time. Where the first is a question of discursive compatibility, the second is partly a practical question: how much can possibly be implemented in the direction of those developments that matter to each power. Then it is unproblematic that, for example, the German version of creating a 'vision of itself' – with a low political profile, emphasising economy, and the downgrading of borders – is seen as mildly ridiculous in France. Actually 'disagreement', where the powers define Europe differently, is not necessarily a weakness; it is very likely a precondition for the process. The parties 'get' Europe in different registers and therefore one's gain is not necessarily another's loss (Fig. 1.5).

The Russian part has been gradually weakened, probably due to the excessive attention of the West to its own problems such as the Maastricht ratification, Bosnia, and NATO debates. The Russian loss of an honourable role was realised too late by the West – only when Yeltsin stated this in words indicating that Russia had already slid out of the grand bargain. In practice, Russia became

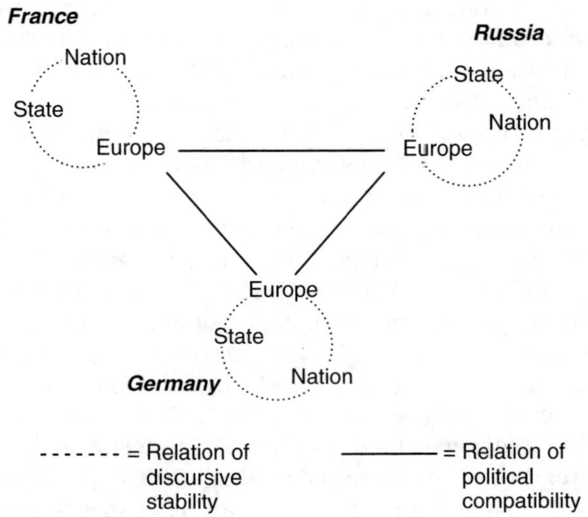


*Figure 1.5* Three competing Europes

a centre in its own regional, ex-Soviet system, and Germany and France became the decisive countries in a Europe, reaching to at least the Eastern border of Poland, Turkey, and increasingly Northern Africa (Buzan and Wæver, 2003).

The main question for the future stability and peace of Europe is not directly about relations among the major powers, but the *inner* struggles over national identity/Europe projects in France, Germany, and Russia. In each country, strong competitors to the project that functioned in the comprehensive quid pro quo of 1990 have emerged.

To assess how stable this constellation is, one has to enter into the constructions in order to judge from the inside. This is of course a quite demanding task, and we will here take only a brief look at the two most important countries, France and Germany. This leads among other things to the somewhat surprising conclusion that Europe does not primarily have a German problem, but a French problem.

France has witnessed increasingly worried debates, partly due to the lack of success for some parts of the French vision (defence, for instance), partly due to successes. As so often in the history of European integration, French second thoughts on their own schemes is one of the main risks. The Mitterrand strategy of 'doubling' France at the European level – a partial *aufhebung* of the French state-nation – led to worries about the resulting 'France', especially its 'banalisation', regionalisation, and loosened ties to the ground, the *patrie* (Holm, 1992, 1996, 1997, 2002). Also, the European project itself was doubted: did it really bind Germany, or was Germany so strong that only

France was tied, and therefore more wisely should secure its manoeuvrability (that is, move towards the left part of the model). The issue of migration questions the political (and secular) concept of the state-nation and reactivates *patrie* in problematical ways.

In the case of France – in contrast to Germany – the three main competing rationales for French foreign (and domestic) politics represent the different basic structural options (level 2 in Fig. 1.2). This implies that French policy is so deeply politicised and challenged that there is no level 2 consensus. Radically different articulations of the basic state-nation idea compete on the political scene. Whereas Mitterrand, 15 to 20 years ago, had a solid consensus around his position of the doubling of France as EU, and therefore transferring state-qualities to Europe, problems and challenges have increased. Particularly during the 1992 Maastricht referendum and the 1995 Presidential election, ideas of more strictly Gaullist derivation were present as the main challenger (much stronger than the federalist alternative occasionally represented by Giscard d'Estaing). Chirac represents a coalition that mixes Mitterrand continuation with strong elements of French independence, including state-based alliance politics both with and against Germany. Various internal as well as external problems have made the 'Mitterrand line' increasingly difficult to present convincingly and, therefore, a meaning vacuum threatens in France. Up to the EU's Inter-Governmental Conferences in 1996–97 and since, France, which normally represents 'the vision thing' found it unusually difficult to come up with any concept for Europe.

Those who assume that 'talk is cheap' will say that you can always come up with a narrative for France to suit any policy. Believing, in contrast, that language is structure(d) and that a large part of politics is about structuring the national conceptual landscape, options are not so abundant. In French political culture, especially, one is very conscious of what concepts are used and whether politicians change well-known formulae. France has three basic structural routes, and each of these can be given different concrete policy formulations, but the question is whether any of them on current conditions can establish harmony between the existing France and the emerging Europe. Possibly, there is a need (cf. Kissinger, 1957) for larger statesmanship that reshapes either France or Europe to make the two compatible again.

At least it is obvious that many of the suggestions made by people who do not take national traditions seriously (Americans) are completely unrealistic (such as Atlantic visions that allocate a hopeless role to France). Even if the actual resources of France make most of the grand visions hard to carry through, it is more likely that the winning line will either be a self-defeating grand policy (or even the far-reaching federalism that at least takes a French political *form*) rather than an unheroic, Anglified policy without any vision for France and for Europe.

The current situation is captured by Ulla Holm's (2003) analysis of Chirac's speech to the ambassadors on 29 August 2003 (see also Chirac, 2004). He plays a dangerous balancing act of hinting at a policy of alliance with Germany, while talking about 'reconciliation' and a 'refounding' of the EU. The key term is a 'strong France', which enables Europe to represent values in international politics that are needed in the light of the Iraq war. As witnessed by the Derrida–Habermas (2003) intervention in the Europe debate, the emphasis on Europe as foreign policy can be linked to another new accent: core Europe. The EU's failure for a while to agree on a constitution triggered an almost hopeful French tone while exploring a 'plan B' that combines increased 'great power' emphasis (Franco-German as well as 'big three') with a nostalgia for the old EU of the original six. The situation allows for a sudden bridge between Gaullist state-to-state logic and a 'refounding' of the EU. Suddenly a 'federation of nation-states' is a credible strategy for reinventing 'Europe'. While the terminology is striking and the logic therefore suddenly clear, it is a highly precarious and temporary possibility to combine in a harmonious way the previously contradictory elements of Chirac's Europe. As long as this dualism continues, France will be severely constricted in formulating visions and initiatives for the EU.

Germany after the cold war has witnessed an increasing presence of alternative lines of more nationalist suggestions for a more German, less European policy. But basically the very Europe-oriented version of what Germany is, where Germany is going, and thereby what German 'interests' are, has kept its solid hold on the political elite.

The struggles in the 1990s that took up most of the attention and created worries about German orientation – notably the possibility of sending German troops abroad – actually happened among two versions of the same conception of the state, nation, and relation to Europe (the same position at 'the second tier'). They divided between, on the one hand, semi-pacifist Greens and (some) social democrats who wanted a continuation of total abstentionism and, on the other, the (then) Kohl government, which also emphasised integration as the rationale for Germany, but was interested in gradually taking on more 'normal tasks' (not least to make Germany fit more smoothly into Western structures).

The differences as well as the resemblance are important. Kohl and other Christian-Democrats are, much less than the SPD (and centre-left intellectuals), driven by the anti-power state argument in its *moral* form (Holocaust nation), but a *rationalistic* argument of more or less geopolitical nature. This produces much the same result: we have to avoid a German power state in a balance-of-power Europe. The centre-right argument is more outside-in and argues from geography and history that if Europe returns to a pattern of power politics – which corresponds to a German state that acts on its own according to a calculus of power – Germany as the power in the Centre will be the loser. Therefore, Germany has an interest in avoiding this Europe but thereby also in avoiding this Germany. Instead, Germany must strive for a different Europe (beyond the nation-state) and a different Germany (not a power state) (Stürmer, 1989). The SPD (especially before Schroeder),

Greens, and left-intellectuals argue more inside-out, by directly addressing and criticising a possible German power state, which they see as morally indefensible and politically dangerous, because it will lead to a Europe of power politics, nationalism, and wars. Both main positions end up pursuing a policy of anti-power state for Germany and anti-balance of power for Europe. Of course, as the two leading parties, they conduct heated debates among themselves, creating the impression of deep divisions and radically different approaches, especially to German security and military policy. Their closeness is, for most purposes, more important.[18]

In contrast, a more radical challenger decisively breaks with European integration as the basic foundation for the future of Germany. At first, this position was curiously formalistic and empty. A nation-state has to have political space for manoeuvre and a political-military profile *because, as nation-state, it has to*. At the turn of the twentieth century, concrete aims (colonies for instance) were to be realised through a position of political power. Because Germany is unified, the argument now goes, one has to realise that a nation-state is a nation-state and it demands political room of manoeuvre and a political-military profile. More strongly: a great power is a great power and it had better realise this. This first appeared as criticism of various elements of the policy of the anti-power state: Europe of the regions, EU integration, continued acceptance of foreign troops, and NATO integration. The strongest expression of this restless search for new ideas is a lively debate on 'normality'. It is striking how the metaphor of 'normality' and even that of 'growing up' have been all over German debates. The debate about moving the capital from Bonn to Berlin brought this out very clearly (Staun, 2001, pp. 589–624).

Normalisation has been articulated most markedly at a more philosophical level by a strand that we might call the neostatists. This is not primarily about nationalism, rather about rehabilitating the state.[19] Post-war Germans are criticised for being unpolitical consumer animals without sense for the big questions (Bohrer, 1990–91). 'Big' means 'big politics', art, and action and thus reconnects aesthetics and politics. For a power state, foreign policy is the arena where the great statesman displays his creative will. These new intellectuals of the right are the ones who explicitly attack the anti-power state and want to repeal the negation involved in this concept.[20]

If the existing political main line should break down for one reason or another, the neostatist conservatives have a solid basis for articulating a complete and coherent political self-conception for the Germans. Whereas they, in an early manifestation, lost the so-called *Historikerstreit*, they in turn won a number of post-unification debates (on GDR literature and so forth), which broke the moral-political hegemony of the Holocaust nation.

Increasingly, observers argue that this logic has taken hold of official policy, particularly through the person of Gerhard Schroeder. However, it is important to remain structural!

Here is a key question worth a close reading. This chapter did not leave space for documenting every element of the analysis by quotations, but the work needed for a full-scale analysis can be illustrated by a targeted answer to this key question.[21] Chancellor Schroeder, in particular, has adopted terminology and metaphors close to neostatism or at least clearly about sovereignty, normalisation, and 'growing up': 'Our Germany is a self-assured country... We do not therefore have to hide our national interests. This is our German way' (Schröder, 2002).

This has triggered a discussion in German research about whether to view this as a victory for 'normalisation' in the far-reaching sense of ending the anti-power state, or if it was a more opportunistic borrowing of words, with the underlying policy untouched.[22] However, it is important to remember that the defining structural element in German state thinking is not 'the state' but 'the *power state*'.

Politicians more or less everywhere deny an interest in 'power' and prefer 'responsibility', but this might be of genuine significance in Germany. Perhaps it is more profitable to ask: *what concept of the state*? Any concept of the state is tied to a specific kind of international system. In France, more emphasis on 'own state' implies *a kind* of state policy related to a classical 'state system' Europe of shifting alliances and balance of power. In Germany, this link is reserved for the 'new right', not the government. To foreign minister Fischer, Germany becoming more 'self-conscious' suggests more actively promoting its Bonner-based policy of 'civilian power'.[23] Chancellor Schroeder, in contrast, has put more emphasis on the German right to push through its national interests 'just like the others do' (speech, 8 December 1998). His 'German way' includes giving up the 'cheque book diplomacy' of Kohl and Genscher, which implies a willingness to send troops instead. However, the most provocative German action so far was its *refusal* to send troops to Iraq in 2003. Thus, the key is a right to have its own views, in contrast with previously following automatically the wishes of key allies (the US in NATO and France in the EU). However, these German interests are thoroughly defined in terms of a European vision: it is only possible to take care of German interests if European integration succeeds. Germany is a better European partner when more normal. 'Wir sind europäisch sozialisiert und groß geworden. Wir sind davon überzeugt, daß Deutschland Teil Europas sein muß' (Schroeder, *Der Spiegel*, 9 March 1998)

Still, it can be appropriate to warn (as does Hellmann, 2004a) against uncritically pursuing normality. This threatens to legitimize the view that all 'normal' great power behaviour is good. So far, the government is far from reinstalling a German power state logic. On the contrary it is an anti-power state defined more by Europe and less by military abstention.

Based on opinion polls and isolated quotations from this or that chancellor, it could easily be concluded that Germany was moving in the direction of neostatism. However, if approached more structurally – not looking at opinion but public discourse – the paradoxical result is that the leading elite has continued to support the anti-power state and has actually become *more* dependent on the EU in recent years. Constructing a narrative for the future of Germany, some basic dilemmas must either be solved on the basis of the EU – or by a radical shift. In a more integrated Europe, for example, German troops can more easily participate in joint operations because they do it not as Germans but as Europeans. Independent German action always risks triggering suspicion. Any solution for Germany is European in a far-reaching sense. In the discussion about the capital moving from Bonn to Berlin, this lead to the accusation that Kohl 'in the long run does not want to move to a renewed Berlin but to Brussels'. Currently, the continued anti-power-state line is the one that most easily makes sense on the German scene. The neostatist one is not a real challenger but it has found a foothold. Should the anti-statist line fall, the neostatist line is the most likely replacement. First of all because it is hard to see why the dominant line should fall, unless Europe failed, in which case all moderate alternatives would also become impossible. The challengers have changed some accents, but they have not been able to change German policy on their own. The most likely trigger that could call them in would be a breakdown of integration, although one also has to reflect on the possible effects of a deepening of Germany's economic crisis.

The inner stability of a cooperative, parallel realisation of the different Europes has already been broken on the Russian side, and Russia has slid out of the grand bargain to a mixture of confrontation and cooperation. In Germany an alternative story is available, but it is not able to break the hold of the dominant one – nor is there any need for this, because the dominant one continues to produce a convincing vision for Germany's future. France is the weak point of the European scene – the Europe-oriented self-interpretation of France is challenged. If France turns away from this line, Germany's overall concept of Europe *and therefore of itself* will lose its rationale. The alternative narratives in Germany will suddenly have the chance of filling a vacuum and German 'interests' and 'orientations' could change drastically. This interaction of domestic struggles over the meaning of state, nation, and Europe is where the direction of developments will be decided. The regional identity 'Europe' clearly has become more important and today plays a key role *in* self-conceptions. Its meaning is not settled once and for all, but most of the concepts of state and nation that compete are thoroughly Europeanised.

If the risk is correctly located, the most important policy advice must be to ensure that the French vision survives. This is actually in line with classical realist diplomacy. Kissinger's concept of 'legitimate order' was aimed at a nineteenth-century formulation of a wise policy towards the loser of the war (in our case: the losers of the post-war peace, France and Russia). Christensen (1993) has introduced the useful concept of 'most vulnerable significant actor'. In terms of order, the most important states are not the most powerful (they are usually happy), nor the weakest (they can only do limited harm), but the most vulnerable of those who are powerful enough to upset an international order. Only if they all can live with the emerging order – which means they can picture themselves in it – do we have a 'legitimate order' (Kissinger, 1957) and, therefore, stability. By combining classical diplomatic virtues with a discourse analysis of the situation today, one conclusion is concern about French visions because Europe has not a German but a French problem, not least because developments in France can trigger the classical German problem.

## Where does it lead?

### Where does it take Europe?

'Europe' has become increasingly powerful; not as an alternative polity out-competing the nation-states, but as a concept increasingly embedded *in* these nation-states who themselves change as a result. Since we are not on the verge of a new sovereign Euro-state, analysis cannot take the comfortable position of a new sovereign observation post – simply moving from the state to the EU. Instead, we have to operate in a perspectival mode, understanding the *different* ways that meaningful worlds are constructed which all include 'Europe' but in different forms. The internal dynamics of each of these narrative struggles, as well as their mutual relations, have to be grasped to understand the stability and fragility of the complex constellation called Europe.

### Where does it take IR theory and foreign policy analysis?

It is indeed possible to develop a foreign policy theory from the surprising departure point of discourse analysis. The theory can explain why some options that seem obvious from abstract theory of abstract states are actually completely unrealistic (incompatible with national traditions of political thought); and, more systematically, it can establish a few main scenarios for each nation and measure how stable each country is in relation to its current commitments. By combining several main countries (in this case only two), we gain a certain power to predict European possibilities.

### What does this analysis hold for discourse analysis?

I have two suggestions, one comfortable and one less so. First, it suggests that international affairs can fruitfully be studied with inspiration from discourse theory. It takes some additional theoretical elaboration to get at the relationship between domestic discourses and inter-state discourses and practices, but these should not, in principle, cause difficulties. Secondly, this chapter has suggested some possibilities for remobilising structuralist elements that are innate to the approach. To some this move will be seen as spelling out theoretical elements already present and thus making these more useful.

To others it will probably be a case of allowing a danger to grow to full size. Maybe this is yet another instance of the classical IR habit of cultivating one monster in order to drive out another.

## Notes

1. This is slightly more complicated in the case of 'small states', who might also use 'Europe' as part of their self-definition but do not believe that they can decide on Europe, and, therefore, sometimes see it as more of an external condition. Still, they have to construct political visions that marry some rendition of current Europeanisation with national traditions, possibly with the inclusion of additional, in-between 'we's, as with the Scandinavian countries, who see themselves as co-constitutive of 'Norden' (Hansen and Wæver, 2002).
2. This corresponds to Niklas Luhmann's basic distinction between social and psychic systems, where the former are about communication, the latter about consciousness. My point is not that the two are unconnected; consider, for example, Lacanian psychoanalysis studying 'the unconscious structured as a language' and discourse psychology studying the role of non-individual discourses in individual psychology. However, one should always be very precise about making claims about either. In IR, especially, it is common to study speeches and then state what George Bush's motive for going to war was. This kind of inference is deeply problematic. We know the *justification* – and that is interesting in itself, but another matter. Either one should focus on reconstructing individual perceptions and motivations – which demands either access to sources not aimed at the public or to very sophisticated methodologies for using indirect sources to such inner mechanisms – or one should stick to public discourse as an important reality in itself. Discourse matters in its own right because it has powers and effects as it exists *in-between* actors, irrespective of how deeply they individually agree or disagree. This does not conflict with Lacan- or Žižek-inspired analysis that includes paradoxes of the subject as a dynamic factor in the analysis, because such arguments are still structural and mostly organised around the unconscious, not about the consciousness of singular individuals. (See, for example, Stavrakakis in this volume.)
3. A hierarchy of depth over surface marks many structuralisms because the code is seen as constant, only to be transformed in correspondence to its own rules of transformation, and the relationship between code and manifestation is seen as one of perfect correspondence (or isotopy). Thus these structuralisms contain assumptions about stable, self-present meaning which are drastically subverted by various forms of post-structuralism. Generally, structuralism can be seen as a science of the sign and post-structuralism as a critique of the sign. Structuralism is optimistic about the possibility of finding the codes and mechanisms that actually produce the manifestations we meet, whereas post-structuralism works from the attitude that meaning is always precarious, transient, and self-contradictory. Post-structuralism is, however, not (as is often implied in American playful postmodernisms) a negation of structuralism – it is 'post-structuralism' exactly because it has grown from and through structuralism. Thus, this study will tread a line between structuralism and post-structuralism by using the methods and ideas of structuralism but with a general attitude to language that is closer to post-structuralism. The various mechanisms of meaning generation that structuralists analyse can be registered but they will never be seen as full, complete, or self-confirming. Meaning is always

an attempt, a process, a move that temporarily counters the indeterminacy of signification.

4. John G. Ruggie explains how the levels (in his case the *international political structure* of neorealism) constitute successive depth levels, and the concept of structure is generative, meaning that 'They are not visible directly, only through their hypothesized effects. [The 2nd tier] mediates the social effects of the deep structure [1st tier], but within a context that has already been circumscribed by the deep structure... [The 3rd tier] comes closest to the surface level of visible phenomena, but its impact on outcomes is simply to magnify or modify the opportunities and constraints generated by the other (two) structural level(s)' (Ruggie, 1983, pp. 266, 280). Concretely, the three international tiers are: (1), the basic organising principle, is it anarchic or hierarchic?; (2) the principle of separation of units, that is, Sovereignty, in the modern system or some other pre- or post-modern principle; and (3) the distribution of capabilities interpreted in terms of polarity (the number of great powers). This structure can be depicted in the same format as figures 1.2 and 1.4 below (see, for example, Wæver, 1994).
5. See Wæver, 2003, for a discussion partly in terms of these other discursive analyses of European integration (Diez, 1999; Jachtenfuchs, Diez, and Jung, 1999; Marcussen, et. al., 1999) that operate with fixed 'ideal types' of 'Europes', which to me seems to violate discourse theory assumptions both of context-dependent concepts and of mutual influence of political rivals.
6. Studies of specific states and their foreign policies are starting to emerge along lines more or less similar to those outlined here. Studies of the following countries: France: Holm, 1992, 1997, 2002; Larsen, 1997, 1999; more fully developed in Wæver, Holm, and Larsen, forthcoming; Germany: Wæver, 1991, 1995; and Wæver, Holm, and Larsen, forthcoming; Russia: Neumann, 1996, 2002; Turkey: Kazan, 1994; and Kazan and Wæver, 1994; Finland: Joenniemi, 1993; the UK: Diez, 1999; and Larsen, 1997; Slovenia: Hansen, 1996; Greece: Stauersböll, 2000; the Nordic Countries: Hansen and Wæver, 2002; Algeria, Ulla Holm, forthcoming; the US (as a European power): Sørensen, 1998; the US (as a global power): Ruggie, 1997; Egypt and India: Banerjee, n.d.; India: Banerjee, 1997.
7. It is therefore easiest in cases where a political unit is also the core of a language area – France and Germany – in contrast to political units that share language and traditions of political thought with other units – Austria, or worse, Belgium.
8. For more extensive discussion of the selection of texts, see Sørensen, 1998, pp. 44–6; Holm, 1999; Neumann, 2000; Hansen, forthcoming.
9. The brief summary below (in section 4) will not, because of limited space, be able to demonstrate the usage of sources, especially not type-2 sources. For fuller discussions, see Holm, 1992, 1997, 1999, 2002; Wæver, 1990, 1991, and 1995; and, most systematically, Wæver, Holm, and Larsen, forthcoming.
10. Does any theory account for ultimate causes? You can always ask another 'why?' the 'independent variable' of any explanation. A good theory is not the one that tries to include the next layer, and the next, and so on, but one that has a very clear conceptualisation of (at least) one layer of reality and, with greater consequence, investigates exactly what this layer can and cannot do.
11. The concepts of nation/state are peculiarly stable, because they were hammered into each country at a specific formative moment (France in the late eighteenth century, Germany in the nineteenth century, and – most likely – some of the East-Central European countries and, for instance, Norway – around the turn of the twentieth century). Since then, they have formed the framework of interpretation and,

therefore, they have been changing only incrementally in an evolutionary mode, on the basis of their own internal components.

12. The French conception of the state-nation has many other dimensions than this – for example, related to secularism and civilisation. The simple graphic display (Fig. 1.1) is meant to represent this complex whole in condensed form.
13. Logically, a relationship of dominance (Napoleon) would also be possible. This option is not included in the figure because it is not relevant today.
14. As always, my analysis of France is greatly indebted to Ulla Holm. The basic diagram is our joint creation from 1989. See Holm, 1992, 1996, 1997, 2002, 2003.
15. Romantic nationalism first took root among the peoples not living in nation-states, Germans and East Europeans in particular (Nipperdey, 1986, pp. 141ff.). It did not, however, remain limited to Central and East Central Europe. 'Even' in France, romantic nationalism became a strong – at times dominant – challenger to the individualistic-civic Western conception.
16. According to Friedrich Meinecke (1976 [1915], pp. 409–21), the political interpretation (the need for a state) and idealistic philosophy were mutually reinforcing.
17. The state is now at the centre in the form of the guiding problem, where previously it was the meaning and energy of everything. In post-war FRG's thinking, the task has been to control the state and stabilise the political order. The German constitution seeks to prevent concentration of power at any point: parliament, president, people, any. Therefore, Germany has no room for referenda, and certain elements of the constitution cannot be changed even with the largest majority in the Bundestag. Political participation is feared rather than encouraged, and it is clearly secondary to the detailed arrangement of the state as a self-stabilising system. Democracy is conceived of in a radically different manner than in the US, for example, because it is not the aim in itself, but a way of dealing with the state. 'Streitbare Demokratie' for instance, as noted by Gregg Kvistad (1989, p. 114), does not rely on mobilising politically conscious citizens to defend democracy, but relies on the state, the rule of law and the civil servants. It trusts the constitution to be so well designed that all dangerous impulses are captured by other instances. Kvistad quotes Kurt Sontheimer's harsh words: 'Germans tend to go about democracy as an affair of the state, in the style of a democratically organized authoritarian state... [because it] has not been possible to make the citizens understand that democratic order is a mechanism by which the people, by delegating representatives, rule themselves' (ibid., p. 114).
18. There is not a total correspondence between the (majority) SPD position and the (majority) CDU line, but there is a *structural* affinity worth noting. If one used cognitive mapping or some other technique that reflects the *arguments* used, the two would appear very different. But from a structural perspective the difference is much smaller.
19. The nation is rehabilitated, too. A symptomatic and influential debate was triggered by a Botho Strauss essay, documented in Schwilk and Schacht, 1994. This rehabilitation primarily means 'a right to the normalcy of self-confidence', thereby equipping the German state with a nationalism as normal as any other. It is emphatically not a plea for a strengthened German nationalism, or any of the ideas we find in the nationalism of neonazi circles. The neoconservative, intellectual 'national consciousness' is careful not to make nationalism a motor of policy as such; it only removes a road block to becoming a normal *state*: the 'unnatural' separation of Germans from their nation. Therefore, this is not a thinking organised around the nation, but a thinking primarily about the state (neostatist)

with a supporting concept of the nation, just like the anti-power state had the 'Holocaust nation'.

20. Probably, one should distinguish between, on the one hand, *general* neostatists like these mainly cultural intellectuals who link up to the deep codes of state, aestheticised politics, and power and, on the other, various historians and foreign policy experts who are *narrow* 'neostatists'. They also reintroduce the logic of the state as such, but often tied to geopolitics and without the whole philosophical construct of aesthetics and ethics. They stress Germany's position, its new *Mittellage*, the legitimacy of Germany rediscovering geopolitics like everybody else, and, thus, a rational interest policy derived from German state interests (see Hellmann, 1996).
21. It would be easy to provide a number of citations in the text to illustrate each of the above points, but it would not be much proof of anything, because isolated quotes can be found for more or less anything. For the broader analysis, it is necessary to study systematically and completely a relevant corpus of texts. However, the way to read these texts can be illustrated by a targeted addressing of this one specific question, whether Schroeder has carried through a 'normalisation' that breaks with the anti-power state.
22. The most convincing analyses of this have been conducted by Gunther Hellmann (2002, 2003, 2004a, 2004b). I draw on these in the following, although his interpretation – at first, at least – points to the opposite conclusions of what my basic analysis would expect and 'hope for' (see also Harnisch, 2000; Peters, 2001; Hacke, 2002).
23. Fischer played a key role in dragging – with Srebnica in mind – his own Green party towards accepting that occasionally the use of military force was the only defensible position (Dalgaard-Nielsen, 2003). However, he has also been the main governmental voice pressing the need to continue radical Europeanisation in order to avoid balance-of-power Europe and a German power state (Fischer, 2000).

## Bibliography


Alker, H. (1996) *Rediscoveries and Reformulations: Humanistic Methodologies for International Relations* (Cambridge, Cambridge University Press).

Anderson, B. (1983) *Imagined Communities: Reflections on the Origin and Spread of Nationalism* (2nd revised edition, 1991) (London, Verso).

Ash, T. G. (1993) *In Europe's Name: Germany and the Divided Continent* (New York, Vintage).

Banerjee, S. (n.d.) 'National Identity and Foreign Policy' (unpublished).

Banerjee, S. (1997) 'The Cultural Logic of National Identity Formation: Contending Discourses in Late Colonial India', in V. M. Hudson (ed.), *Culture and Foreign Policy*, (Boulder, Colorado, Lynne Rienner).

Bartelson, J. (1995) *A Genealogy of Sovereignty* (Cambridge, Cambridge University Press).

Bertramsen, R. B., J. P. F. Thomsen, and J. Torfing (1991) *State, Economy and Society* (London, Unwin Hyman).

Bohrer, K. H. (1990–91) 'Provinzialismus', *Merkur* (501), pp. 1,096–1,102; (504), pp. 255–62; (505), pp. 348–56; (509), pp. 719–27; (512), pp. 1,059–68.

Brunner, J. (1991) 'The Narrative Construction of Reality', *Critical Inquiry*, 18 (2), pp. 1–21.

Buzan, B., and O. Wæver (2003) *Regions and Powers: the Structure of International Security* (Cambridge, Cambridge University Press).

Chirac, J. (2004) *Allocution lors de la presentation des voeux du corps diplomatique*, available at www.france.diplomatie.fr (viewed 8 January 2004).
Christensen, T. J. (1993) 'Conclusion, System Stability and the Security of the Most Vulnerable Significant Actor', in J. Snyder and R. Jervis (eds), *Coping with Complexity in the International System* (Boulder, San Francisco; Oxford, Westview Press).
Dalgaard-Nielsen, A. (2003) 'Gulf War: the German Resistance', *Survival*, 45 (1), pp. 99–116.
Derrida, J., and J. Habermas (2003) 'Nach dem Krieg: die Wiedergeburt Europas/Europe: plaidoyer pour une politique étrangère commune', *Frankfurter Allgemeinen Zeitung* and *Libération*, 31 May 2003.
Diez, T. (1999) *Die EU lesen: Diskursive Knotenpunkte in der britischen Europadebatte* (Opladen, Leske & Budrich).
Dreyfus, H. L., and P. Rabinow (1982) *Michel Foucault: Beyond Structuralism and Hermeneutics* (New York, Harvester Wheatsheaf).
Elshtain, J. B. (1987) *Women and War* (New York, Basic Books).
Fischer, J. (2000) 'Vom Staatenverbund zur Föderation – Gedanken über die Finalität der europäischen Integration', speech on 12 May 2000, at the Humboldt University, Berlin, available at http://www.europa-digital.de/aktuell/dossier/fischer/rede1205. shtml
Foucault, M. (1972) *The Archaeology of Knowledge* (London, Pantheon).
Gellner, Ernst (1983) 'Nationalism and the Two Forms of Cohesion in Complex Societies', *Proceedings of the British Academy*, London vol. LXVIII (Oxford: Oxford University Press).
Giesen, B. (1993) *Die Intellektuellen und die Nation: eine deutsche Achsenzeit* (Frankfurt am Main, Suhrkamp).
Grosser, A. (1980[1978]) *The Western Alliance: European-American Relations since 1945* (translated by Michael Shaw) (French original 1978; New York, Continuum).
Hacke, C. (2002) 'Die Außenpolitik der Regierung Schröder/Fischer: Zwischenbilanz und Perspektiven', *Aus Politik und Zeitgeschichte*, B48, pp. 7–15.
Hansen, L. (1996) 'Slovenian Identity: State Building on the Balkan Border', *Alternatives*, vol. 21 (4), pp. 473–95.
Hansen, L. (forthcoming) *Security as Practice: Discourse Analysis and the Bosnian War* (London, Routledge).
Hansen, L., and O. Wæver (eds) (2002) *European Integration and National Identity: the Challenge of the Nordic States* (London, Routledge).
Harnisch, S. (2000) '*Deutsche Außenpolitik nach der Wende: Zivilmacht am Ende?*, paper for 21st DVPW Congress, Halle, in October 2000.
Hellmann, G. (1996) 'Goodbye Bismarck? The Foreign Policy of Contemporary Germany', *Mershon International Studies Review*, vol. 40, supplement 1, pp. 1–40.
Hellmann, G. (2002) 'Deutschland in Europa: eine symbiotische Beziehung', *Aus Politik und Zeitgeschichte*, B48, pp. 24–31.
Hellmann, G. (2003) 'Agenda 2020: Krise und Perspektive deutscher Außenpolitik', *Internationale Politik*, 2003 (9), pp. 1–12.
Hellmann, G. (2004a) 'Wider die machtpolitische Resozialiseriung der deutschen Außenpolitik: ein Plädoyer für offensiven Idealismus', *WeltTrends* (42) April, pp. 79–88.
Hellmann, G. (2004b) 'Von Gipfelstürmern und Gratwandern: "Deutsche Wege" in der Außenpolitik', *Aus Politik und Zeitgeschichte*, B11, pp. 32–9.
Holm, U. (1992) *Det Franske Europa* (The French Europe) (Aarhus, Aarhus University Press).
Holm, U. (1996) 'Den franske nationalstat: en urolig magt', *Militært Tidsskrift*, vol. 125 (1), pp. 53–68.

Holm, U. (1997) 'The French Garden Is Not What It Used to Be', in K.-E. Jørgensen (ed.), *Reflective Approaches to European Governance* (London, Macmillan).

Holm, U. (1999) 'Det franske Europa: Et retrospektivt perspektiv. Metode og teori', PhD dissertation, University of Aarhus.

Holm, U. (2002) *The Implication of the Concept of the French State-Nation and 'Patrie' for French Discourses on (Maghrebi) Immigration*, AMID Working Paper Series (6) (Aalborg University, Academy for Migration Studies in Denmark).

Holm, U. (2003) The French Concept of Europe – Before, Now and in the Future', lecture to Master Course on European Studies, 17 September 2003.

Holm, U. (forthcoming) *A Study on Algeria*.

Holm, U., H. Larsen, and O. Wæver (1990) 'Forestillingen om Europa: en studie i fransk og tysk tænkning efter revolutionerne i Øst', *Vandkunsten: Konflikt, Politik og Historie* (3), pp. 212–36.

Jachtenfuchs, M., T. Diez, and S. Jung (1999) 'Which Europe? Conflicting Models of a Legitimate European Order', *European Journal of International Relations*, 4 (4), pp. 409–45.

Joenniemi, P. (1993) 'Euro-Suomi: rajalla, rajojen, välissä vai rajaton?', in P. Joenniemi, R. Alapuro, and K. Pekonen, *Suomesta Euro-Suomen: Keitä me olemme ja mihin matkalla*, Tampere: Occasional Papers of Tampere Peace Research Institute (53).

Kazan, I. (1994) 'Omvendt Osmannisme og Khanaternes Kemalisme: Tyrkiets udenrigspolitik – en diskurs udfordret af EFs integration og Sovjetunionens opløsning', MA thesis, Institute of Political Science, University of Copenhagen.

Kazan, I., and O. Wæver (1994) 'Tyrkiet mellem Europa og europæisering', *Internasjonal Politikk*, vol. 52 (2), pp. 139–75.

Kissinger, Henry A. (1957) *A World Restored: Castlereagh, Metternich and the Restoration of Peace, 1812–1822* (Boston, Houghton Mifflin Company).

Koselleck, R. (1985 [1979]) *Futures Past: On the Semantics of Historical Time* (Massachussets, MIT Press).

Kvistad, G. O. (1989) 'Radicals and the State: the Political Demands on West German Civil Servants', in James A. Caporaso (ed.), *The Elusive State: International and Comparative Perspectives* (Newbury Park, Sage).

Laclau, E. (1990) *New Reflections on the Revolution of Our Times* (London, Verso).

Laclau, E., and C. Mouffe (1985) *Hegemony and Socialist Strategy: Towards a Radical Democratic Politics* (London, Verso).

Larsen, H. (1997) *Foreign Policy and Discourse Analysis: France, Britain, and Europe* (London, Routledge).

Larsen, H. (1999) 'British and Danish European Policies in the 1990s: a Discourse Approach', *European Journal of International Relations*, vol. 5 (4), pp. 451–83.

Marcussen, Martin, Thomas Risse, Daniela Engelmann-Martin, Hans Joachim Knopf, and Klaus Roscher (1999) 'Constructing Europe? The Evolution of French, British, and German Nation-State Identities', *Journal of European Public Policy*, vol. 6 (3), pp. 614–33.

Marx, K. (1956 [1867]) *Das Kapital: Kritik der politischen Ökonomie*, vols 1–3 (Berlin, Dietz).

Meinecke, F. (1976 [1915]) *Die Idee der Staatsräson in der neueren Geschichte* (München, R. Oldenburg).

Neumann, I. B. (1996) *Russia and the Idea of Europe: a Study in Identity and International Relations* (London, Routledge).

Neumann, I. B. (2000) *Makt, Mening, Materialitet* (Bergen, Fagbok for laget).

Neumann, I. B. (2002) 'From the USSR to Gorbachev to Putin: Perestroika as a Failed Excursion from "the West" to "Europe" in Russian Discourse', in Mikael af

Malmborg and Bo Stråth (eds), *The Meaning of Europe* (Oxford and New York, Berg), pp. 191–214.

Nipperdey, T. (1986) *Nachdenken über die Deutsche Geschichte: Essays* (München, Beck'sche Verlagsbuchhandlung).

Onuf, N. G. (1989) *World of Our Making: Rules and Rule in Social Theory and International Relations* (Columbia, University of South Carolina Press).

Pedersen, O. K. (1970) *Udenrigsminister P. Munch's opfattelse af Danmarks stilling i international politik* (Copenhagen, Gad).

Peters, D. (2001) 'The Debate about a New German Foreign Policy after Unification', in V. Rittberger (ed.), *German Foreign Policy since Unification: Theories and Case Studies* (Manchester, Manchester University Press).

Popper, K. (1963) *Conjectures and Refutations* (London, Routledge and Kegan Paul).

Ricoeur, P. (1995) 'Reflections on a New Ethos for Europe', *Philosophy & Social Criticism*, 21(5–6), pp. 3–14.

Ringmar, E. (1997) 'Alexander Wendt: a Social Scientist Struggling with History', in I. B. Neumann and O. Wæver, *The Future of International Relations: Masters in the Making?* (London, Routledge).

Ruggie, J. G. (1983) 'Continuity and Transformation in the World Polity: Toward a Neo-Realist Synthesis', *World Politics*, 36(2), pp. 261–85.

Ruggie, J. G. (1997) 'The Past as Prologue? Interests, Identity, and American Foreign Policy', *International Security*, vol. 21(4), pp. 89–125.

Schröder, G. (2002) 'Meine Vision von Deutschland', *BILD-Zeitung*, 8 August 2002, available at http://www.bundeskanzler.de/-.7698.78497/Gerhard-Schroeder-Meine-Vision-von-Deutschland.htm

Schwilk, H., and U. Schacht (eds) (1994) *Die selbstbewußte Nation: 'Anschwellender Bocksgesang' und weitere Beiträge zu einer deutschen Debatte* (Berlin, Frankfurt am Main).

Skinner, Q. (2002) *Visions of Politics 1: On Method* (Cambridge, Cambridge University Press).

Sørensen, J. M. (1998) 'The Coming Hegemony? A Constructivist Interpretation of the Future Direction of the US' Security Role in Europe', MA thesis, Copenhagen: Institute of Political Science, University of Copenhagen.

Stauersböll, H. (2000) 'Between Byzantium and Hellas: Understanding the Greek Policy towards Macedonia in the 1990s', MA thesis, Copenhagen: Institute of Political Science, University of Copenhagen.

Staun, J. (2001) *Mellem kantiansk patriotisme og politisk romantik: det tyske stats- og nationsbegreb i to århundreder*, PhD thesis, Department of Political Science, University of Copenhagen.

Stürmer, M. (1989) 'Die Deutschen in Europa: Auf dem Weg zu einer zwischenstaatlichen Innenpolitik', *Europa Archiv* 25 (12), pp. 721–32.

Wæver, O. (1990) 'Three Competing Europes: German, French, Russian', *International Affairs*, 44 (2), pp. 477–93.

Wæver, O. (1991) 'Det tyske problem i 1990erne' (The German Problem in the 1990s), *Internasjonal Politikk* (Oslo), 1991 (4), pp. 401–19.

Wæver, O. (1994) 'Resisting the Temptation of Post Foreign Policy Analysis', in W. Carlsnaes and S. Smith (eds), *European Foreign Policy: the EC and Changing Perspectives in Europe* (London, ECPR/Sage).

Wæver, O. (1995) 'Hvordan det hele alligevel kan gå galt . . .', in H. Gottlieb and F. P. Jensen (eds), *Tyskland i Europa* (Copenhagen, SNU).

Wæver, O. (1996) 'The Rise and Fall of the Inter-paradigm Debate', in S. Smith, K. Booth and M. Zalewski (eds), *International Theory: Positivism & Beyond* (Cambridge, Cambridge University Press).

Wæver, O. (1997) *Concepts of Security* (Copenhagen, Politiske Studier).

Wæver, O. (1998a) 'The Sociology of a Not So International Discipline: American and European Developments in International Relations', *International Organization* 52 (4), pp. 687–727.

Wæver, O. (1998b) 'Insecurity, Security and Asecurity in the Western European Non-War Community', in E. Adler and M. Barnett (eds), *Security Communities* (Cambridge, Cambridge University Press).

Wæver, O. (2003) 'Discursive Approaches', in A. Wiener and T. Diez (eds), *European Integration Theory* (Oxford, Oxford University Press).

Wæver, O., U. Holm and H. Larsen (Forthcoming) *The Struggle for 'Europe': French and German Concepts of State, Nation and European Union.*

Waltz, K. (1979) *Theory of International Politics* (New York, Random House).

Žižek, S. (1992) 'Eastern Europe's Republics of Gilead', in C. Mouffe (ed.), *Dimensions of Radical Democracy: Pluralism, Citizenship, Community* (London, Verso).

# 2
# Passions of Identification: Discourse, Enjoyment, and European Identity

*Yannis Stavrakakis*

## Introduction

Without doubt, our contemporary world is marked throughout by the importance of questions of identity, something increasingly reflected in the directions of contemporary social-scientific research. It would be bizarre if the broad field of international relations were to stay untouched by this trend. In fact, no one is surprised any more by the fact that 'the discipline of international relations (IR) is witnessing a surge of interest in identity and identity formation' (Neumann, 1999, p. 1). The same applies to the subdiscipline of European Studies – affecting both marginal and mainstream approaches. As Anthony Smith has pointed out, one of the fundamental reasons for the current interest in 'European unification' is, undoubtedly,

> the problem of identity itself, one that has played a major part in European debates over the past 30–40 years. At issue [among others] has been the possibility and legitimacy of a 'European identity', as opposed to the existing national identities. (Smith, 1999, p. 226)

This development is hardly surprising given that, at least since the 1970s, processes of European integration have been explicitly linked with an identity problematic. As far back as 1973, when the member states of the European Community agreed to define European identity in a 'fundamental declaration' released at the Copenhagen summit, the construction of European identity was officially recognized as a crucial policy issue in the process of strengthening the profile and safeguarding the future prospects of the European Community (Commission, 1974). Undoubtedly, the extent to which 'European identity' is something to be discovered or constructed (or both), something that should be viewed 'in opposition to' or 'side by side with' national identities (or even within a post-national framework), something to be celebrated or resisted (or, simply, ignored); all these are still contentious points. What is clear, however, is that identity is firmly positioned at the centre of intense European policy and research interest.

This is not to say, however, that the question of Europe (European integration, unification, or European identity) has been adequately addressed from a perspective focusing on processes of identity formation. As Gerard Delanty has put it in his book *Inventing Europe: Idea, Identity, Reality*, 'little thought is actually given to the meaning of the term Europe and its relationship to problems in contemporary political identity' (Delanty, 1995, p. 1). For example, more than forty years after the European project in its current form began, 'it is striking how little we know about its... identity-shaping effects' (Checkel, 2001, p. 50). This is not merely a matter of limitations in our empirical research; it has to be linked to the fact that it is rarely clear what such an identity approach implies. Identity is becoming fashionable as a word but its meaning as a theoretical category and a tool for analysis remains unclear. Such problems in conceptual clarity and theoretical rigour have serious analytical repercussions. For example, they make it extremely difficult to account in a sustained way for what may be the most pressing problem affecting the European Union today; namely, that although Europe is now undoubtedly an economic, and increasingly a political, entity, identification with Europe has so far failed to acquire 'a wider cultural or affective meaning' for the different European peoples (Pagden, 2002, p. 33). As has been observed, 'apart from a flag, a hymn and a few festivals... the European Union offers little that can inspire collective enthusiasm' (Chebel d'Appolonia, 2002, p. 190), something that seems to be corroborated by recent *Eurobarometer* statistical data (Dunkerley et al., 2002, p. 120).

The aim of this chapter is to focus on some 'paradoxical' dimensions of political identity and identity formation in general, dimensions which are often neglected but remain essential if we want to arrive at a thorough and rigorous conceptualization of identity and identification. Clearing the ground for a more sophisticated and effective discussion of identity formation is surely a prerequisite for any serious discussion of the questions around European identity and for the development of an appropriate set of research directions and hypotheses in this area. In particular, beyond the trivial use of 'identity', we will try to explore what accounts for the appeal of an identity construction, what makes people collectively identify with particular identity formations, and what implications such identifications entail. Here, discourse theory (as elaborated by Laclau and Mouffe) constitutes an important theoretical resource. However, we will not present discourse theory as some sort of panacea, as a fully developed theoretical perspective with limitless empirical applications; we are rather interested in tracing certain limitations of the discursive research programme and in suggesting directions for its future development both in terms of theoretical innovation and new research agendas. In particular, we will focus on the way the psychoanalytic problematic of enjoyment can diversify the discourse-theoretical account of identification, encompassing not only its formal/discursive but also its substantive/affective conditions of possibility, what one could call its *obscene* dimension. If, however, the first part of this chapter is developing a primarily theoretical argument, the second part will comprise an attempt to *articulate* a set of discourse-theoretical and psychoanalytic concepts with the research context of discussions around European identity. Our main hypothesis here will be that the view of identity and identification resulting from a blend of discourse theory and psychoanalysis *can* provide plausible and innovative explanations for the current difficulties in constructing European identity as a collectively appealing object of identification, and thus *can* redirect the debate around this issue in an uncharted but clearly promising direction.

## Passions of identification I: discourse and enjoyment

### Discourse theory, identity, and identification

Generally speaking, it is possible to discern at least two theoretical movements leading to the current preoccupation with identity. First, the social character of identity is recognized. Within modernity, human identity cannot be but a social identity. More specifically, this implies an awareness of the socially *constructed* character of identity. Hence, from a discourse theory perspective, the problem of identity is not a question of people *discovering* or *recognizing* their true, essential identity but of *constructing* it (Laclau, 1994, p. 2). As soon as the obviousness and essentialism of social identities is put into question, the political dimension of identity formation, its reliance on contingent hegemonic plays, and processes of inclusion/exclusion, also comes to the fore. Moreover, it is also revealed that the continuous political construction of social identities can never result in a closed, self-contained, and absolute identity. Identity, at both the personal and political levels, is only the name of what we *desire* but can *never fully* attain.[1]

What is the political practice that supports and sustains this desire for identity? What is the name of this practice which, although it always fails to produce a full identity, plays a crucial role in structuring our lives? In Laclau's view,

> the key term for understanding this process is the psychoanalytic category of *identification*, with its explicit assertion of a lack at the root of any identity: one needs to identify with something [a political ideology or ethnic group for example] because there is an originary and insurmountable lack of identity. (Laclau, 1994, p. 3)

Indeed this has become a central insight for discourse theory (Howarth and Stavrakakis, 2000, p. 14). The ultimate impossibility of identity renders *identification* central for contemporary political analysis and destabilizes any identitarian metaphysics: *political subjectivity* (both at the individual and the collective levels) depends on identification but identification never results in the production of full identity. In fact, it is because it proves unable to cover over lack and dissimulate social antagonism that identification remains the horizon of political subjectivity. Its ultimate failure is its biggest success.

**Aspects of identification: from discourse to affective investment**

Now, the crucial question is at what level does one locate this play of identification. What exactly is at stake in identification processes? What drives, for example, the endless repetition of identification acts? Is it only imaginary fullness and symbolic coherence? Is identity construction merely a semiotic play? Is the transformation taking place in a subject during identification of an exclusively cognitive nature? And, most crucially, what accounts for the pervasive character, the long-term fixity of certain identifications? Questions such as these have attracted the attention of a variety of disciplines. Social psychology, for example, has long been puzzled by the process through which 'identifications become a salient basis for cognitions and behaviour' (Chryssochoou, 1996, p. 299).

It might be possible to illuminate these questions by paying some attention to Freud's comments on identification and group formation. Undoubtedly, Freud's account bears the marks of its own historicity. It alerts us, however, to something which is often foreclosed or downplayed in discussions of identity and identification – even within discourse theory. What I have in mind is the crucial Freudian insight that what is at stake in assuming a collective identity is something of the order of *affective libidinal bonds*. As Freud points out in *Group Psychology*, 'a group is clearly held together by a power of some kind: and to what power could this feat be better ascribed than to Eros, which holds together everything in the world?' In that sense, what is at stake in collective identification is not only symbolic meaning and discursive fullness but also 'the libidinal organization of groups' (Freud, 1985, p. 140). This is also the case in the two examples Freud uses, the Church and the Army: 'It is to be noticed that in these two groups each individual is bound by libidinal ties on the one hand to the leader (Christ, the Commander-in-Chief) and on the other hand to the other members of the group' (Freud, 1985, pp. 124–5). Furthermore, true to Freud's commitment to the duality of the drives, every *passionate* affective investment also entails a more sinister dimension, that of hatred and aggressiveness: 'it is always possible to bind together a considerable number of people in love [to create, in other words, a libidinally invested shared "identification"], so long as there are other people left over to receive the manifestations of their aggressiveness' (Freud, 1982, p. 44).

Freud's account points to a crucial dimension which is constitutive of identification: the dimension of passion, of affective attachment, and libidinal investment, something which presupposes the mobilization of the *energetics of the body*, of libido as a 'quantitative magnitude' (Freud, 1985, pp. 118–19). Lacan will redirect this Freudian focus on the affective side of identification processes onto the *obscene* paths of enjoyment (*jouissance*). In Lacan's work, *jouissance* – a satisfaction so excessive and charged that it becomes painful – seems to occupy a place overlapping with what is associated with libido in Freud. In that sense, it could be argued that Lacan prefers to 'reconceptualize sexual energy [Freud's libido] in terms of jouissance' (Evans, 1996, p. 101). Indeed the Lacanian distinction between the plane of the signifier and discourse – the symbolic – and *jouissance* – the real – parallels, to some extent, the Freudian one between representation and affect:

> The subject of representation can be associated here with the unconscious, and thus with the articulation and development of unconscious desire – Lacan's subject of desire or desiring subject – whereas the subject of affect or 'emotive' subject is the subject of *jouissance*, or 'enjoying subject'... where there is affect, there is *jouissance*. (Fink, 1997, p. 212)

Thus, identification has to be understood as operating on both of these distinct but interpenetrating fields: discursive structuration/representation and *jouissance*.

### Logics of enjoyment

The problematic of enjoyment helps us answer in a concrete way what is at stake in socio-political identification and identity formation, suggesting that support for particular identifications is partially rooted in the *jouissance* of the body. What is at stake in these fields, according to Lacanian theory, is not only symbolic coherence and discursive closure but also *enjoyment*, the *jouissance* animating human desire. This passage from a consideration of the symbolic aspect of identification to an analysis at the level of desire and *jouissance* is clear, for example, in Lacan's 1961–62 unpublished seminar on *Identification*. The seminar starts with a consideration of the 'signifier and its effects': 'From the processes of this language of the signifier, from here alone can there begin an exploration which is fundamental and radical of how identification is constituted' (seminar of 29 November 1961). This plane of signification is gradually linked with the logic of desire: 'identification has to be made with this something which is the object of desire' (seminar of 24 January 1962). Desire, however, can only be properly understood through the Lacanian logics of enjoyment. In order to illuminate this connection, it is necessary to distinguish between different types of *jouissance* present in Lacan's work. The emergence of desire is primarily related to the process of symbolic castration: desire presupposes the sacrifice of a pre-symbolic *jouissance qua* fullness, which is prohibited upon entering the social world of linguistic representation. It is only by sacrificing her/his pre-symbolic enjoyment that the social subject can develop her/his desire (including the desire to identify with particular political projects, ideologies, and discourses).

The fact, however, that this enjoyment is excised during the process of socialization does not mean that it stops affecting the politics of subjectivity and identification. On the contrary. First of all, it is the imaginary promise of recapturing our lost/impossible enjoyment which provides the fantasy support for many of our political projects and choices.[2] But this is not the full story. Apart from the promise of fantasy, what sustains desire, what drives our identification acts, are at least two further dimensions: our ability to go through limit-experiences related to a *jouissance* of the body, and the fact that desiring itself entails a *jouissance* of its own – an enjoyment beyond the anticipation of fantasmatic fullness. In the *Identification* seminar, for example, Lacan argues that the subject can momentarily experience something akin to an attainment of her identification: 'at this unique instant demand and desire coincide, and it is this which gives to the ego this blossoming of identificatory joy from which jouissance springs' (seminar of 2 May 1962). However impressive, this *jouissance* remains *partial*: '"That's not it" is the very cry by which the jouissance obtained is distinguished from the jouissance expected' (Lacan, 1998, p. 111); its momentary character, unable to fully satisfy desire, fuels dissatisfaction. It reinscribes lack in the subjective economy, the lack of another *jouissance*, of the sacrificed *jouissance qua* fullness, and thus reproduces the fantasmatic promise of its recapturing, the kernel of human desire.

In that sense desire – and social life as we know it – presupposes the impossibility of fully recapturing our lost *jouissance*; at the same time its appeal depends on the possibility of partial *jouissance* (encountered in momentary limit experiences and in desiring itself). This paradox is also reflected in the peculiar structure of fantasy. What is crucial to understand here is that fantasy sustains desire by performing a delicate balancing act. This has been very well highlighted by Slavoj Žižek. On the one hand fantasy promises a harmonious resolution of social antagonism, a covering over of lack. Only in this way can it constitute itself as a desirable object of identification. On the other hand, this beatific dimension of fantasy 'is supported by a disturbing paranoiac fantasy which tells us why things went wrong (why we did not get the girl, why society is antagonistic)' (Žižek, 1998, p. 210). This second – obscene – dimension which 'constructs the scene in which the *jouissance* we are deprived of is concentrated in the Other who stole it from us' (Žižek, 1998, p. 209) is instrumental in perpetuating human desire and reproducing the centrality of identification. By focusing on the 'theft of enjoyment', by conveying the idea that somebody else – the Jew, for example, or the national Other – has stolen our enjoyment, it succeeds on both fronts. It preserves our faith in the existence and the possibility of recapturing our lost enjoyment – a faith enhanced by the partial enjoyment we get from our experience – but projects its full realization onto the future, when we will manage to get it back from the Other who has stolen it from us. This way enjoyment is kept at a 'healthy' distance, not too far but not too close either; close enough to support the appeal of an object of identification but far enough from letting us entertain the vision of full satisfaction as an imminent possibility, something that would kill desire and put identification in danger. Nevertheless, there is an important by-product in this balancing act: the exclusion/demonisation of a particular social group.[3]

It is possible now to understand the importance of Lacanian theory in broadening the scope of the Freudian idea of identification and in enriching a discourse-theoretical approach to identity formation and identification. First, by elaborating his complex problematic of *jouissance*, Lacan points to the important connection between love and hate, libido, and death drive, in accounting for the complexity of identification:

> to understand the concept of jouissance in Lacan as unique, is to understand that it concerns at the same time libido and death drive, libido and aggression, not as two antagonistic forces external to each other, but as a knot forming an internal cleavage. (Miller, 1992, pp. 25–6)

As we have seen this is also reflected in the limit-experiences of (partial) *jouissance* – uniting satisfaction, and dissatisfaction – as well as in the paradoxical (dual) structure of fantasy – of a fantasmatic, imaginary *jouissance* that can operate as an object of desire only insofar as it is posited as lacking/stolen and thus causing the hatred of the Other.

Secondly, by locating the basis of *jouissance* outside representation, in the real of the body, Lacan has distanced himself from a dry interpretation of his work which reduces the complexity of his teaching to a mere moment in the passage from structuralism to semiotic post-structuralism. With his complex theory of *la substance jouissante* (Lacan, 1998, p. 23), Lacan 'locates the reality of the body in his thought and militates against any purely "intellectualist" reading of his work' – discourse theorists should perhaps try to articulate a similar strategy in responding to the banal criticism regarding the supposed idealism of discourse theory. This is not to say, however, that the somatic acquires the character of a positive essence, reintroducing some sort of biological essentialism. Lacan guards against such a development by pointing to our inability to master the real (either in our knowledge constructions or in our practice and action):

> The indeterminate exigence of the somatic is every bit as central to Lacan as it is in Freud, although by relegating it to the domain of the real Lacan insists on its irremediable mysteriousness and emphasizes the distance between the psychoanalytic theory of the drives and the specific subject matter of biology. (Boothby, 1991, p. 223)

True to Freud's foundational distinction between (biological) instinct and drive, Lacan will highlight the relation between *jouissance* and the signifier, the symbolic and the real, language and affect. All these are distinct but not isolated realms. The affective and *jouissance* have to be seen as shifted and directed by the symbolic order, by the order of representation, which is in turn dislocated and distorted by their pressure, by the persistence of the drive and the irreducibility of enjoyment. In some of his most enigmatic moments, Lacan will go as far as to proclaim 'the union between the imaginable of flesh and word' (Boothby, 1991, p. 228), by stressing that 'the signifier is situated at the level of enjoying substance', being both the cause and the limit of *jouissance* (Lacan, 1998, p. 24).[4] In any case, Lacan's theoretical trajectory becomes clearer when examined in its diachronic unfolding. Everything is first approached through a structuralist/post-structuralist stress on the symbolic register. Then the real dimension is added, the dimension of *jouissance*. In a final synthesis, albeit an enigmatic and incomplete one, both these dimensions are explored in their essential connection.

Hence, from a psychoanalytic point of view, in order to account in a coherent and effective way for identification it is necessary to redirect our attention from the formal to the substantive/affective dimension, from discourse to enjoyment, from a drier to a stickier conception of the politics of subjectivity. Lacan offers us the possibility of doing that in a way that enriches discourse theory without reoccupying the ground of an outmoded essentialism, in a way that incorporates into the same theoretical/analytical logic discourse and *jouissance*, desire and aggressivity. Discourse theory should not be seen as alien or antithetical to such a problematic. It may be the case that in some of its early formulations discourse theory emphasized 'contingency and discourse at the expense of jouissance' (Lane, 1996, p. 112), but this seems to be changing and this chapter is designed to further encourage such a change.[5] In her recent work, for example, Chantal Mouffe has stressed that 'passions and affects' play a crucial role in securing allegiance to particular political projects (Mouffe, 2000, p. 95). She clearly considers 'passion' – meaning the passions 'which produce collective forms of identification' – as one of the moving forces of political action (Mouffe, 2001, p. 11). At the same time she points out that 'reciprocity and hostility cannot be dissociated and we have to realize that the social order will always be threatened by violence' (Mouffe, 2000, p. 131).

### Example: national identification

What are the implications of such a theoretical and conceptual redirection of discourse theory for concrete political analysis? An example will help illuminate what is at stake here and what the advantages are in terms of broadening the scope of political research. Let us examine national identity. There is no doubt, of course, that nations are discursive constructs with particular historical conditions of possibility. To what extent, however, is this sufficient explanation of the pervasive nature of national identification? In Benedict Anderson's words 'it is doubtful whether either social change or transformed consciousness, in themselves, do much to explain the *attachment* that peoples feel for the inventions of their imagination [or] . . . why people are ready to die for these inventions' (Anderson, 1991, p. 141). It is here that one also has to take note of the fact that national identification is supported by affective bonds, which account for its persistence and hegemonic success. Freud's Eros, which plays a key role in the construction of every collectivity, seems to be crucial in understanding nationalism: 'it is useful to remind ourselves that nations inspire love, and often profoundly self-sacrificing love' (Anderson, 1991, p. 141). No doubt nationalisms are produced through complex social and political processes, but these processes are 'premised on the activation of social and cultural relationships and emotional attachments' (Jenkins and Sofos, 1996, p. 11; also see Billig, 1995, p. 18). In other words the mobilization of symbolic resources has to be coupled with an affective investment grounded in the body in order for national identity to emerge: 'References to sentiment, attitude, and loyalty underscore the very visceral dimension of identity. Nationalism works through people's hearts, nerves and gut. It is an expression of culture through the body' (Jusdanis, 2001, p. 31). The strength of national identity – or of any other identity for that matter – is not wholly attributable to the structural position of the nation as a nodal point (or of other signifiers and discursive elements). The discursive dimension is certainly important in structuring national desire, something persuasively captured in certain Lacanian analyses of nationalism (Easthope, 1999), but it is not enough. There is also a much more 'substantive' – but not essentialist – dimension that has to be taken into account: 'The element which holds together a particular community cannot be reduced to the point of symbolic identification: the bond linking together its members always implies a shared relationship toward . . . Enjoyment incarnated', an enjoyment structured in fantasies and directly linked to the hatred of Others (Žižek, 1993, p. 201). In Mark Bracher's words,

> the bedrock of a group's sense of identity . . . might be said to lie in the unique way in which a group finds enjoyment, the unique combination of particular partial drives that, like a unique blend of spices, gives each group's enactments of libido and aggression a unique particularity. (Bracher, 1996, p. 5)

But how exactly can we recognize the presence of this aspect of enjoyment? Žižek's answer is that

> all we can do is enumerate disconnected fragments of the way our community organizes its feasts, its rituals of mating, its initiation ceremonies,

> in short, all the details by which is made visible the unique way a community organizes its enjoyment. (Žižek, 1993, p. 201)

In any case, the symbolic aspect of national identification is not sufficient: 'A nation exists only insofar as its specific [partial] enjoyment continues to be materialized in a set of social practices and transmitted through national myths that structure these practices' (Žižek, 1993, p. 202). Admittedly, Žižek's analysis leaves a lot of questions unanswered, especially as far as the precise interface between the discursive and enjoyment is concerned (Easthope, 1999, p. 221). It highlights, however, a dimension which is central in accounting for the resiliance of (national) identification. It draws our attention to the fact that the mechanism most effective in structuring subjectivity in relation to discourse may not be exclusively or primarily discursive, but linked to the *extimate* real of enjoyment: 'Lacanian theory, unlike poststructuralist theory, posits linguistic meaning as operating not simply in the logic of a system of differences that structure the symbolic, but in relation to the effects of the real' (Alcorn, 1996, p. 83). Hence, contrary to what some postmodern theories of 'multiple' or 'fluid' identity imply, 'national identity cannot be exchanged like last year's clothes':

> Perhaps the postmodern consumer can purchase a bewildering range of identity-styles. Certainly, the commercial structures are in place for the economically comfortable to change styles in the Western world... One can eat Chinese tomorrow and Turkish the day after... But being Chinese or Turkish are not commercially available options. (Billig, 1995, p. 139)

Moreover, due to the fact that enjoyment is a knot between libido and the death drive, owing to the fact that is by definition excessive – either too little or too much – every identification is bound to produce its obscene Other. Hence the fantasies of the Other's special enjoyment, such as 'the black's superior sexual potency and appetite... the Jew's or Japanese's special relationship with money and work' (Žižek, 1993, p. 206). The Other is hated because he is fantasized as stealing our lost enjoyment. This is what accounts for the ever-present potential for violence, aggressiveness, and hatred marking national identification: nationalism is 'both Pandora's box and Hephaestus' hammer, capable of unlatching evil and chaos while also creating novel forms of social life'. It can inspire people to seek justice, autonomy, or other noble ideals, but it can also 'incite them to murderous violence' (Jusdanis, 2001, p. 13).

### Strategies of control: the politics of repression

If, however, the dimension of affect and enjoyment is so crucial in collective identification, why has it gone unnoticed by so many social theorists, political analysts, and modern politicians? Enlightenment philosophy and political theory – as well as politics itself – have largely seen their role as drawing a sharp distinction between the discursive/symbolic dimension of identification and its affective/obscene support. In the age of reason and rational administration there was no room for 'irrational' forces and libidinal bonds; the aim was either to control or, even better, to eliminate passion, affect, and enthusiasm, to drain from political practice and political theory the *jouissance* of the body. In its attempt to ground politics on reason and nature, the Enlightenment was 'led to present an optimistic view of human sociability, seeing violence as an archaic phenomenon that does not really belong to human nature' (Mouffe, 2000, p. 130). Passion and enthusiasm were also seen as dangerously pathological conditions, to be eradicated by the progress of human civilization (Ruby, 1996). Elements of such a stance are still implicit in some traditions of democratic theory (including some aggregative and deliberative models) and even in certain versions of postmodernism (Mouffe, 2000).

There are, however, at least two major problems with such a strategy. First, it is very difficult to sustain a strict separation between affect and reason, to disengage the symbolic aspect of discursive organization and identification from libidinal investment and enjoyment. Let us briefly return to the example of national identification. It is obvious for anyone studying nationalism that both dimensions are crucial here. Nevertheless, literature on nationalism is replete with attempts to distinguish a *benign*, drier form of nationalism (usually named 'patriotism') from the *malignant* nationalism of hatred and affective cathexis. Hence, one sees the prominent dichotomies between civic and ethnic, political and cultural, Western and Eastern, benevolent and malevolent nationalism. All these moralistic dichotomies are so many attempts to exorcize the obscene dimension of national identification. Many rationalists, liberals, and cosmopolitans consider this aspect of national identification as anathema, as 'straitlaced, illiberal and vulgar' (Jusdanis, 2001, p. 28). For these politicians and academics 'nationalism can be seen almost anywhere but here' (Billig, 1995, p. 15); their motto is 'Our patriotism – Their nationalism' (Billig, 1995, p. 55).

Such a view obviously neglects the fact that the frontiers between a supposedly benevolent nationalism and an ugly hypernationalism are never clear-cut and certainly do not preclude the transformation of one into the other. As Jenkins and Sofos have argued, it is wrong 'to see nationalism in terms of simple dichotomies – "good" and "bad", "open" and "closed", "Left" and "Right", "French" and "German". The reality is much more nuanced and complex, and in practice the two "models" are not mutually incompatible' (Jenkins and Sofos, 1996, p. 15). The juxtaposition of cultural and political nations, of civic and ethnic nationalism, seems to be based on an idealization of the histories of France, England, and the United States, which are conceptualized as realizing the enlightenment principles (Jusdanis, 2001, p. 136; also see Smith, 1995, p. 16). Such an idealization presupposes the disavowal of the fact that, in the final analysis, 'all nationalism takes on a cultural dimension' (Jusdanis, 2001, p. 162). In Anthony Smith's words, 'every nationalism contains civic and ethnic elements in varying degrees and different forms' (Smith, 1991, p. 13), to the extent that, in practice, territorial nations also have to be cultural communities (Smith, 1986, pp. 136, 149), communities that structure in their own distinct way their modes of enjoyment. The possibility of 'a purely civic (uncultural) conception of nationalism – that a nation-state can be based on an idea, that it can flourish in a purely political sense, that it can be held together by its constitutional documents and democratic institutions' (Jusdanis, 2001, p. 10) has to be put into question simply because no identity with the resiliance characteristic of nationalism can be constructed without effectively dealing with libidinal investment and *jouissance*. As Chantal Mouffe has put it, 'to make sense of nationalism one has to understand the role of "passion" in the creation of collective identities' (Mouffe, 2001, p. 11). This not to say, however, that it is impossible to construct political projects with minimal affective content; it is merely to point out that such projects will be unable to mobilize popular support on a large scale and form the basis of pervasive identifications (as has been the case with national identification).

There is, though, a second significant complication with such a strategy. When politics or theory manage to construct political projects almost devoid of affective 'substance', another problem appears. The repression of signifiers cathected with libidinal and affective value does not repress affect itself. In Freud, repression does not touch affects directly but only ideas (signifiers): affects, however, are displaced and transformed as a result of repression. Repression 'takes place via a withdrawal of the affect (quantum of energy) from [an] event's psychic representation, through which the event itself is transformed into an unconscious memory trace, while the affect is displaced to another representation' (Nobus, 2000, p. 23). In repression, in other words, affect and thought are detached from each other. While, however, the representation is directed to the unconscious, affect remains and gets attached onto another substitute representation. It is not difficult to understand the political significance of this logic. It implies that the more we repress the affective dimension of political subjectivity and identification, the signifiers associated or invested with political passion within a certain socio-political configuration, the more this dimension will seek expression through substitute political formations ('social symptoms').

An excellent example of this play is provided by Mouffe's analysis of the rise of right-wing populism, one of the explosive political phenomena that challenged discourse theory to broaden the scope of its analytical tools. According to Mouffe, the increasing appeal of right-wing populist parties in countries like Austria cannot be comprehended without exploring the link with the current depoliticization of politics advocated by Centrist political projects (Third Way politics, etc.). Putting the stress on a neutral 'politics without adversaries', on the depoliticized administration of what they accept as unavoidable – almost natural – forces and trends (such as globalization), Third Way theorists and politicians have downplayed the 'primary reality of strife in social life' (Mouffe, 1998, p. 13). This has significant effects on political identification: 'Major contemporary political passions cannot find an outlet ... as there is no debate in which different forms of identification could be provided around which people could mobilize. We are therefore witnessing the growth of other forms of collective identification' (Mouffe, 1999). In that sense, at the root of the rise of neopopulist parties, one finds a refusal to recognize the political in its antagonistic dimension and 'the concomitant incapacity to grasp the central role of passions in the constitution of collective identities' (Mouffe, 2002, p. 2).

Very often, right-wing populist parties are the only ones that try to mobilize passions and to construct collective forms of identification:

> Against all those who believe that politics can be reduced to individual motivations and that it is driven by the pursuit of self-interest, they are well aware that politics always consists in the creation of an Us versus a Them and that it implies the creation of collective identities. Hence the powerful appeal of their discourse because it provides collective forms of identification around 'the people'. (Mouffe, 2002, p. 8)

This approach has been fruitfully applied in the case of Flanders (De Vos, 2002). It is, however, the case of Le Pen in France which provides the best example so far, both in terms of the content, but also in terms of the style of his political discourse. Le Pen's discourse is marked throughout by

> passion, conflict, wit, playfulness, exaggeration, a willingness to name the enemy (or multiple enemies, in his case), and a mixture of literary references with pure vulgarity, physicality and action. By comparison politicians of the Centre Left and Centre Right look cautious and wooden, devoid of genuine feeling, creatures of their respective machines. (Budgen, 2002, p. 45)

The inability of both the political class and political analysts to predict or comprehend Le Pen's success in the 2002 French presidential elections can safely be attributed to their disavowal of the affective dimension, to the repression of the signifiers of political passion, and the inability to realize that such a repression can only lead to a displacement of affective energy and to the 'return of the repressed' in a new (pathological) form infused with obscene enjoyment and aggressiveness.

## Passions of identification II: constructing European identity

### From political practice ...

The argument that I would like to put forward in the second section of this chapter is that political and academic debates on 'European identity' and

Europeanization often reproduce the problematic strategies of repression and disavowal highlighted above. First, they purport to create a salient identification of European peoples with Europe, but neglect the crucial role of affect and passion in this process. Second, by repressing this often obscene dimension of identification, by focusing exclusively on institutional arrangements and symbolic ideals, they force the expression of passionate attachment through a variety of anti-European discourses; in that sense, they are not only ineffective but they actually harm the prospects of constructing a strong European identification. In what follows I will treat political documents, scholarly texts, and – towards the end of the chapter – newspaper articles, three very different types of discursive instantiations, simply as surfaces for the inscription of discourse. Treating academic discourse as a privileged – more or less reliable – discursive source would obscure the – often unconscious – 'complicity' between mainstream (European) politics and academia, two discursive domains which, in a typically modernist fashion, are interimplicated in the formulation and reproduction of a particular standpoint vis-à-vis European identity. As for the group of newspaper articles that will be discussed in the closing section of our discussion, they merit our attention because they constitute the surface for the discursive inscription of the affective dimension largely excluded from or downplayed in mainstream political and academic discussions.

Let us first explore the way 'European identity' is promoted and conceptualized in European political practice and theoretical analysis. There seems to be little doubt that the preoccupation with 'European identity' emerges as a primarily top-down strategy to foster popular support for the project of European integration and unification. At a stage – during the early 1970s – when the EEC was faced with bleak economic prospects within a major international crisis (Strath, 2000b, p. 401), and given the 'distinct lack of heartfelt support from ordinary Western Europeans' (Wintle, 1996, p. 10), European institutions saw, in the issue of identity, a new recipe for fostering popular support and social legitimacy, for creating a sense of common belonging and identification with European institutions and the Europeanization programme at all levels.

The fundamental declaration 'Concerning European Identity', agreed in the 1973 Copenhagen summit, was the first concrete discursive crystallization of this strategy. It is impossible to analyse in detail this document within the limits of this chapter. We can focus, however, on one essential aspect. The way 'European identity' is envisaged and discussed in the document clearly draws on a dry, institutional, symbolic conception of identity. What are the 'fundamental' or 'essential' elements of European identity according to the document? They range from the rule of law, social justice, and respect for human rights through to the common market, the customs union, and all the other 'common policies and machinery for cooperation' (Commission, 1974, p. 492). Apart from these concrete but rather unimaginative references, the document is full of big words and boring jargon about a 'common European civilization', assurances of progress and international equilibrium, and promoting the 'deepest aspirations of [the European] peoples' (Commission, 1974, pp. 492–3). Even when it is accepted that identity presupposes asserting Europe's differences from other countries and parts of the world (see especially Commission, 1974, p. 496), this is expressed in a naively pacifist, neutral, even unreal language:

> European unification is not directed against anyone, nor is it inspired by a desire for power. On the contrary, the Nine are convinced that their union will benefit the whole international community since it will constitute an element of equilibrium and a basis for cooperation with all countries, whatever their size, culture or social system. (Commission, 1974, p. 494)

Since Copenhagen, identity has appeared in a variety of official documents and declarations – including the 'Solemn Declaration of the European Union' (1983), the 'Single European Act' (1987), up to the Maastricht Treaty, where European identity is given an important role in the external relations of the Union, but is conceived as limited by the national identities of the Member States. During this period a variety of more practical reports was also produced: in 1975 the Tindemans report pointed to the importance of creating a European identity; in 1985 the Adonnino reports put forward the idea of introducing common symbols in order to enhance the identity of the EEC – hence the adoption of a standardized passport, an official European flag, etc. – and, in 1993, the De Clerq report discussed the importance of an effective communication of Europe to its citizens (Pantel, 1999, p. 53; Strath, 2000a; Strath, 2000b). Of course today, the Euro can be singled out as the most important development in this trend of unification. Simultaneously, sustained attempts have been made to promote European identity through education, with the introduction of a variety of student exchange and other educational programmes (such as Erasmus, Leonardo, Socrates, and Tempus).

All these policies and actions have had considerable effects. They failed, however, to deepen popular identification with the European Union and European identity. How can one explain this apparent failure? Many commentators have observed that all these processes and declarations, no matter whether premised on pragmatic concerns or a genuine euro-enthusiasm, have been, to a large extent 'contrived and shallow' (Wintle, 1996, p. 10), limited to big words and a dry institutional jargon. It is a common conclusion that what is really missing here is, so to speak, the substance behind the projected image of Europe. From our point of view, this lack of substance can clearly be associated with the libidinal/affective dimension of identification. When this is lacking, identifications cannot acquire any salience or deep hegemonic appeal. In that sense, one could argue that the problem lies in the fact that the stress has been clearly and exclusively on fostering 'identification with the EU as a political [and economic] entity' (Billig, 1995, p. 125). Fortunately or unfortunately, however, as Delors has put it, 'you don't fall in love with a common market; you need something else' (Delors in Bideleux, 2001, p. 25). Thus, it also 'seems unlikely that a European identity, with the EU as its political foundation, will generate the sorts of passions and loyalty that people feel towards their nations' (Billig, 1995, p. 121). Indeed the prospects will be bleak for Europe if it remains 'a patchwork, memoryless scientific "culture" held together solely by political will and economic interest' (Smith, 1999, p. 245).

**. . . to academic analysis**

Let us now move to an exploration of the way academic analysis has dealt with these problems of European identity. Faced with the normative/formal/institutional and mostly top-down attempts of European institutions to foster a strong popular identification with Europe and their poor results, most academics were led to recognize the existence of the two crucial dimensions of identity formation, the procedural and the substantive, the *drier* and the *stickier*. There is an increasing acceptance of the fact that 'Europeans do not recognize the EU as an appropriate sphere for politics, as they do the nation state', that the EU is deficient in terms of 'levels of affective attachment and identification', although this does not necessarily mean that they don't recognize it as a framework for politics alongside the national arena (Banchoff and Smith, 1999, pp. 1–2). Now, there are, broadly speaking, three ways to deal with the recognition of this split:

1. One can adopt a moralistic framework and attempt to abolish the darker side in favour of the brighter. A lot of the research on European identity is predicated upon a strict distinction between a positive (*benign*) and a negative, exclusionary (*malignant*) form of identification, implying that it is possible to cultivate the former and abolish the latter. Delanty, for example, criticizes 'the largely unreflective idea of Europe based on self-identity through negation and exclusion' – proposing its replacement 'with one based on autonomy and participation' (Delanty, 1995, p. 15). He grounds this claim on a sharp distinction between *positive* and *negative* difference: in the first case identity is founded on the positive recognition of otherness (leading to solidarity), in the second it is based on the negation of difference (leading to exclusion) (Delanty, 1995, p. 5). Such a view has also affected what is known as the postnational agenda. As Shaw has put it:

   > Postnationalism may be seen as . . . the attempt to recover and rethink some of the core values of nationalism as lending meaning to a particular community with shared practices and institutions, *without the*

> *necessary institutional baggage or ideological weight of the modern (nation) state or a negative sense of nationalism as exclusion.* (Shaw, 2000, p. 74, my emphasis)

As we have seen this is an impossible strategy which, due to the inherent paradox of identification, is unable to produce any sustainable results. It is impossible to fight or displace processes of social or political cathexis and exclusion with a theoretical or analytical exclusion or *repression* (of the 'obscene' side of identification).

2. One can alternatively adopt a 'multiple identity' or 'dual identity' framework that tries to keep the two dimensions present but strictly separate. This option is more alert to the irreducibility of the two dimensions involved in identification but fails to understand their close interconnection. For example, most of the theorists adopting a 'multiple identities' standpoint seem to subscribe to a quasi-relativist version of constructionism. They conceptualize identity as something in 'permanent flux where boundaries are constantly contested and negotiated': 'European – and national – identities are always fluid and contextual, contested, and contingent' (Malmborg and Strath, 2002, p. 5). According to such a view, 'the most essential part of identity is its multiple nature' (Wintle, 1996, p. 22; also see Banchoff and Smith, 1999, p. 7): 'The adjectives "European" and "national" are not alternatives but are articulated in the recognition of multi-identification' (Malmborg and Strath, 2002, p. 6). But here is where the first problems enter the horizon.

   'Multiple identity' or 'multi-identification' is typically predicated upon a model of peaceful coexistence between different but equally valid subject-positions. Of course, one can have multiple identifications at different levels, but that 'does not mean that such ties are entirely optional and situational, nor that some among them do not exercise a greater hold and exert a more powerful influence than other'. We have seen in this paper how 'national identity does in fact exert today a more potent and durable influence than other collective cultural identities' (Smith, 1991, p. 175). Nationalism 'commands popular support and elicits popular enthusiasm. All other visions, all other rationales, appear wan and shadowy by comparison' (Smith, 1991, p. 176). Hence, a series of legitimate questions presents itself. What *organizes* multiplicity? What determines the movement between different subject positions? Are all the components of a multiple identity equally important? The answer psychoanalytic theory provides is that there is always a *fantasy scenario* which organizes and supports the apparent multiplicity of identity and determines the 'rules of engagement' between its different levels, a *mapping* which prioritizes particular modes of enjoyment, particular libidinally invested components and nodal points (*points de capiton*) and not others, which remain structurally and emotionally peripheral.[6]

Two further points are crucial here. First, without the intervention of these nodal points, subjective structure can easily disintegrate into a psychotic state. This has to be taken very seriously into account by some 'chaotic' conceptions of 'multiple identity', primarily because 'the total disintegration of personal identity into identity atoms [components of a multiple identity] might not be psychologically manageable' and thus 'multiple identity' might not be the most promising solution for the Europeanization of national identities (Wilson and van der Dussen, 1995, p. 207). This also explains why, when a conflict of loyalties arises, certain components or levels are always assigned higher priority than others, the process that has sustained most nationalist identifications so far. As we read in a recent textbook on Europe, 'people always were many things, but in the epoch of nationalism, one identity was the trump card . . . the national identity was the primary one in cases of conflict between loyalty to the different identities' (Wilson and van der Dussen, 1995, p. 207). Second, 'multiple identity' arguments often presuppose a fluid conception of identity, which is ultimately premised on a certain voluntarism. It seems, in other words, to imply that the particular profile of an identity is a matter of conscious, instrumental or even rational choice on the part of the subject, a matter of shopping around for interesting components for inclusion. It is clear that discursive structuration and affective investment, set precise – although contingent – limits to such movements.

3. As far as the 'dual identity' framework is concerned, the model European citizen would hold, in this respect, two distinct national loyalties: one political (at a European level) and the other ethnic (Goldmann, 2000, p. 42). In other words, every European citizen would be *split* between a political state identity (along the lines of the so-called 'French' model) and a cultural identity (along the lines of the so-called 'German' model) (Wilson and van der Dussen, 1995, p. 208). I am using the term 'split' because according to such a model 'identity and politics are *delinked* and *refocused*' and what is introduced is 'a dualism, with Europe as the civic nation-state and our old nation-states as organic people-nations' (Wilson and van der Dussen, 1995, p. 208, my emphasis). This split is also one of the premises of certain versions of the 'postnational' agenda. Here again the link implied by nationalism between cultural integration (the ethnic, substantive aspect of nationalism) and political integration (the formal, procedural aspect) is deconstructed (Curtin in Shaw, 2000, p. 74).

Given our argument so far, it is very difficult to imagine how it would be possible to de-link politics from identity, discourse from enjoyment. Furthermore, even if it would be possible to separate them, what would be the 'rules of engagement' between them? A conflictual scenario, that of a spill-over of affect/aggressivity from the national to the European sphere, seems probable – even more probable than a peaceful one: 'the greater the distance between the models of different countries and the more emotionally involved the populations are with their respective models, the more unlikely it is that a common policy on a supranational level can be established, accepted and implemented' (Zetterholm, 1994, p. 7). Furthermore, if such a contamination would be unavoidable, then another question becomes crucial: which of the two dimensions would dominate the other? Given the deficiencies of a dry conception of 'European identity' or 'Europe', once more prospects look a bit gloomy. Engaged in such an unequal 'battle' it is difficult to see European identity ever acquiring a salient role in the lives of European citizens.

At this point, it is important to make clear that this analysis is not premised on some sort of a priori privileging of national or state identity. Of course we can and should envisage a strong European Union beyond traditional statist and nationalist models, but such a development cannot materialize and will never succeed without dealing with the affective dimension of identification in a non-repressive way. If theory and political analysis continue to repress or disavow this dimension 'Europe' will, of course, develop in various directions but will never become a really salient identification, winning the hearts rather than merely the pockets of European citizens. To put it in Georges Bataille's poetic language, 'the reduction to order fails in any case: formal devotion (devotion without excess) leads to inconsequence' (Bataille, 1991, p. 161). Current research using a multiplicity of other methodologies seems to support our conclusions: feelings of national identity directly influence support for the European Union. In particular, 'there is a clear indication that a strong national identity leads to a decrease in support for the EU' and that the effects of national identification 'are at least as significant as utilitarian explanations, such as income, education, and subjective economic evaluations' (Carey, 2002, pp. 397, 407). However, this is not because national identity is a priori invested with such a privileged position. This affective investment is a contingent, historically determined reality associated with the shifts in collective identification within modernity. It provides an opportunity to study the intricacies of the relation between affect, enjoyment, and identity but does not preclude the possibility of articulating alternative administrations of enjoyment in the future.

## Europe's obscene Other

What is even more crucial is that repressing the dimension of enjoyment does not only affect the future prospects of European unification, it also produces a series of indirect results of major political importance. As we have already argued, the repression of signifiers cathected with libidinal and affective value never leads to the disappearance, but merely to the displacement, of psychical energy and to the 'return of the repressed' through the emergence of symptomatic formations. We have seen the relevance of this logic in explaining political phenomena such as the rise of right-wing populism in Europe. If our hypotheses are correct, then a similar loop must be in operation with relation to discussions around European identity and integration. Indeed, it seems that the neglect of the affective side of identification leads to a displacement of cathectic energy which is now invested in anti-European political and ideological discourses. In fact, a whole separate level of charged debate is erected, in which dry European identity, its institutional arrangements and big words are seen as agents of castration, not only indifferent but also hostile to the structures of enjoyment operating in the various nationalisms and engaged in a process of standardization which has to be resisted. These discourses of resistance differ from the standard euro-jargon not only in terms of their content but also in terms of their style: they are aggressive, visceral, and funny ranging from the obscene to the violent, often via the grotesque. This is, however, the secret of their success.

In fact, these discourses are so incommensurable with standard political and academic debates on Europe that both the political class and the research community have preferred to avoid taking them into account. This, however, will not make them disappear; quite the contrary. Thus it is more prudent to explore their constitution and functioning. A lot of very good examples are available; Le Pen again, religious populist discourse in Greece, and others. But the most graphic example is offered by some versions of British Euro-scepticism. I am particularly interested in the type of Euro-scepticism which attracts millions of people, that of the British popular press, which will comprise the last discursive reservoir to be analysed in this chapter. In general, research on the treatment of European integration by the British media suggests that they are particularly negative and resistant to the idea of European integration and European identity (Cinnirella, 1996, p. 263). What is most important, however, is that this hostility towards Europe typically takes a particular form. According to our schema we would expect it to be articulated in a way antithetical to the dry, normative, and detached form the debate takes in official political circles. Is this the case? Indeed resistance speaks a different language; it is played out at a completely different level, one founded on affect, passion, ridicule, and obscenity. It is difficult to ignore the fact that, on 1 November 1991, when respectable politicians were discussing the pros and cons of federalism and national independence, Britain's most widely read national newspaper, *The Sun*, simply read, 'Up yours Delors!' (Cinnirella, 1996, p. 263). This type of discourse, characteristic of the right-wing popular press, has indeed become so successful that it now comprises one of the major pillars on which Euro-sceptic influence is built (Forster, 2002, p. 111).

What are the basic parameters of this resistance to Europe, which is articulated in the British popular press? Its most salient feature seems to be the depiction of the European Union as an alien regulating agency which somehow intervenes in the particular way we have organized our lives, in the particular way we have structured our enjoyment. In other words, the EU is primarily represented as an agent of castration. Some examples are in order here. 'Brussels bureaucrats' have been accused of wanting to scrap the traditional British loaf (*Daily Mail*, 27 October 1997, p. 29), of forcing Britain to change its three-pin plugs to the continental version, costing domestic electricity users a fortune in rewiring and allegedly jeopardizing UK safety standards (*Daily Star*, 27 May 1994, p. 2), and of pushing Britain to replace the traditional British lavatory with the 'Euro-loo' (*The Sun*, 4 May 1999, p. 11). Other titles and news-flashes read: 'Eurocrats sparked outrage among the Welsh on St. David's Day yesterday by ordering that all leeks sold in the future must look the same' (*Daily Express*, 2 March 2002, p. 36), 'EU Meddlers ready to outlaw smacking' (*The Sun*, 16 June 1998, p. 15), 'Brussels plan to scrap our passports' (*The Mail on Sunday*, 29 October 2000, p. 1). What is even more extraordinary, from our point of view, is the abundance of sexual connotations and obscene metaphors which mark this discourse throughout. This is obvious, for example, when the EU is accused of deciding that 'bananas must not be excessively curved' (*The Sun*, 4 March 1998, p. 6) and that 'Cucumbers have to be straight' (*The Sun*, 4 March 1998, p. 6), or when stories like these appear: 'Crackpot Euro chiefs have decreed British rhubarb must be straight' (*The Sun*, 24 June 1996, p. 11). Not to mention of course the alleged harmonization of condom dimensions and the 'Euro threat to kill the British Banger'. One could go on recounting such stories *forever*. What is important is that such grotesque stories seem to provide the obscene support to a resistance against a Europe that has failed to inspire and function as an object of identification, a Europe that has failed to engage with the visceral, obscene dimension of identification, which is increasingly seen as devoid of substance and appeal.

Two further points are crucial here. First, one should be very careful before dismissing these stories as marginal or unimportant. Not only are they depicting the basic editorial line of some of Britain's major newspapers, they also occasionally surface in more serious newspapers and increasingly influence more mainstream public discourse. In the first book-length account of British Euro-scepticism, Forster argues that due to the predominance of pro-integrationists in the academic community most discussions have 'routinely overlooked Eurosceptics and Euroscepticism and by design or default have often failed to treat it as a serious phenomenon or object of study' (Forster, 2002, p. 3). If this is the case with respectable forms of Euro-scepticism you can imagine what has been happening along the obscene dimension of the debate. Fortunately, this complacent indifference is slowly coming to an end. It is indicative that pro-European institutions – including the representation of the European Commission in the UK and the 'Britain in Europe' campaign, an initiative supported by Tony Blair, Gordon Brown, Ken Clarke, Michael Heseltine, and Charles Kennedy – are increasingly becoming conscious of the need to deal somehow with this avalanche. Hence, a whole section of the European Commission British website is devoted to the various euro-myths we have presented, while the 'Britain in Europe' campaign has produced a booklet characteristically entitled *Straight Bananas? 201 Anti-European Myths Exposed.*[7] In both instances, however, the focus is on revealing how untrue these stories are. What is thus missed is that people do not enjoy these stories because of their truth-value but because they identify with the fantasy implicit in them, because 'European identity' does not offer them any other *real* choice. Why is the British press operating at this 'level of argument'? Why is the British public – as well as other European public spheres – still susceptible to such a rhetoric? Mainstream social and political analysis should perhaps start entertaining the possibility that all these are the vicissitudes of a construction of European identity based on the exclusion of certain dimensions crucial in the reproduction of social and political identification: affect, enjoyment, passion.

## Conclusion

So, simply put, what is to be done? Readers unfamiliar with types of argumentation such as psychoanalysis and discourse theory could be easily led to the conclusion that what naturally follows from this analysis is that people should surrender to aggressiveness and obscene enjoyment, that European studies should refocus their research attention on the size of fruits and the castration fantasies of the European peoples, and that Europe will only become really appealing as an object of identification if it starts a sexual – if not an S&M – revolution! In actual fact, the conclusion we envisage is much more modest: *European policy and European studies obviously don't have to reproduce the obscene reactions and identifications we have described. It is, however, in their interest to take into account their causes and implications. Only by taking seriously the dual nature of identification (discursive and affective, symbolic and libidinal) will they gradually become able to reflect on their own contribution – through their strategies of repression or disavowal – in phenomena such as Euro-scepticism and the lack of pervasive popular identifications with 'Europe'.*

Both in terms of theoretical consistency and in terms of political productivity, it is important to accept that contamination of one from the other dimension is ultimately inevitable and that any viable European project must involve both in a hybrid construction transcending both of them, a hybrid combining formal procedures with an administration of enjoyment capable of winning not only the political or academic argument but also 'the hearts' and 'the guts' of the peoples of Europe. What is at stake then is neither the elimination nor the glorification of antagonism, exclusion or *jouissance*, but a modified relation to these constitutive dimensions. As Neumann has put it vis-à-vis exclusion, 'integration and exclusion are two sides of the same coin, so the issue here is not *that* exclusion takes place but *how* it takes place' (Neumann, 1999, p. 37). What is at stake is to find a way to *relate ethically to antagonism and* jouissance, as opposed to the unethical, unproductive, and even dangerous standpoints of *eliminating* or *mythologizing* them: to sublimate instead of repressing or disavowing, to inject passion into the radicalization of democracy and the reinvigoration of political discourse instead of reducing politics to the unattractive spectacle of the neutral administration of unavoidable necessities.

## Notes

1. For a more detailed analysis of identity along these lines, see Stavrakakis, 2001.
2. I elaborate further on that in Stavrakakis, 1999, especially ch. 3.
3. See Stavrakakis, 1999, ch. 4.
4. This intimate relation is also behind Lacan's neologism 'enjoy-meant' [*joui-sens*].
5. Also see, in this respect, Glynos and Stavrakakis, 2003.
6. This is especially the case when 'multiplicity' involves the articulation of apparently contradictory elements.
7. In fact, some of the examples we have cited above originate from there.

## Bibliography

Alcorn, M. (1996) 'Talking with Jesse Helms: the Relation of Drives to Discourse', *Journal for the Psychoanalysis of Culture and Society*, 1:1: 81–9.

Anderson, B. (1991) *Imagined Communities* (London, Verso).

Banchoff, T., and Smith, M. (1999), 'Introduction', in T. Banchoff and M. Smith (eds), *Legitimacy and the European Union* (London, Routledge).

Bataille, G. (1991) *The Impossible* (San Francisco, City Lights Books).

Bideleux, R. (2001), 'What Does It Mean to Be European?', in M. Smith and G. Timmins (eds), *Uncertain Europe* (London, Routledge).

Billig, M. (1995) *Banal Nationalism* (London, Sage).

Booker, C. (1996), 'Europe and Regulation – the New Totalitarianism', in M. Holmes (ed.), *The Eurosceptical Reader* (London, Macmillan).

Boothby, R. (1991) *Death and Desire* (New York, Routledge).

Bracher, M. (1996) 'Editor's Introduction', *Journal for the Psychoanalysis of Culture and Society*, 1:1.

Budgen, S. (2002) 'The French Fiasco', *New Left Review*, 17: 31–50.

Carey, S. (2002) 'Undivided Loyalties: Is National Identity an Obstacle to European Integration?', *European Union Politics*, 3:4: 387–413.

Chebel d'Appolonia, A. (2002), 'European Nationalism and European Union', in A. Pagden (ed.), *The Idea of Europe* (Washington, Woodrow Wilson Center).

Checkel, J. (2001), 'Social Construction and European Integration', in T. Christiansen, K. E. Jorgensen, and A. Wiener, *The Social Construction of Europe* (London, Sage).

Chryssochoou, X. (1996), 'How Group Membership Is Formed: Self Categorisation or Group Beliefs? The Construction of a European Identity in France and Greece', in G. Breakwell and E. Lyons (eds), *Changing European Identities: Social Psychological Analyses of Social Change* (Oxford, Butterworth Heinemann).

Cinnirella, M. (1996), 'A Social Identity Perspective on European Integration', in G. Breakwell and E. Lyons (eds), *Changing European Identities: Social Psychological Analyses of Social Change* (Oxford, Butterworth Heinemann).

Commission (1974), 'Concerning European Identity', in *Seventh General Report on the Activities of the European Communities in 1973* (Brussels–Luxemburg).

Connolly, W. (1991) *Identity/Difference: Democratic Negotiations of Political Paradox* (Ithaca, Cornell University Press).

Delanty, G. (1995) *Inventing Europe: Idea, Identity, Reality* (London, Macmillan).
De Vos, P. (2002) 'The Sacralisation of Consensus and the Rise of Right-Wing Populism in Flanders', *Studies in Social and Political Thought*, 7: 3–29.
Dunkerley, D., Hodgson, L., Konopacki, S., Spybey, T., and Thompson, A. (2002) *Changing Europe: Identities, Nations and Citizens* (London, Routledge).
Easthope, A. (1999) *Englishness and National Culture* (London, Routledge).
Evans, D. (1996) *An Introductory Dictionary of Lacanian Psychoanalysis* (London, Routledge).
Evans, D. (1998), 'From Kantian Ethics to Mystical Experience: an Exploration of Jouissance', in D. Nobus (ed.), *Key Concepts of Lacanian Psychoanalysis* (London, Rebus Press).
Fink, B. (1997) *A Clinical Introduction to Lacanian Psychoanalysis* (Cambridge, Mass., Harvard University Press).
Forster, A. (2002) *Euroscepticism in Contemporary British Politics* (London, Routledge).
Freud, S. (1982) *Civilization and Its Discontents* (London, The Hogarth Press and the Institute of Psychoanalysis).
Freud, S. (1985), 'Group Psychology and the Analysis of the Ego', *The Penguin Freud Library, vol.* 12, *Civilization, Society and Religion* (London, Penguin).
Glynos, J., and Stavrakakis, Y. (2003) 'Encounters of the Real Kind: Sussing Out the Limits of Laclau's Embrace of Lacan', *Journal for Lacanian Studies*, 1:1: 110–28.
Goldmann, K. (2000) *Transforming the European Nation-State* (London, Sage).
Hansen, L., and Wæver, O. (2002) *European Integration and National Identity: the Challenge of the Nordic States* (London, Routledge).
Howarth, D., and Stavrakakis, Y. (2000), 'Introducing Discourse Theory and Political Analysis', in D. Howarth, A. J. Norval, and Y. Stavrakakis (eds), *Discourse Theory and Political Analysis* (Manchester, Manchester University Press).
Jenkins, B., and Sofos, S. (1996), 'Nation and Nationalism in Contemporary Europe: a Theoretical Perspective', in B. Jenkins and S. Sofos (eds), *Nation & Identity in Contemporary Europe* (London, Routledge).
Judt, T. (1996) *A Grand Illusion? An Essay on Europe* (New York, Hill and Wang).
Jusdanis, G. (2001) *The Necessary Nation* (Princeton, Princeton University Press).
Lacan, J. (1961–62) 'The Seminar of Jacques Lacan, Book IX, Identification 1961–1962', unpublished transcript (trans. Cormac Gallagher).
Lacan, J. (1998) *The Seminar of Jacques Lacan, Book XX, Encore 1972–1973* (New York, Norton).
Laclau, E. (1990) *New Reflections on the Revolution of Our Time* (London, Verso).
Laclau, E. (1991) 'God Only Knows', *Marxism Today*: 56–9.
Laclau, E. (1994), 'Introduction', in E. Laclau (ed.), *The Making of Political Identities* (London, Verso).
Laclau, E. (1996) *Emancipation(s)* (London, Verso).
Laclau, E. (2001) 'Democracy and the Question of Power , *Constellations*, 8:1: 3–14.
Laclau, E., and Mouffe, C. (1985) *Hegemony and Socialist Strategy: Towards a Radical Democratic Politics* (London, Verso).
Lane, C. (1996) 'Beyond the Social Principle: Psychoanalysis and Radical Democracy', *Journal for the Psychoanalysis of Culture and Society*, 1:1: 105–21.
Malmborg, M. A., and Strath, B. (2002), 'Introduction: the National Meanings of Europe', in M. A. Malmborg and B. Strath (eds), *The Meaning of Europe* (Oxford, Berg).
Marcussen, M., Risse, Th., Engelmann-Martin, D., Knopf, H. J., and Roscher, K. (2001), 'Constructing Europe? The Evolution of Nation-State Identities', in T. Christiansen, K. E. Jorgensen, and A. Wiener, *The Social Construction of Europe* (London, Sage).
Miller, J.-A. (1992) 'Ethics in Psychoanalysis', *Lacanian Ink*, 5: 13–28.

Mouffe, C. (1998) 'The Radical Centre: a Politics without Adversary', *Soundings*, 9: 11–23.
Mouffe, C. (1999) 'Ten Years of False Starts', *New Times*, 9.
Mouffe, C. (2000) *The Democratic Paradox* (London, Verso).
Mouffe, C. (2001) 'Democracy – Radical and Plural', interview in CSD Bulletin, 9:1: 10–13.
Mouffe, C. (2002) 'The "End of Politics" and the Challenge of Right-wing Populism', unpublished paper.
Neumann, I. (1999) *Uses of the Other: the 'East' in European Identity Formation* (Manchester, Manchester University Press).
Nobus, D. (2000) *Jacques Lacan and the Freudian Practice of Psychoanalysis* (London, Routledge).
Pagden, A. (2002) 'Europe: Conceptualizing a Continent', in A. Pagden (ed.), *The Idea of Europe* (Washington, Woodrow Wilson Center).
Pantel, M. (1999), 'Unity-Diversity: Cultural Policy and EU Legitimacy', in T. Banchoff and M. Smith (eds), *Legitimacy and the European Union* (London, Routledge).
Passerini, L. (2000) 'The Last Identification: Why Some of Us Would Like to Call Ourselves Europeans and What We Mean by This', in B. Strath (ed.), *Europe and the Other and Europe as the Other* (Brussels, PIE – Peter Lang).
Ruby, C. (1996) *L'enthusiasme: Essai sur le sentiment en politique* (Paris, Hatier).
Shaw, J. (2000), 'The "Governance" Research Agenda and the "Constitutional Question"', in European Commission, *Governance and Citizenship in Europe: Some Research Questions* (Luxembourg, European Communities).
Smith, A. (1986) *The Ethnic Origins in Nations* (Oxford, Blackwell).
Smith, A. (1991) *National Identity* (London, Penguin).
Smith, A. (1995), 'The Dark Side of Nationalism: the Revival of Nationalism in Late Twentieth Century Europe', in L. Cheles, R. Ferguson, and M. Vaughan (eds), *The Far Right in Western and Eastern Europe* (London, Longman).
Smith, A. (1999), 'National Identity and the Idea of European Unity', *Myths and Memories of the Nation* (Oxford, Oxford University Press).
Stavrakakis, Y. (1999) *Lacan and the Political* (London, Routledge).
Stavrakakis, Y. (2001), 'Identity, Political', in J. Foweraker and B. Clarke (eds), *Encyclopaedia of Democratic Thought* (London, Routledge).
Strath, B. (2000a), 'Introduction: Europe as a Discourse', in B. Strath (ed.), *Europe and the Other and Europe as the Other* (Brussels, PIE – Peter Lang).
Strath, B. (2000b), 'Multiple Europes: Integration, Identity and Demarcation to the Other', in B. Strath (ed.), *Europe and the Other and Europe as the Other* (Brussels, PIE – Peter Lang).
Todorova, M. (1997) *Imagining the Balkans* (Oxford, Oxford University Press).
Wilson, K., and van der Dussen, J. (1995) *The History of the Idea of Europe* (London, Routledge & Open University Press).
Wintle, M. (1996) 'Cultural Diversity & Identity in Europe', in M. Wintle (ed.), *Culture and Diversity in Europe* (Aldershot, Avebury).
Zetterholm, S. (1994), 'Introduction: Cultural Diversity and Common Policies', in S. Zetterholm (ed.), *National Culture and European Integration* (Oxford, Berg).
Žižek, S. (1993) *Tarrying with the Negative* (Durham, Duke University Press).
Žižek, S. (1998), 'The Seven Veils of Fantasy', in D. Nobus (ed.), *Key Concepts of Lacanian Psychoanalysis* (London, Rebus Press).

Websites: http://www.cec.org.uk/press/myths/index.htm

Newspapers: *The Sun, Daily Mail, Daily Star*

# 3

# Polity as Politics: Studying the Shaping and Effects of Discursive Polities

*Allan Dreyer Hansen and Eva Sørensen*

## Introduction

Traditional governance research tends to treat political units of governance, such as the polity, as pre-given. The polity is perceived as the framework for governance processes rather than its outcome. This traditional perception of the role of the polity in governance processes is closely linked to core ideas of the traditional research approach of the 'old' institutionalism, according to which governance is perceived as the activities that take place within formal governance institutions (March and Olsen, 1989, pp. 1–2). The image of the polity as pre-given is also found in traditional theories of liberal democracy, which are concerned with the regulation of governance processes that apply to a clearly demarcated people.

The traditional approach to the study of governance and democracy has lead to a downgrading of two important questions: how is a polity produced in and through governance processes, and how do the specific features of a given polity influence governance outcomes? In order to obtain the best possible understanding of societal governance, both questions must be addressed. In other words, we need research that focuses on the polity as an outcome, as well as an input in governance processes (see also Hajer, 2003).

As we argue later in this chapter, the strong interrelatedness between politics and polity is a constituting feature of the political. The fact that traditional research has put so little focus on this interrelatedness is a result of the hegemonic position of the nation-state as polity. The nation-state polity has for many years appeared as pre-given. However, in recent years, studies of governance and democracy have, to an increasing extent, focused on the interrelatedness between policy and polity. This new turn has both empirical and theoretical grounds. With regard to the former, radical transformations of governance institutions in Western democracies have taken place in the last decades of the twentieth century. What is more, there are no signs that we have seen the last of them.

Governance researchers describe this transformation as a change 'from government to governance' (Rhodes, 1997; Pierre, 2000; Mayntz, 1999; Scharpf, 1997; Jessop, 1998). In this phrasing the term 'government' points to a situation in which governance is exercised through a vertical chain of command involving legislative, executive, and administrative powers. 'Governance', in contrast, refers to a situation in which governance takes place within horizontal networks, involving a multitude of public and private actors. The main ingredients in the transformation from government to governance are, first, a simultaneous decentralization and globalization of the political system, which challenges the sovereign position of the nation-state by transforming it into one among several territorial levels of governance in a multi-layered governance structure. Secondly, there is an increased differentiation of public policy actors. Thirdly, there is a growth in governance networks that involve different public and private actors. Currently, governance researchers debate how far this process towards 'governance' has actually advanced (Hirst and Thompson, 1996; Jessop, 1998; Van Effen, Kickert, and Thomasson, 2000). However, regardless of the position that is taken in this debate, the traditional image of governance as the outcome of sovereign nation-state rule has lost its hegemonic position. Today, nation-states must justify their right to govern in competition with other potential territorially or functionally demarcated polities. Consequently, the question 'what polity is the legitimate body of authoritative decision-making?' has become an integrated and prominent issue in many governance processes. The emergence of the principle of subsidiarity in the EU debate can be seen as one of the few attempts to deal with this question. Another attempt is the principle of affectedness. The identification of stakeholders is increasingly used as a point of reference in the dynamic identification and demarcation of a polity, and thus in the political legitimization of the patterns of inclusion and exclusion that it establishes. As a consequence of the still more flexible and dynamic interaction between politics and polity caused by the transformation from government to governance, it has become still more evident that governance research must include studies of the polity as an outcome of politics.

However, there are also theoretical grounds for the increased interest in the interrelatedness between polity and politics. Governance research has, in the last twenty years, been strongly influenced by a 'neo-institutionalist' wave. What unites the many neo-institutionalist schools is the claim that 'institutions matter' in politics as well as in other aspects of societal life (Powell and Dimaggio, 1991; March and Olsen, 1989; Hall and Taylor, 1996). Institutions matter because they regulate human behaviour. The neo-institutionalists share this view with old institutionalists such as Finer (1932), Duverger (1959), and Johnson (1973), but they criticize their narrow focus on formal institutions, and broaden the definition of institutions to include their regulative, normative, cognitive, and/or imaginary characteristics (Rhodes, 1995). Neo-institutionalists argue that institutions regulate behaviour by structuring interaction. They focus on the way the interests, preferences, capacities, and identities of those who participate in governance processes are conditioned by the institutions in which they are embedded. Rational choice neo-institutionalists such as Fritz Scharpf see governance institutions as game structures that govern behaviour through the framing of utilitarian rational choices (1994). Constructivist neo-institutionalists such as James G. March and Johan P. Olsen regard governance institutions as relatively fixed universes of meaning that condition the way actors perceive themselves, other people, and the rule-governed situations in which they are placed (March and Olsen, 1995, p. 7). However, despite the considerable differences between them, the two neo-institutionalist approaches share an interest in how a given polity – be it a game structure or a fixed universe of meaning – affects policy outcomes.

Neo-institutionalists have comparatively less to offer when it comes to analysing how a polity – regardless of its political impact – is in itself an outcome of politics. A few hints can be found in the theorizing of constructivist neo-institutionalists such as March and Olsen. They argue that a central element in the governing of society is the construction of images of commonality and collective identity (March and Olsen, 1995, pp. 49–60). This argument conceives of the polity as an imagined community which is constructed in and through political processes. In what follows, we define such an imagined community a 'discursive polity'.

A discursive polity differs from a formal polity as defined by the old institutionalists in that it is not constituted by a set of formal organizational features, but by a relatively stable structure of meaning that regulates behaviour in governance processes. The focus on structures of meaning does not indicate that formal organizational features do not matter in governance processes. Instead, it indicates that it is the meaning that actors attach to them that matters, not their formal characteristics. Hence, there is an asymmetrical relationship between a discursive and a formal polity. In the end, it is the discursive polity that conditions the impact of the formal polity on governance processes. The asymmetrical coexistence of discursive and formal polities does not entail them being identical. A discursive polity might cross the borders of formally separated entities, but a formal organization might also contain more than one discursive polity.

To sum up: empirical and theoretical advances in recent years show that important steps have been taken in order to make way for studies of the interrelatedness between politics and polity. However, further steps are needed, not least because of the limited interest that neo-institutionalists have shown in analysing the discursive polity as an outcome of politics. Hence, we need to know more about the role of the discursive polity in the exercise of political power. We need answers to two questions. How is a discursive polity constructed in and through political battles? and how do specific discursive polity constructions condition political battles?

The discourse theory of Ernesto Laclau and Chantal Mouffe offers valuable insights into these questions (Laclau and Mouffe, 1985; Laclau, 1996). Regarding the first question, Laclau and Mouffe introduce the concepts of dislocation, hegemony, and floating signifiers. Dislocation denotes a situation in which a discursive construction of meaning – in this context a discursive polity – collapses and leaves the scene open for a political battle about the nature and scope of the polity. This battle takes the form of a battle for hegemony. The struggles for hegemony continue until a new discursive polity has gained ground as the dominant point of reference in the ongoing policy processes. This battle for hegemony is structured around more or less floating signifiers – or as we denote them – *organizing metaphors*.

In the political process that leads from dislocation to a new hegemony the content of the discursive polity tends to become more and more fixed. In the wake of dislocation, by contrast, the meaning that is attached to the polity is very loose. In such situations the organizing metaphor functions as a relatively empty signifier. However, as a new discursive polity achieves hegemony, the new hegemonic metaphor gains some content and becomes floating. Consequently, as the new hegemony is stabilized, the organizing metaphor aquires more of a structuring function in the governing process. As we argue later, the concepts of dislocation, hegemony, and organizing metaphors are valuable analytical tools in the analysis of how a discursive polity is constructed in and through political processes.

Discourse analysis also offers important conceptual tools that can help us to understand the political effects of a hegemonic discursive polity. Such concepts are sedimentation and social antagonism. Sedimentation can be seen as the counter-concept to dislocation since it denotes a stable discursive system in which meaning is relatively fixed. Because of this fixity, sedimented meaning attached to a hegemonic discursive polity becomes de-politicized. Although it is the outcome of former political battles, the discursive polity appears as natural, pre-given, and self-evident, as do the answers that the discursive polity gives to a number of questions regarding the collective identity of the polity such as: 'what are we?', 'who are we?', and 'what is our relationship to others?'. However, while the answers to these questions might appear as non-political, their political effects are considerable. Hence, they constitute a discursive structure, which through its considerable impact on patterns of inclusion and exclusion in political life is basically antagonistic.

Many approaches to the study of inclusion and exclusion in governance processes tend to focus exclusively on 'who' are excluded from/included in processes of political decision-making. In comparison, discourse analyses focus not only on 'who' is included or excluded, but also more basically on 'what' is being included or excluded. Discourse analysts ask: 'what forms of meaning are discursively excluded and included?' and read those processes as essentially political, that is, as antagonistic.

Accordingly, the notion of a discursive polity, which we introduce in this article, does not only focus on the discursive polity as a structure of meaning that serves as a framework for politics (as indicated by constructivist neo-institutionalists such as March and Olsen). Rather, it places specific emphasis on the way a sedimented structure of meaning conditions battles for political power. A sedimented discursive polity can be analysed in terms of a prevailing 'logic of appropriateness', but this specific logic partly works through the exclusion of other alternative logics.

The above presentation of the conceptual contributions of discourse analysis might give the impression that the construction of a discursive polity and the political effects of a sedimented hegemonic polity are separate elements in a policy process, and can be studied as such. This is evidently not the case. Even in a situation characterized by widespread sedimentation, politics always contributes to the shaping of a discursive polity through ongoing processes of disarticulation and re-articulation. And, even in the event of dislocation, politics is always to some extent conditioned by former discursive polities.

In short, there is always a certain combination of discursive change and discursive stability. The balance between change and stability varies according to the depth of dislocation. In more stable situations, changes in the discursive polity take the form of small disturbances that are handled through minor political re-articulations. We choose to call these political processes of re-articulation 'day-to-day politics'. By contrast change prevails in the face of large-scale dislocation. The higher the degree of dislocation of the discursive polity, the more there will be a need for all-encompassing political reconstructions of the discursive polity. The political battle for hegemony that this state of affairs initiates we call 'radical politics'. However, even at these moments of radical politics, some level of stability is maintained, since efforts to reconstruct meaning always start from former constructions of meaning that have not been dislocated. Since dislocation is never total, the shaping of meaning is always to some extent path dependent. To sum up, day-to-day politics is about incremental change in a relatively stable discursive polity, while the relatively rare moments of radical politics denotes political battles about the reconstruction of a discursive polity in the wake of dislocation.

In order to investigate the extent to which discourse theory can contribute to studies of the interaction between polity and politics in processes of societal governance we present an empirical study of two closely linked local governance processes. One purpose of the case study is to assess how much added value discourse theory concepts contribute in a concrete study of local governance. The case study involves an analysis of the construction of two discursive polities in the wake of a moment of dislocation, and the way these discursive polities condition governance processes when they have become sedimented. Hence, the study involves both radical politics that leads to the construction of a new discursive polity and processes of day-to-day politics that are conditioned by a sedimented hegemonic discursive polity. Before we venture into the presentation of the case study, however, we need to reflect on a few methodological issues that arise when using a discourse-analytical approach to conduct empirical studies of the interplay between politics and polity.

## Considerations on method

When conducting discourse analysis, one is confronted with a set of difficulties concerning method. The first difficulty derives from the traditional perception of 'method' as a procedure for testing theoretical claims. According to this methodological approach, it is crucial to make sure that the steps taken in empirical analysis are firmly grounded inter-subjectively and are, in principle, reproducible by all other members of the scientific community. The aim of method in this sense is an instance of what Ernesto Laclau terms 'the death of the subject' (Laclau, 1996) and suggests that good science produces knowledge that is not influenced by those who produce it (Hansen, 2003a, p. 54). Discourse theorists stress the constructed character of data and renounce the idea that it is possible to produce research that is not affected by the eyes that see and the hands that produce data. Hence, discourse theory – again employing the words of Ernesto Laclau – calls for 'the death of the death of the subject'; that is, the steps taken are not neutral vis-à-vis the theoretical point of departure, but always include an element of construction. This consideration applies equally to the operationalism of theoretical concepts and problems, for selection of data, and the analysis of the collected data (Taylor, 2001, pp. 11–14).

However, while discourse theory challenges positivist approaches to questions of method, it does not reject methodological considerations as such. Questions regarding what data to collect, how to collect them, and eventually how to analyse them are just as crucial for discourse analysis as for other research approaches within the social sciences. But some of the answers discourse analysis gives to these questions differ considerably.

With regard to the question of *what* type of data to collect, discourse theory shares its privileging of qualitative data with a wide range of other theoretical approaches, including hermeneutics and phenomenology. The common ground that these approaches share is the claim that 'context matters' if we are to gain a fuller understanding of social phenomena. Discourse analysts have traditionally focused on the analysis of written documents, since they are seen as the only reliable evidence of discursive rules in a given social or political context. In our view, documents are an important ingredient for uncovering discourses, but other forms of data are available and should also be used. Discourse theory analyses text, but the notion of 'text' covers much more than just 'written documents' (Silverman, 2001, p. 177). In fact, document data suffers from a series of shortcomings and should therefore be supplemented by other forms of data. To begin with, the level of detail in written material is often not very high. They often present a very schematic description of the discursive framework that is being studied. Secondly, documents are often messy and unclear, because they are the outcome of processes of negotiation and compromise that provide little information about existing discursive patterns of conflict. Thirdly, they often have a formalized nature that delimits the informal and more spontaneous expressions of existing discourses. Finally, without contextualizing the documents selected, it is hard to know whether they can be seen as emblematic of the discursive set up. In order to make such a contextualization, one would often have to use other forms of data.

For these reasons, discourse analysts, as well as social science researchers in general, should seek to combine document studies with studies of other forms of data. These include qualitative data like interviews and observation, as well as quantitative survey data (Taylor, 2001, p. 10; Yates, 2001, p. 105). It might come as a surprise to defend even the use of surveys in discourse analysis, but the point is that surveys are also a form of textual material. From a methodological perspective, different forms of text each exhibit different strengths and weaknesses. The strength of surveys is that they give the researcher an impression of the number of actors who identify with particular ideas, conceptions, and idioms. On the negative side, surveys cannot uncover discourses which have not already been identified. Accordingly, they can only function as a supplement to more context-oriented qualitative research methods. The observation method is powerful, in providing the researcher with important knowledge about the discursive patterns of interaction between actors. More negatively, there are problems in respect of the choice of situations to observe and because it does not provide any knowledge about how the participants experience the observed interaction. Finally, there are both strengths and weaknesses with respect to the use of qualitative interviews. On the strong side, interviews present discursive images of the world that are much less sanctioned, formalized, and rationalized than documents. In an interview situation, respondents provide spontaneously formulated individual expressions of the discursive patterns of meaning that exist in a given social field. Furthermore, knowledge is obtained about the ways individuals in different positions within a given discursive structure construct meaning and identity – and thus knowledge – about themselves and the other actors, and how and where they draw discursive patterns of inclusion and exclusion. Finally, interviews allow the researcher to search for more detailed and specific information about the discursive articulation of a specific issue among those involved. One of the problems with interviews is similar to the problems arising from the use of documents and observations: how do you select your sources – in this case the respondents? A second problem regarding the use of interviews is how to interpret the statements that informants make, that is, the old problem of concluding from what was said what was done. In short: how do we know that the informants do not lie in order to please or tease the interviewer? These problems are of course not exclusive to discourse analysts, but to all social researchers who make use of interviews. However, as we shall see below, because of differences in the analytical focus, the rearticulation of the 'said vs. done' distinction means that the 'lying' problem is less troubling for discourse analysis than for hermeneutics and phenomenologists.

Two conclusions concerning method can be drawn. First, there are no a priori limits on the forms of data available for discourse analysis, as all available research methods have something to offer in the search for data. However, and this is the second conclusion, they all suffer from serious shortcomings. For those reasons, we recommend a multi-data approach where different data types can supplement each other. We employ this approach in the case study presented below: we use surveys, documents and observation, and interviews to generate data. Each of these methods throws its own colour upon the picture we can paint of the dynamic interplay between politics and polity in two Danish localities.

As we note, one of the most general methodological problems facing a discourse analyst is the problem of selection, that is, how to select the texts, the events, and the interview respondents? We approached this problem by using a very open method of selection in the initial part of the case study. Hence, we started the data collection with a pilot period of extensive newspaper reading and by using the snowball method (Hjern and Porter, 1981, p. 274) to select respondents for the interviews. We initially studied ten years of the local newspapers in order to find events that were described as important for the local community, and to uncover the names of actors who were involved in these events. Informed by the newspaper reading, we started a process of snowball interviewing. First, we interviewed two respondents who appeared not to be directly connected with each other, but seemed to be involved in events that seemed relevant to our study. They then provided further names who, in turn, suggested additional interviewees. Ideally this process continues until no new names are mentioned in the interviews. It is, of course, impossible to be certain when to stop interviewing and the decision to limit the investigation is precisely one of the multiple instances of the return of the subject. However 'snowballing' is a way of minimizing the risk of crucial omissions owing to pre-given images of who is relevant and who is not. We stopped at 60 interviews, as at that point very little new information was produced.

However, the newspaper reading and the snowball interviewing does not only produce relevant names of respondents. They also produce knowledge of *which* events and documents are regarded as important by those involved. While some documents and events seem relevant from a formal point of view, the analysis of newspapers and the interviewing furnishes an important understanding of the meanings the involved parties attach to them, and hence of the degree to which they represent a central point of reference in the discursive constructions of meaning among those involved in the policy process. Thus we were able to select a number of documents and events that seemed of specific importance in the policy process, and pay them specific attention in the analysis.

The methodological problems, associated with the assumption that you can obtain knowledge about how respondents actually act from how they describe their actions, are rearticulated in discourse analysis. Hence, Laclau and Mouffe's theory of discourse collapses the distinction between 'said and done' by viewing both as practices of articulation. The methodological problems concerning the relation between what is being said in an interview and the practice of the respondent in the situations the interview is about therefore appear rather as problems of relations between two different contexts. Both contexts are discursive, for instance, articulations of specific rules for 'saying and acting'. But these rules for production of statements are (probably) different in the two contexts: what is possible to say-and-do in an interview situation is different from what is possible in the context that the interview seeks to represent (Hansen, 2000, pp. 53–60; Hansen, 2003b, pp. 309–10). In our study of Skanderborg and Hylke we coped with this problem by making a number of process-oriented policy analyses. This approach ensures that you obtain knowledge not only about the way individual actors describe a specific event and the role that they and others played in it but also about how other actors perceive the same event. Hence, you are able to get an impression of the level of consistency between the way the participants describe their own actions and those of others, and the way other actors describe them. The purpose of this exercise is not so much to uncover whether individual respondents lie about their actions but rather to study the degree to which the involved actors are telling the same story. This gives you an impression of how different events in the policy process have been given hegemonic meaning, or whether the content of the policy process, and the role that different actors play in it, are discursively contested.

With these remarks we finally approach the question of the specificity of a discourse-theoretical approach to the analysis of the collected data. It is in this ontological respect that discourse analysis differs most from other research approaches. As we have already noted, a criticism often levelled against interview data is that there is a risk that respondents lie. If respondents have views or perform actions that they think are illegitimate, they are likely to tell the researcher a more sanitized story. Our claim is that this might be true in the sense that respondents might lie about their views and practices. However, from a discourse-analytical approach, the main objective is to uncover the patterns of meaning that structure social and political life in a given setting. Accordingly, the respondents' views and practices are seen primarily as signs of the overall pattern of meaning. Our claim is that what respondents might say about their views and practices in the course of an interview might well differ substantially from what they say and do in the settings under analysis. But even such a distance may reveal significant features of the meanings we are interested in. One cannot lie about the discursive structuring, so the discursive conditions of possibility that structure lying are revealed, regardless of the actual lie that is made.

It is the uncovering of these discursive conditions of possibility that has guided our analysis of the data collected in the case study presented below. However, this uncovering of implicit, contingent images of the world is not an easy task. It raises the question: how does the researcher get from interview statements to analytical claims about discourses and strategies? One way is to focus on what the respondents define as evident, natural, and indisputable. In theoretical terms, the task is to look for organizing metaphors and the way they function as points of legitimization, in the promotion of concrete political objectives for various respondents. In the case study of Skanderborg and Hylke, two such metaphors are revealed through the qualitative data study: 'Skanderborg on the map' and 'We can do it ourselves'.

How and when, then, do we identify an organizing metaphor? In some cases, the metaphor is more or less self-evident because all responses and documents contain it. This is the situation in Skanderborg. At other times, as is the case in Hylke, it is more difficult to identify because it is expressed in a less direct manner in a community song.

In conclusion, we have argued that, if possible, discourse analysis should make use of a multi-data method that includes a plurality of 'texts' such as interviews, observation, document studies, and surveys. Hence, with regard to data types, the method of discourse analysis does not differ radically from that of other forms of social science research. The methodological differences between discourse analysis and other research approaches concern the way the data are analysed and the status of the results that are reached. We hope that the case study presented below will illuminate the added value of a multi-data discourse-analytical approach to the analysis of governance processes understood as the interplay between polity and policy.

## The case study: polity and politics in Skanderborg and Hylke

In order to produce knowledge about the interplay between politics and polity in actual governance processes, we have studied political life from the middle of the 1980s until 1999 in two localities in the centre of Jutland in Denmark. One locality is Skanderborg, which is a provincial town with 6,000 inhabitants. The other is the village Hylke, which has 800 inhabitants and is located a few kilometres from Skanderborg. The two localities are interconnected because of the short distance between them, and because they are part of the same formal polity – the municipality of Skanderborg.

However, as we shall see, their interconnectedness does not simply follow formal lines.

As mentioned above, we used a multiple data-collection method. Among the people we interviewed were local politicians, public administrators, grassroots activists, citizens, businessmen, and members of a number of different voluntary organizations. Important documents we used included the municipal business plan and Hylke's local magazine, *HUGin*, which often contained accounts from the committee meetings in the Hylke Council. Furthermore, four policy processes were chosen as objects of a policy analysis: the building of a culture house, the promotion of a sports club in Skanderborg, plans to build an amusement park, and the formation of 'Project Hylke'. Furthermore, we observed a number of meetings in the city hall in Skanderborg and in the Hylke village council. Finally, two surveys were carried out: one among all voluntary organizations and the other among a representative sample of 200 citizens. In what follows, we present the results of this case study.

### 'Skanderborg on the map'

The town of Skanderborg was, until recently, located in a rural area dominated by farmers. For that reason, its role as a collective point of identification in the locality was limited. The farmers identified themselves with the rural districts and the small villages. This pattern of identification was supported by the way the formal governance institutions were traditionally organized. Hence, the area around Skanderborg was formerly divided into a number of small rural municipalities. However, at the beginning of the 1970s, the many rural municipalities merged into one large municipality, with a city hall located in Skanderborg. Initially, this did not markedly affect the discursive point of identification of the inhabitants. The farmers still saw themselves as a part of a farmers' community constituted by small villages in the countryside. This state of affairs lasted well into the 1980s when the town of Skanderborg slowly but steadily began to develop into a strong discursive polity. In what follows, we will try to explain, first, how this transformation can be seen as an outcome of politics and, secondly, what political implications it has had for policy-making in Skanderborg.

The point of departure in the construction of Skanderborg as a strong discursive polity was a dislocation of the traditional farmers' community in the late 1970s and early 1980s. The dislocation was started by a severe growth in unemployment among the farmers. Because of the heavy industrialization and centralization of agriculture, ever fewer jobs were available, with a similar lack of alternative jobs, resulting from the limited number of firms in the area. This increasing unemployment triggered a whole series of disasters in the mid-1980s. In short, the municipality experienced a severe economic crisis. The hospital and the cinema closed down; a youth gang terrorized the town; many young people moved to larger cities; and a new state highway bypassed the town, resulting in great financial loss for local trade. The devastating effects of these dislocating events on the collective self-consciousness and identity of the inhabitants were considerable. In an interview with the mayor, he neatly summarized what many other respondents told us about the widespread feeling of dislocation in Skanderborg at that time: 'We walked around agreeing with each other that Skanderborg was a dump.' However, it was not only the self-confidence and self-esteem of the people in Skanderborg which was dislocated, so was the traditional image of the polity.

By the end of the 1980s, the dislocation of the traditional self-image of the people in Skanderborg had triggered the slow emergence of a new strong self-conscious 'we' identity. As one of the respondents put it, 'Nothing is so bad that it is not good for something', and she went on to explain how one of the big upheavals in the end of the 1980s became a turning point for her:

> As I was participating in the demonstration protesting against the closure of the hospital I suddenly became aware that we were a lot of people who wanted to defend Skanderborg, and the thought hit me that if only we were able to stick together we could do something to turn the tide.

Another respondent describes this moment as a collective experience: 'in some way all good forces in the town decided to work together in order to change things'. A third informant explains: 'It reminded me a little of a war situation where the whole community is threatened. It makes you stick together.' Hence, out of the experience of dislocation, there emerged a sense of common destiny among a large group of active and resourceful citizens. This image of a common destiny formed the basis for the construction of a new discursive polity that saw the promotion of the town of Skanderborg as a central strategic element in a long-term political strategy of survival.

Many informants regarded the emergence of this feeling of a common destiny among the more resourceful citizens of Skanderborg as the main reason why the negative image, of a farmers' community in decline, was gradually replaced by an image of Skanderborg as an attractive modern community. One of the respondents described the effects of this feeling of a common destiny in the following terms: 'It is as if we in Skanderborg work towards a common goal, and with deeper bonds between us than you would find it in any other town.' A respondent who has recently moved to the town agrees: 'I have a strong feeling that people work for Skanderborg as a common project.'

As these quotations demonstrate, references to the well-being – not of the farmers' communities but of the city of Skanderborg – began to function as a point of identification in the local policy processes. This point of identification finds its verbal expression in the shape of a metaphor that is repeated by nearly all the interviewed respondents when they claim that the overall policy goal is to 'put Skanderborg on the map'. This phrase is not only used by many informants, but also appears in the most important policy document of the 1990s – a municipal plan for the development of business life in Skanderborg (Erhvervsplan T20-10, Skanderborg Kommune, 1996). In this plan, the ability to put Skanderborg on the map is seen as the means, not only to promote a prosperous business life in Skanderborg but also to pave the way for a healthy municipal economy, a high level of public services, good leisure life facilities, an attractive town centre, a beautiful nature environment, and, as a sum of all these good things, a general improvement of the quality of life and well-being for all. Not only does the municipal business plan formally authorize the 'Skanderborg-on-the-map' metaphor, and thereby consolidate its already hegemonic position on the political scene in Skanderborg, but it also refers to it as the remedy for all evils.

One of the factors that seem to have laid the ground for the hegemonic position of the 'Skanderborg-on-the-map' metaphor was the fear of future dislocations. This fear was expressed by some of the important politicians and municipal administrators, including the mayor and the chair of the business council. They were both afraid that a future reorganization of the municipal structure in Denmark would lead to the establishment of larger municipalities. A question was thus raised about the future of Skanderborg in this process. It was possible that another town would be chosen as the centre in a new and larger municipality, thus placing Skanderborg on the periphery rather than at the centre of the polity. The 'Skanderborg-on-the-map' metaphor can therefore be understood quite literally as a proactive strategy aiming to develop the town into a suitable centre in a new larger municipality, both with regard to infrastructure, governing capacity, and overall reputation.

As we have seen above, the dislocation of the traditional image of the community made way for the establishment of a new discursive polity with the 'Skanderborg-on-the-map' metaphor as its point of signification. This metaphor became the hegemonic point of reference for many of the central political actors in Skanderborg, including the mayor, the business council, and a number of local business men and the grassroots. Attempts were made by people from the small villages to challenge the hegemonic position of the metaphor, as they feared that it would lead to a marginalization of the political position of the villages. However, this battle was lost because the opponents did not succeed in offering an alternative discursive image of the polity. Hence, the moment of radical politics in Skanderborg was swift and hegemony easily won.

We shall now see how the hegemonic position that the 'Skanderborg-on-the-map' metaphor quickly obtained in the course of the 1990s became sedimented and began to condition the political processes in the locality. The impact that the 'Skanderborg-on-the-map' metaphor made on policy-making in Skanderborg throughout the 1990s was considerable. That is to say, in order for any political project to succeed, it had to demonstrate how it would contribute to putting Skanderborg on the map. In our study of policy processes in Skanderborg, we identified several political projects that were legitimized through this logic. One of these projects was the establishment of a prestigious culture house in the town centre. The network of people who promoted this project included the mayor, a public administrator, and a number of central grassroots' activists and businessmen. They argued that a prestigious culture house would help to promote Skanderborg as an attractive place where exciting things happen. In this case and others, the 'Skanderborg-on-the-map' metaphor served as an important political resource. All that was required was that participants were able to link their concrete political project to this hegemonic metaphor. By contrast, those who either would not or could not inscribe their political projects within this discursive framework had a hard time obtaining influence in the policy processes. Hence, a given metaphor – in this case the 'Skanderborg-on-the-map' metaphor – has important political effects in terms of inclusion and exclusion of political projects that are part of day-to-day politics.

To begin with, the metaphor makes it difficult for those actors who do not regard Skanderborg as a homogenous community with common interests. Among these are the labour unions. Not surprisingly, they argued that what was to the advantage of business life was not always to the advantage of the community as a whole. In addition, the inhabitants in the rural areas and small villages located outside Skanderborg also tended to reject the image of Skanderborg as an undivided unity with common interests. They constantly sought to challenge this image by pointing to a conflict of interests between the town, on the one side, and the villages, on the other. By stressing these conflicts of interest, the labour unions as well as the village people automatically excluded themselves from the political scene in Skanderborg. Secondly, the 'Skanderborg-on-the-map' metaphor tended to exclude ordinary citizens from political processes. The metaphor appealed more to the social and political elites, who were capable of inventing grand futures, than to ordinary citizens who were primarily interested in finding solutions to the concrete problems of every day life. Thirdly, the metaphor excluded, or at least marginalized, political actors who had little to offer when it came to the promotion of a positive image of Skanderborg in the eyes of the surrounding world. This included weak social groups, such as the elderly and the unemployed, who had great difficulties in getting political attention in the public debate and from grassroot activists. It was also difficult for actors in rural areas and the villages to garner political attention, because they tended to bring about negative memories of the breakdown of the traditional farmers' community. However, as we shall see in the case of Hylke, it is possible for a village to prosper in Skanderborg's new hegemonic discursive polity – so long as it is willing to give up its traditional image as a farmers' community and reconstruct itself as a modern attractive community, which can contribute to placing Skanderborg 'on the map'.

The Skanderborg case illustrates a situation in which dislocation leads to a moment of radical politics that produces a new discursive polity. Former collective political identities lose their meaning and new ones are created and become sedimented. The analysis shows that this process of reconstructing a discursive polity is not necessarily hard or protracted. If a new collective identity is offered and no alternatives are visible, the battle for discursive hegemony is swift. Hence, radical politics does not necessarily indicate the presence of a tough political battle. It is only 'radical' in the sense that it brings about a new discursive battlefield for future processes of day-to-day politics in the wake of a moment of dislocation.

Once the hegemonic battle is won and a new discursive polity gradually becomes sedimented, as is the case in Skanderborg, it has considerable impact on the patterns of political inclusion and exclusion in day-to-day-politics. Actors who will not or cannot relate to the floating signifier that condenses the content of the hegemonic discursive polity are excluded, and so are those who are unable to argue how their project contributes to the promotion of what is defined as the common good. By contrast, actors who are willing and able to inscribe their political projects in the hegemonic discourse and are capable of arguing how their project contributes to the common good pass easily into political power.

However, it is important to underline that the presence of a hegemonic discourse does not lead to the end of politics. Hence, if a discourse is to maintain hegemony over time, it must be flexible in the sense that it is possible for a multitude of shifting political projects to inscribe themselves in it. In other words, the signifier has to be floating. This is clearly the case in Skanderborg, where the 'Skanderborg-on the-map' metaphor provides a vague and abstract framework for inscribing a variety of political projects. Moreover, these day-to-day efforts to inscribe concrete political projects in the hegemonic discourse incrementally disturb and transform it, through constant reinterpretations and displacements. Accordingly, there is always a little element of transformative radical politics in day-to-day-politics. The analysis of the interplay between politics and polity in Hylke will reveal how this is so.

### Hylke: 'we can do it ourselves'

During the late 1960s and 1970s, Hylke experienced a whole series of dislocatory events.[1] Owing to the industrialization and centralization of agriculture, there was an increasing number of lay-offs and the local dairy was closed down. Later, the local school and the train station also closed. As part of the major reform of the Danish municipal system in 1970, the former 'parish commune' was merged with five other parishes, and the borough of Skanderborg became the town centre of the new municipality. In this process the village even lost its vicar. The death of the village was a realistic possibility.

However, from the mid-1980s things started to change. The turning of the tide, inaugurating a period of 'radical politics', was set off by a particularly dislocating event; namely, when the municipality chose not to visit the village as part of a round trip to the different villages in order to debate a municipal plan about the future infrastructure in the area. This aroused much local criticism, and led to the organization of an alternative meeting for the inhabitants of Hylke. Another triggering event was the planning of an amusement park close to the village – a plan that was initially approved by the municipality. The plan was met with huge protests from many residents in Hylke who saw it as a threat to rural peace and harmony. A working group was formed with the task of 'lobbying' against the project, and the whole affair became a hot issue in the local press. As a result of the lobbying, the plans for the amusement park were finally abandoned. After these initial victories, efforts were made to reopen the school, which again were successful. The reopening of a closed-down village school is a very rare achievement in Denmark, and it soon became a crucial point of reference in the self-representations of the villagers.

The next step in the slow but steady transformation of Hylke into a self-conscious and resourceful modern village polity was taken when a group of local inhabitants made a development application to the Ministry of the Interior. Their aim was to establish 'Project Hylke': a set of activities that would make Hylke a good place to live for existing inhabitants and an attractive place for newcomers. Money was granted for the employment of a project secretary for six months, and various activities followed. The outcome of the project (1989–90) was a whole range of ideas concerning the development of the village into an attractive community. One idea was to form a village council. A questionnaire had shown the need for a (more) formalized forum, where local topics could be debated. The idea came from the central working group of 'Project Hylke'. The village had – and has – several voluntary associations, but apart from the 'Inhabitants' Association' (*Borgerforeningen*) they all have specific aims (sports, horse riding, and so forth). The council was formed and quickly filled the void engendered by the various dislocations. As a result of a number of successful interventions by members of the council, it became the new collective point of political identification, just as it became a site for representing 'the village as such'. After this, the discursive polity in Hylke entered a relatively long period characterized by 'day-to-day' politics.

One of the arguments that led to the establishment of the Hylke Council was that a more formal regulation of the local democracy was needed in the wake of the sedimentation of a new, stronger discursive polity. However, the actual degree of formalization was limited. A set of formal rules was devised, stating that the aim was to create a forum for the discussion of all topics of common interest, to help solve problems, and to manage the external relations of the village. Nevertheless, the actual workings of the council cannot be characterized as 'formal'. Moreover, the Hylke Council did not become a part of the official municipal organization and the members expressed no desire to move in that direction. In juridical terms, the council was a 'private association', although it was obviously recognized as something more, both by the citizens in Hylke and by the municipality. With regard to its internal organization, a steering committee and a chairman are formally elected by the citizens of Hylke, but there have never been more candidates than seats. The actual issues are often dealt with through working groups, consisting of both members and non-members of the steering committee. The working groups are concerned with applying for financial or other types of support for various projects and, when they have succeeded, with implementing the project. The number of successful projects has been quite impressive (Neufeld, 1999). They have ranged from establishing a kindergarten and a crosswalk, to building a fountain and a local meeting place for the community. Furthermore, the Hylke Council also articulated village policies in relation to the municipality, and functioned as a mediator between the municipality and the local associations, as well as between the municipality and the citizens of Hylke. The members were proud to inform us that they had never received a definite rejection of any application for support. They had received many 'nos', but repeated attempts had always yielded a positive result.

What, then, was the collective identity of the rearticulated village polity that the council represented? The meaning and representation of the polity were condensed in the metaphor 'we can do it ourselves'. The first thing to be noted is that the discursive polity seemed to have undergone a change from a 'farmers' village' to a village for reproductive and recreational activities, intrinsically linked to the city. The former chairman of the council expressed this new village identity in the following manner: 'Hylke is a village, and shall remain a village, because that is what people have moved out here for.' Hylke is not seen as a village one is necessarily born in, but is a picturesque place to which one decides to move. This way of representing the village indirectly pointed to a conflict between the Village Council, which was dominated by newcomers, and the Citizens' Association dominated by older inhabitants. However, this conflict seemed to be waning, and we were not able to detect any visible signs of it.

From the middle of the 1980s until the end of the 1990s, Hylke changed its dominant collective identity from a traditional farming village to a village one moves to because it is attractive and a place to raise children. This new discursive polity changed the relationship between the village and the town of Skanderborg considerably. Since a large number of the inhabitants was commuting to Skanderborg every day either to shop or to work their point of identification was two-sided. This tended to lower the level of antagonism between the two communities. This does not mean that the inhabitants in Hylke saw the relationship between Hylke and Skanderborg as purely harmonic. Some level of antagonism was partly revealed by the way inhabitants insisted that they had explicitly decided not to live in a town ('life is nicer out here') and partly shown by the way they saw decisions made in Skanderborg as a potential threat to Hylke. This complexity in the perception of the relationship between Hylke and Skanderborg was to some extent institutionalized in the conflicts between the Village Council and the municipality. However, before turning to this issue we will present some lines from, 'A Song about Hylke and Its Surroundings' reprinted in a local 'magazine' (*HUGin*, November 1996, for a reprint see Hansen and Neufeld, 2000, p. 231). The first verse articulates the fact that Hylke has become 'the place we've decided to settle'. Then the 'we-can-do-it-ourselves' spirit is presented:

> It's quiet and easy and pretty nice
> But if something is to be done, it should be done in a hurry
> Sometimes we fight over many issues
> But if we want something, we get going
> Then we do a lot, we do all we can
> To fight for the things we want!
> We meet, we talk, we write, are ready
> With shovel and hammer, with brush, we have
> A lot of resources we use, so that
> Our community, Hylke, won't come to a stop.

These lines suggest that people in Hylke have a strong collective identity, a strong feeling of reliance and a high level of self-confidence. They see themselves as a capable and united polity. However, as the lines suggest, this unity does not rule out conflicts. Conflicts are legitimate not only within the community but also between the village and its surroundings. The relationship to Skanderborg is presented in the following manner:

> If 'the town' teases us, we know what to do
> Stick together and act – that is something we can do
> If we don't, we won't get anything
> We have fought for all that we've got.

Hence, the song points to the presence of considerable conflicts of interests with the town, which the villagers construct as equivalent with the municipality. However, the presence of conflicts between Hylke and Skanderborg/the municipality did not lead to the establishment of an antagonistic relationship between them, as seemed to be the case between Skanderborg and some of the other villages in the area. The relationship between the two communities is better described as one of difference. The Hylke Council considered the municipality as an important place to which to direct their demands, but only as one point among many others (the others including national ministries, EU-funding, regional funding, and so on). Furthermore, the municipality was seen as an ally because it supported 'Project Hylke'. For its part, Skanderborg regarded Hylke as a place of which to be proud – a place that helped to put Skanderborg on the map. The privileged position that the alliance with Skanderborg gave Hylke was signalled by the negative way some of the active Hylke residents characterized some of the other surrounding villages. Hence, one of them described a nearby village as a place where people 'are not active'. Owing to this 'lack of action', they regarded it as fair that this village did not receive the same support from the municipality as did Hylke. This other village was also much more directly a part of a fierce conflict between a number of villages and the strong network of actors who wanted to build the culture centre in Skanderborg. The village claimed that it was a typical case of giving priority to the town at the cost of the villages. In this regard, Hylke chose to take a much more neutral stance, indicating that 'we've got our share. You can spend your share as you please.'

All in all, from the point of view of the Skanderborg polity, Hylke fitted well into the self-image produced by the 'Skanderborg-on-the-map' metaphor. However, from Hylke's point of view, the relationship was more complex. Hylke did not only see itself as an integral part of the overall discursive strategy of the town, it also regarded the 'Skanderborg-on-the-map' metaphor as a potential threat to Hylke. In discourse analytical terms the relation of difference to Skanderborg sometimes threatened to become adversarial. However, most of the time the 'Other' of the 'we-can-do-it-ourselves' metaphor was the nearby villages, which were seen as places 'where people do not act'.

What, then, were the effects of the establishment of this strong discursive 'we-can-do-it-ourselves' polity on the policy-making in Hylke? First, it created a strong need for voluntary action in relation to the concrete issues that are dealt with by the council. Most of the policy issues were of a highly concrete kind: building a kindergarten, establishing a crosswalk, and so on. Each of them called for voluntary action. Secondly, a less apparent but no less significant effect of the discursive polity concerned the handling of conflict. Even though internal conflicts were mentioned as a legitimate element in the harmonious polity portrayed in the Hylke song discussed above, the absence of conflict in the political processes in Hylke and in the committee was striking. One reason for this might be the fact that political action depends on voluntary activity. Hence, the case study indicates that efforts to realize overly contested projects would lead to the end of the council. The way that 'we can do it ourselves' could be achieved was by making sure that the political projects and issues that were pursued were accepted as being in the interest of the community at large. This limited the number of issues that could legitimately be dealt with in the council to issues that were relatively uncontroversial. A clear example of this occurred when the first chairman stepped down, because of criticism regarding decisions about where to place a fountain. The fact that he had to resign points to a limited (democratic) ability to deal with internal conflicts in the council. This limited ability could be seen as an effect of the implicit but strong emphasis on the unity of the 'we' in the 'we-can-do-it-ourselves' metaphor. So if the metaphor strengthened the ability of the polity to get things done, it also carried the risk of eliminating politics, in terms of contests between conflicting images of the content of this 'we'.

### Hylke and Skanderborg: differences, similarities and interrelatedness

A comparison between the policy processes in Skanderborg and Hylke reveals both differences and similarities. In terms of similarities, we have shown, first, how a dislocation of the traditional discursive polities in both localities opened a space for the rearticulation of the discursive polity through a process we call radical politics. Secondly, we have shown how this space was eventually closed by hegemonic projects, which are expressed by the organizing metaphors 'Skanderborg on the map' and 'We can do it ourselves'. We have argued that the sedimentation of these organizing metaphors had considerable impact on what we call day-to-day politics in Skanderborg and Hylke. In Skanderborg, the sedimentation of the 'Skanderborg-on-the-map' metaphor resulted in an exclusion of political projects from the political scene because the actors who pursued them did not link them to the metaphor. In Hylke, projects that were not presented as being obviously in the interest of all simply never made it to the political scene. A final similarity concerns the need for a certain formalization of a sedimented discursive polity. In Skanderborg, a central element in the sedimentation of the 'Skanderborg-on-the-map' metaphor as the floating signifier in the discursive polity is the formalization of its position in a formal policy document: the Municipal Business Plan. This plan establishes a close discursive relationship between the municipality and the discursive polity of Skanderborg. In Hylke, we also witness a need for a formalization of the position of the discursive polity in the formation of the Hylke Council.

Although there are many similarities there is also an important difference between the two discursive polities concerning the way the two discursive polities understood conflict. In Skanderborg, the discursive image of the policy seemed to be formed by the aggregative imaginaries of state and market, while the discursive imaginary in the Hylke policy was much more that of civil society. While conflict, opposition, and competition were accepted, and even regarded as a positive thing in the discursive policy in Skanderborg, consensus and dialogue was the name of the game in Hylke. This might result from the fact that the processes that lead to the construction of the two discursive polities, and the actors who contributed to it, differed considerably. With regard to the construction of the 'Skanderborg-on-the-map' metaphor, it was the outcome of an effort to develop a new municipal business strategy. For that reason, the network of actors who contributed to the construction of the metaphor came from the formal political system, from the local business world, and from strong and well-organized organizations within the area of elite sports and culture. Against this background, it is not surprising that core values of the political system and of business life, such as difference, opposition, and conflict, were given a positive connotation. As one of the businessmen in the network states: 'We agree too much in the network. We need more conflict in order to make new things happen.' If political actors accept the discursive framework – that legitimate political projects must contribute to placing Skanderborg on the map – conflicts regarding the nature of these projects, and about the priority that should be given to them, are regarded as acceptable and even positive.

By comparison, the construction of the discursive polity in Hylke took place primarily as a part of a reconstruction of a dislocated civil society. The overall goal was to put Hylke back on its feet as a local village community, and the actors who contributed to the construction of the 'we-can-do-it-ourselves' metaphor were all local inhabitants. Accordingly, it is no wonder that the set of core values that came to characterize the discursive polity in Hylke was inspired by the core values of civil society: inclusiveness, dialogue, and conflict avoidance. These values did not only exist informally, but were a central characteristic of the formal set up of the Village Council.

One final issue to be dealt with concerns the interrelatedness between the discursive polities in Skanderborg and Hylke. Formally, Skanderborg and Hylke are part of the same municipality, and inhabitants from both places are representatives in the municipal council. Hence, the two discursive polities are part of the same formally demarcated polity. Most of the time, the two discursive polities coexist peacefully within this formal framework, mainly because the metaphors that organize them are easily linked. However, when the Hylke Council does not get things its own way, it tends to construct the municipality and the 'Skanderborg-on-the-map' metaphor as the adversary. The complex relationship between Skanderborg and Hylke indicates that not only is it possible for two different discursive polities to coexist within one formal polity, with a certain degree of overlap, but also that the discursive polities do not follow the lines of the formal institutions in any neat and simple way.

## Conclusion

One of the central objectives of this chapter was to show how discourse analysis contributes to the theoretical redefinition of a polity. Discourse analysis shares the argument presented by a range of constructivist neo-institutionalists that a polity, like any other social institution, should not merely be defined by its formal features. It is a structure of meaning that constructs images of communality and collective political identities, and adds meaning to formal organizational structures. The case study revealed how two strong discursive polities were constructed and became hegemonic points of reference in political life in Skanderborg and Hylke. Furthermore, it showed how two discursive polities can coexist within the limits of one formal polity and ascribe different meanings to it. The close ties between the 'Skanderborg-on-the-map' metaphor and the establishment of the Hylke Council raise a question that calls for further study: is it necessary for a discursive polity to establish a formal basis of power in order to obtain or maintain hegemony?

A second objective has been to stress the interrelatedness between a discursive polity and politics. Traditional governance research leaves us with little knowledge about how a discursive polity is produced in and through governance processes, and how specific discursive features of a given polity influence policy outcomes. While constructivist neo-institutionalists have produced valuable insights concerning the way a stable discursive polity structures meaning, they have said little about the implications of this structuring on the distribution of political power within a discursive polity. Furthermore, neo-institutionalists have not dealt with how a discursive polity is constructed as an outcome of politics. A central objective of the case study was to show how discourse analysis can help to shed light on this issue. Hence, the case study shows how the discourse theoretical concepts of dislocation, hegemony and organizing metaphors, can facilitate concrete studies of radical politics, while concepts of sedimentation and hegemony focus attention on political processes of inclusion and exclusion in periods of relative stability, that is, day-to-day politics.

A third objective of the article has been to contribute to the development of a discourse theoretical method. We have argued that what separates a discourse-analytical method from other methods in the social sciences are not the forms of data it uses, but the way the data is selected and analysed. Regarding the selection of data, like a number of other constructivist analytical research approaches, discourse analysis insists that the selection of data must build on a considerable amount of knowledge about the context. Hence, discourse analysis claims that considerable knowledge is needed about the discursive patterns of meaning that are in play in a given social setting. Accordingly, decisions about what data to select should not be taken in advance but during the research process itself. The snowball and multi-data collection methods that we used in our case study have proved to be fruitful means to qualify the data collection in this way.

With regard to the way data is analysed, discourse theorists call for a focus on what is implicitly said about the discursive conditions of possibility in a given governance process. This analytical focus on discursive conditions of possibility represents a serious methodological challenge to the researcher, since it is not often the explicit content of the data material that is examined. For us, the future methodological challenge confronting discourse analysis is the development of analytical tools that can qualify our search for the discursive conditions of possibility that are implicitly present in the data material.

## Note

1. This section is based on Hansen and Neufeld, 2000. For a more detailed presentation of the village council in Hylke, see Neufeld, 1999.

## Bibliography


Duverger, Maurice (1959) *Political Parties* (London, Methuen).

Finer, H. (1932) *The Theory and Practice of Modern Government* (2 vols) (London, Methuen).

Hajer, M. A. (2003) 'Policy without Polity? Policy Analysis and the Institutional Void', *Policy Sciences*, 36, pp. 175–95.

Hall, P. A., and Taylor, C. R. (1996) 'Political Science and the Three New Institutionalisms', paper presented at MPIFG Scientific Board.

Hansen, A. D. (2000) 'Diskursteori, demokrati og lokaludvalg', PhD thesis, Københavns Universitet.

Hansen, A. D. (2003a) 'Diskursteori – konstruktivisme og negativitet', in A. D. Hansen and K. Sehested (eds), *Konstruktive bidrag: Om teori og metode in konstruktivistisk videnskab* (Frederiksberg, Roskilde Universitetsforlag).

Hansen, A. D. (2003b) 'Diskursteori i et videnskabsteoretisk perspektiv', in L. Fulgsang and P. B. Olsen (eds), *Videnskabsteori i samfundsvidenskaberne: På tværs af fagkulturer og paradigmer* (Frederiksberg, Roskilde Universitetsforlag).

Hansen, A. D., and Neufeld, J. J. (2000) 'Vi kan selv: Politisk demokratisk fællesskab under governance betingelser', in H. Bang, A. D. Hansen, and J. Hoff (eds), *Demokrati fra neden: Casestudier fra en dansk kommune* (København, Jurist og Økonomforbundets Forlag).

Hirst, P., and Thompson, G. (1996) *Globalization in Question* (Cambridge, Polity Press).

Hjern, B., and Porter, D. (1981) 'Implementation Structures: a New Unit of Analysis', *Organizational Studies*, vol. 2, pp. 211–27.

Jessop, B. (1998) 'The Rise of Governance and the Risk of Failure: the Case of Economic Development', *Unesco/155* (London, Blackwell Publishers).

Johnson, Nevil (1973) *Government in the Federal Republic of Germany: the Executive at Work* (Oxford, Pergamon Press).

Laclau, E. (1996) *Emancipation(s)* (London, Verso).

Laclau, E., and Mouffe, C. (1985) *Hegemony and Socialist Strategy* (London, Verso).

March, J. G., and Olsen, J. P. (1989) *Rediscovering Institutions: the Organizational Basis of Politics* (New York, The Free Press).

March, J. G., and Olsen, J. P. (1995) *Democratic Governance* (New York, The Free Press).

Mayntz, R. (1999) 'New Challenges to Governance Theory' (paper, Max-Planck Institut für Gesellshaftsforschung).

Neufeld, J. J. (1999) 'Village Idiots? A Study of a Village Council and Its Significance for the Local (Political) Community' (Dissertation, Department of Social Sciences, Roskilde University).

Pierre, J. (2000) *Debating Governance: Authority, Steering, and Democracy* (Oxford, Oxford University Press).

Powell, Walter W., and Dimaggio, Paul J. (1991) 'Introduction', in Powell and Dimaggio (eds), *The New Institutionalism in Organizational Analysis* (Chicago, University of Chicago Press).

Rhodes, R. A. W. (1995) 'The Study of Political Institutions', in G. Stoker and D. Marsh (eds), *Theories and Methods in Political Science* (London, Macmillan, now Basingstoke, Palgrave Macmillan), pp. 47–65.

Rhodes, R. A. W. (1997) *Understanding Governance: Policy Networks, Governance, Reflexivity and Accountability* (Buckingham, Open University Press).

Scharpf, F. W. (1994) 'Games Real Actors Could Play: Positive and Negative Coordination in Embedded Negotiations', *Journal of Theoretical Politics*, vol. 1 (6), pp. 27–53.

Scharpf, F. W. (1997) *Games Real Actors Play: Actor-centred Institutionalism in Policy Research* (Oxford, West View Point).

Silverman, D. (2001) *Interpreting Qualitative Data: Methods for Analysing Talk, Text and Interaction* (London, Sage).

Taylor S. (2001) 'Locating and Conducting Discourse Analytic Research', in M. Wetherell, S. Taylor, and S. J. Yates (eds), *Discourse as Data* (London, The Open University).

Van Heffen, O., Kickert W. J. M., and Thomassen, J. J. A. (2000) *Governance in Modern Society* (Dordrecht, Kluwer Academic Publishers).

Yates, S. J. (2001) 'Researching Internet Interaction: Sociolinguistics and Corpus Analysis', in M. Wetherell, S. Taylor, and S. J. Yates (eds), *Discourse as Data* (London, The Open University).

# 4

# Problematizing the Mobilization of Hospital Directors[1]

*Steven Griggs*

For much of the post-war period, narratives of health policy change characterized public health care systems in Europe as stable professionalized policy networks, dominated by medical professionals and typified by incremental change, if not policy inertia, and political consensus (Harrison, Hunter, and Pollitt, 1990, pp. 6–8). Hospital managers were content to work as 'diplomats' (Hunter, 1994, pp. 441–2), concentrating on conflict-avoidance and consensus-building in public hospitals, whilst developing alternative administrative hierarchies that did not encroach into the domain of medical freedom (Steudler, 1973). However, the changing policy priorities of cost containment and efficiency have called into question many of the assumptions structuring this 'shared vision' of public health care systems. Indeed, the politics of cost containment has become widely synonymous, not with stability and consensus, but rather with the driving antagonisms of competing elites, not least the emerging challenge posed by managerial rationalizers to the dominance of medical professionals. No longer content to work as 'diplomats' or hospital managers, and keen to maximize their collective interests through the sponsorship of cost containment, they have contested the professional autonomy and control of the workplace exercised by medical professionals (Alford, 1975; Wistow, 1992).

This chapter questions how, if health policy networks were highly stabilized and characterized by medical predominance, challenging managerial elites emerged in public health care systems. It analyses one such group of managerial rationalizers: public hospital directors in France. Through the 1980s, the French civil service *corps* of hospital directors emerged as a new actor in health policy networks. The vehicle for this mobilization of the *corps* was the hospital director trade union, the *Syndicat National des Cadres Hospitaliers* (SNCH) and the collective mobilization within it of a generation of hospital directors from the French national school of public health, the *École Nationale de la Santé Publique* (ENSP). These directors transformed the SNCH into a health policy lobby in the late 1970s and early 1980s. This chapter thus sets out to understand how and why this clique of modernizing French civil servants engaged in a collective attempt to upgrade the standing of their *corps*, while dragging the majority of their colleagues behind them. The first part of the chapter problematizes the emergence of discourse coalitions and the emergence of corporate rationalizers in public health care systems. The second analyses the emergence of French hospital directors as a new actor in policy networks through the study of a modernizing discourse coalition in its dominant trade union, the SNCH.

## Forging discourse coalitions

The policy process is not populated by individual actors but by collective actors 'functioning in interaction with other actors in a system regulated by institutions' (Jobert, 2001, p. 3). The unitary 'public policy actor' is in fact an 'internal coalition of groups occupying different positions in the social structure' (Jobert, 2001, p. 3). Such internal coalitions will be predicated upon the perception of a collective or group identity. Indeed, Patrick Dunleavy recognizes group identity as 'the something more' necessary for those deciding whether or not to join a group – without it the strategic actor has 'no basis for contributing to the group's activities because of its collective benefits' (Dunleavy, 1991, p. 55). However, standard accounts of such internal coalitions simply appeal to common interests as the 'glue' that holds these disparate groups of actors together. Even Dunleavy's recognition of group identity cannot escape the primacy of interests. He defines the perception of a 'group identity' as 'sharing a subjective self-interest with others': a group identity is a common interest (Dunleavy, 1991, p. 57). Yet, no explanation is offered as to how individuals come to perceive this subjective self-interest. Common interests are given, read off the structural locations of agents or the apparent logic of institutions.

Thus, the seminal work of Robert Alford (1975) on the politics of health care in New York identifies three broad heterogeneous coalitions of interests within public health care systems: hospital managers characterized as corporate rationalizers, challenging interests to dominant professional monopolizers, and repressed community populations. Each heterogeneous coalition occupies a distinct structural location, defined by how their interests are 'served or not served by the way they "fit" into the basic logic and principles by which the institutions of society operate' (Alford, 1975, p. 14). Despite short-term conflicts within and between these three broad coalitions, common structurally-determined interests ultimately hold them together. The respective organizational interests of corporate rationalizers may well 'often require that they compete with each other for power and resources', but they will nonetheless 'share an interest in maintaining and extending the control of their organisations over the work of the professionals' (Alford, 1975, p. 192). The 'inherent antipathy' (Harrop, 1992, p. 166) of bureaucrats and professionals thereby substitutes for, or rather as, the process of group identity.

Drawing upon recent ideational accounts that recognize how ideas structure social actors' understanding of their interests and the world around them, I argue here that the empirical world is given meaning and constructed by ideas. The ambiguity of much of policy-making obliges social actors to work within the likes of a policy frame, storyline, or paradigm, which establishes a hierarchy of values, norms, and codes for interpreting problems and guiding behaviour within the policy process (Jobert, 1992; Hall, 1993; Rein and Schön, 1991; Fischer, 2003). Broad discourse coalitions will thus unite groups of actors who 'agree upon the cognitive frame and institutions to manage their conflict' (Jobert, 2001, p. 5). Actors construct their identities in relation to this predominant policy frame; the definition of interests and ideas thus cannot be separated (Jobert and Muller, 1987). Through the mediation of new policy discourse, actors will adopt new or revised group identities, elaborating new forms of action as well as repositioning themselves in the division of labour (Muller, 1997).

However, while discourse coalitions agree a cognitive frame, it does not follow that groups of actors will necessarily share either a common belief system or for that matter common motives (Jobert, 2001, p. 5). Successful discourse coalitions will not only draw boundaries between 'insiders' and 'outsiders', defining membership through identifying a common enemy or 'other', but will also cover-over the differences that exist between their members. Only this construction of such a group identity will enable group members to accept internal differences while maintaining their united opposition to an external 'enemy'. Indeed, the key to understanding the emergence of discourse will be the process of hegemony, the process by which particular frames and meanings come to dominate policy sectors, and coalitions emerge around these particular discourses (Griggs and Howarth, 2002).

So, how do we explain the emergence of a new discourse coalition? First, actors will mobilize initially not because of some conception of shared interests or positive affirmation of group identity, but because of a perceived failure of identity or the perception that their identity was 'blocked' within a given structure (Howarth, 2000; Torfing, 1999). That is to say, new identities or coalitions will emerge when existing structures are dislocated and no longer confer identity on agents. In such periods of crisis, 'the cognitive and normative frame which structures the meaning of politics and the actions of the actors concerned no longer, or badly, expresses the place, the role and the status of the groups concerned' (Muller, 2000, p. 196).

Second, during such moments of dislocation, strategically placed entrepreneurs will act as policy brokers between groups, engaging in alternative frame-shaping strategies based on different interpretations or readings of events. During this process of discussion and negotiation for leadership of the policy subsystem, such hegemonic forces will strive to structure relations of cooperation and antagonism with other actors and between other actors, drawing boundaries between 'insiders' and 'outsiders' (Torfing, 2001). They will thereby seek to simplify policy arenas into two hostile discourse coalitions that perceive each other as 'blocking' their own identities and interests (logic of equivalence). They will also integrate previously hostile opponents into emerging discourse coalitions by negating existing antagonisms and spreading 'equivalential chains' beyond existing boundaries (logic of difference). Indeed, much of this hegemonic conflict will involve second-order reflections, in that actors will be preoccupied less with policy form and content than with 'the tactical question of what they can do in order to remove obstacles to their path-shaping strategies and to turn the new conjunctural opportunities into the institutionalized supports of a new policy path' (Torfing, 2001, p. 291).

Third, as I said above, policy entrepreneurs will seek not only to identify a common enemy but also to cover-over the differences that exist between the potential memberships of emerging discourse coalitions. This will hinge in part upon their capacity to produce empty signifiers. Indeed, discourse coalitions will bring together actors with different storylines in which elements of the various ideas, concepts, and categories are combined into a more or less simplified coherent whole (Hajer, 1993, p. 47). Such storylines convey meaning even in a single phrase, and summarize values, norms, and operating codes. However, these multiple storylines can only be held together by the production of empty signifiers, images, or phrases, which are unlike storylines because of their lack of signification, and can thus enable the articulation of internal differences, while simultaneously showing the limits of a group's identity, and its dependence on the opposition to other groups (Howarth, 1995).

Thus, it is during moments of dislocation that new identities or coalitions are possible as actors engage in hegemonic struggles for leadership of a policy subsystem. However, this should not lead us to believe that the entrepreneurial skills and strategies of actors during moments of dislocation make all policy frames possible. The institutional legacies of previous policy frames will mediate hegemonic struggles between actors and condition the formation of new policy frames; for although during moments of dislocation previous patterns of 'normal politics' no longer make sense, this decline in the structured coherence of a policy frame does not create an institutional void. As Torfing (2001, p. 291) argues, institutional legacies will indeed be strategically selective, ruling out some strategies and modifying others, while limiting the availability of potential empty signifiers. It is thus both the availability of potential signifiers within the confines of existing institutional legacies and the capacity of strategically placed entrepreneurs to combine old and new policy elements through the 'delivery' of credible empty signifiers that will condition the possibility and success of discourse coalitions. It is to the interaction of these conditions that I now turn.

## The transition of the SNCH to health policy lobby

In 1991, public hospital directors formed collectively one of the category A 'management and conception' *corps*[2] of the French public hospital civil service (Quermonne, 1991, pp. 149–51; Stevens, 1992, pp. 122–33). They exercised a virtual monopoly over all public hospital management posts (Griggs, 1999), part of the leading 27 per cent of French civil servants recruited at graduate level or above (Quermonne, 1991, p. 150). Indeed, over the previous thirty years, the *corps* had accumulated many of the trappings of the French elite civil service *grands corps*. However, the vehicle for the emergence of hospital directors as a new actor in French health policy networks in the 1980s and 1990s was not, as might be expected, a *corps*-based association, but the hospital director trade union, the SNCH. Trade unions are traditionally associated with battles to improve the pay and conditions of their members. Here, however, the SNCH accommodated the construction of a substantive knowledge base for the *corps* with the development of organizational resources and the delivery of pecuniary and policy rewards throughout the *corps*. Indeed, the *200 Propositions*, the trade union's 1985 manifesto for hospital reform formed the backbone of the 1991 Hospital Law that saw a modernizing discourse coalition of hospital directors from the SNCH capture the Health Ministry and pilot the 1991 Hospital Law through the National Assembly (Griggs, 1999).

This section analyses the construction of this modernizing discourse coalition in the SNCH. It argues that this coalition was forged by a generation of hospital directors trained at the national school of public health, the ENSP, who swung the SNCH away from its traditional function as a defender of pay and conditions into that of a lobby for health policy reform in the late 1970s and early 1980s. Indeed, this transition was complete when, at its Mâcon conference in 1982, the SNCH elected one of the modernizing ENSP generation to its presidency, who then proceeded to use his election to push through conference support for the key pillars of the then socialist government's programme to remodel public hospitals.

### Methods

The study offers a 'thick descriptive' analysis of organizational and policy changes within the *corps* of hospital directors and the SNCH. In doing so, it adopts a process-orientation that does not reduce policy changes to narrow exemplary moments of decision-making (Hassenteufel and Martin, 1999, pp. 145–6). Rather, it examines over time the series of organizational processes, interactions, and actors that structured decision-making in the *corps* and its predominant trade union from the 1960s to the early 1980s. Institutions are read as discourses that form the identities of actors and objects. This is not, however, to reduce the study of institutions to a narrow focus on texts and language. On the contrary, it is to abandon the 'misconception that argumentative research just deals with languages' and to conceptualize the institutional setting as an 'argumentative field', investigating 'the ways utterances relate to the specific institutional contexts and practices in which they can be meaningfully stated and understood' (Fischer, 2003, p. 90). More importantly, it is to support an 'institutional constructivism' (Hajer, cited in Fischer, 2003, p. 90) that emphasizes the importance of wider meaningful institutional practices, sedimented norms, and informal and formal rules, and how such embedded practices favour specific patterns of policy change.

As befits anti-foundational approaches, the study employs qualitative research tools to generate and analyse data (Bevir and Rhodes, 1999). Thus, its thick description is informed by semi-structured interviews with nodal actors, supported by the textual analysis of internal trade union documents, professional journals and newsletters, official publications, and articles in the specialized medical and national press.

Semi-structured interviews were used to generate actors' own accounts and representations of events. In total, 62 interviews were undertaken with leading personalities of the SNCH and the *corps*, as well as actors from the relevant ministries, government departments, and public hospital lobbies. Each interview lasted on average between one and two hours. A number of these interviews were accompanied by informal conversations with hospital doctors and nurses and observations of hospital directors in their working environments. Interviewees were primarily selected from a survey of internal trade union documents, press reports, and official publications. Those engaged in the factional politics of the SNCH in the 1970s and 1980s were identified by a survey of the membership of the unions' national executive from 1976 and 1991, and conference proceedings and interventions detailed in the SNCH quarterly journal, *L'Hospitalier* (which later became *Le nouvel hospitalier*). In addition, a random sample of hospital directors working in different hospital environments and at different classes within the *corps* was identified by breakdowns of graduations of hospital directors from the ENSP and listings of directors in the *Bottin Administratif*. Later interviews were also undertaken with actors named in the course of the first round of interviews.

The accounts generated by the semi-structured interviews were set against a systematic and detailed survey of *Hospitalier-Actualités*, the monthly information newsletter for members of SNCH, and its quarterly journal, *L'Hospitalier* (see above). These publications were the voice of the SNCH leadership and grassroots members. They contained regular minutes of the meetings of its national executive and editorials from the leadership as well as policy declarations, conference reports and proceedings, and open forums for debate within the *corps* of hospital directors. Surveys of the medical press (notably the leading daily newspaper for doctors *Le Quotidien du Médecin*), the national press (notably *Le Monde*), and official publications served to contextualize the changing storylines of the *corps* and the SNCH.

The reliance on semi-structured interviews by discourse analysts does not raise concerns as in other approaches of how to separate out in interviews the representation of events from what can be deemed to be factual information (Bachir, 1999, pp. 96–100). However, interviews do pose a number of challenges for discourse analysts, not least the creation of 'monuments' (Bachir, 1999, p. 98), the reconstructions of interviews by researchers, and the individualization and simplification of events. During interviews, individuals may over-simplify the course of events as they strive to impose order on complex and ambiguous policy and organizational developments. This disappearance of ambiguity can equally befall discourse analysts who search themselves to impose or create emerging storylines against the background of their own experience of earlier interviews. Equally, the accounts that emerge during interviews may over-accentuate the role of individuals. Actors attach events to the actions of individuals. They can, therefore, underestimate or fail to recognize the structural constraints imposed on individuals. Some individuals might even overrate their own importance in the course of events, as they seek to assert their place in history (Bachir, 1999, p. 98; Hassenteufel and Martin, 1999, p. 145).

Such challenges posed by the use of semi-structured interviews have a number of consequences for discourse analysts. First, discourse analysts should refer directly to extracts from interviews so as to minimize as far as possible the contamination or reconstruction of interviews (Bachir, 1999, pp. 96–100). Second, they should recognize both the constraints facing actors and the significance of dislocation to explanations of the role of individuals. Third, they should analyse the divergent as well as convergent interpretations that emerge during interviews. And, finally, discourse analysts should not simply rely on interviews but cross-reference and contextualize interview data with detailed textual analysis. Such analysis will help to substantiate the representation of events constructed by individuals.

## The ENSP identity

The ENSP, the national school of public health, began life in October 1945 as a government training department within the *Institut National d'Hygiène* in Paris. It opened its doors to public hospital directors in 1958; the same year that government increased the powers of hospital directors and transferred the formal nomination of hospital directors from the local Prefect to the Minister of Health. However, it was not until the early 1960s that the strong school-*corps* bond was established. In 1960, the school took responsibility for the first national competitive entrance examination and training programme for hospital directors, and thereby gained its monopoly over the training of future hospital directors. Two years later, it moved to its own premises in Rennes, reinforcing the institutional and physical ties between the school and its graduates, without which 'the idea of the *corps* would be diluted; the dynamic School-Profession would disappear. The teaching...would no longer have a common physical base: a place, a school, specialized teachings' (Jahan, 1992, p. 11).

In fact, the ENSP created a multi-dimensional school-*corps* dynamic that facilitated the forging of common professional networks. At its lowest common denominator, the school-*corps* dynamic manifested itself as no more than the common experiences of teachers, classrooms, and corridors. However, the ENSP monopoly over training gave an important institutional and physical focus for hospital directors: 'We have all gone through the same training, we have all had the same discourse at the School about who we were, and what we should be in the profession' (interview). First, success at the competitive entrance examination, the *concours*, furnished a common reference for all directors; reinforced as it was by the selection of a nucleus of individuals with common backgrounds and educational standards (In 1966, university graduates accounted for the first time for over 50 per cent of the annual intake of the ENSP). Second, graduation from the school defined the parameters of group membership and came over time to symbolize common interests and values: 'the homogeneity of the *corps* of directors is true... because we all have this common training' (interview). Thus, the ENSP tag enabled other hospital directors to short-cut information constraints and automatically categorize fellow directors.

However, this identification with the ENSP was symbolic of ENSP directors' 'fantasy' of belonging to one of the *grands corps* of the French civil service. Each civil service *corps* monopolizes a specific task or set of tasks, with all its members enjoying the same terms and conditions of service (Stevens, 1992, p. 123). However, the seven *grands corps*[3] at the summit of the French civil service hold claims to a monopoly of expertise as well as possessing a degree of self-management with their own councils managing internal affairs. They are characterized by their historical origins, their small membership with limits on annual entries, their interministerial controls, and their mobility and ability to traverse public and private sectors under the practice of *pantouflage* (Kessler, 1986; Birnbaum, 1982). Their expertise rests in part upon a certain generalism qualifying them for leadership posts and allowing them to define a conception of national interests and to manipulate multiple discourses (Jobert and Muller, 1987, pp. 217–18). Entrance into these *corps* is primarily through the *grandes écoles* of the *École Nationale d'Administration* (ENA) or the *École Polytechnique*.

The discourse of the *grands corps* induces a balkanization of the civil service, symbolized by competition and rivalry for territorial control of services and functions (Dupuy and Thoenig, 1985; Stevens, 1978; Suleiman, 1974, 1978; Thoenig, 1973; Wright, 1989). Fuelling this balkanization are the distinct identities, which are attributed to *corps* along with an *esprit de corps* which 'is first the awareness of belonging to a specific group; it is next to have a sense of solidarity with this group; it is finally the tendency to adhere to the objectives that it pursues, to identify with it' (Chevallier, cited in Quermonne, 1991, pp. 151–2). *Corpsards* are part of the same elite with common values and identities enforced by success at national *concours*, and training at a common institution where personal networks which tie individuals together are forged. Indeed, Thoenig (1973) showed how members of the Bridges and Highways *corps*, who shared common training, entrance examinations, and 'language' and traditions, demonstrated group cohesion and a certain 'homogeneity'. In a study of industrial policy, Schmidt (1996, p. 424) alludes to *corpsards* as a 'small club of like-minded, arrogant, but competent individuals'. 'Like-minded because like-trained' (Schmidt, 1996, p. 335), the *corps* allegiance brings individuals together beyond the ties of substantive policy interests, political allegiances, and recruitment from a narrow social and educational base. Indeed, allegiance to the *corps* can claim to reduce the difficulty of collective action because 'belonging to the *corps* takes on almost metaphysical connotations. It is the integration into a continuum which transcends the individual, integrates him into a chain which gives understanding to his actions' (Kessler, 1986, p. 167).

These codes and practices of the French civil service elite were replicated in the codes and practices of the ENSP directors. They moulded and exploited their actions upon the rules and norms of the *corps* structures imposed by the French state from the 1960s. Upon entry into the *corps*, the first ENSP graduates began to organize as a distinct group of hospital directors with its own codes and conventions:

> One put in the same saucepan [the ENSP], a community of people who integrated through the reality of professional *corps*, therefore... the necessity to distinguish themselves from those who preceded them, to find working rules which were common to the *corps* and to lead a truly autonomous *corps* with its own internal rules, its culture and its methods of identification. (interview)

Indeed, ENSP graduates alluded both to the ENSP as a *grande école* like ENA and the prerequisite *esprit de corps* that it generated: 'you have been to a *Grande École* [ENSP], therefore, you have come out of this *Grande École*, therefore, you have a sense of belonging which federates energies, which attenuates differences' (interview). And, as they took up posts in public hospitals, this *esprit de corps* motivated their decisions to appoint candidates to vacant posts as they fought off competition both from non-ENSP hospital directors already in post and the *corps* of *chefs de bureaux*, the middle-ranking clerical staff who had colonized hospital administrations with the aim of gaining access to management posts through internal promotion:

> A director from the ENSP who found himself opposite candidates of whom certain were graduates of the ENSP, ..., he would favour, independently

> of the quality of the individual and of the quality of the training, he would favour those graduates, that is definite. (interview)

After all, the previously weak selection procedures had produced a disparate recruitment into the *corps*, with appointments depending upon 'the fortune of their past history and the institutional history of the hospital' (interview). ENSP graduates possessed:

> a different basic training, people who had already been through further education, who had done *Sciences Po*, who had prepared the entrance exam for ENA, who had a higher education diploma. (interview)

However, this emerging *corps* of ENSP graduates did not have the history, self-management, monopoly of expertise, and cultural authority attached to the *grands corps* of the French civil service. First, its entrants came not from ENA and the *École Polytechnique* but were trained at the less reputed ENSP, 'a school for second lieutenants' (interview). Indeed, the history of the school was punctuated by a series of conflicts between the school's administrators and hospital directors who believed that:

> The School is not, in terms of the quality of training, at the required level of the ambitions that it should have. And, precisely because it is not this privileged place of reflection, of doctrinal construction, in relation to the occupation of director, it is more at the back of our evolutions than in the avant-garde of them. (interview)

Even the progressive dominance, at *corps* entrance examinations, of *Sciences Po* graduates from the prestigious Institutes of Political Science deserved qualification. Paris, the most prestigious of the seven institutes, prepared candidates for ENA and their top students took positions there. Although Paris graduates dominated the entry into the hospital directors' *corps*, this option was often their second choice. Indeed, many entrants also sat the ENA entrance examination, with the ENSP relegated to a 'safe-bet'.

Second, there was no immediate influx of ENSP graduates into the *corps*, nor any overnight coup, which seized its commanding heights. It was not until the June 1969 circulars introduced the *assistanat* training programme for hospital directors that the number of student directors entering the ENSP expanded significantly. The *assistanat* extended the training period of student hospital directors to three years, adding two years as trainee directors in public hospitals to the one year spent in the classroom at Rennes (*L'Hospitalier*, 1972, 281, p. 30). At a stroke, the government increased the prestige of the *corps* within the universe of the civil service – for prestige tends to be based not only upon the entry requirements of the *corps* but also upon the length of training undergone by its new recruits. From graduations of 20, the annual intake increased over sevenfold, with a series of graduations of over 100 student directors between 1974 and 1981 (with a peak of 148 in 1978) (*L'Hospitalier*, 1986, 390, p. 71). Thus it was only the entry of the 1974–81 *assistanat* generation into the *corps* that enabled ENSP graduates to use 'the arrival in mass of these young graduates in health to overthrow, to effectively take, let's say, all the sectors in hospitals' (interview).

Overall, therefore, the origins of the mobilization of hospital directors lie not in a challenge to medical predominance in public hospitals. Rather, it lies in the failure of these aspirant ENSP graduates to live out their 'fantasy' of belonging to a *grands corps*. The enemy or 'other' blocking this identity was not the medical profession but non-ENSP hospital directors, the ENSP in certain respects, and rival *corps* in central government. In fact, this failure of identity had its origins for some directors in their failure at the entrance examinations to the *grands corps*. They entered the *corps* with a failed identity that the ENSP and non-ENSP directors were unable to resolve. Paradoxically, however, it was the French state, through its progressive imposition of the administrative organization common to civil service *corps*, which triggered the mobilization of hospital directors. Once the ENSP took sole responsibility, in 1960, for the hospital director training programme, a school-*corps* dynamic was put in place (Jahan, 1992, p. 11). It in turn brought with it both the intake of university and *Sciences Po* graduates and identification with a discourse of *esprit de corps* (drawn from success at a specialist national *concours* and passage through a *corps*-based school) that were common throughout the elite French civil service (Stevens, 1992, pp. 122–7). Thus the system of competitive civil service *corps*, which was initially a cause of dislocation for those entrants into the ENSP, was subsequently to offer them new points of identification. Key signifiers such as 'the ENSP' and 'the *corps*' became an available and credible means to forge a group identity. Its assertion, however, was to take place within the SNCH. It is to the entry of ENSP hospital directors into the trade union that I now turn.

## Forging a modernizing coalition within the SNCH

The ENSP graduates of the *assistanat* generation had yet to coalesce around a distinct political project. This was to take place outside the formal structures of the *corps* in the hospital director trade union, the SNCH – a trade union forum traditionally associated with pecuniary gains and defence of interests rather than the construction of a substantive knowledge base and the development of organizational resources. This section first examines why ENSP graduates entered into the SNCH. It then analyses the dislocation of the model of SNCH trade unionism that made possible the radical transformation of the SNCH into a health policy lobby by the ENSP graduates. Finally, it examines the forging of the modernizing coalition within the trade union, symbolized by the support of the SNCH at its 1982 conference for the global budget reform of hospital financing.

### Entry into the SNCH

The SNCH adopted the dual organizational principles of an occupation-based trade unionism and political neutrality. These principles hinged upon the belief that hospital directors, like lower-ranking hospital administrators, faced occupational challenges that could not be bracketed together with those of other hospital personnel or, for that matter, with any other occupation. Although it opened its ranks to other hospital administrative staff, it remained none the less 'the' hospital director trade union, both in terms of directors' numerical weight within the SNCH (over half of its membership) and their control of its decision-making bodies. Hospital directors monopolized the presidency of the trade union and overwhelmingly dominated its national executive committee, the Bureau National (BN). From 1976 onwards, only one of the BN's 12 members was not a hospital director. In short, its constituency was clearly that of public hospital directors.

This constituency and its organizing principles accounts for the decision of ENSP graduates to join its ranks. They joined the SNCH because their ENSP-*corps* identity dictated that they recognize themselves within its constituency. It did so by laying down conditions of group membership, which the internal structure and constituency of its chief rival, *Force Ouvrière* (FO) could not meet. First, as part of a wider trade union confederation, FO could not satisfy the focus of these ENSP graduates upon the occupation of hospital director. Indeed, recounting his reasons for joining the SNCH rather than FO, one ENSP graduate explained: 'As a director, I think that there is, nevertheless, one difference between these two trade unions. It is that there is one which is, above all, a general trade union and the other is a *corps* trade union' (interview). The SNCH was the only hospital director trade union that was capable of supporting the *grands corps* professionalization 'fantasy' of ENSP of hospital directors. The institutional constraints of belonging to a wider confederation meant that FO was perceived by ENSP graduates as being unable to develop such a political project: 'quite simply, because it belongs to the... confederation. This means that in joining FO, you support the policies of the confederation, and as for any far reaching discussions, you are prevented from having them between directors' (interview). In addition, as the traditionally dominant trade union within the *corps* of hospital directors, FO was more clearly associated with pre-ENSP hospital directors than the SNCH. Its links with this constituency hampered its acceptance by ENSP graduates who saw themselves as members of a constituency that was defined by generation and graduation from the ENSP. Even for one of its former general secretaries, the attractiveness of the FO for potential members suffered because it was perceived by ENSP graduates as 'the trade union for grandfathers' (interview). Conversely, the SNCH was able to distance itself from any association with such a constituency so that for ENSP graduates: 'It is definite that the SNCH incarnated a certain modernist character' (interview).

Thus, the practices of institutions, the operating codes and electoral mechanisms of the SNCH and the FO, were coded by ENSP graduates as barriers to or opportunities for identity formation. Those ENSP graduates who entered the SNCH were those graduates who had the most distinct hospital manager *corps* identity: 'Me, when I joined the SNCH, it was because it was a trade union of hospital directors' (interview). They 'felt better in a trade union of managers' (interview). And, once within the SNCH, they asserted once again their own codes and conventions:

> There was never a rejection of those who had not been to the School [ENSP]. But, in fact, it was those who had gone to the School who dragged the trade union along, who pushed the trade union towards the top. (interview)

**An exhausted model of trade unionism**

The SNCH leadership went into its annual trade union conference at Strasbourg in April 1976 under pressure to redefine its practice of collective bargaining. Its established pattern of consensual 'behind-closed-doors' negotiations with the Health Ministry had failed to deliver sufficient improvements in pay and conditions to satisfy the growing demands of its rank-and-file membership. Claude-Guy Charlotte, the trade union's president, voiced concerns that the model of trade unionism adopted by the SNCH was at a crossroads, if not at the end of its life span, informing delegates that 'it is absolutely crucial that we find another path along which to centre our demands' (*L'Hospitalier*, 1976, 326, p. 48).

In the months leading up to Strasbourg, the SNCH toyed with a strategy of overt confrontation in its negotiations with the Health Ministry. Twelve months earlier at La Baule, delegates had voted for strike action for the first time in the union's history (*L'Hospitalier*, 1976, 326, p. 55). As a result, on 17 October 1975, the SNCH held its first national day of action with approximately 1,500 hospital directors demonstrating on the streets of Paris (L. Giraldé, cited in *L'Hospitalier*, 1976, 327, p. 5). However, this policy of overt confrontation clashed with the SNCH president's brand of 'responsible' trade unionism and placed unsustainable demands upon the organizational resources at the union's disposal. The national executive, the Bureau National (BN), did not initiate the radicalization of the SNCH stance in negotiations with the Health Ministry, but was forced by the rank-and-file into overt confrontation:

> The willingness to abandon a certain passive attitude – indeed, a fatalistic attitude – in favour of attacking stances, going as far as to take to the streets, proves that the times have changed and the BN can no longer today modify the speed of change except under threat of being accused of backtracking. (G. Poisson, cited in *L'Hospitalier*, 1976, 323, p. 9)

This crisis of the SNCH leadership and its model of trade unionism opened a pathway for ENSP graduates to transform the hospital director trade union. At the 1976 annual conference, Jean-Paul Fischer, socialist member of the national executive, the BN, and ENSP graduate (1974–76) tied the lack of progress of the SNCH in furthering the demands of its membership not only to its consensus-led and 'behind closed doors' patterns of negotiations but also to its lack of a distinct programmatic base. For Fischer, the SNCH leadership could not continue 'to veer from left to right according to circumstances, events and [external] pressures' (*L'Hospitalier*, 1976, 326, p. 51). On the contrary, if the SNCH was to defend adequately the interests of hospital directors, it was obliged to anchor its demands within its own platform of health policy reforms and values. He consequently moved from the conference floor at Strasbourg that the BN or conference delegates establish an internal working party to study health policy issues. After an initial rebuttal, Charlotte, the president of the union, conceded to Fischer's demand, putting in place a health policy working group – the SNCH's first step towards developing its own platform of health policy reforms. Indeed, Fischer and his co-supporter from the floor, Guy Vallet, both ENSP *assistanat* graduates, had a rival conception of the trade unionism to that of the Charlotte leadership. They coupled its role as trade union negotiating improved pay and conditions to that of learned society, expanding the knowledge base of the *corps* and that of lobby delivering legislative change.

This dislocation of the SNCH discourse of 'responsible trade unionism' took place against the background of a wider crisis of public hospitals, as the Barre government swung towards cost containment. The government's imposition of top-down controls on hospitals led Charlotte to accept the shift towards health policy debate as a necessary prerequisite of the continued defence of the *corps*. Along with other senior figures in the trade union, Charlotte argued that it was impossible to ignore the threats of top-down spending controls on the function of hospital director and the environment of public hospitals. The SNCH had thus to react, to enter into the fray, not to launch a programme of managerial reform but to counter the cost containment agenda of the Barre government:

> We talk now of widening the debate ... we are orientating ourselves towards proper political-economic problems ... I would say that, in fact, we have only reacted, that in these circumstances, the initiative comes from the Ministry. (G. Barsacq, cited in *L'Hospitalier*, 1979, 353, p. 25)

So, for Charlotte, the health policy commitment was a defensive reaction to perceived external threats, best characterized as an 'externalist' strategy that engaged the SNCH in the on-going public debate to defend the existing status and working conditions of hospital directors. There was no desire to transform the SNCH into a lobby for hospital management reform. Rather, the union confined debate to a defensive counter-attack on the policies implemented by the Barre government.

From the Strasbourg conference onwards, it was this 'externalist' strategy, led by Charlotte, which dominated the SNCH, a strategy that 'welcomed' health policy working groups, but took no concrete steps to formulate a programme of managerial reform. However, this externalist strategy failed to respond to the dislocation of the SNCH discourse of responsible trade unionism that no longer expressed the place, role and status of the groups concerned. The Charlotte strategy, although pacifying opposition in the short-term, was to become increasingly untenable as the dislocation of the SNCH discourse of trade unionism made possible the radical transformation of the SNCH into a health policy lobby. In brief, although both the 'externalist' strategy of Charlotte and the strategy of confrontation were available, they were not credible. By contrast, the strategy of transformation was to become both available and credible. It is to the breakdown of the 'externalist' strategy that I now turn.

## The modernizing coalition takes shape

By 1976, ENSP graduates occupied approximately half of the seats in the BN. Graduates of the *assistanat* accounted for 3 of these posts. Their number subsequently rose to 4 in 1978 and 6 in 1980. Parallel to their progressive rise in the BN, ENSP graduates entered the national working groups that the SNCH established on an *ad hoc* basis to report on the chosen themes for debate at annual conferences. At Strasbourg in 1976, ENSP graduates, all from the *assistanat* programme, provided 5 out of 8 hospital directors in the working group on the future of hospital directors in the civil service. At Pau in 1977, ENSP graduates provided 17 of the 30 hospital directors involved in health policy working groups, including 12 graduates from the *assistanat*. Their predominance was temporarily lost at the following conference in Rouen in 1978. However, at Metz in 1979, they represented 7 out of 10 directors in the health policy working group, including 6 graduates from the *assistanat*.

However, if the shift towards the SNCH as a health policy lobby began from the floor of the Strasbourg conference in 1976, it was not until the 1980 Grenoble conference that the first organized grouping or internal faction of directors went beyond the declarations of enlightened individuals and formally promoted the development of a health policy doctrine by the SNCH. 'Grenoble 80' (named after the conference venue) challenged the weak accountability of the BN and argued that the SNCH had to act as 'social mediators' defending the interests of its members in the arena of political parties through the promotion of wider social transformations (*'Projet de Charte Grenoble 80'*, in *L'Hospitalier*, 1980, 362, p. 33). The driving force behind the faction came from an ENSP network of graduates between the years of 1974 and 1976 revolving around Vallet and Fischer, 'the one who brought in [to *Grenoble 80*] the whole current of thought' (interview) and later Jacques Coz. This network of ENSP graduates argued that through the development of a health policy platform the trade union would be able to propose reforms rather than suffer from projects inspired by others (*'Projet de Charte Grenoble 80'*, in *L'Hospitalier*, 1980, 362, p. 33). It was thus 'the first to say that if the SNCH did not have a doctrine, that if we did not propose a project, we would not be...the SNCH was going to die a beautiful death' (interview).

Support for the aims of 'Grenoble 80' came from a group of hospital directors gathered around the vice-president and leading 'modernizer', Gérard Vincent. At the end of the 1970s, he mobilized within Paris an informal health policy think-tank which was encouraged by the internal debate over strategic planning within the hospital of the *Assistance Publique* (interview). Those hospital directors alongside Vincent were all aged roughly between 27 and 35 years old and graduates of the *assistanat* programme. Indeed, Vincent was 'through his age and his charisma...the animator, in effect, of a group, you could say, which was of young Parisian intellectuals' (interview). Emerging from their socialization within the *corps* was the collective ambition to professionalize the *corps* through the assertion of the autonomy of hospital directors as fully-fledged managers. As one Paris modernizer recalled, 'If we chose this occupation, it was not by chance. We wanted to work in the civil service, but we did not want to be civil servants...In fact, we wanted to be managers' (interview). The means to this common goal was perceived to be the transformation of the SNCH from a traditional trade union defending pay and conditions into the champion of managerial reform. Indeed, recounting internal discussions over strategy and tactics, modernizers underlined the shared commitment to the transformation of the SNCH:

> At that time, what struck me was more the lobby aspect of the SNCH: we wanted to make it a lobby. And I believe that we were aware that lobbying needed the constitution, the creation, the affirmation, of a collective discourse. (interview)

These organizational principles, inspired by the modernizing discourse of Vincent, demonstrated a certain discursive affinity with the discourse of 'Grenoble 80'. Held together by their common critique of the 'externalist' leadership, both groups argued that the development of a platform of health policy reforms would increase the SNCH's unity, improve its credibility in the eyes of other actors, and encourage managerial change within public hospitals (interview). More importantly, the alliance was facilitated by the *effet de génération* that bound together the leading members of 'Grenoble 80' and the Vincent group. They were all ENSP graduates imbued with the same ENSP identity. Thus signifiers such as 'ENSP' and *corps* were able to mask the internal differences between the two emerging factions within the SNCH.

However, 'Grenoble 80' was primarily composed of left-wing activists and supporters of the French *Parti Socialiste*, the PS, which polarized its relations with the SNCH leadership and BN. Its left-leaning health policy commitments employed a socializing discourse advocating, for example, 'the adaptation of man to his environment and not simply the repairing of his productive force' (*'Grenoble 80: Qui sommes-nous?'*, in *L'Hospitalier*, 1981, 367, p. 15). Mirroring the policy shifts within the PS in opposition in the 1970s, it gave prominence to preventative medicine, improved patient rights, decentralized planning, and increased staff participation in the running of hospitals to 'make the hospital a more democratic hospital, a place of autonomy where decisions could be made in favour of the user up against a statist system which did not appear to take the interests of the hospital into account' (interview). By contrast, the Vincent network had no formal organization or policy commitments in the mould of 'Grenoble 80'. At best, it drew upon the organizational culture of the *Assistance Publique* and demonstrated a more pronounced openness than other directors to the integration of doctors into multidisciplinary management teams (interview). It retained a marked *ad hoc* character when compared to the collective ranks of 'Grenoble 80':

> The team of Gérard Vincent was more a team of men, you could say of quite brilliant individuals, but who were all promoters of individual projects. Whereas I think that *Grenoble 80* (with, however, the phenomena of charisma as well, in particular, Jean-Paul Fischer who was an important character at the time) was, even so, in my opinion, . . . more a team effort, that is to say, that somewhere, it had a collective discipline of reflection. (interview)

However, after Grenoble, Vincent mobilized increasing support, emerging as a strategically placed mediator. One of his lieutenants entered the BN on the back of the presidential majority at Grenoble and those modernizers in the national executive equally threw their support behind the leader of the Paris modernizers. Indeed, the polarization between the Charlotte and 'Grenoble 80' factions cast Vincent as a bridge builder between the rival camps. For the rising generation of ENSP graduates, Vincent was very much 'the identikit profile of the ideal hospital director' (interview). Upon graduation from the ENSP, he entered the *Assistance Publique* in Paris where, in 1977, at the age of 28, he was appointed head director of *Hôtel-Dieu*, one of the oldest and most symbolically important hospitals in France (*Le Monde*, 20 December 1983). His embracing of pragmatic and centrist positions within the BN 'very quickly gave the impression of someone who was serious, obviously competent and moderate . . . He, thus, avoided all excesses' (interview). Progressively, therefore, Charlotte's hold over the presidency waned as Vincent, already vice-president, was increasingly accepted within the BN as his natural successor: 'He was institutionally more than a Number Two, he was almost a co-President' (interview).

In fact, Charlotte's position as the incumbent president became untenable as delegates at Monaco in 1981 voted to introduce proportional representation for elections to the BN. Charlotte reinforced his hold over the SNCH at Grenoble partly because of the vagaries of the electoral system, which shut 'Grenoble 80' out of the BN despite its substantial minority vote. After Grenoble, the demands of this official opposition persisted. The decision at Monaco to introduce proportional representation paved the way for 'Grenoble 80' candidates to continue their attacks from within the BN. It reinforced the impression that Charlotte was no longer in control of the changing agenda both within and outside the trade union. Having given ground on this issue at the conference, and then been progressively sidelined within the BN, he formally resigned from the presidency of the SNCH. At Mâcon, the BN elected Vincent as President, who was also the chosen successor of Charlotte. At the same conference, the first director went on to enter the BN on the 'Grenoble 80' ticket. With the election of Vincent, a clique of a dozen ENSP *assistanat* graduates seized control of the leadership of the SNCH. The backbone of the group was formed by the leading members of the Paris modernizers and 'Grenoble 80', as Vincent took his circle of directors into an informal alliance with the former opponents of Charlotte. Symbolically 'Grenoble 80' continued to abstain at conference when it came to voting the annual report of the president. However, Vincent integrated the faction fully into the workings of the BN.

This modernizing clique broke with the indecision of the externalist strategy. At the Mâcon conference, and upon his election, Vincent swung the SNCH's support behind the global budget and the introduction of departments in public hospitals, the twin pillars of the health policy formulated by the Mauroy government elected in 1981. The trade union had opposed the global budget at its previous conference and throughout its trials in the late 1970s. However, in the short-term, Vincent bargained that support for hospital management reform would deliver improved pay and conditions for hospital directors. In the long-term, he wagered that the modernization of public hospital management would reinforce the line-management function and the 'strategic apex' within public hospitals. So Vincent tied the SNCH to a discourse which integrated the demands for improved pay and conditions with managerial change within public hospitals – the final step towards the transformation of the SNCH as a health policy lobby. Indeed, the personal engagement of Vincent swung conference behind the SNCH endorsing the global budget:

> The membership as a whole would certainly not have followed it [global budget], but the people who were at the conference, I would say that, in

> the crowd of the conference and with the weight of the president [Vincent] and then, his election, it went through. Gérard took a position for it. (interview)

Thus, by 1982, the key transition of the SNCH to a health policy lobby was complete, driven by the ENSP graduates of the *assistanat* programme. To a certain extent, the ENSP identity offered chains of equivalence between 'Grenoble 80' and the Paris modernizers. However, Vincent was a key mediator in the forging of a modernizing discourse coalition at the head of the trade union. As Muller (1997, p. 165) argues, 'the mediator . . . is the actor, group or individual, who produces the . . . "truth" of the moment'. As such, the function of the empty signifier was played out by the career and image of Vincent. Defining 'the truth of the moment', he was the bridge-builder between 'Grenoble 80', his Paris modernizers, the BN, and indeed the rank-and-file. He symbolized the aspirations of the *corps* and held together through all he symbolized the modernizing discourse-coalition of the SNCH. As a leading protagonist at the time remarked, the strength of Vincent's leadership was:

> To conceive of the role of hospital director, but in a renovated hospital, and to never dissociate this from the individual stature of hospital directors themselves . . . I believe that Vincent was a visionary for that . . . He knew how to provoke in his entourage and in the profession an understanding that . . . 'We keep that which is good for me but what is also good for the hospital.' I believe that that was truly an innovative discourse and a cultural revolution. (interview)

## Conclusions

This chapter set out to question how, if health policy networks were highly stabilized and characterized by medical predominance, challenging managerial elites emerged in public health care systems. In the first instance, it problematized the emergence of hospital directors as a modernizing discourse coalition, laying down key conditions for the emergence of new discourse coalitions. It then analysed the emergence of a modernizing discourse coalition in the SNCH. Standard accounts of health policy change dismiss the emergence of managerial elites as the inevitable outcome of either the 'inherent antipathy' of bureaucrats and professionals, the interest-maximizing calculations of opportunistic actors, or the functional demands of changing social, political, and economic structures (Harrison, Hunter, and Pollitt, 1990; Harrop, 1992, p. 166; Klein, 2001, p. 112).[4] They thereby gloss over the whole process of preference and identity-formation. However, this study has demonstrated the importance of the social construction of group identity. Hospital directors from the ENSP mobilized not against hospital doctors but against the non-ENSP directors in the *corps*. Theirs was the 'fantasy' of belonging to the French civil service elite, not necessarily tackling medical predominance. Indeed, the gradual imposition by the French state of the administrative organization common to civil service *corps* triggered the mobilization of hospital directors. Graduation from the ENSP came to define group membership and short-cut the information constraints facing hospital directors. It was the subsequent dislocation of the responsible model of trade unionism within the SNCH that then enabled hospital directors to forge a common political project. This modernizing discourse coalition at the head of the SNCH was eased by the ENSP identity of its participants; however, the role of strategically placed individuals and their capacity to symbolize and thus hold together coalitions was fundamental to organization and policy change within the SNCH. This leadership capacity of individuals raises questions for the role of empty signifiers and the role of individuals in the construction of discursive coalitions. More importantly, the study asks questions of the significance of group identity for mainstream theories of bureaucratic behaviour. Budget-maximizing and bureau-shaping are collective endeavours and, as such, will be predicated upon the process of group identity that cannot simply be dismissed as common interests.

## Notes

1. I would like to thank David Howarth and Jacob Torfing for their valuable comments on earlier drafts of this chapter.
2. There were four categories of *corps* which were broadly concerned with executive management and decision-making (the top-ranking category 'A' *corps*), implementation (category 'B'), and routine administrative and clerical tasks (categories 'C' and 'D'). Entrants required degree-level qualifications for category 'A' *corps* as opposed to baccalaureate (equivalent to A-level) qualifications for category 'B' *corps*.
3. The seven *grands corps* are the Council of State, the Court of Accounts, the General Finance Inspectorate, the Corps of Mines, the Corps of Bridges and Highways, the Prefectoral Corps, and the Diplomatic Corps.
4. Although focusing on neo-Marxism and elitist positions, Harrison, Hunter, and Pollitt still argue that 'administrators were swift to seize the opportunity to turn themselves into general managers' (1990, p. 156).

## Bibliography

Alford, R. R. (1975) *Health Care Politics* (Chicago, University of Chicago Press).

Bachir, M. (1999), 'Les registres et répertoires d'action de l'élite du welfare', in P. Hassenteufel (ed.), *L'émergence d'une 'elite du welfare'? Sociologie des sommets de l'état en interaction* (Paris, CNRS/IEP de Rennes/Université de Rennes 1).

Bevir, M., and Rhodes, R. A. W. (1999) 'Studying British Government: Reconstructing the Research Agenda', *British Journal of Politics and International Relations*, 1 (2), pp. 215–39.

Birnbaum, P. (1982) *The Heights of Power* (Chicago, University of Chicago Press).

Dunleavy, P. (1991) *Democracy, Bureaucracy and Public Choice* (London, Harvester Wheatsheaf).

Dupuy, F., and Thoenig, J.-C. (1985) *L'administration en miettes* (Paris, Fayard).

Fischer, F. (2003) *Reframing Public Policy: Discursive Politics and Deliberative Practices* (Oxford, Oxford University Press).

Griggs, S. (1999) 'Professionalisation, Policy Networks and the Development of French Health Policy: the Rise of Hospital Directors, the Syndicat National des Cadres Hospitaliers, 1976–1991' (Unpublished PhD thesis, London School of Economics, University of London).

Griggs, S., and Howarth, D. (2002), 'The Work of Ideas and Interests in Public Policy', in A. Finlayson and J. Valentine (eds), *Politics and Post-Structuralism: an Introduction* (Edinburgh, Edinburgh University Press).

Hajer, M. (1993), 'Discourse Coalitions and the Institutionalisation of Practice: the Case of Acid Rain in Britain', in F. Fischer and J. Forester (eds), *The Argumentative Turn in Policy Analysis and Planning* (London, UCL Press).

Hall, P. (1993) 'Policy Paradigms, Social Learning and the State: the Case of Economic Policymaking in Britain', *Comparative Politics*, 25 (3), pp 275–94.

Harrison, S., Hunter, D. J., and Pollitt, C. (1990) *The Dynamics of British Health Policy* (London, Unwin Hyman).

Harrop, M. (1992), 'Health Policy', in M. Harrop (ed.), *Power and Policy in Liberal Democracy* (Cambridge, Cambridge University Press).

Hassenteufel, P., and Martin, C. (1999), 'Forumlation des politiques et intervention dans les processus décisionnels – politiques familiales et de protection maladie (1981–1997)', in P. Hassenteufel (ed.), *L'émergence d'une 'élite du* welfare'? *Sociologie des sommets de l'état en interaction* (Paris, CNRS/IEP de Rennes/Université de Rennes 1).

Howarth, D. (1995) 'Complexities of Identity/Difference', *Journal of Political Ideologies*, 2 (1), pp. 55–78.

Howarth, D. (2000) *Discourse* (Buckingham, Open University Press).

Hunter, D. (1994) 'Managing Medicine: a Response to the Crisis', *Social Science and Medicine*, 32 (4), pp. 441–2.

Jahan, P. (1992) 'Quo vadis ENSP?', *Le directeur d'hôpital*, 5, pp. 6–11.

Jobert, B. (1992) 'Représentations sociales controverses et débats dans la conduite des politiques publiques', *Revue française de science politique*, 42 (2), pp. 219–34.

Jobert, B. (2001) 'Europe and the Recomposition of National Forums: the French Case', paper presented to 'Ideas, Discourse and European Integration' conference, European Union Center, Harvard University, 10–11 May 2001.

Jobert, B., and Muller, P. (1987) *L'état en action: politiques publiques et corporatismes* (Paris, Presses Universitaires de France).

Kessler, M.-C. (1986) *Les grands corps de l'état* (Paris: Presses de la FNSP).

Klein, R. (2001) *The New Politics of the NHS*, 4th edn (Harlow: Pearson Education/ Prentice Hall).

Muller, P. (1997) 'Les politiques publiques comme construction d'un rapport au monde', in A. Faure, G. Pollet, and P. Warin (eds), *La construction du sens dans les politiques publiques: débats autour de la notion de* référentiel (Paris, L'Harmattan).

Muller, P. (2000) 'L'analyse cognitive des politiques publiques: vers une sociologie politique de l'action publique', *Revue française de science politique*, 50 (2), pp. 189–207.

Quermonne, J.-L. (1991) *L'appareil administratif de l'état* (Paris, Seuil).

Rein, M., and Schön, D. (1991), 'Frame-reflective Policy Discourse', in P. Wagner, C. Hirschon Weiss, B. Wittrock, and H. Wollman (eds), *Social Sciences and Modern States: National Experiences and Theoretical Crossroads* (Cambridge, Cambridge University Press).

Schmidt, V. A. (1996) *From State to Market? The Transformation of French Business and Government* (Cambridge, Cambridge University Press).
Steudler, F. (1973) 'Hôpital, profession médicale et politique hospitalière', *Revue française de sociologie*, 14, pp. 13–40.
Stevens, A. (1978) 'Politicisation and Cohesion in the French Administration', *West European Politics*, 1 (3), pp. 69–80.
Stevens, A. (1992) *The Government and Politics of France* (Basingstoke, Macmillan now Palgrave Macmillan).
Suleiman, E. N. (1974) *Politics, Power and Bureaucracy in France* (Princeton, Princeton University Press).
Suleiman, E. N. (1978) *Elites in French Society* (Princeton, Princeton University Press).
Thoenig, J.-C. (1973) *L'ère des technocrats* (Paris, Les Éditions d'Organisation).
Thoenig, J.-C. (1987) 'Pour une approche analytique de la modernisation administrative', *Revue française de science politique*, 37 (4), pp. 526–38.
Torfing, J. (1999) *New Theories of Discourse* (Oxford, Blackwell).
Torfing, J. (2001) 'Path-dependent Danish Welfare Reforms: the Contribution of the New Institutionalisms to Understanding Evolutionary Change', *Scandinavian Political Studies*, 24 (4), pp. 277–309.
Wistow, G. (1992) 'The Health Service Policy Community: Professional Pre-eminence or under Threat?', in D. Marsh and R. A. W. Rhodes (eds), *Policy Networks in British Government* (Oxford, Clarendon Press).
Wright, V. (1989) *The Government and Politics of France* (London, Unwin Hyman).

# 5
# Political Administration

*Niels Åkerstrøm Andersen*

## Introduction

One of the major academic discussions of the 1990s has concerned the relation between politics and administration. The themes of these debates have been many and varied. It has been suggested that the level of politics should concentrate on the general direction of policy – the 'big picture' – and leave matters of detail and implementation to the administration. Politicians have been criticized for basing their decisions on single cases, which ought to be an entirely administrative matter. Another issue has concerned the belief that efficient operations can be created only by creating a clear difference between politics and administration. Such questions have been raised in most of the OECD countries and have been grouped under the label: 'New Public Management'. The same situation appeared in Denmark, which provided the case on which this chapter is based.

What triggered my curiosity was a series of statements made by the Danish Ministry of Finance. The Danish Ministry of Finance has time and again questioned the political field. The Ministry of Finance has been in the lead of many reforms and concrete initiatives with the purpose of reining in the political in preference for the administrative, and giving the public institutions the independence to make a number of decisions free from political interference. Among others, one may mention the transformation of state institutions into state PLCs, leasings, contract management and so on. The concept of 'excessive control' has been mentioned and it has been argued that politicians should concentrate on the general and the 'genuinely political', and that the relation between political and administrative institutions should be changed from one of hierarchy to one of dialogue and mutuality, where the political only decides in the last resort.

It seems to me that this is a sign of an administration (the Danish Ministry of Finance) that politicizes the relation between politics and administration. We are dealing with an administration that has arrogated to itself the right to question the relation between administration and politics and also to have a role in initiating policy. It seems like a paradox: politics are intensified in the administration when the administration (in this case the Ministry of Finance) attempts to delimit, and free the administration of, the political. How did this become a possibility and in what way does it change the political system? That is the central concern of this chapter.

The purpose of the article is not to determine where the line between politics and administration should be drawn. It is not a normative critique of either New Public Management (NPM) or the Danish Ministry of Finance's view on the relation between politics and administration. I will not formulate a definition of 'democracy' or any other alternative norm and present it as superior to New Public Management or the Danish Ministry of Finance. The interest of this article is sociological, as it intends to withdraw from the present discussion of the relation politics/administration, not to determine what is true, false, right or wrong in the discussion, but to question the discussion itself, its emergence, its construction, and its function in the political system.

Though its focus is Danish administration, my research problem is more general. This chapter deals with the effect of NPM on the possibilities and impossibilities of separating administration from politics. In this regard Danish administration is typically European, picking up ideas, practices, and concepts from the international NPM debate and from the OECD in particular. My thesis is that with the new public management discourse – or managerial discourse as Clark and Newman (1997) call it – we get a discourse organized around an ideal, or nodal point, of constant change. Classically, stability is the opposite of change, but, in the new discourses about the public sector, only turbulence, growing complexity, and uncertainty are, themselves, 'stability' (Andersen and Born 2000). 'The only continuity is change itself', say Clark and Newman (1997, p. 45). This conception radically challenges the relationship between politics and administration.

This chapter raises three questions:

1. What is the difference politics/administration, and what function does the distinction have in the modern political system? Is it a boundary between two different systems, each with their own separate logics, or is the difference an internal one within the political system?
2. How did it gradually become an option for the Danish Ministry of Finance to politicize the relation between politics and administration in the way that it does? How has the semantic space of options for the politicizing of the difference politics/administration changed, especially with NPM?
3. How does the politicization of the difference politics/administration in itself change the political system? Does the change on the semantic level bring on any changes in the system? My assertion is that the semantic development of the difference politics/administration in modern administrative policy results in a political system that has obtained a high degree of self-reflexivity as a political system.

The chapter comprises four parts. The first part introduces the starting point of the article's analytical strategy. The second part discusses the character of the political system and conducts a formal analysis of the difference politics/administration. The third part engages in the semantic history of the difference politics/administration in Denmark. The final part analyses this differentiation and addresses the way that semantic development has opened up space for greater reflexivity in the political system's own appraisal of the boundary between politics and administration.

## Analytical strategy

This chapter focuses on the difference politics/administration – not on politics or administration themselves – but on the relation between them. Bearing that in mind I have chosen Luhmann's theory of systems of communication, as this specific theory is based on a certain constructivist philosophy of difference.

Discourse analysis is a form of second order observation; it articulates discursive articulations and points to their regularities. Systems theory is similar and, fundamentally speaking, Luhmann's systems theory is a method of observing observations as observations.

To Luhmann, an observation is an operation of differentiation. An observation is an indication within the boundaries of a difference (Spencer-Brown 1969, p. 1). The operation of observing the administration means to indicate the phenomenon, but in a way in which administration becomes indicated not by the administration itself but by the difference, which establishes the framework of the observation. It makes a difference to observe administration by means of oppositions such as efficient/inefficient, public/private, democratic/undemocratic, or politics/administration. The difference establishes the blind spot of the observation. The observation sees what it sees but it cannot see that it does not see what it does not see. Systems theory is about the observation of the blind spots of other observations. But, of course, even systems theory has a blind spot of its own. It reduces everything to observations and only observes within the framework of the difference indication/difference. Within systems theory, the observer functions as an ascription to observation. There is no observer before observation. As the observation indicates something in the world, so the world is divided into system (observer) and environment (observed).

In social systems, observation happens through the operations of communication. Communication is produced backwards. It is later connections to earlier articulations and statements which make them into social communication. Every articulation produces a horizon of connectivity, but only the next connection fixes for a moment its social meaning, thus making it communication. A statement can always be interpreted as serious, flippant, and so on. Therefore it is the connection by the next statement, which selects and decides the form and content and transforms the first statement into communication. The connection produces itself a new horizon of connectivity which becomes communication only through new selective connections. Participants in communication can therefore never control communication. Communication becomes a recursive flowing stream of connections, of potentializations and actualizations. In this way, communication takes on a life of its own. It becomes autopoietic. Accordingly, a social system can be observed as a network of recursive communication operations, which consist of pure actuality.

According to Luhmann's reasoning I have chosen and developed three complementary strategies of analysis, which I will recount in brief. The three strategies are: analysis of form, analysis of semantics, and analysis of differentiation.[1]

## Analysis of form

Generally, Luhmann's analysis of form corresponds to Jacques Derrida's method of deconstruction (Luhmann 2002; Stäheli 2000). Analysis of form observes the unity of the differentiation of an observation operation. Form is defined as the unity of a difference (Luhmann 1999). The analysis of form pertains to the analysis of single differences. The question is which difference is employed and which unity keeps the form together. The analysis of form is an analysis of those *conditions of impossibility*, which relate to the communication within a particular form given a particular difference. In other words, it is a study of the paradoxes of communication given a particular difference. Apart from this general concept of difference, I shall distinguish between boundary and re-entry as two 'particular' kinds of difference-making operations.

Actually, any observation creates two differences at the same time. One is the difference which the observation establishes between the marked inside of the difference (m) and the unmarked outside (for instance, it is a man, therefore, not a woman). The sign for this difference is shown in figure 5.1.

The other difference is established with the observation as the difference between the observer and the observed. This difference is the boundary between the system and the environment, which Luhmann calls *the boundary*

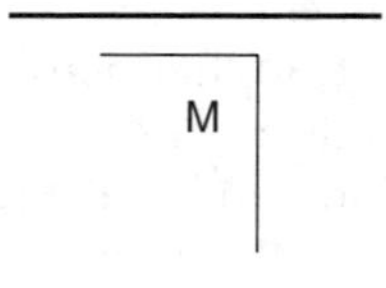


*Figure 5.1* The sign of difference

*of meaning*. Neither the system nor the environment exists before the observation. On the contrary, it is the operation of observing which creates both of them. The boundary of meaning is the horizon of meaning of the system of communication. The boundary of meaning determines that there are other conditions for the creation of meaning outside the system beyond those which are inside it. Therefore, the possibility of talking about a boundary between politics and administration relies on the fact that both of them can be identified as independent systems with their own boundary of meaning. Thus, meaning is based on conditions in the political system fundamentally different from those in the administrative system, and hence politics and administration cannot communicate with each other. To argue, therefore, that the issue at hand involves a boundary of meaning may be a very demanding statement.

The final kind of difference I shall introduce is what Spencer-Brown calls re-entry. Re-entry concerns the way a difference is sometimes copied and reintroduced in the space as created by the difference itself (Spencer-Brown 1969, pp. 69–76). A reintroduced difference is a difference that occurs in the space created by the difference (Luhmann 1993a, p. 484). This is the Luhmannian way of describing the infinity of a distinction. The separation of the political sphere into government and opposition is an example. Every day, when watching the news, we can see how this difference is reintroduced on both sides of the division. We can see how, when viewing the government, it contains both a governing wing and an opposition. Often, we can see that the opposition contains both a governing opposition and an opposition to the governing opposition. If we take a look at any government and its constituent wings we will see that they, at the same time, must have the same relation to the same external environment (us = the government, them = the opposition), but they also construct their own individual environment, for example, their own group of friends. Furthermore, they also construct each other as the environment. The opposition inside the government constructs the government itself as its own environment. On one hand, this increases the government's possibilities of communication and its sensitivity to the environment, for example, by providing the government with contact with more groups and issues. On the other hand, it installs a paradox within the system, since re-entries are both identical with and different from the system, and the system can never determine which one is the re-entry (copy) and which is the original. It installs an infinite game of communication (parallel to Derrida's definition of discourse (Derrida 1978, pp. 278–94). So 'the heart' of any communication system is the impossibility of the system, which forces it to continually attempt to fixate itself in new operations. Does the opposition in the government or the government in the government represent the 'right' line, the 'genuine' government? The sign for re-entry is shown in figure 5.2.

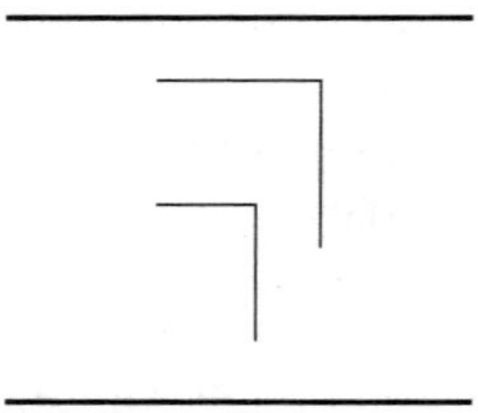

*Figure 5.2* The sign of re-entry

## Analysis of semantics

Whereas Luhmann's analysis of form corresponds to Derrida's concept of deconstruction, his analysis of semantics corresponds with Michel Foucault's or Ernesto Laclau's discourse analysis. And whereas deconstruction is supposed to open the political space by dismantling central difference such as freedom/power, and present the logic of their way of reasoning, discourse analysis is, subsequently, supposed to pursue the unfolding of these logics in historically concrete discursive struggles for hegemony.

In Luhmann there is the same division: whereas the objective analysing form is to present the paradoxes that form the basis of central differences such as right/wrong and true/false, the purpose of analysing semantics is to study the creation of these paradoxes and the ensuing relevant historically concrete attempts to circumvent the paradoxes through continuous attempts to fix the meaning of the particular difference.

Thus, Luhmann distinguishes between a system of communication and semantics. Semantics are defined as special structures which connect communication with communication by providing different forms of meaning, which the system of communication treats as worthy of preservation (Luhmann 1995, p. 282). Semantics are the reserve of generalized forms of differences (concepts, ideas, images, symbols, and so forth) which can be used in the selection of meaning in the systems of communication. Semantics are, in other words, condensed and replicable forms of meaning available to communication. These generalized forms of meaning are relatively independent of the situation and obtain their concrete content in the communication which selects them (Luhmann 1993b, pp. 9–72). In short, the strategy of the analysis of semantics is about studying how meaning is created and sought, fixated, and condensed in the form of new concepts, shifts in the concepts and their relations, including the replacement of the concepts' counter-concepts and so on. Nevertheless, this process is marked by struggle and involves what Foucault calls productive power. Luhmann will, less sentimentally, refer to it as a process of construction.

The relation between analysis of form and analysis of semantics can be illustrated as in figure 5.3.

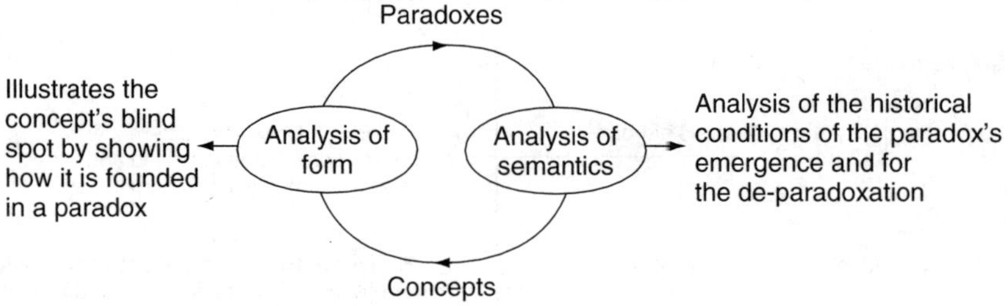


*Figure 5.3* The relationship between form analysis and semantic analysis

## Analysis of differentiation

Following the analysis of form and the analysis of semantics I make an analysis of differentiation. What comes closest to Luhmann's analysis of differentiation, in the discourse theoretical tradition, is probably the analysis of inter-discursivity. When discussing Foucault, this may be understood as discourse formations' mutual exclusion and, when dealing with Laclau, it may be interpreted as antagonistic chains of equivalence.

The purpose of the analysis of differentiation is to analyse the system of communication's unity of difference. This unity is called the form of differentiation; in short, the analysis of differentiation can be described as an analysis of the similarities of the difference between systems, for instance, the similarity in the way in which the systems make themselves differ from each other, and the likeness in the way in which the systems construct themselves through the difference system/environment. The analysis of differentiation, therefore, tells us something fundamental about the space of possibilities for the creation of communication systems.

The form of differentiation determines the systems' fundamental form of sensitivity to their environment; for example, the basic manner in which the systems of communication let themselves be disrupted by their own internally constructed environment.

The relation between semantics and form of differentiation is that the semantic development always follows society's form of differentiation, which means that the condensation of meaning in concepts in various systems of communication follow each other as parallels. Luhmann calls it a joint transformation of society's semantic apparatus. Concerning the strategy of analysis, this means that the emergence of a new form of differentiation is first seen in a semantic rupture. Inevitably, a new form of differentiation must show that a new semantic space of possibilities is being established. Thus, the analysis of semantics is the entrance to the analysis of differentiation. In

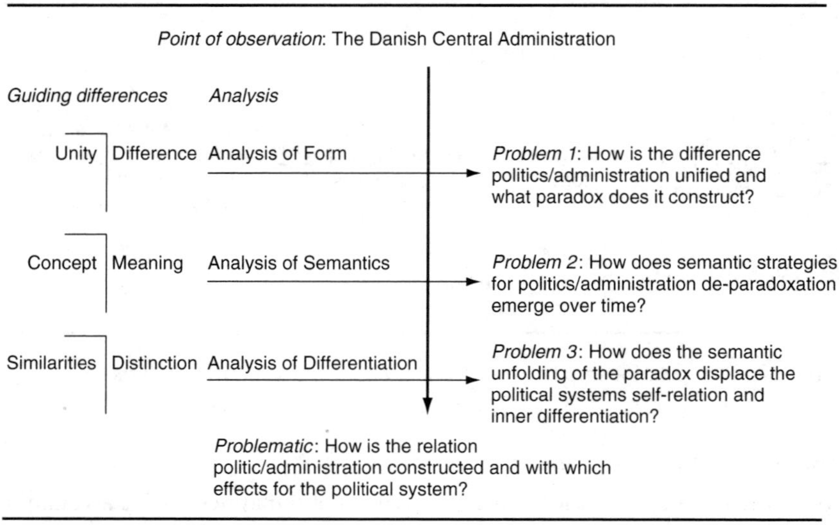


*Figure 5.4* The analytical strategy

this way the analysis of semantics is placed horizontally on the relation between sensitivity to the environment and the form of differentiation (Luhmann 1993b, p. 34).

The three analytical strategies and the questions connected to them can be summarized as in figure 5.4.

## The archive

In a Foucaultian sense, the archive consists of approximately 400 monuments from the public sector from 1850 until today. The archive has not been established solely for this chapter but in the context of three more comprehensive genealogies of the history of the Danish central administration, the history of outsourcing in Denmark, and the history of the public employee. The texts are all so-called reflexive administrative texts. Reflexive texts do not comprise single cases or individual decisions, but policy considerations in which concepts appear in a developed and justified form. These are mainly commission reports, public reports, campaign papers, extensive contributions to debates and articles in ministerial journals. This chapter draws on the archive without presenting it in its entirety. This has been done elsewhere (Andersen, N. Å., 1995, 1997; Andersen and Born 2001).

What is important for a systems theoretical reading of the archive is the following:

- A text represents a fixed communicative observation and must only be observed as such. What matters is to grasp the observations in their 'momentality', in their singularity, not reducing them to anything else, such as intention, motives or structures, not commenting on them, not explaining them, only describing them as pure operations.

- A text is always inherent in a net of recursive texts. A text is not in itself communication, but becomes communication by recursive references by the next text. One must read texts through their later articulations.
- One ought to focus not on meanings, but on the differences drawn in the texts. What is marked, what is unmarked, and what is excluded as the unmarked state of the difference (the constitutive outside).

## An analysis of form of the difference

### Politics/administration

Let us now return to the article's theme: the relationship between politics and administration. I shall begin with an analysis of the form of the difference politics/administration and shall start off by assuming that the difference is not a boundary of meaning, but a re-entry. Whether this is a profitable consideration cannot be determined within the analysis of form but only through the subsequent analysis of semantics. It is the analysis of the semantic unfolding of the form that proves the form's empirical status as discursive machinery. Therefore, the strategic analytical problem of the analysis of form ('why this specific difference') really cannot be answered until the analysis of semantics has been completed.

In the following, I shall assume that politics and administration are *not* two systems but, on the contrary, that the line between politics and administration is a difference within the political system. This choice is, of course, disputable.[2]

My view is that there is no reason to argue that meaning is based on conditions in politics that are different from those in administration. It is not possible to find such a boundary of meaning.

I define the political system as a special system of communication characterized by a particular function and a particular code. The political system emerges as a functional differentiation: for instance, it stands out as a special communication, which differentiates itself from other types of communication in society, not by referring to a certain area or a special part of society, but by referring to a specific function. Political communication differs from other forms of communication as a system that appoints itself to function as a decision-maker on collectively binding decisions. Compared to the political system, the State is nothing but the semantic of the political system. This means that the State is the semantics through which the political system attempts to describe itself (Luhmann 1990). The State is the political system's self-description.

As a system of communication, the political system constantly distinguishes between itself and its environment, between what is political and non-political. This is made possible by using a binary code. The binary code marks the political system's boundary of meaning. Before the breakthrough of democracy, the code of the political system was governing/being governed. This is a code of preference with a positive and a negative side to it: it is better to govern than to be governed. In the area of political communication the world is divided in two, the governing and the governed. The political system secures its identity by continuously connecting to one side of the code or the other.

With the breakthrough of democracy the top of the political system divides in two, for instance, the positive side of the code (governing) becomes divided between government/opposition, where it is always better to be the government than the opposition. Thus, democratic and political communication is characterized by two codes: governing/being governed and government/opposition. According to Luhmann, democracy is exactly the unity of the difference government/opposition. This means that all democratic, political communication connects to one of the sides in the two differences. Subsequently, politicizing means to subscribe to either of the two codes of politics. Politicizing, accordingly, implies a communicative thematization within the code of the political system. The division between government and opposition had great consequences for the political system, the distinction between the political and administrative systems being one of them. Formerly, the purpose of administration was to gain power. Political and administrative power were identical. There was a constant struggle for administrative power at both national and local levels. An example of this is the articulation of the occupation of office during the period of absolute monarchy in Denmark. During this period there was a constant struggle between the king and leading officials for the right to appoint new officials. Being in a position to appoint officials meant possessing administrative power, and having administrative power meant possessing the State. To the very end, absolute monarchs fought for the right to appoint officials, and they always made sure that the appointed officials were loyal to the king. The officials were meant to know that they owed their appointment to the king himself (Jensen 1987). After the division of the political summit, the matter of office becomes articulated in a totally different manner. Officials are no longer appointed with the aim of sustaining or conquering the administration of the State and thereby the power of the State. Appointments are ostensibly objective, in the same way that an official's professional conduct is regarded as being separate from his private views. A precondition for democracy among others is the development of political parties that are capable of surviving the transformation from government to opposition and vice versa. Another precondition, however, is that the administration implements legislation impartially, and is not directly persuaded by different political interests. Thus, the route to the administration of the State goes through the power of the State. Here we see the distinction between politics and administration, or, as it is stated in the Danish Constitution, between the juridical and the executive powers.

In this regard, the most important point is that the difference politics/administration does not indicate the outer boundary of the political system. The difference is a difference *inside* the political system of communication – not a coincidental difference, but a difference that is necessary for the reproduction of the political system's democratic form (the unity of government and opposition). Without a distinction between politics and administration, and between juridical and executive powers, the political struggle becomes a struggle for the direct conquest of the administration of the State, which would cancel the division at the political summit and thereby the meaning of the difference government/opposition.

The difference politics/administration is not a boundary of meaning, but a reintroduced difference. The difference between what is political and what is non-political is copied and reintroduced in the political communication. This is illustrated in figure 5.5.

In the reintroduction, the unmarked outer side of politics (non-politics) is marked as administration. This means that politics/non-politics becomes politics/administration: for instance, it becomes a difference between what is really political and what is less political. The difference politics/non-politics is copied and reintroduced as the difference politics/administration on the inside of the space created by the difference politics/non-politics, and in this way the difference becomes part of its own unity. Thus, the difference is simultaneously the same and not the same. It can be illustrated as in figure 5.6.

Thus, the political system faces a paradox in which the political and the administrative basically remain indefinite. When 'administration' becomes separated *inside* the political, it follows logically that it cannot be separated clearly *from* the political at the same time. The problem is the 'difference in the same', for instance, the necessity of treating the administration as something different from politics while the administration is, at the same time, political. The problem is the necessity of treating the same difference as if it was a different difference. The paradox is insoluble, but can and *must* be handled through de-paradoxation and unfolding.

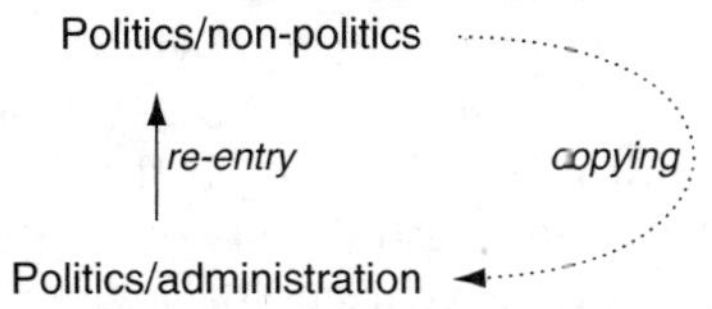


*Figure 5.5* A difference becoming a part of its whole

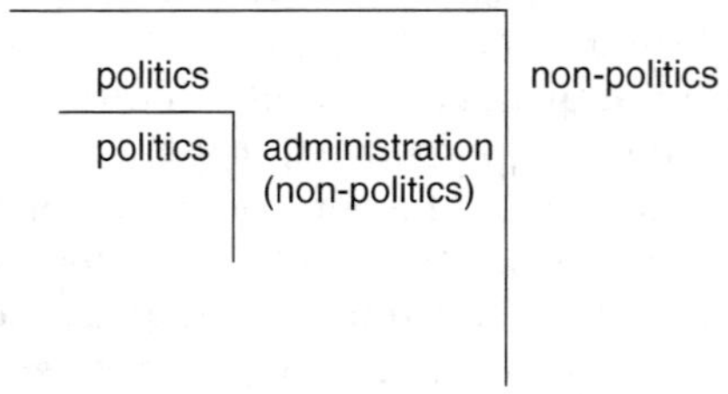


*Figure 5.6* The re-entry of politics

The most obvious way to solve a situation in which the paradox blocks political communication is a continuous *unfolding* of the paradox. The political system is forced to unfold the paradox of the reintroduction, and the manner in which the system unfolds the paradox is through still more reintroductions on *both* sides of the difference politics/administration. In this way, for example, the environment of an administration always appears political (seen from the point of view of the administration), even though the 'same' administration, from the point of view of a hierarchically subordinated organ, naturally appears as this organ's political environment. However, the handling of the paradox through unfolding is only successful if the unfolding does not appear to be what it is in the political communication, namely, a reintroduction. *De-paradoxation* can be described as a strategy for hiding and forgetting a re-entry, as in a 'naturalization' of the environment (Luhmann 1993c; Andersen, N. Å, 2000, 2003b). For example, the administration might begin to describe its political environment; it might characterize it as a structural framework, characterize it eventually by, for example, describing how politics seems to move more and more in one specific direction, describe politics as something that presses on from the outside with the urgency of an imperative. At the same time the administration becomes naturalized as an administration. Facing this naturalized political environment the administration does not doubt itself as administrative and as non-political. The administration becomes identical with itself as administration in negation of the political – at least as long as the de-paradoxation is successful in hiding the paradox. The paradox of the political nature of the administration disappears from the field of vision of the communication. That it concerns a re-entry is forgotten and this oblivion opens for the continuation of the political communication. The establishment of what is actually politics and what is administration is an impossible division to make. It always depends from which system's point of view we see it. In a scientific second-order observation, we are still not able to distinguish the original from the copy simply because the original is a copy already by definition;

there is no 'first time' difference between politics and non-politics; the re-entry of politics/non-politics as politics/administration is always already a re-entry.

I will, briefly, give some examples of re-entries of the difference politics/administration. The difference is, for example, reintroduced on the political side as the distinction between the party-political work and the party organization, but it is also reintroduced as the distinction between cases of principle which, of course, belong in the political area, and the individual cases which never should have been made a political issue, but should have remained strictly administrative.

On the administrative side of the difference, the difference is re-entered in every single administration and at all levels, for example, as the difference between what is politically given for us, and the content with which we can decide to fill in the frame. What can be characterized as the frame and what is content is not always obvious, leaving the decision-makers *in* the administration with a heavy and continuous workload. On the administrative side, the difference is also reintroduced as a difference between political and administrative cases. In the administration it is a constant problem to determine which cases are administrative and can or must be decided by the administration itself, and which cases should be referred to someone higher in the hierarchy in the political area. Furthermore, it is also a reoccurring problem for the administration to determine which cases are political and whether there is a risk of politicization. The cases, in the administration view, can be so politically 'explosive' that they, more than anything, must remain administrative and dealt with as such. However, it becomes a problem for the administration to decide how to present the cases as objective, avoid statements that provoke a political reaction and, in short, keep the cases at a distance from the political world.

The difference politics/administration also becomes interesting when responsibility is being divided. Again, the difference re-enters on both sides of itself. On the political side, for example, there is a distinction between political responsibility, which incorporates political consequences, and administrative responsibility, which incorporates disciplinary consequences. On the administrative side, there is a distinction between our responsibility for executing and implementing decisions and their (political) responsibility for taking the initiative, acting, and making decisions.

But these re-entries of the difference are all political in the sense that they are part of a political communication, which forms the code government/opposition. It is only within the political that the difference between what is a matter of principle and thereby political and what is an individual case and thereby administrative, between what is a political decision and what is just a practical implementation of a decision and so on can be made. The place from where an administration draws the line between politics and administration is always the political system. It is always a line of political balance but this is hidden by the never-ending operation of re-entries. It is a *necessary secret*. It is precisely the function of the never-ending re-entries to hide the source of the difference, for instance, the paradox of the difference. If the administration in its administrative operations realized the political nature of its operations, it would imply a simultaneous marking of both sides of the difference politics/administration, which would be a cancellation of the difference between politics and administration – and that would be a threat to democracy itself; in the sense of the unity of the difference government/opposition.

No matter where we enter the political system, we will find the difference politics/administration but never in exactly the same shape. It is always the same, yet somehow another difference. There is never total coherence between the re-entry of the difference on the political side and the re-entry of the difference on the administrative side. It can never mean the exact same. The difference will always be determined locally, but the fact that the difference is local will always remain concealed. Therefore, the difference politics/administration is not the outer boundary of the political system and neither is it a clear dividing line within the political system, and it never will be.

## An analysis of the semantics of the administrative policy as politics about the difference politics/administration

If my form analysis of the difference politics/administration is correct it must appear semantically in the continuous development of new strategies of de-paradoxation, in still more new ways of condensing and fixating the difference politics/administration.

But what would happen, then, if the political system not only (continuously) operates with the difference politics/administration alone and emphasizes first one side of the difference then the other side of it, but *frames* it and makes it the subject of political communication? What will happen if the difference, at one and the same time, is the subject of politicization *and* the difference which builds the frame for political observation of the difference?

We now move away from emphasizing the difference politics/administration as a fundamental re-entry in the political system to emphasizing the historically varying semantics, which the operation of re-entry has at its disposal, exact meanings which have been given to the difference politics/administration throughout history. We move from analysis of form to analysis of semantics. The initial thesis of this part of the chapter is that the re-entry of the difference politics/administration creates a paradox, and that the continuous de-paradoxation, which the political system is subsequently forced into, appears as a constant semantic renovation of the difference politics/administration. I shall now focus on the condensation of certain forms of meaning regarding the difference politics/administration and then I shall discuss how the semantic development influences the political system's possibilities of relating to itself, for instance, the political system's form of internal differentiation.

### Administrative Law: 1860–1945

The semantic development of the difference politics/administration was initiated with the discussions of the constitution, and in the twentieth century unfolded the Administrative Law. At the same time, we see the distinction discussed in individual pieces of legislation such as administrative directives, which specify the principles under which administrations should administrate. However, the development of the difference did not really accelerate until the Administrative Law was introduced as a separate law.

The first feeble dispositions to enact an administrative law appeared at the end of the nineteenth century. In 1870 *The Danish State's Administrative Law*,[3] by Carl Georg Holck, professor in jurisprudence, was published. The book was the first complete and systematic publication of Danish State Administrative Law. In retrospect, the book obtained importance primarily by setting out Administrative Law as an independent issue in regard to constitutional law, under the generic term 'the state law' (Holck 1870, p. 2). In 1893, the book *Concerning Determination of Disputes with the Administration, Especially Concerning Administrative Laws*,[4] by Johannes Ussing, was published. With Ussing, the distinction between a constitutional state and a police state was introduced into Danish Administrative Law. By the constitutional state, Ussing means law enforcement that emanates from recognition of the inviolability of the citizens' private sphere of jurisdiction without pursuance of existing law (Ussing 1893, p. 3). The problem was how to establish the frames of the independent administrative settlement, a settlement free of political influence.

An answer was given in 1924, in Poul Andersen's doctoral dissertation 'On Invalid Administrative Documents with Special Reference to Sources of Invalidity'. It was a juridical dissertation which dealt with the juridical code justice/injustice, and it indicated, first and foremost, the reflexive side of the code (injustice) by considering the criteria under which an administrative document could be claimed to be invalid. An administrative document was defined as a one-sided statement from an administrative organ of a certain juridical binding content (Andersen, P., 1924, pp. 22f.). Now, why was this relevant? It was relevant because politics is a considerable source of invalidity. Politics occurs as a more or less central aspect in all the sources of invalidity which Poul Andersen identified (Andersen, P., 1924, pp. 77–88). This means that politics plays the part of 'injustice' in administrative documents in contrast to the independent administration, which plays the part of 'justice'.

What was constructed in the period 1860–1945 was a legal semantic dealing with the difference politics/administration as a difference between legal adminstrative decisions on the one side and political decisions on the other. Politics was here constructed as the counter-concept of objective administrative decision-making.

**The rationalization policy: 1946–60**

After the Second World War, the Administrative Commission of 1946 was established. The terms of reference of the Administrative Commission were wide and included, among other things, public administration, decentralization, and rationalization. From 1947, the Administrative Commission turned the question of rationalization over to the Administrative Tribunal, which was established for the very same purpose. When the Administrative Commission was abolished in 1952, the Administrative Tribunal was installed permanently. Later, in 1964, the Administrative Tribunal was abolished.

In the first years of the Administrative Commission, the aim was to create an administrative policy, which also thematized the basic premises of the administration, among these the difference politics/administration. Later, with the Administrative Tribunal of 1947, the themes were limited to questions of rationalization. We get an administrative policy that is placed in the administration but at the same time has the explicit norm to be non-political. The object is a policy which can assist the administration with advice and consultation in the project of rationalization. Typically it concerns administrative techniques, filing, and the organization of casework.

The Administrative Tribunal thus assumed the difference politics/administration but only indicated the administration side. By marking it in this way the Administrative Tribunal distinguished between political policy regarding the administration and technical-administrative policy regarding administration. The latter presumed that the Administrative Tribunal could delimit the specifically political in administrative policy. This was, of course, no simple task and was obviously a pressing problem for the Administrative Tribunal. The problem was presented most clearly in 1953 by Bent Christensen. Christensen saw the efficiency of the administration as the objective of the Administrative Tribunal. Efficiency meant a rating of the relation between procedure and results. An efficient administration is subsequently one that uses procedures which lead to the best possible result with the least possible effort. According to Christensen, the efficiency consideration is developed in relation to private companies, where it functions without problems. But the problem was that the Administrative Tribunal could not draw up objectives for the administrative operations on its own because this was a legislative, political function. In contrast, no precise objective for administrative activity on the basis of the existing law could be given (Christensen 1953, p. 344). According to Christensen, the problem was insoluble unless single working units inside the administration were focused upon, for example, that the accountancy function in a specific department was made the object of attention (Christensen 1953, p. 345). To keep the political out of the rationalization policy, the difference politics/administration re-entered on the administration side as a difference between the administration as a whole and single working units, where the former was politically determined and the latter was technically determined. Parallel to this difference, the difference politics/administration also re-entered as a difference between form and content (Christensen 1953, p. 357). According to Christensen the Administrative Tribunal could only engage in the form of administration, that is, the procedure in the separate working unit, and not in the content of the administration, for instance, the object of the administration. The problem was a dilemma: either there was an efficient rationalization policy which arrogated to itself political rights concerning the objective of the administration (and that, of course, would not do), or there was an administrative policy that was not particularly efficient (while being non-political), which only observed the form of the administration in relation to the separate working units, and, therefore, did not pursue extensive and costly objectives (Christensen 1953, p. 357). What materialized, however, was politics about administration which was placed in the administration and tried to delimit the political in the rationalization policy.

**The planning policy: 1962–82**

From the end of the 1950s, the narrow definition of the Administrative Tribunal, as concerning itself merely with the separate working units, was questioned. In 1957, the Labour Market Commission approached the Administrative Tribunal with the intent of discussing the problem of the administrative separation of a number of colleges. The Administrative Tribunal rejected the problem by referring to it as a question of content, and hence, a political problem. In 1959 the Commission of Technicians made a report. The commission pointed out a sectorial problem of co-ordination of the technical colleges and stated that the problem could not be solved through adjustments of the legal basis of the individual colleges, but demanded a larger administrative reform which might enable a continuous concurrence and planning of the individual colleges in relation to general sectorial considerations. The Commission of Technicians simply demanded a new administrative commission which included the content of the administration and which took a stand on its planning problems.[5]

This demand was made by the Administrative Committee of 1960 (A60). A60 made five reports in all. The reports concerned the demarcation of the substance of planning. It happened through the construction of sectors or problem fields. The general discursive figure in which the problems of the sectorial demarcation were formulated can be formalized like this: (1) originally there was an administrative whole; (2) development in the form of an increase in the extent and complexity of the administration had brought with it administrative separation; (3) thereby, overall unity was lost by means of which imbalance and co-ordination problems emerged; and (4) unity was reinstated through planning and unification of the administration in sectors (The Administrative Committee of 1960, 1962a, 1962b, 1963, 1965, 1966; Andersen, N.Å., 1995, pp. 150–78).

In the first report, the difference politics/administration was explicitly framed and a model for how the difference should be made as a difference, between the consideration of cases and planning, was formulated. In the following reports the difference was no longer explicitly framed, but the difference was implicitly rewritten when the question of which problems belonged to which sector fields was discussed, and when these sector fields were given a new organizational structure which often, but not unambiguously, drew on the first report of the A60. One could say that the difference was always an implicit part of the discussion when the Administrative Committee decided which administrative assignments, policy problems, institutions, and interests were included and excluded, respectively, in a particular sector because the committee also decided the level of access to different ministers that these assignments, problems, institutions, and interests each had.

What was achieved with the Administrative Committee of 1960, which continued with the Administrative Council and later with the Administrative Department until the end of the 1970s, was a planning policy that was placed on the administration side, a policy that implicitly enacted the difference politics/administration and sought to do that in a non-political manner through the overall consideration of the difference politics/objective.

### The administrative policy (NPM): 1982–2004

From the end of the 1970s, the administrative political semantic changed again. By the end of the 1960s, the generalized notion of sectors was already being questioned, because one sector was elevated above the rest of the sectorial units, namely, the economic unit. It was realized that public sector growth created considerable economic imbalance (The Ministry of Labour 1971). During the 1970s, a semantic regarding the planning of planning was developed. The combination of the sectorial units into bigger unities was proposed, first and foremost as an economic whole. A general, and above all long-term plan, which could produce a frame for the shorter-term sector plans, was constructed. In 1975, this idea culminated in the report *Planning in the Civil Services*, which, on top of the sector planning, envisioned the establishment of four centres of planning and above these a central centre of planning. One of the planning centres was established in the shape of the Department of Budgets. The rest were never established (still, they were the starting point for several administrative-political strategies in the 1990s, for example, the Ministry of Coordination).

By the end of the 1970s, the idea of the planning of planning broke down. It began with difficulties in the collecting and preparation of the information necessary for building a planning system, and eventually the idea emerged of rewarding the administrative units that pursued an active policy of adaptation, contrary to the administrative unit, that pursued a passive policy of aversion regarding the debit side (Thygesen 1980). In 1981, a new ideal was introduced concerning an adaptation-efficient administration which aimed at removing barriers for the individual administrations' adaptation of themselves (The Department of Administration 1982). So the new ideal was an ever self-changing administration. Or, to be even more clear, an ideal about change towards constant readiness for change, change for the sake of capacity to change, that is always to be ready to become something else.

Planning Account no. 3 and the Modernization Programme emphasized the shift. The planning policy was determined explicitly, and a new administrative policy was beginning to take form on the horizon (The Planning Information Committee 1984; The Minister of Finance 1983). From then on, a new administrative policy was created concerning the entire public sector. It aimed at increasing the public sector's ability to adapt itself by changing the public sector's borders. The traditional borders were seen as a barrier for adaptation and change. The boundary between public and private was explicitly put at stake, for example, through statements concerning different forms of privatization. The boundary between administration and the individual citizen was also put at stake, for example, in programmes about service-oriented self-management, simplification of rules, and de-bureaucratization. And finally, the difference politics/administration was put at stake too; in many reports, in many sketched designs, and in many themes, the difference politics/administration was framed and made the object of administrative policy. Contract management and leasing were examples of this. In this chapter, however, I shall only emphasize a single example, which was more articulated and pinpointed the problem more than most documents concerning administrative policy. The subject was the report by the Ministry of Finance: *A New View on the Public Sector*, published in 1993.

Where A60 was primarily about introducing a differentiation between the planning part of the administration, with access to the minister, and the case-working part of the administration, without access to the minister, *A New View on the Public Sector* was largely about creating more freedom of action in operational decisions within the public sector, without political interference. For example, the report stated:

> The political responsibility is a fundamental premise in the public sector. But that does not necessarily show through *direct* political management. Direct political management is appropriate in situations where the political aims are expressed and where it becomes secured that the political decisions are followed up. However, regarding the majority of the public sector, the political management is inconsistent with the demands of quality. Here, the management must become more general and fundamental. Here, it is

> often appropriate that the political management is supplemented with, or partly replaced by, other forms of management. (The Ministry of Finance 1993, p. 90)

Thus, we are dealing with an administration (the Ministry of Finance), which frames the difference politics/administration in order to get the administration's operational ability in focus and the political issues in it withdrawn. The staging of the problem has several dimensions. First, through a difference in time:

> Traditionally, the public sector has been viewed on the basis of the idea that the politicians can survey and manage the public sector in all its particulars top-down. This precondition is no longer in place and the renewal of the public sector must be made in the light of that. Instead, the heart of the matter must be the public institutions, whose leaders and employees must supply the services and the quality, which the citizens, the trade industry and other industries need... The management can no longer build on hierarchy and centralistic solutions. On the contrary, it has to build on principles of dialogue and co-operation. (The Ministry of Finance 1993, pp. 6–7)

The Ministry of Finance illustrated the change as seen in figure 5.7, along with which appeared the comment:

> The hierarchical model, which has been the carrying element in the public sector, is replaced by a model which, to a higher degree, is based on

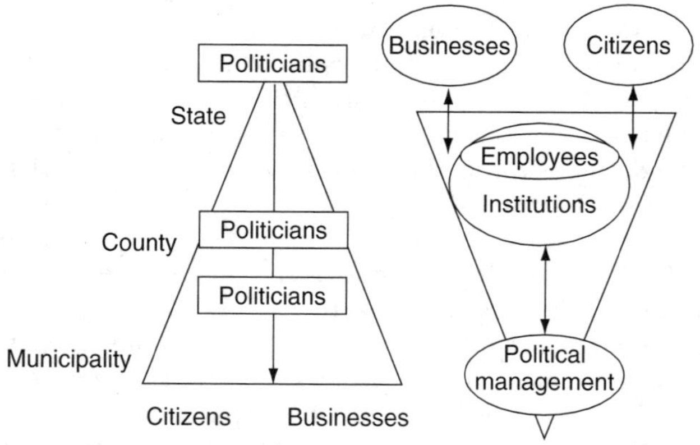


*Figure 5.7* Hierarchy in transformation

> dialogue between the State, the municipalities, and the counties, and between the politicians and the institutions. The politicians' detailed management disappears in this model. (The Ministry of Finance 1993, p. 111)

Thus, the report highlighted a natural development where the Ministry of Finance was a temporal instrument, that is, a temporal instrument by which not only the boundary between politics and administration was moved slightly to one side or the other and the hierarchy was turned upside down so that future political management is placed at the bottom, but also the relation between politics and administration became marked by dialogue rather than authority. In some places it was even underlined that the relation between politics and administration should be an 'equal relation' even though the formal hierarchy was preserved as a 'last resort' (The Ministry of Finance 1993, pp. 91–2).

Secondly, the difference politics/administration was seen as a problem of balance between over-steering and under-steering, in parallel with other problems of balance, for example, between inflation and employment, or between imports and exports:

> There is a risk of 'over-steering' if major parts of the traditional management system is maintained in spite of the formal decentralisation and the involvement of the market and users in the management... On the other side, there is a risk for under-steering if the traditional system is removed without anything replacing it. The institutions can end up in a situation where they are managed neither from the top (politically) nor from the bottom (market and users). The renewal of the management in the public sector has the aim to give the necessary freedom of action to the institutions and their employees in order to work efficiently in relation to businesses and citizens. To do this a clarification is needed of how far the political management should go and where the responsibility of the independent operation begins. It should lead to the establishment of a new balance between political and operational responsibility so that both over-steering and under-steering are avoided. (The Ministry of Finance 1993, pp. 87–8)

The problem of balance was specified in a number of instances. At the top was the balance between politics and operations, followed directly by the balances between conflicting objects and precise objects; between carefully defined means and freedom of action; between political leaders and administrative and professional leaders; between staffing and local freedom of action regarding staff; and, finally, between specified appropriations and framework appropriations (The Ministry of Finance 1993, p. 89).

How could it be that a Ministry of Finance was able to deal with the contents of the administration as well as politics, when the same situation was totally unthinkable in the Administrative Tribunal of the 1950s? Concerning

A60, the answer was about the difference politics/the objectivity of the whole. Today, adaptation and readiness for self-change has become a value above politics. In 1979 the Ministry of Finance reflected upon the possibility of more self-adaptability in the administration but rejected the idea. The argument was that the function of politics was change and that this function demanded a stable administration through which change could be implemented. If the administration were changing itself it might threaten a move toward the function of politics. This concern has been totally forgotten.

The political must not stand in the way of the change and adaptation of the public institutions. That is why the institutional freedom of action must be 'shielded' from politics. There are considerations concerning adaptation which mean that politicians must step back and enter into dialogue with the institutions instead of using the formal hierarchy. At the same time, it puts high demands on the institutions which cannot relinquish responsibility by referring to the political level. Generally, it is an attempt to define some limits for the administration's possibility of reintroducing the difference politics/administration, with the intention of pushing responsibility upwards in the hierarchy.

An example in *A New View on the Public Sector* concerns quality. It says: 'The citizens have a right to quality. But quality cannot be secured through decision-making or laws and rules alone' (The Ministry of Finance 1993, p. 55). The citizens' right to quality is, thus, in one sense more important than the political. What we have here is a right that must not be violated by politics, but cannot be secured through politics either. Furthermore:

> The responsibility for this (the quality) lies on the individual institutions. Therefore, the individual institution has to specify the aims which should be reached within the given framework *through dialogue with the politicians*, and create clarity concerning the users' needs and expectations *in dialogue with the users*. (The Ministry of Finance 1993, p. 56)

Figure 5.8 shows how the Ministry of Finance illustrated this.

What was experienced from the beginning of the 1980s was an administration (The Ministry of Finance) which produced politics concerning the administration by framing the difference politics/administration, and by continuously and *explicitly* putting the difference at stake in different reforms concerning contract management, concern management, the institutions' independence in the public sector, and so on It was, among other things, a matter of shielding the administration from the political, getting the political Function to draw back from the zone that is named the 'actually political' in order to give the institutions not only freedom of action but also the responsibility to adapt. Furthermore, it is an administrative policy that is accepted as being above politics and representing the highest value of that time: adaptation. In this way, the administrative policy becomes

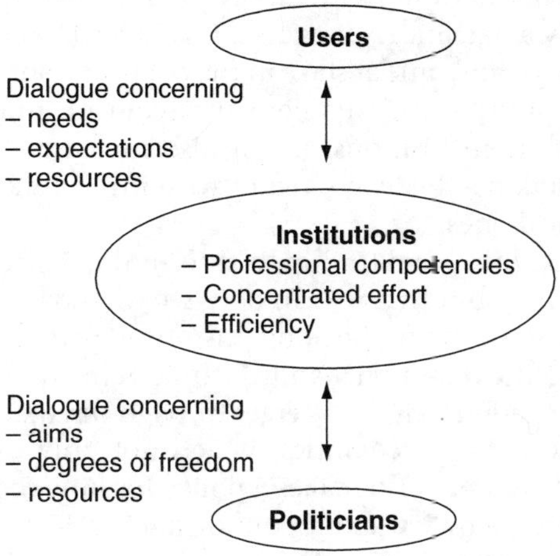


*Figure 5.8* Precondition for Quality

| **Period** | **Semantics** | **Ideal** | **Politics/administration difference** |
|---|---|---|---|
| **1860–1945** | Administrative law | Objective administrative decisions | Political/legal |
| **1947–60** | Rationalization policy | Effiency work and administration | Result/procedure Content/form |
| **1960–82** | Planning policy | Parts are a part of a whole | Politics/objective overall considerations |
| **1983–today** | Administrative policy (NPM) | Reconversion and readiness for change on all administrative levels | Generel policy/strategies of single institutions |

*Figure 5.9* The history of semantics

*non-political* to the extent that it operates with the difference politics/adaptation.The semantic history is sumed up in figure 5.9.

## Conclusion: differentiation of a reflexive subsystem

Now my last argument is that the dislocation in the semantic strategy of de-paradoxation regarding the politics/administration paradox merely exchanges one strategy for another. What is at stake is the very self-relation of the political communication system. My point is that new public management is not simply a 'technical' discourse. It is indeed 'political', in the sense that it put the rules of the game at stake in the political communication system. It withdraws the politics of parliament in favour of innovative strategies of singled-out public institutions. But it also increases the self-reflexivity in the system, making it always ready to reinterpretate administrative decisions as political ones.

The semantic ruptures seem to show a shift in the *differentiation of form* in the political system, a shift that we can only see when we view the semantics of politics/administration in the long historical perspective, a shift that cooperates the political system's ability to be reflective about itself. The politics' reflective relation to itself emerges through three steps and peaks with the administrative policy's semantics, which not only uses the difference politics/administration but also makes a policy for how the difference ought to be: in other words, a policy about politics, a second-order policy. Level by level, the emergence of politics's reflective relation to itself can be described as follows. The first level is announced with the rationalization policy. With the semantics of the rationalization policy, only the administration side in the difference politics/administration is marked. The difference itself, from where the administration can become visible in observations, which is the difference politics/administration, is not framed and made the object of discussion, but is the blind spot of the rationalization policy. We have observations of the first order, but not observations of the second order on how the political system makes its observations. The semantics of the rationalization policy opens, allowing the political system to refer to itself or its environment, but it does not open up for the system's possibility of seeing from *where* it observes itself. The semantics of the rationalization policy do not involve the possibility of the political system questioning its own blind spots as limitations in its own system of communication and way of describing itself. In the semantic of the rationalization policy it is possible to operate with the difference politics/administration, but it is not an option to question it.

The next level, which is announced with the planning policy, frames the difference politics/administration. The difference is made the object of discussion only to be fixated in a new semantic figure (the department–directorate model) immediately after, which is not questioned later on. Subsequently, the difference is only treated implicitly, when area after area has been analysed with sectorial problems of coordination as the starting point and rearranged in the image of the department–directorate model. This means that the difference politics/administration is not the centre of attention and reflection, but it is treated implicitly, by being pointed out by an external necessity (usually an imbalance in the unity). The semantics of the planning policy gives us the possibility of self-reflection via external reference.

At the third level the administrative policy frames the difference politics/administration. The difference is explicitly put at stake through a long line of politicizations. The relation politics/administration is continuously questioned in relation to a long line of areas and problems. What the rationale of the separation of politics and administration should be is continuously debated and the relation politics/administration is made the object of choice. The semantic of the administrative policy does not open for reflection concerning the organization of politics only; it opens up for reflectivity and for a reflection on how the difference should be discussed and made. I have called this self-relation a reflection on one self as reflective. The history of the differentiation form is summed up in figure 5.10.

Thus, the semantics of the administrative policy opens for the political system to view itself, to see the difference politics/administration, which rules the communication, thereby making it a possible object of choice and management.

However, in a system perspective we have to accept that there is no place *outside* the political system from where it can see itself. For a system to be able to see itself (become visible in itself), it must divide itself between the observer and the observed (Spencer-Brown 1969, p. 105). The establishment of the reflection of politics on its own semantics and differences is only possible because a subsystem appears in the political, which assigns itself the right of being the one to describe the political system. In this subsystem of a higher order the semantic is the administrative policy, and the system consists of all of the communication that refers to this semantic. This system of higher order, which closes itself communicatively around the function of reflecting on the rest of the political system's basic differences, brings an asymmetry into the political system, because the communication of these higher orders ascribes to itself the right to be the active observer of the rest, who become the passively observed.

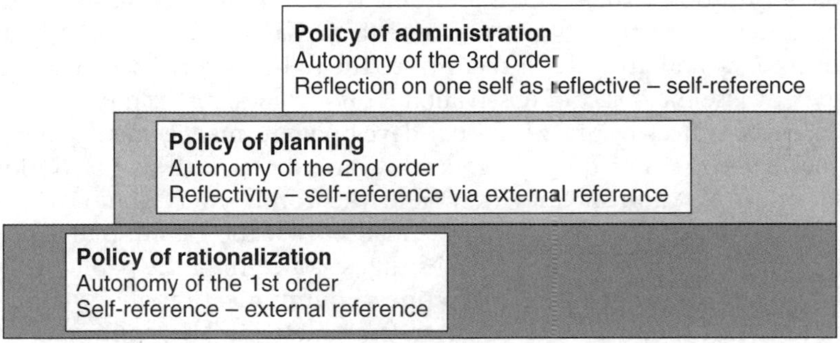


*Figure 5.10* Politic's relation to itself

The higher order of the administrative policy communications arrogate to themselves the right to describe the political system, to simplify it in images of the public sector, and to ascribe meaning to the political system and its many organizations in general. Consequently, the other subsystems can be viewed as having been ascribed meaning. They observe themselves being described and simplified by others. Reports on 'The Public Sector' are part of this simplification, where individual organizations are regarded as of one kind; but also different types of ranking in the public institutions contribute to these simplified descriptions, for example, descriptions of 'the best in the State' or public awards for quality. Balance sheets, staffing accounts, and bench-marking are also part of the schemata, through which institutions in the political system must view themselves being simplified. The observed get an identity ascribed to them through observations and descriptions, for example, in capacity of aims and functions, they get a position ascribed to them in relation to other institutions, a past and a future – often divided between threat and possibility, they get strong and weak sides ascribed to them, problems and solutions, responsibilities and expectations. All in all, the act of observation and description implies ascriptions, which also tie the observed ones to certain expectations.

Furthermore, the asymmetry consists of the existence of a place, which is not described and is not observed, namely, the place from where the observations are made. In this sense, the position of the observer of the administrative policy becomes a 'non-place', a place 'taken-for-granted', which by the power of description is not included. It can also be explained in a more formal manner: the political system is only able to view itself by hiding behind a difference that it cannot see. This difference appears to be + Adaptation /– Adaptation.

By the mid-1980s, the higher order system of the administrative policy seems to have the Ministry of Finance as the absolute centre. Today, a long line of organizations has been built that refer to the administrative policy and have arrogated to themselves rights to observe and describe the rest of the public institutions. Today, we find municipal and state organizations on all levels and in all sectors, which subscribe to the same semantics of administrative policy and arrogate to themselves the rights of an observer to make everybody else the object of observation. This includes, for example, financial secretariats, offices of organizational development, management, and personnel divisions, and then, of course, organizations such as the National Association of Municipalities (KL)[6] and the Forum of Personnel Policy,[7] which, very much like the Ministry of Finance, view the administrative policy as a central battlefield in the general struggle concerning the public sector's future. They all seek to take a step up as communication about communication, and they wish to install an asymmetry in the political system between the observer and the observed. In this sense, the higher order system of the administrative policy is a polycentric system and the power connected with a higher order's reflective position is dispersed (Andersen, N. Å., 1995; Andersen and Born 2000).

However, the Ministry of Finance still assumes an exceptional position among many of the organizations in the field of administrative policy. This is partly because the Ministry of Finance has also arrogated to itself the right of observing, describing, and ascribing by making general guidelines for personnel policies, legal frames for new wages, and of being a part of the negotiation process in all state contract agencies and so forth (Andersen, N. Å., 1995, p. 210ff.). Again, we have to remind ourselves that every single observation is an indication within the frame of a difference. The observations we ascribe to the Ministry of Finance, and the observations the Ministry of Finance ascribes to itself, do not express any particular sovereign subject, but as any other observations they are connected with a difference; in this case with the difference + Adaptation /– Adaptation. As any other observer, the Ministry of Finance does not realize that it cannot see what it cannot possibly see. Furthermore, even though the Ministry of Finance and others have arrogated to themselves the right to observe, describe, and prescribe the public sector, the Ministry of Finance does not observe from a position where it can represent 'the unity.' First, one part of the public sector is placed outside of that particular public sector, which is the object of observation, in order to enable the observation. We have already discussed this subject. Secondly, the political system of communication divides itself into subsystems all the time, which all distinguish between the system and the environment. If the world is the unity of the system and the environment and if the political system of communication divides itself into subsystems all the time, then there are *many* political worlds. The political system's environment is in this way polycontextual and therefore cannot be represented in any kind of unity. The Ministry of Finance and others are able to construct 'the public sector' as its own internal environment (through descriptions), but it will never be able to make a representation that corresponds to the polycentric and polycontextual political system. The Ministry of Finance, the financial secretariats, and others have, for their own advantage, to constantly put aside 'the many worlds' with the risk of being reduced to 'noise' instead of meaning in the observed parts, and with the risk of causing serious interruptions in the observed systems.

Thus, the semantics of the administrative policy enable the subsystems in the political system to break away and arrogate to themselves rights as observers of the rest, who then become observed. But even though the administrative policy's semantic supplies forms of meaning that can frame the difference politics/administration, the semantic does not change the fact that all political communication has to refer to the difference politics/administration and that it has to unfold the paradox of the re-entry. This way, the subsystems (the Ministry of Finance, financial secretariats, and so on), which subscribe to the semantic of the administrative policy mark the administration side themselves as the side from where they observe and conduct politics. Even though the administrative policy specifically enables the political system to be reflective about the relation politics/administration, administrative policy is defined as a political fact in the arrangement of the relation politics/ administration. How the emergence of the administrative policy itself changes the relation politics/administration and especially the 'game' concerning the relation is not discussed. Here too, the re-entry paradox is unfolded: only by defining the political, which means avoiding the perception that administrative policy is political politics, can the administrative policy avoid the administrative policy's relation to the political becoming politicized as well.

When observing how the administration has been able to create limits for politics, it is tempting to conclude that the difference politics/administration has been cancelled. In order to claim this, one would claim also that the power of the State can be conquered again via the state apparatus. That would be claiming that in reality democracy is cancelled. That is not the case, however. As never before, references are made to the difference politics/administration. Previously, the difference politics/administration was made by structural ties. The political aspect would, for example, exist all the time as an external structure in a civil servant's career. From the perspective of the individual communication, the difference appeared to be given externally. Before, the difference politics/administration was an external tie to, for example, the administrative communication. Now, the difference has been moved into the administration, so that it is no longer perceived as an external structure, but, on the contrary, exists in every single administrative communication, which includes any administrative ruling as a question that has to be settled constantly. Now, one does not automatically land on the administration side of the difference politics/administration just because one enters a civil servant's career. Regardless of where one is situated, one can fall on either side. The administration can no longer take it for granted that the administrative decision it makes is not a political decision. The administration can no longer politicize under the cover of a wealth of administrative prescriptions and routines. Not even the more or less court-like administrations, such as the Refugee Tribunal, can make political decisions concerning asylum under the cover of administrative objectivity, but is instead constantly forced to consider whether it is concerned with politics or administration. That does not cancel the difference politics/administration, but it increases the tension concerning where the difference is made. Even administrative arguments, which are accepted as administrational arguments, contain the constant insecurity that the administrative argumentation is rhetoric covering over politics in reality. The structural characteristics of the difference has been deconstructed from within the political system itself and possesses the character of an inner dynamic instead.

## Notes

1. For further discussion and comparison of these strategies of analysis with other discursive strategies of analysis see: Andersen, N. Å , 2003b.
2. Torstein Haaland, for example, argues that Norway during the nineteenth century 'had two different systems – a political and an administrative one – marked by two different kinds of rationality or "logic"' (Haaland, 1998, pp. 162–77).
3. 'Den Danske Statsforvaltningsret.'
4. 'Om Afgørelsen Af Tvistigheder Med Forvaltninger, Særlig Om Administrative Retter.'
5. Teknikerkommissionen [Commission of Technicians] (1959) 'Teknisk og naturvidenskabelig arbejdskraft', *Betænkning nr. 229* [Technical and Scientific Working Capacity, *Report nb. 229*; in Danish only], Copenhagen. For further examination of the conflict between the Administrative Tribunal, the Labour Market Commission and the Commission of Technicians see Andersen, N. Å. (1995), pp. 50–3 (only in Danish).
6. KL is a non-governmental organization representing the municipalities. KL has been given the competence to negotiate with the State on behalf of the united municipalities in relation to a long list of subjects; for example, level of municipal taxation and municipal budget frames. Furthermore, KL is an import organization concerning policy formulation in a large number of subject areas that concern the municipalities.
7. The Personnel Political Forum is a policy institution that consists of KL, the Association of Counties (ARF, which is an equivalent to the KL at county level), and the umbrella organization for public employees. It formulates general strategies of personnel policy, initiates projects, and organizes discussions.

## Bibliogaphy


Administrationsdepartementet (1982) *Beretning 1980*, Copenhagen.

The Administrative Committee of 1923 [Administrationskommissionen af 1923] (1924) *2. betænkning*, Copenhagen.

The Administrative Commission of 1946 [Forvaltningskommissionen af 1946] (1950) *2. betænkning*, Copenhagen.

The Administrative Committee of 1960 [Administrationsudvalget af 1960] (1962a) '1. betænkning', *Betænkning nr. 301*, Copenhagen.

The Administrative Committee of 1960 [Administrationsudvalget af 1960] (1962b) '2. betænkning: Administration af Arbejds- og Sociallovgivningen, 1. del', *Betænkning nr. 320*, Copenhagen.

The Administrative Committee of 1960 [Administrationsudvalget af 1960] (1963) '3. betænkning: Administration af Told- og forbrugslovgivningen', *Betænkning nr. 342*, Copenhagen.

The Administrative Committee of 1960 [Administrationsudvalget af 1960] (1965) '4. betænkning: Administration af Arbejds- og Sociallovgivningen, 2. del', *Betænkning nr. 380*, Copenhagen.

The Administrative Committee of 1960 [Administrationsudvalget af 1960] (1966) '5. betænkning: Revisionsdepartementernes og hovedrevisionens forhold', *Betænkning nr. 408*, Copenhagen.

Andersen, N. Å. (1995) *Selvskabt forvaltning: Forvaltningspolitikken og centralforvaltningens udvikling i Danmark 1900–1994* (Copenhagen, Nyt fra Samfundsvidenskaberne).

Andersen, N. Å. (1997) *Udlicitering – strategi og historie* (Copenhagen, Nyt fra Samfundsvidenskaberne).

Andersen, N. Å. (2000) 'Public Market – Political Firm', *Acta Sociologica* vol. 43 (1): 43–63.

Andersen, N. Å. (2003a) 'The Undecidability of Decision', in Bakken and Hernes (eds), *Autopoietic Organization Theory* (Oslo, Abstrakt forlag).

Andersen, N. Å. (2003b) *Discursive Analytical Strategies – Foucault, Koselleck, Laclau, Luhmann* (Bristol, Policy Press).

Andersen, N. Å., and Born, A. (2000) 'Complexity and Change: Two 'Semantic Tricks' in the Triumphant Oscillating Organization', *System Practice and Action Research* vol. 13 (3).

Andersen, N. Å., and Born, A. (2001) *Kærlighed og omstilling: Italesættelsen af den offentligt ansatte* (Copenhagen, Nyt fra Samfundsvidenskaberne).

Andersen, P. (1924) *Om ugyldige Forvaltningsakter med særligt Henblik paa Ugyldighedsgrunde* [On Invalid Administrative Documents with Special Reference to Sources of Invalidity] (Copenhagen, Arnold Buscks Forlag).

Andersen, P. (1943) 'Politik og forvaltning', *Nordisk Administrativt Tidsskrift.*

Bredsdorff, J. (1951) 'Rationaliseringsarbejdet indenfor stat og kommuner', in Hjort-Nielsen and Mikkelsen (eds), *Kommunal Aarbog 1951* (Copenhagen).

Bredsdorff, N. (1996) 'Forvaltningshistorie og forvaltningsvidenskab – en undersøgelse af efterkrigsårenes forvaltningshistorie og Forvaltningskommissionen af 1946', Ph.D.-afhandling, Roskilde Universitetscenter.

Clark, J., and Newman, J. (1997) *The Managerial State* (London, SAGE Publications).

Christensen, B. (1953) *Forvaltningskommissionen og Forvaltningsnævnet: Mål og midler* (Copenhagen, Nordisk Administrativt Tidsskrift).

Derrida, J. (1978), 'Structure, Sign and Play in the Discourse of Human Science', in Derrida (ed.), *Writing and Difference* (Chicago, The University of Chicago Press).

Günther, G. (1976) *Beiträge zur Grundlegung einer operationsfähigen Dialectic* (Hamburg, Felix Meiner Verlag).

Haaland, T. (1998) *Seculum Primum – den norske sentraladministrasjonens første århundre 1814–ca. 1900*, i Nordisk Administrativt Tidsskrift, Jurist og Økonomforbundets forlag, Copenhagen, nr. 2, pp. 162–77.

Holck, C. G. (1870) *Den Danske Statsforvaltningsret* [The Danish State's Administrative Law] (Copenhagen, Forlaget af Den Gyldensdalske Boghandel).

Jensen, B. B. (1987) *Udnævnelsesretten i enevældens magtpolitiske system 1660–1730*, Administrationshistoriske studier nr. 12, Rigsarkivet, G. E. C. Gads Forlag, København.

Luhmann, N. (1990) *Political Theory in the Welfare State* (New York, WdeG).

Luhmann, N. (1993a) 'Observing Re-entries', *Graduate Faculty Philosophy Journal*, vol. 16 (2).

Luhmann, N. (1993b) *Gesellschaftsstruktur und Semantik*, Band 1 (Suhrkamp, Frankfurt am Main).

Luhmann, N. (1993c) 'Die Paradoxie des Entscheidens i Verwaltungs-Archiv: Zeitschrift für Verwaltungslehre, *Verwaltungsrecht und Verwaltungspolitik*, 84 Band, heft 3, pp. 287–99.

Luhmann, N. (1995) *Social Systems* (Stanford, Stanford University Press).

Luhmann, N. (1999) 'The Paradox of Form', in Baecker, D. (ed.), *Problems of Form* (California, Stanford University Press).

Luhmann, N. (2002) 'Deconstruction as Second-order Observing', in Luhmann, N., *Theories of Distinction* (California, Stanford University Press).

Ministry of Employment [Arbejdsministeriet] (1971) *Perspektivplanlægning 1970–1985* (Copenhagen).

Minister of Finance [Finansministeren] (1983) *Redegørelse af 30/11 83 om regeringens program for modernisering af den offentlige sektor*, Redegørelse nr. R 4, Folketingstidende: 2379–92.

Ministry of Finance [Finansministeriet] (1993) *Nyt syn på den offentlige sektor* (Copenhagen).

The Planning Information Committee [Planinformationsudvalget] (1984), *Al den planlægning – hvordan og hvorfor? Planredegørelse 3* (Copenhagen, Finansministeriet).

Sachs, A. (1925) *Forholdet mellem lovgivningsmagten og administrationen*, Nordisk Administrativt Tidsskrift, pp. 217–77.

Skjerbæk, O. J. (1925) *Anmeldelse*, Nordisk Administrativt Tidsskrift Copenhagen, pp. 77–88.

Spencer-Brown, G. (1969) *Laws of Form* (London, George Allen and Unwin).

Stäheli, U. (2000) *Sinnzusammenbrüche: Eine dekonstruktive lektüre von Niklas Luhmanns Systemtheorie* (Weilerswist, Velbrück Wissenschaft).

Teknikerkommissionen (1959) 'Teknisk og naturvidenskabelig arbejdskraft', *Betænkning nr. 229*, Copenhagen.

Thygesen, I. (1980) 'Flerniveau-planlægning af det offentliges udgiftspolitik', *Indlæg på Nationaløkonomisk Forenings konference om Økonomisk planlægning*, vol. 3 (9).

Ussing, J. (1893) *Om Afgørelsen Af Tvistigheder Med Forvaltningen, Særlig Om Administrative Retter* [Concerning Determination of Disputes with the Administration, Especially concerning Administrative Laws] (Copenhagen, P. G. Philipsens Forlag).

Von Foerster, J. (1981) *Observing Systems* (Seadside, CA, Intersystems Publication).

# 6

# The Human Rights Act: Politics, Power, and the Law

*Anthony M. Clohesy*

## Introduction

In 1998, the Human Rights Act (HRA),[1] which incorporated the European Convention of Human Rights (ECHR) into British law, was passed by the United Kingdom Parliament, giving British citizens a form of protection taken for granted in virtually every Commonwealth country and Western democracy (Dyer, *The Guardian*, 12 November 1998). The Act, which some have argued is the most important constitutional development in Britain since the signing of the Magna Carta, is intended to deliver 'a modern reconciliation to the inevitable tension between the democratic right of the majority to exercise political power and the democratic need of individuals and minorities to have their human rights secured' (Klug, Singh, and Hunt, 1997, p. 2). Anyone living within the jurisdiction of the UK, regardless of citizenship or nationality, can claim the protection of the convention. If one is a victim, in other words, if one's rights have been or would be violated by a public authority, one can bring proceedings in any court or tribunal in the land. Provided someone can show that they are 'personally affected' by the decisions or actions of a public body they can bring a case for judicial review on convention grounds alone (Klug, Singh, and Hunt, 1997, p. 3).

At first sight, this legislation represents something of an oddity in British politics in that it implies a significant shift of power from the executive.[2] Although, at the time of writing, the New Labour Government is keen to present itself as a modernizing force, committed to democratizing the British state, the evidence so far suggests that behind this apparent reformist zeal lurks a deeply conservative and centralizing instinct. Witness, for example, the initiatives of devolution, reform of the House of Lords, and the Freedom of Information Act. All of these can and have been interpreted as the government using change as a means of maintaining or enhancing its own power. However, although prior to the HRA the courts wielded considerable power by means of judicial review, the relationship that now exists between the executive and the judiciary is quite different:

> The unequivocal requirement that all public authorities comply with the Convention means that present restraints on the judicial review of the actions or decisions of officials will no longer apply. Currently these can only be overturned on grounds of illegality, procedural impropriety or what is known as Wednesbury irrationality, where a decision is so outrageous in its defiance of logic or accepted moral standards that in the court's view no sensible person could have arrived at it. Now it is the Government's stated intention that this will change. This means that it is expected that the courts will import the 'doctrine of proportionality' in reviewing whether restrictions on fundamental rights are justiciable or not. Even if such restrictions are deemed rational (in the Wednesbury sense) they will be liable to be overturned if they are not aimed at meeting a pressing social need and are not proportionate to the aim of meeting that need. This is what is meant by the requirement in many articles in the Convention that limitations on rights must be 'necessary in a democratic society'. (Klug, Singh, and Hunt, 1997, p. 4)

This shift towards what Lord Hoffman has called a 'bipolar sovereignty' does not, however, follow the Canadian example. Here the courts can overturn Acts of Parliament unless that legislation is passed, by means of the 'notwithstanding clause', in specific defiance of the Charter of Rights.[3] Nor does it adhere to the New Zealand model where the courts have little formal power. Here, where legislation cannot be reconciled with the Bill of Rights, the courts are bound to uphold the legislation and there is no further consideration of the case.[4] The key to understanding the uniqueness of the British system is in the procedure known as the 'declaration of incompatibility'. If a court decides that it cannot interpret legislation as compatible with convention rights then a declaration will be made and a special fast track procedure can then follow to allow the government to make the necessary legislative amendments.[5] However, crucially, because there is no formal obligation for Parliament to accede, its sovereignty is preserved.[6] The new situation has been summarized as follows:

> The Human Rights Act does not, therefore, give the judiciary the power to overrule 'inconsistent' Acts of Parliament but it does give the judges new responsibilities to protect and respect Convention rights in the domestic courts. The act makes it unlawful for the courts, as public bodies, to act incompatibly with Convention rights. It also requires that judges interpret and give effect to primary and secondary legislation, as far as possible, in a way that it is compatible with Convention rights. If legislation cannot be read in a manner compatible with the Convention, the higher courts can make a 'declaration of incompatibility' which may prompt the Government and Parliament to change the law. (Croft, 2000, p. 44)

## Introduction of the HRA: competing interpretations

In this chapter, I argue that discourse theory allows for a critical examination of what I consider to be one of the central questions surrounding this development, namely, why a Labour government, traditionally sceptical about the value of rights-based approaches to politics, introduced the HRA in the first place. This question is intriguing when one considers that there was no public clamouring for it. Indeed, from the outset, there was significant opposition to it. Prince Charles, for example, in a letter to the Lord Chancellor, expressed his concern that the Act posed a serious threat to a sane, civilized, and ordered existence (Klug, *The Guardian*, 3 October 2002). Within sections of the legal profession there was, from the outset, open hostility. Lord McCluskey, for example, commented that the HRA represents a 'field day for crackpots, a pain in the neck for judges and a goldmine for lawyers' (Travis and Dyer, *The Guardian*, 11 September 2000). Lord Denning was equally critical:

> it is framed in a style that is quite contrary to anything to which we are accustomed. There are broad statements of principle and broad statements of exception ... which are so broad that they are capable of giving rise to an infinity of argument ... that are so general that they will give rise to a multitude of cases. (Betten and Grief, 1998, p. 32)

Within much of the right-wing press a marked scepticism was similarly evident. The *Daily Mail*, for example, condemned the measure as a 'criminals' charter', more proof, if it were needed, that the government remained more concerned with protecting the rights of the guilty than those of the innocent. The opposition of the Conservative Party was partly informed by its instinctive belief that Britain's 'anti-rationalist' (or uncodified) constitution remains the most apposite arrangement for dealing with the exigencies and contingencies of politics. The more specific argument from this quarter, however, was summarized by ex-Home Secretary Michael Howard, who said that 'balancing individual rights against the exercise of power on behalf of the community at large often involved difficult judgements better made by politicians accountable to voters than by unelected judges who cannot be dismissed' (Travis and Dyer, *The Guardian*, 11 September 2000). This is a serious point about which there is widespread concern beyond the Conservative Party and I return to a discussion of it at the end of this chapter. Indeed, from within the judiciary itself there was little desire to usurp the role of Parliament in this regard. The important constitutional issue at stake here has been summarized as follows:

> We could therefore have a situation where there is increased impetus to develop the common law without the sense of illegitimacy that at present accompanies significant changes unapproved by Parliament. This will decrease the legal and political capacity of Parliament to exercise its

theoretical sovereignty by passing legislation that can decisively override common law developments. (Campbell, 1999, p. 25)

This anxiety goes some way to explaining the ambivalence to the HRA that exists within sections of the Labour Party. However, there is a more fundamental source of opposition to the HRA from within this constituency. This has been summarized as follows:

> Where human rights are asserted, they are asserted as claims by *individuals* and against the power of the *state*, or against other individuals. But to assume that rights are needed against the state is to assume that there must always be antagonism between the interests of the state and the interests of individuals and this is a denial of the kind of ideal society envisaged by socialism and communitarianism alike. (Mendus, 1995, p. 12)

Yet, despite these reservations, the government remained determined to get the HRA onto the statute book. The official justification for the HRA is that it was introduced to promote an authentic rights culture. Times had changed and, from a moral or ethical perspective, it was simply considered to be the right thing to do. It is important to remember, however, that from the beginning the government message was that rights had to be considered in the context of duties. This remains explicit within all government statements given at the time. Consider, for example, the following:

> [T]he rights we enjoy reflect the duties we owe; rights and opportunities without responsibility are engines of selfishness and greed. Human nature is co-operative as well as competitive, selfless as well as self-interested; and society could not function if it were otherwise . . . all our lives are enriched or impoverished by the communities to which we belong. (Blair, 1998, p. 4)

> [B]uilding a true human rights culture means much more than legal rights you can enforce in the UK courts. It means learning to understand and accept personal responsibilities and the rights of others in the community. (Straw, 27 October 1999)

> [R]ights flow from duties – not the other way round. One person's freedom is another person's responsibility. And the Convention – and the Act – contains many rights that have to be carefully balanced – one with another. (Straw, 18 May 1999)

There is, however, another way of understanding the introduction of the HRA. This does not see it as issuing from a normative concern about promoting rights and duties but as part of a carefully calculated strategy to enhance the power of the government and enable it to achieve other objectives. Considered from this perspective, the important theoretical context is not norms but instrumentality. How might such a 'cost-benefit' analysis deepen our understanding of this issue? Well, it is clear that the HRA offered a range of potential benefits to the government. Consider, for example, that incorporation significantly reduced the number of high profile and highly embarrassing cases being brought before the Strasbourg authorities. The resultant rebukes from the European Court of Human Rights were not only damaging to Britain's reputation. It could be argued that they also had the effect of further alienating the British public from the project of closer European integration. Although the ECHR was established by the Council of Europe and has, therefore, nothing to do with the European Union, it may well have been felt that such a catalogue of negative findings from this body was reinforcing the British public's negative attitude to 'all things European'. This would not have been seen as conducive to the government's broader federalist aims.

Consider also that the HRA could be seen as bolstering rather than hindering New Labour's electoral prospects:

> Cabinet secrecy means that it will be many years before we can discover precisely the political considerations which finally tilted the balance in favour of incorporation... [However], incorporating the Convention is more likely to disembowel the Adam Smith ship of state than New Labour's flotilla. (Clements, 1999, p. 83)

In this context we can understand ex-government minister Peter Mandelson's observation that the essential rationale of the HRA was to preclude any future attack on New Labour's willingness to sacrifice individual rights on the altar of collectivist ideology (Mandelson and Liddle, 1996, p. 196). Consider also that the government remained confident that, in addition to these benefits, it could limit any adverse effects of the new legislation. For example, 'Section 19' of the HRA obliges the government to confirm that all legislation passing through Parliament is 'HRA-friendly'. This gives grounds for supposing that a genuine rights climate may now emerge. However, according to rights group Liberty, this is a procedure open to widespread abuse:

> The government's approach to Section 19 statements significantly reduces its usefulness. In assessing whether a particular provision complies with the Act, those advising the Government assume that all those public authorities that have to implement the provision will act in compliance with the Convention if they have the power to do so. So for instance a Bill that gave wide discretion to the police to act in ways which would clearly violate the Convention would still be assessed as complying with the Convention because the discretion given to the police would be constrained by the Human Rights Act... [T]his approach to Section 19 ousts Parliament's role in ensuring that legislation complies with the Act.

> Instead of Parliament having the duty to ensure that legislation complies with the Convention the duty is left with those who have to implement the legislation and to the courts if they get it wrong. (Wadham, 2001, pp. 3–4)

However, the most damning analysis of the government's normative pretensions comes from Luke Clements who regards the HRA as a cynical attempt to bolster government power. He points, for example, to how, under the HRA, the domestic courts can ignore European Court precedent whenever it suits them, a practice known as 'Strasbourg-proofing' – paying lip-service to fundamental freedoms but coming to the same reactionary common law conclusions (Clements, 1999, p. 77). In fact, the 'margin of appreciation' is an established mechanism whereby a national judiciary can defer from legal precedent set by the European Court on the grounds that doing otherwise would offend national sensitivities or interests. This means that the Strasbourg institutions have to be sensitive to the 'need for subsidiarity, ensuring that the member states' own political and cultural traditions are respected. For example, what may offend religious sensitivities in one country may be deemed an essential aspect of free speech in another' (Wadham and Mountfield, 2000, p. 22).

Clements also claims that the government's refusal to set up a Human Rights Commission to promote rights awareness was a cynical ploy to keep people as ignorant as possible about how they can claim their rights. In addition, he draws our attention to how tight restrictions on the provision of legal aid will dramatically limit litigants' access to the courts. Finally, he asserts that the requirement that any prospective plaintiff be a 'victim' amounts to a severe and entirely unjustified restriction of *locus standi*. In conclusion he states that:

> The Human Rights Act provides the state with a number of politically symbolic benefits and imparts an intellectual rigour to the reform agenda that at times has appeared lacking. It has, however, all the hallmarks of an opiate; it appeases the intellectual 'Charter 88' elite clamouring for constitutional reform and diverts attention from the new government's failure to 'open up the state' and its abandonment of a radical Freedom of Information Act. 'New Labour' has gone native: the Establishment has created a new and subtle ideological discourse ensuring its continued vitality. (Clements, 1999, p. 85)

This is a compelling criticism of the government's claim that its motivation for introducing the HRA reflected moral concerns and a desire to promote an authentic rights culture. While not implying that morality has *no* explanatory value, it suggests, rather, that the HRA should be understood in a Downsian rather than a Kantian context. Thus, from this perspective, criticisms of the HRA, such as those of Clements, would undoubtedly have been anticipated and weighed against the benefits the legislation would offer. However, an important question remains, namely, how far can instrumentalist approaches such as this deepen our understanding of the wider politics of the HRA? To examine the matter further let me consider the HRA in the historical context of the first, second, and third waves of rights.

## 'Generations' and 'waves' of rights

The 'tripartite' conceptualization of rights is normally associated with T. H. Marshall. He famously argued that the development of citizenship in England proceeded with the establishment of civil rights in the early nineteenth century, for example, those rights necessary for the freedom of the individual, such as the right to free speech and the right to own property. This was followed by the slow evolution throughout the nineteenth century and early twentieth century of political rights culminating in universal political citizenship in 1918. Social rights by contrast were, he argues, the last to be realized. By social rights Marshall refers to the 'whole range from the right to a modicum of economic welfare and security to the right to share to the full in the social heritage and to live the life of a civilized being according to the standards prevailing in the society' (Marshall, 1992, p. 8). This way of understanding rights in terms of 'generations' is criticized by contemporary rights theorists, such as Francesca Klug, who argue that it creates too rigid a distinction between different forms of rights. Thus, she argues that the upholding of *negative* civil liberties invariably required the state to do more than merely leave people alone. In the instance of the right to a fair trial, for example, it was necessary for the state to take a range of positive steps to uphold rights such as spending money on a criminal justice system (Klug, 2001, pp. 362–3). This is an important argument because it allows us to blur the overly neat distinction between the different generations of rights implicit in approaches such as that of Marshall. Klug's argument, by contrast, is that rather than thinking of rights in the context of generations, it is more appropriate to consider them in the context of 'waves'. This allows for a more subtle appreciation of the complexity and dynamism involved in the evolution of rights thinking in the post-Enlightenment period. For the purposes of my argument here, however, Klug's work is important as it makes possible a more nuanced theoretical insight into the specifically contingent nature of the relationship between rights, duties, and responsibilities. This, as I shall show, allows us to see more clearly the limitations of the instrumentalist approach to the HRA.

First wave accounts are usually associated with the 1789 'Declaration of the Rights of Man' in France and the 1791 'Bill of Rights' in the United States of America. The inspiration of these documents is the Enlightenment idea that individuals are endowed with natural rights that have to be protected from state tyranny and religious persecution. Within these documents, however, we find an implicit appeal to the notion of duty:

> A rousing Preamble to the French Declaration demanded that it be a 'perpetual reminder of both rights and duties'. Tom Paine, the English radical who witnessed the French Revolution, tells us that the issue of rights and responsibilities was addressed by members of the French Assembly in terms not unfamiliar to today's debate. (Klug, 2000, p. 23)

However, it was not long before the natural law legacy articulated by Locke, Paine, Voltaire, and Rousseau was challenged by, among others, Bentham, Burke, and Marx. Marx's criticism is important and can be summarized as follows:

> None of the so-called rights of man . . . go beyond egoistic man, beyond man as a member of civil society, that is, an individual withdrawn into himself, into the confines of his private interests and private caprice and separated from the community. In the rights of man . . . society appears as a framework external to the individual, as a restriction of their original independence. The sole bond holding them together is natural necessity, need and private interest, the preservation of their property and their egoistic selves. (Marx, 1843, p. 43)

These two conceptions of rights, what we might call the individualist and collectivist versions, competed with each other until the end of the Second World War when the idea of the individual with inalienable rights emerged considerably the stronger. However, this did not persuade the authors of the United Nations Charter to include a rights-based treaty within its terms. This omission was partly rectified by the signing of the United Nations Declaration of Human Rights (UNDHR) in 1948.[7] The UNDHR, though non-binding, has been hugely influential and has been described as 'truly the mother and father of all second-wave rights documents' (Klug, 2000, p. 96). What distinguishes it from the natural law tradition is its articulation of rights in negative *and* positive terms.[8] Francesca Klug has observed that this shift signifies how the notions of 'dignity, equality and community' replaced the idea that the foundation of rights was God or nature (Klug, 2000, p. 101). This change is most evident in Article 29 of the UNDHR. This states that 'everyone has duties to the community in which alone the free and full development of his personality is possible'. The gradual shift from first to second waves of rights receives its clearest articulation in the following:

> In essence the transition from the first to the second wave of rights is represented by a shift from a preoccupation with the rights and liberties of individual citizens within particular nation states to a preoccupation with creating a better world for everyone. Both waves were aimed at protecting individuals from tyranny but the vision of how to achieve that goal had shifted. In the earlier era the main target was to set people free; in the later period it was to create a sense of moral purpose for all humankind.

> Since this time, the struggle for human rights has in large measure been a quest to create a better world for everyone. (Klug, 2001, p. 364)

However, within the international body responsible for drawing up the UNDHR, there was considerable disagreement over this thorny issue of *how* the relationship between rights and duties should be theorized. The eventual decision not to enumerate duties in the UNDHR meant that, by strong implication, responsibilities were presented as flowing from the rights upheld. One of the interesting questions Klug and others are now examining is whether, with the HRA, Britain has moved into a *third wave* in which rights, having been freed from the intellectually stifling and politically constrained environments of the second wave era, can assume a new cultural and political significance. Klug is optimistic that we may be witnessing the emergence of this new era:

> Whilst there is still the same recognition of the values of dignity, equality and community as in the second wave (and liberty, autonomy and justice in the first) there is now a growing emphasis on participation or mutuality. In legal terms the net of liability is spreading ever wider under international human rights law. Corporations, charities and even private individuals in some circumstances are increasingly held responsible for upholding the rights of others. (Klug, 2001, p. 369)

The essence of Klug's argument here is that the HRA paves the way for a new legal and political culture in which rights are at the centre of a new and more inclusive dialogue between government, Parliament, and the courts. This culture of deliberation is at the heart of what she terms the third wave, which in time promises an even wider debate within society about how to proceed in the event of rights colliding or rights and duties clashing with each other. As she notes: 'this is different from the second wave approach that tends to assume that this is the concern only of judges or UN enforcement bodies' (Klug, 2001, p. 370). However, there is a considerable obstacle preventing such a transition, namely, New Labour's stated objective of integrating rights into a 'third-*way*' discourse of *reciprocity* that seeks to link rights even *more* closely to duty and responsibility. More specifically, what we find in this third-way formulation is the idea that it is only after the satisfactory performance of duty that rights can be claimed. This has been most evident in the debate about work. New Labour's approach to this issue is that, if able, everyone has a responsibility to work that, if neglected, will rightfully result in the foregoing of any right or entitlement to welfare benefits. This is one of the reasons why advocates of the third wave are concerned about the government's particular fixing of the relationship between duties and rights. They argue that if this new discursive configuration, which privileges duty over rights, is successful it will be even more difficult to achieve their central aims, to put rights centre stage and to ensure a more open and democratic debate. However, Klug remains sanguine about this development as she sees these attempts as *part* of the new dialogue. In any event such judgements are subject to the wider provision in the HRA, that you can only 'lose those rights that are necessary to protect the rights of others and the broader community. Furthermore, if rights are limited for those reasons, this must happen in a proportionate way to meet a legitimate aim in a democratic society' (Klug, 2001, p. 371).

## Methodological considerations: the value of a discourse theory approach

Now, let me return here to the question of methodology. It could be argued that this narrative is quite within the explanatory range of a cost-benefit, or instrumentalist, methodological approach. Thus, the government articulated a new rights/duty relationship precisely to promote a particular ideological agenda. In other words, it was calculated that the communitarian/third-way philosophy favoured by the 'Christian-Right' within the New Labour hierarchy could best be achieved by integrating it into a discourse of rights. This would have the benefit of appeasing the rights lobby at the same time as effectively neutralizing its potentially destabilizing agenda. Viewed from this perspective, the purpose of the HRA was the promotion of *duty* at the *expense* of rights. This, in my view, may be to put the matter too strongly. However, it allows us to appreciate the sentiment, shared by many who would not be natural New Labour supporters, that society works best when the claiming of rights is understood in the context of community and responsibility.

However, whatever the political merits of this argument, there is a methodological problem here, namely, that the focus on instrumentality, in which the rational, calculating subject emerges as the primary independent variable, deflects our attention from a number of other important dimensions of this debate. My argument here is that attempts to answer 'why questions' or, more specifically, attempts to provide explanations about *why* a particular strategy emerged have to be considered in a broader theoretical context examining *how* such a strategy became *possible* in the first place. In order to consider this in more detail let me examine the above 'three waves' narrative detailing the successive decontestations[9] to the rights/duties relationship in the context of discourse theory. In Laclau and Mouffe's seminal 1985 text, *Hegemony and Socialist Strategy*, they argue that all claims to identity are predicated on what they term a 'constitutive outside'. This is, they claim, the condition of possibility *and* impossibility for the production of meaning. It makes meaning possible because identity requires the presence of something other than itself in order for it to be intelligible. Yet, at the same time it forbids the prospect of transparency or closure. Why? Because of the same stipulation that identity must always rely on something outside of itself, on something, literally, other than itself. If this is the case, then all claims to positivity or universality are immediately subverted. This is because the identity of a structure can never be fully present to itself if it requires supplementation from outside. From the perspective of discourse theory, structure can thus be understood as a non-totalizable openness that requires a decision to inscribe a decidable hierarchy through acts of power. The significance of this for my argument can be understood more clearly by examining it in the context of Derrida's 'infrastructure of iterability'. Gasche has summarized this as follows:

> Repetition thus hinges on the *structural* possibility of an absence of the repeated. If the unit to be repeated were totally present and present to itself, if it were not breached by a certain lack of plenitude, no repetition could ever occur. This absence, however, is not to be understood as a continuous and ontological modification of presence. It is not the absent presence of a full plenitude, of a once or, at one time self-present presence; it is an absence owing not to an empirically effective and hence accidental occurrence of absence but, on the contrary, to the *possibility* of being absent. This possibility, as Derrida has argued in 'Signature, Event, Context' and even more powerfully in 'Limited Inc', is what breaches and divides the plenitude or self-presence of even the most unique and singular event. (Gasche, 1986, p. 213)

Let me try to unpack this rather dense formulation to show how it is relevant to my argument. Derrida's argument is that signifiers can be repeated because their meaning is, and can never be, exhausted. They are, therefore, always subject to rearticulation into other contexts. However, when this rearticulation happens, the meaning of the signifier is modified. This is because meaning is only intelligible in the context of a particular system of differences. Thus, when the context in which the sign appears changes, its meaning also changes. This has important implications for how we understand politics as it allows us to see that political identities and settlements, while appearing natural and necessary, are always the product of this wider system of differences. How is this related to power? The important point here is that the integration of a signifier into a new system of differences is always the result of a specific act of power that excludes other possible interpretations. This is the case whether the attempt to recast the terms of a debate is successful in hegemonic terms or not. This relates specifically to my argument about the introduction of the HRA. It is precisely because the meaning of the relationship between rights and duties is never, could ever, be exhausted that it is always possible (although not always easy) to recontextualize and reconfigure it. In other words, it is because the context in which meaning is derived is always the result of power that it is always then subject to the future exercise of power. More specifically, following the three-waves argument of Klug, it was because the terms of these particular waves were always fluid and precarious that they were always subject to new political attempts to reconfigure them.

It is in this specific sense that I make the argument that any attempt to create a broader understanding of the reasons why the government chose to introduce the HRA has to be understood in terms of *how* that act of reconfiguration was possible in the first place.

Sceptical voices may still want to argue that this adds little to our understanding of the central issue at stake here, namely, that the government introduced the HRA to further its interests and that this must remain the cornerstone of our approach to it. As I have argued, it is important that we remember the realist dimension in our understanding of political action. However, to paraphrase Marx, it is also important to remember that although states pursue their interests relentlessly they do not do so in conditions of their own making. It *is* important, therefore, to understand action in a broader framework that allows us to see interests and action outside the context of an originary subject position. By addressing the question of *how* the rearticulation of the terms of earlier waves of rights was possible it is clear that the rationalist approach to understanding the *why* question (for example, that the HRA can be explained solely in instrumentalist terms) is problematized.

This is because an examination of the 'how question' allows us to see that, because interests, rights, and duties (and the relationship between them) are so saturated with power and contingency, an instrumentalist conception of the subject claiming and exercising them simply cannot stand alone as a reliable starting point, much less a foundation, for political analysis and research. In other words, we always have to take a *step back* from the subject as the site of the articulation of interests. However, once this is done, all we find are yet more complexes of power, all equally beyond any rationalist process of disentangling. It is in this sense that the how and why questions become less and less distinct, almost interchangeable, to the extent that one cannot be addressed outside the context of the other.

To repeat, this is important because it means that politics has to be understood in a context that does not reduce, or imply the reduction, of action to a fully constituted, sovereign subject. Rather, while recognizing the realist dimension of politics, which does not, incidentally, imply accepting the ontological and epistemological assumptions of rational choice theory, it is vital that we understand that the articulation of interests and the pursuit of political objectives and strategies is always internal to what Wittgenstein called a 'language game', a discursive recursivity in which neither the subject nor the socio-economic structures into which she is thrown is given any necessary priority. Failure to recognize this broader dimension will result in an impoverished understanding of political action.

Let me now move on from these broader questions of ontology and focus on how discourse theory can help us understand the politics of the HRA in a more concrete or empirical way. My argument thus far has been to show the value of discourse theory in terms of showing the implication of power and contingency in the *inception* of the strategy to introduce the HRA and in the inception of the strategy to oppose it. Thus, rather than understanding the respective interests served by these strategies as *given*, their dimension of temporality must be acknowledged. From here we can proceed to an examination of how a discourse theory methodology, uniquely, affords an understanding of how, once the decision to introduce the HRA had been made, the pro- and anti-HRA strategies were actually constructed. This focus on strategy will allow us to see how the tactics of the groups opposed to the introduction to the HRA differed from those of its advocates with both sides using subtly different rhetorical devices to persuade the wider public of the integrity of their respective interpretations of the legislation. On one side of the newly constituted hegemonic terrain, we find the opponents of the legislation arguing that the post-HRA situation would be characterized by, for example, administrative chaos, an erosion of the principle of precedent,[10] a culture of criminality, a deepening of the democratic deficit with the judiciary usurping the will of Parliament and the downgrading of community. It was specifically against the last of these charges that the government chose to focus its strategy. Thus, throughout the period of the passage of the HRA through Parliament, the government focused on the relationship between rights and duties. More specifically, it focused on how the HRA would lead, not to the diminution of duty, but to a strengthening of it.

We can get a sense of the general tone of government thinking in this regard by considering the following speeches from two leading cabinet ministers:

> The Act will create and promote a culture of human rights in Britain. It will make citizens more aware of their rights and make it much easier for them to enforce them... Of course with rights come responsibilities and the Act will encourage greater awareness of, and respect for, the rights of others. It will help to create a society in which rights and responsibilities are properly balanced. (G. Hoon, cited in Croft, 2000, p. 12)

> The culture of rights and responsibilities we need to build is not about giving the citizen a cudgel to beat the State. That's the old-fashioned individualistic libertarian idea that gave the whole rights movement a bad and selfish name. The idea that forgot that rights don't exist in a vacuum, that forgot about the relationship between the individual and the group. That's not the culture of rights and responsibilities we want or need. (J. Straw, cited in Croft, 2000, p. 12)

If the strategy of the opponents of the HRA was to link it with a range of negative consequences, the strategy of the government was to promote the view that it would lead to rights and duties interacting harmoniously. Once again, this would appear to be broadly consistent with a rational choice approach. Thus, we find the advocates and opponents of the legislation considering their tactics with a view to how their respective interests would be realized. So, even if the rational choice theorist is prepared to accept the constitutive nature of interests, she would still insist that action always entails adopting the most cost-efficient means to realize them. In other words, we always act rationally to achieve our interests irrespective of their ontological status. Now, at first sight this seems reasonable enough. However, it is problematic because of its implication that the means at our disposal can be ranked in an objective hierarchy, as most likely to produce the highest utility yield. The important point here is that, if our interests cannot be understood as given, neither can the means we adopt to realize them. What, for example, of those strategies that are considered unacceptable for one reason or another? The clear implication of this is that the formulation of any strategy is subject to a range of subjective assessments and judgements that simply cannot be dealt with by a rationalist methodology. In other words, the constitution of interests *and* the strategies utilized to realize them can only be understood in the context of discourse, power, and contingency.

One way to examine this in more detail is to consider the question of strategies in the context of the 'logic of equivalence' and the 'logic of difference'. The former works by establishing a discursive unity between disparate elements by positing the existence of a common threat. Thus, it is a logic that seeks to divide social space by the construction of frontiers, by 'condensing meaning around two antagonistic poles' (Howarth, 2000, p. 107). The logic of difference, conversely, seeks to break down frontiers separating these 'chains of equivalence' by 'incorporating disarticulated elements into the expanding formation' (Howarth, 2000, p. 107). This is important for our understanding of the politics of the HRA because the strategy of those opposed to it can be understood specifically in the context of the logic of equivalence. Thus, we see their attempt to depict rights and duties in a starkly antagonistic way. For the left, the government's emphasis on rights was presented as a betrayal of the socialist dream of a society in which interests coincided. From the right, the HRA was also seen as a threat to community. Here, however, the emphasis was on how it would lead to a breakdown of social and political order. The strategy of the government and the pro-HRA forces, in contrast, was precisely the opposite and can be understood more in the context of the logic of difference. Thus, its objective was to *weaken* the antagonism that existed between rights and duties by articulating them together in such as way as to make them appear as complementary rather than confrontational or contradictory. Certain interventions, however, would seem to incorporate elements of both of these logics. Consider, for example, the following citation from Onora O'Neill:

> The fingerpointing culture is a vulgar extension of the rights culture. It has never been a useful thing to do. The emphasis on rights, not duties, reflects a very big intellectual and political shift of the last 50 years. We have encouraged one another to think a great deal about human rights, and then not getting one's rights and then blaming someone or other for

> it – usually the government. I do criticize the trivialising attitude to human rights which forgets that you and I would never have rights but for others having duties. (O'Neill, *The Guardian*, 7 May 2002)

This is a formulation that could be used to good effect by opponents of the HRA and the Labour government that introduced it. On the one hand it can be read as meaning that the rights agenda has gone too far and that the HRA will lead to an erosion of responsibility and duty. On the other hand, with its appeal to the intimate relationship between rights and duties, it sells the government's communitarian message perfectly. It is this possibility of double reading that shows once again the limitations of a rationalist methodology. Even if we were to accept that agents are able to choose the most cost-efficient means to realize their interests it is clear that, once a strategy has been articulated, given a linguistic form, set free from the grip of its authors, it becomes subject to a range of alternative interpretations.

This can be examined further in the context of how to conduct empirical research using discourse theory methodology. This is a vital question so let me here be as clear as possible about the specific methodological position taken by this chapter. The primary focus of this chapter has been to look specifically at interviews, speeches, and texts written by those advocating the HRA as well as those who were opposed to it. By providing a close textual analysis of these primary sources the chapter has sought to make the argument that discourse theory is a vital tool for our understanding of both the inception of the legislation in terms of how it was possible in the first place and the subsequent attempt to give it a particular form in terms of how rights and duties were articulated together. In order to do this I have looked at two specific analytical devices provided by the discourse theory approach. First, I looked at how the category of iterability allows for an understanding of how the HRA was possible in the first place. The argument here was that it was only because the earlier articulation of rights and duties within the 'second wave' was itself so structured by power and politics that it was open to new interpretations. The second argument sought to show how the logics of equivalence and difference allow us to examine interviews, statements, and texts and see how particular rhetorical strategies were used in order to promote a new conception of how the relationship between rights and duties can be understood. In the time that has ensued since the HRA was finally enforced in 2000 the Prime Minister, Tony Blair, has continued this attempt to break down the space that exists between rights and duties. In a recent speech, he argued that the central task of the centre-left was not to replace the crude individualism of the Thatcher years with an overbearing paternalistic state. Rather it was to rebuild a strong civic society where rights and duties go hand in hand. In his speech to the Progressive Governance conference (London, 2002) he made the same point: 'Partnership is not a soft word. It implies give and take on both sides. It implies that the individual has responsibilities as well as rights; that they have to do as well as to receive.'

The important and general methodological point at stake here is that, in its attempt to provide us with an exhaustive account of politics, a blue-print of causality, a 'big picture' of how action and choice can be reduced to interests and the maximization of utility, instrumentalist methodologies end up telling us very *little* about politics. One of the things I have tried to show above is how, by focusing on the specificity of how a particular discourse is constructed, we gain far more insight into how the business of politics actually works. So, for example, we can see how signifiers such as rights and duties can be presented as mutually confirming, almost as metaphors or, by contrast, as starkly oppositional terms. This is an important point not least because, all too often, the methodology of discourse theory is seen as overly abstract and inattentive to the minutiae of politics. What I hope I have shown in the above is that, if anything, the opposite is true.

There is one other issue that needs to be considered. At the beginning of this chapter I argued that one of the important criticisms of the HRA was that it would lead to an increase in the power of the judiciary at the expense of Parliament. It is now possible to consider this important question concerning the relationship between law and politics in the context of the HRA and discourse theory. One of the important contributions to this debate has been made by Derrida who makes the following distinction between law and justice:

> Every time that something comes to pass or turns out well, every time that we placidly apply a good rule to a particular case, to a correctly subsumed example, according to a determinate judgement, we can be sure that law (droit) may find itself accounted for, but certainly not justice. Law (droit) is not justice. Law is the element of calculation, and it is just that there be law, but justice is incalculable, it requires us to calculate with the incalculable. (Derrida, 1992, p. 16)

The important point being made here is that the politics must always be prioritized because implicit within it is a recognition of the essential contestability and contingency of decision-making. The obvious target of this position is the legal positivism advocated by, among others, Ronald Dworkin which maintains that law is knowable, capable of moral certainty and that the role of the judge is to identify the principles and liberal ideals implicit within law that protect individual rights. This view has been most recently attacked by Richard Bellamy who makes the argument that there is a serious problem with the view of rights that sees them as entrenched constitutional principles designed to protect individuals against the public good. From this perspective, he argues, there seems to be no room for acknowledging different points of view. The collective simply has no business expressing an opinion or interfering with the individual's legitimate sphere of personal choice. The role of the courts becomes the defender of the individual against the illegitimate incursions of the collectivity. He goes on to ask if this collective process would be improved it if was undertaken with regard to a bill of rights? Would not political debate be improved by having some sort of statement of public standards as a reference point? His answer to this is 'no', as formal systems of rights protection tend in time to have the effect of closing down democratic debate (Bellamy, forthcoming, pp. 42–6).

This is clearly a wide-ranging debate that goes way beyond the concerns of this chapter. However, it is worth considering that the existence of rights legislation need not have the effect identified by Bellamy in terms of a closing down of debate about the meaning of rights and their relationship to the good of the collective. Indeed, as we have seen, Francesca Klug's argument is precisely that, with the HRA, we may be witnessing the emergence of a third wave of rights in which the idea of an open and ongoing dialogue between a broad range of actors within civil society about how this relationship should be theorized is axiomatic. It could be argued, therefore, that from a discourse theory perspective, the HRA should be supported precisely on the grounds that it has the capacity or potential to promote the primacy of politics and counter the tendency of law to eclipse it.

This can be considered in a broader ethical context. Discourse theory methodology is often criticized for being relativist. That is, that it is unable to provide a 'solid foundation' for criticism of injustice and inequality. Furthermore, it is said that, unlike realist methodologies, it precludes or obscures our understanding of the nature of power, thus providing protection or cover to those who exercise it illegitimately. However, it is useful to remember that the exposure of power and contingency, made possible by discourse theory's attention to how political settlements are constructed, is a necessary condition for the deconstruction of 'false necessity' arguments that all too often seek to deny legitimate social and political rights. In this sense discourse theory remains an important tool in the struggle for a more democratic rights debate in Britain.

## Conclusion

In this chapter I have argued that discourse theory is vital for our understanding of the introduction of the HRA in two distinct senses. First, it allows us to consider that contingency and power are the conditions for the constitution of interests. It is in this sense that I argued that theories claiming to answer why questions have to be understood in a context of *how* action becomes possible in the first place. Thus, in the context of the HRA, the government was able to introduce a new discourse precisely and only because the relationship between rights and duties was already dislocated and, therefore, subject to rearticulation. Second, I argued that discourse theory allows us a critical insight into the 'nuts and bolts' of politics and the vital role of power in constructing and maintaining the unity of discourses. Here I was particularly concerned to challenge the perception that discourse theory remains at the meta-theoretical level of analysis. What I hope I have shown is that this charge is wholly unjustified.

## Notes

1. The Act, which came into force on 2 October 2000, guarantees a range of basic rights and freedoms. Included are the right to life, the right to a fair trial, the right to privacy and family life, the right to education, the right to practise religion and the right to marry and found a family. Also included are freedom from discrimination, freedom from torture, inhuman or degrading treatment, freedom from slavery, arbitrary arrest and detention, freedom from retrospective penalties, and freedom from discrimination. A. W. B. Simpson has commented that, in the cold-war context of 1950, the ECHR has to be understood as a declaration of ideology – 'in a non-derogatory sense its function was propagandist' (C. Gearty, 2001, p. 10). The ECHR is different from the United Nations Declaration of Human Rights (UNDHR), the European Social Charter (ESC), and the European Union's 1989 Community Charter of Fundamental Rights (CCFR). These are primarily concerned with the protection of social and economic rights. The 1989 Charter, revised in 1995, was famously dismissed by Mrs Thatcher as a 'socialist charter'. Britain won the right to opt out of it when it was included as part of the 1992 Maastricht Treaty. It has since been fully implemented.
2. This is the point made by Clements: '[T]he reforms heralded by the White Paper reach further than the traditional response of changing the power relations between the key stakeholders in the state in that they appear to give non-stakeholders the power to attack the state itself' (Clements, 1999, p. 73).
3. It is argued that such defiance is so unlikely that, in practice, the Canadian courts enjoy the same powers as their United States counterparts. In the context of the UK, Lord Hoffman has noted that, in practice, a declaration will be equivalent to a judicial review finding against the government. This has led Michael Beloff, QC, to conclude that a 'declaration of incompatibility will present the government with a constitutional hobson's choice effectively making refusal to comply out of the question' (Dyer, *The Guardian*, 3 April 2001).
4. In the UK the courts will be required to interpret legislation, both existing and proposed, 'as far as is possible to do so' in a way that is compatible with convention rights: '[T]hey are required to take into account the opinion and rulings of the European Commission and the Court of Human Rights but are not bound by previous domestic interpretations of legislation where these are considered to be incompatible with the Convention. This approach is unique. It is not replicated in any other country with a bill of rights or incorporated human rights treaty' ( Dyer, *The Guardian*, 3 April 2001).
5. It should be noted here that the constitutional limitation to the courts declaring 'incompatibility' applies only to primary legislation. In the case of secondary legislation (statutory instruments and regulations issued by government departments) the courts will have the authority to override the government. It should also be noted that, in the event of a UK court finding against them, litigants can still take their case to the ECHR in Strasbourg. However, this will remain a time-consuming

and expensive process taking on average up to five years and costing on average £30,000.

6. The principle of parliamentary sovereignty was upheld in the Kebilene case in which Lord Steyn commented that: '[I]t is crystal clear that the carefully and subtly drafted Human Rights Act preserves the principle of parliamentary sovereignty. Where legislation is seen as incompatible, which cannot be avoided by interpretation under section 3(1), the court may not disapply the legislation' (Croft, 2000, p. 37).
7. The provisions of the UNDHR were given legal standing in 1966 with the adoption of two international covenants covering both civil/political rights and social, economic, and cultural rights. These covenants were ratified in 1976.
8. This distinction was first made by Isaiah Berlin in his celebrated essay 'Two Concepts of Liberty', published in 1969.
9. This idea of decontestation has been developed in the work of Michael Freeden who sees the role of ideology as attaching a single meaning to a political term: '[U]ltimately, ideologies are configurations of decontested meanings of political concepts…in concrete terms, an ideology will link together a particular conception of human nature, a particular conception of social structure, of justice, of liberty, of authority etc.' (original emphasis, Freeden, 1996, p. 76).
10. Precedent remains an important principle in legal theory. However, the view of Lord Symonds, who referred to its binding character, has been challenged by those such as Lord Denning who remained a strong advocate of the judiciary's creative function. One of the concerns of advocates of the HRA is that it will become ensnared in precedent thus depriving it of its moral force. I would argue that one of the reasons the HRA is important is that it may allow us to see more clearly the irreducible political content of all adjudication. For a brief but incisive discussion about precedent see J. A. G. Griffiths, *The Politics of the Judiciary*, Fontana Press, 1997, pp. 281–9. See also Dworkin, 1978, pp. 81–90.

## Bibliogaphy

### Books

Betten, L., and Grief, N. (1998) *EU Law and Human Rights* (London and New York, Longman).

Blair, T. (1998) *The Third Way: New Politics for the New Century* (London, Fabian Society).

Derrida, J. (1992) 'Force of Law: the Mystical Foundation of Authority', in D. Cornell (ed.), *Deconstruction and the Possibility of Justice* (New York, Routledge).

Dworkin, R. (1978) *Taking Rights Seriously* (London, Duckworth).

Freeden, M. (1996) *Ideologies and Political Theory: a Conceptual Approach* (Oxford, Clarendon Press).

Gasche, R. (1986) *The Tain of the Mirror* (Massachusetts and London, Harvard University Press).

Griffiths, J. (1997) *The Politics of the Judiciary* (London, Fontana).

Howarth, D. (2000) *Discourse* (Philadelphia, Open University Press).

Klug, F. (2000) *Values for a Godless Age* (London, Penguin).

Laclau, E., and Mouffe, C. (1985) *Hegemony and Socialist Strategy* (London, Verso).

Mandelson, P., and Liddle, R. (1996) *The Blair Revolution: Can New Labour Deliver?* (London, Faber and Faber).

Marshall, T. (1992) *Citizenship and Social Class* (London, Pluto Press).

Marx, K. (1843), 'On the Jewish Question', in R. C. Tucker (ed.), *The Marx–Engels Reader* (1978) (New York and London, Norton and Company).

Wadham, J., and Mountfield, H. (2000) *Blackstone's Guide to the Human Rights Act* (London, Blackstone).


## Newspapers


Dyer, C., 'Bringing home the basics', *The Guardian*, 12 November 1998.

Dyer, C., 'The rights stuff', *The Guardian*, 3 April 2001.

Klug, F., 'A law fit for a prince', *The Guardian*, 3 October 2002.

O'Neill, O., 'A matter of trust', *The Guardian*, 7 May 2002.

Travis, A., and Dyer, C., 'Power shifts to the judges', *The Guardian*, 11 September 2000.


## Journals and press releases


Campbell, T. (1999) 'Human Rights: a Culture of Controversy', *Journal of Law and Society*, Vol. 26 (1).

Clements, L. (1999) 'The Human Rights Act – a New Equity or a New Opiate: Reinventing Justice or Packaging State Control?', *Journal of Law and Society*, Vol. 26 (1).

Clements, L., and Young, J. (1999) 'Human Rights: Changing the Culture', *Journal of Law and Society*, Vol. 26 (1).

Croft, J. (2000) 'Whitehall and the Human Rights Act', The Constitution Unit, University College London.

Gearty, C. (2001) 'Airy-Fairy', *London Review of Books*, Vol. 23.

Hunt, M. (1999) 'The Human Rights Act and Legal Culture: the Judiciary and the Legal Profession', *Journal of Law and Society*, Vol. 26 (1).

Klug, F. (2001) 'The Human Rights Act – a Third Way or a Third Wave Bill of Rights', *European Human Rights Law Review*, 4.

Klug, F., Singh, R., and Hunt, M. (1997) 'Rights Brought Home: a Briefing on the Human Rights Bill with Amendments', The Constitution Unit, University College London.

Mendus, S. (1995) 'Human Rights in Political Theory', *Political Studies*, Vol. XLIII, pp. 11–25.

Straw, J. (27 October 1999) 'Jack Straw Sets Out New Vision of Society', Press release by the Lord Chancellor's department.

Straw, J. (18 May 1999) 'Jack Straw Announces Implementation Date for the Human Rights Act', Home Office press release.

Wadham, J. (2001) 'The Human Rights Act – One Year On', London, Liberty.

# 7

# Right-wing Populism and the Radical Centre: Explaining the Electoral Growth of the Vlaams Blok in Belgium

*Patrick de Vos*[1]

## Introduction

This chapter engages with mainstream explanations of the electoral growth of the xenophobic and separatist Flemish far-right party, Vlaams Blok, in Belgium from the late 1980s onward. The issue of right-wing populism in Flanders is introduced by briefly outlining the genesis of the current political situation, and subsequently explaining the two dominant political positions held by the Vlaams Blok, separatist nationalism and authoritarian xenophobic populism, as they were articulated in Party manifestos, such as 'Immigration: the Time Bomb Is Ticking!',[2] the 1999 electoral platform 'Masters in Our House', and the current programme summary 'A Future for Flanders'. Thereupon I will summarize and problematize the two foremost types of analysis that have been put forward to account for the electoral upsurge of the Vlaams Blok, and relate them to strategies employed by the mainstream democratic elites to marginalize this party. From this, it is argued that the current dominant frame of thinking is missing a crucial point: for instance, that the rise of an ultra-nationalist and authoritarian-populist party in Flanders, as elsewhere in Europe, can be better understood in the context of a hegemonic consensus around the political centre, resulting from an ideological convergence between the established political parties, characterized by the disappearance of antagonism. Such an alternative account has been developed over the years by Chantal Mouffe, and I shall first summarize and expound her thesis, and explain how and why it is applicable to the case of the Vlaams Blok.

## The electoral upsurge of the Vlaams Blok

On 8 October 2000, Belgium held its most recent (at the time of writing) local elections. Despite most opinion polls and the anticipations of a number of authority figures, the Vlaams Blok scored its sixth consecutive election victory. In the largest city of Flanders, Antwerp, exactly one-third of all enfranchized citizens appointed a candidate from the Vlaams Blok list as their representative on the city council. Prior to these elections, the media, scholars, and politicians hoped and expected that the electoral growth, during the last decade, of the authoritarian populist party would be curtailed. Hence, the polls were seen as a key test of support for the party. The results were blunt: the party gained another 5 per cent and was, with 20 of the 55 seats in the city council, the biggest political party in Antwerp, and therefore entitled to convene a council meeting at any time.

In terms of personal popularity, the Vlaams Blok's leading politician, Filip Dewinter, obtained the highest personal score of all Flemish politicians, attracting 49,975 preferential votes. By way of comparison, the, at that time incumbent, mayor of Antwerp, Leona Detiège, gained 24,854 preferential votes, which was the second-best score. Also remarkable was the fact that the Vlaams Blok could rely upon an exceptionally devoted electorate: in the case of Antwerp, 92 per cent of those who voted for the Vlaams Blok in 2000 also voted for it in 1994, while the average loyalty rate for all parties amounted to 69 per cent.[3]

The authoritarian populists of the Vlaams Blok also took root in most other constituencies throughout Flanders. The average percentage of all votes for the Vlaams Blok in local elections went up from 10.3 per cent in 1994 to 13.3 per cent in 2000.[4] During the general elections for the Flemish parliament in 1999, the party obtained 15.5 per cent of all votes, improving 3.2 per cent on their 1995 performance. It is now the third-largest Flemish party, ahead of the Flemish Social Democrats.[5] Although we might conceive of Antwerp as the epicentre of a shift to the right in Flemish politics, it is obvious that this tendency is not restricted to this or other Flemish urban centres.

During the general elections, held on 18 May 2003, the Vlaams Blok improved its electoral position once again. In the Belgian Chamber of Deputies the party went up from 9.9 per cent in 1999 to 11.6 per cent in 2003.[6] In Belgium the European ballot of 13 June 2004 – when this book was already in its final editorial phase – coincided with the election of their regional parliaments. In Flanders these polls have resulted in yet another victory of the Vlaams Blok. This time one out of four Flemish voters – one million people all together – had appointed the Vlaams Blok as their representative in the Flemish parliament. No less than six percentage points were gained by the party, which now controlled 24.1 per cent of the overall vote. Since no other party in Belgium managed to improve their election results for eight polls in a row, we can conclude that the Vlaams Blok is the most successful political project of the last decade. Therefore the question should be raised: what kind of political party is the Vlaams Blok.

## Separatist nationalism and authoritarian xenophobic populism

The Vlaams Blok is a separatist-nationalist party. Since its foundation in 1977–79 the Vlaams Blok has continuously advocated the dissolution of the Belgian state and the independence of Flanders. For the Vlaams Blok, Belgium is a historical error. This mistake has not been rectified by successive constitutional reforms since 1969, which eventually resulted in a complex federal government structure that, according to the Vlaams Blok, still dictates an improbable alliance with the Walloon region.[7] Both Wallonia and Belgium are socio-political entities perceived as standing in the way of Flemish autonomy, which is largely understood in terms of an unconstrained pursuit of the prosperity of the Flemish economy. The following quotations are from the present Party programme of the Vlaams Blok and illustrate how this position is articulated:

> It is only too obvious that the federal state structure of Belgium has been invented to rescue the Belgian construction. And to secure the annual transfer of more than 11 billion euro from Flanders to Wallonia.[8]
>
> The unemployed in Flanders are handled more stringently than their Walloon colleagues. Although Flanders only represents 32 per cent of the total unemployment in the country, it stands for 56 per cent of all reported cases of work refusal, and 72 per cent of all penalties. Wallonia represents 56 per cent of the total unemployment, yet it stands for only 9 per cent of all reported cases of work refusal, and 10 per cent of all penalties. In other words, Flanders is paying for the unemployment in Wallonia.[9]

It is not uncommon within this Flemish separatism to seek, in the long term, the unification of Flanders with the Netherlands, which belongs to the same language community,[10] even though the latter has no political movements with similar demands at all.

According to discourse theory, the logic of equivalence constructs a chain of equivalential identities among different elements, that are seen as expressing a certain sameness:[11] '[It] functions by a system of difference... instituting a political frontier between two opposed camps.'[12] For the most part, the Vlaams Blok discursively combines its fierce anti-Belgianism with an anti-establishment stance into chains of equivalence: 'us' against the corrupt Belgian political establishment. From the Vlaams Blok magazine of December 1997:

> There is the party with clean hands and there are the parties of the profiteers. There is the party of the people and there are the parties of the establishment. There is the party that gives priority to its own people and there are the parties *of* and *for* the foreigners. There is the party of the

> future and there are the parties of the past. There is a popular, militant and radical nationalist party and there is the Gang of Five [that is, the mainstream parties].[13]

> The Vlaams Blok wants to be the ally and the voice of the man in the street, who's hands are tied by the establishment, the lobbies (the unions, the health insurances, the employers' federation, ...) and their servants: the traditional political parties. The resistance of the citizens must join in one political party: the Vlaams Blok.[14]

Furthermore, the Vlaams Blok has followed a militant political strategy that is explicitly anti-immigrant. It asserts that, in pursuit of a culturally homogeneous Flanders, non-European immigrants in particular, including the second and third generations of immigrants, should either assimilate – in terms of language, religion, values, and norms – or be forced to return to their countries of origin. The Vlaams Blok's political agenda includes plans to close down mosques, to install a separate social security system for immigrants, and to institute separate schools for those immigrants who have failed to integrate. Its hostility towards immigrants in general, and Muslims in particular, is especially apparent where the presence of this foreign population is articulated with the issue of crime and delinquency into equivalential chains:

> The Flemish cities and towns should remain cities and towns of bell-towers and cathedrals, and not become North African ghetto's with mosques... The Vlaams Blok sides with the victims, not with the attackers; the Vlaams Blok sides with the police, not with rapists and criminals; the Vlaams Blok sides with the young, not with paedophiles and other deviants![15]

The same goes for issues like unemployment, social security, and the benefits of the welfare state: the Vlaams Blok resolutely condemns non-European immigrants as parasites or free riders of 'our' welfare system. Its political campaigns have openly played on racist sentiments against immigrants and refugees, the presence of whom it describes as a threat to the economic and cultural security of Flanders:

> The presence of a large number of immigrants is slowly but surely changing our living environment. Street scenes are changing, the quality of our education is decreasing, there is an increase of crime, unemployment keeps on growing.[16]

The Vlaams Blok, however, denies that it is xenophobic and declares that foreigners are welcome to stay, provided they sufficiently adjust and integrate themselves. As Balibar rightly observed, the Vlaams Blok's brand of xenophobia

> is a [neo-]racism whose theme is not biological heredity but the insurmountability of cultural differences, a racism which, at first sight, does not postulate the superiority of certain groups or peoples in relation to others, but 'only' the harmfulness of abolishing frontiers, the incompatibility of life-styles and traditions.[17]

So, as Hossay notes, the Vlaams Blok does not call for a racially pure society, but for an escorted return of the masses of non-European foreigners.[18]

How then does the Vlaams Blok bring its xenophobic populism into line with its separatist nationalism? The following quote is from the leading Liberal-Democratic politician and former State Secretary of Foreign Trade, Annemie Neyts-Uyttebroek. Regarding the logic of equivalence it is nearly self-explanatory:

> For years on end and without much disapproval they have written with impunity about Walloon people that they were lazy, unproductive or less productive, that they were prodigal and less disciplined; which all boils down to the same thing. And then, all of a sudden, we are amazed when a discourse arises in which the same is being said about Moroccans and Turks in particular and about Islamic people in general. All at once we look upon it as xenophobia, racism or hatred of foreigners; which all boils down to the same thing.[19]

In the words of Hossay: 'Anti-immigrant and anti-Belgium feelings reinforce one another under the rubric of nation.'[20]

Besides the two governing positions mentioned here, the Vlaams Blok speaks out for traditional family values, stresses the importance of maintaining cultural traditions, firmly rejects abortions and euthanasia, and is in favour of a repressive zero-tolerance policy towards crime, delinquency, and drugs.

## Explaining the upsurge of the Vlaams Blok

What can account for the parliamentary rise of an extreme right party like the Vlaams Blok in an advanced European democracy like Belgium? There are, obviously, numerous explanations for the rise of right-wing radicalism. Here I shall restrict myself to the two most prominent accounts.

The most prevalent line of explanation correlates the enlarged support of extreme right parties with wider economic problems such as unemployment and personal insecurity, which have created a climate of social disaffection towards governmental policies. It is a widely held view that people gravitate towards extreme right-wing solutions in times of economic recession and/or growing social inequalities. For instance, the leading journalist and former editor-in-chief of the Flemish left-wing newspaper, *De Morgen*, Paul Goossens, wrote in 1992 that he was 'firmly convinced that there is a direct correlation between unemployment and the emergence, success and perseverance of the extreme right'.[21] In the same edition, Jaap Kruithof, a well-known left-wing Belgian philosopher, stated that 'the source of the shift to the right is situated at the economic level...Neoliberalism leads, intended or not, to an unrestrained capitalism, which fortifies the possibilities of racism and fascism.'[22] According to this line of reasoning problems of unemployment, high inflation rates, and large-scale de-industrialization cause widespread anxiety and frustration among those who feel trapped by their lack of skills.[23] This makes them particularly vulnerable to the discourse of resentment characteristic of the radical right.

Commonly, the contemporary radical right in Flanders, as elsewhere in Europe, has been perceived in the context of advanced capitalist economies and the process of transformation from an industrial to a post-industrial and globalized era that is characterized by a crisis of the welfare state, deregulation and privatization, rapid technological changes, a general transformation of the labour market towards flexible employment policies, individualization, and so on.[24] This dramatic transformation has been increasingly felt in the last decade of the twentieth century and has caused a rapid obsolescence of skills, a continuous pressure on the individual to retrain and reskill, a slow or modest increase in real wages and a decrease in protection by the reduced state.

There is a substantial literature that insists there is causality between recession, unemployment or relative deprivation, and personal and/or social insecurity, on the one hand, and support for right-wing extremism on the other. De Witte and Scheepers,[25] for instance, attribute the success of the Vlaams Blok in Antwerp to a combination of social deprivation and the presence of a well-organized group of Vlaams Blok militants. According to De Witte, Billiet, and Scheepers[26] there is a correlation between socio-economic status and the chance that someone will vote for the Vlaams Blok, which they explain as a translation of economic interests into ethnocentric sentiments. Eisinga et. al.[27] draw in part on Lipset's theory of (threatened) economic interests,[28] which claims that a social class will vote for that party which defends its own specific economic interests best. For Lipset, the economic crisis of the 1930s threatened the social position of the German middle classes, which found its political translation in the rise of the NSDAP. Eisinga et. al. found a correlation between districts and towns with a relatively high level of unemployment and the number of votes for right-wing populist parties. In general, these theories and models use a lack of skills, inactivity, and limited educational attainment as explanatory variables for the increasing support for right-wing radicalism. The fear caused by these socio-structural transformations, especially among those threatened by social insecurity, is linked with the increasing number of immigrants and refugees, who are seen as endangering domestic employment, and with the current issue of multiculturalism.[29]

One of the problems with such a structural approach is that it might very well offer us a macro-framework for the drastic socio-economic changes that can account for the existence of social dislocations and frustrations, but it cannot itself explain why these social anxieties are directed towards right-wing extremism and not to other forms of political mobilization.[30] Furthermore, these accounts offer no explanation for the fact that the extreme right has been flourishing in Flanders, with an economy that has done relatively well in comparison with the Walloon region, where, although unemployment has been significantly higher, right-wing radicalism is virtually non-existent.[31] In the 1999 parliamentary elections de Walloon Front National obtained 1.5 per cent of the vote.

The other dominant approach interprets the contemporary extreme right as a form of protest politics, against the climate of corruption, scandals, and favouritism dominant in the 1990s.[32] As the public's confidence in the traditional political parties has steadily eroded, a growing number of voters have chosen either to turn their backs on politics or to use their vote as a means of protest.[33] It is common in Belgian politics to refer to this phenomenon as a 'crisis of confidence' or as 'the gap between citizens and institutional politics'. According to this kind of interpretation, the Vlaams Blok is a party of discontent that has managed to exploit voters' disgust and disillusionment. In the 1990s, quite a number of Belgian politicians were indeed accused of irregularities with regard to party funding, corruption, and favouritism in the allocation of government contracts. For example, in 1995 the Agusta bribery scandal forced Willy Claes – a leading politician of the Flemish Social Democrats (SP) – to resign as Secretary General of NATO. All this has damaged the reputation of the political establishment. This climate of dissatisfaction and suspicion of traditional politics, and a lack of confidence in institutions such as the government, the police, and the judiciary (the Dutroux affair, for instance), have offered the Vlaams Blok the opportunity to promote itself as a viable alternative to a corrupt political establishment.

Discontent has indeed been an important feature of the political discourse of the Vlaams Blok. However, this kind of approach is as insufficient as the previous one when it comes to explaining the differing political developments in Flanders and Wallonia, since Walloon politicians were equally implicated in political scandals; for example, the assassination of the Walloon Social Democratic leader André Cools (PS) in the summer of 1991. Even though, in 1998, the two Tunisian gunmen were sentenced to prison in their own country for the murder of Cools, it took no less than 13 years to try the accomplices who fell within Belgian jurisdiction. Eventually, on 7 January 2004, six people were found guilty and were given a prison sentence. But the main suspect, another Walloon Social Democratic leading politician, Alain Van der Biest, had already committed suicide in March 2002. Therefore, a lot of issues related to this murder remained unsolved. There are several theories about the assassination of Cools, some relating it to the Agusta bribery scandal,[34] but these are beyond the scope of this chapter.

## Defending democracy: counter-strategies

Since the electoral breakthrough of the Vlaams Blok in 1989–91, several counter-strategies intended to silence the party have been considered and discussed at length. These have included the denial of the phenomenon, the political isolation of the party, counter-argument and discussion, protest actions and efforts towards 'the revealing of its true nature'.[35] Furthermore, after the first electoral breakthrough in the local elections of 1988, a government commissioner entrusted with the task of promoting equal opportunities and opposing xenophobia was established. In the aftermath of the general elections of 1991, in which the Vlaams Blok won its first representation to the federal parliament – often referred to as 'Black Sunday' – a Centre for Equal Opportunities and Opposition to Racism was established, taking over the assignments of the commissioner. In 1995 all parties were obliged to stipulate in their statutes that they accepted the European Treaty of Human Rights (with which several items of the Vlaams Blok programme were in contradiction) as a guiding principle, in order to retain government funding. Ultimately, the Vlaams Blok adjusted its enactments, although reluctantly. Until recently (21 April 2004), attempts to convict the Vlaams Blok as a racist organization have failed, primarily because of inadequate legal means.

The most prevalent strategy against the Vlaams Blok, the so-called cordon sanitaire, was established in 1989, when all the traditional parties unanimously declared that they would never enter into an alliance or governing coalition nor cooperate with the Vlaams Blok in any manner.[36] By doing so they affirmed that, as far as they are concerned, the Vlaams Blok is not in any way a regular democratic party with whom they could possibly collaborate, in spite of the fact that its representatives have been democratically elected. The undemocratic character of the Vlaams Blok is revealed, for instance, by the fact that the party's executive committee and chairman are not elected but appointed by their resigning predecessors.[37]

This cordon sanitaire, one might say, is a protocol of isolation and denial, initially inspired by the belief or assumption that the Vlaams Blok will spontaneously disappear as soon as their electors discover that the party will never find a coalition partner and that the rest of the political spectrum will barely be influenced by them. By depriving them of the possibility of governing, the established parties hoped to create dissent within the party, while in the meantime the anticipated economic revival would hopefully undermine their electoral prospects. Although the cordon sanitaire has remained until today, it has never prevented the Vlaams Blok from improving their electoral position. Neither has it stopped the party from participating in various parliamentary committees, sitting on executive boards of government institutions, nor from obtaining government funding and claiming public broadcasting time, all of which it is entitled to according to its electoral size.

Not only has this cordon sanitaire been criticized for condemning the Vlaams Blok to an underdog position from which it has prospered electorally, it has also contributed to its radicalism. In the words of the former Government Commissioner for Equal Opportunities, Paula Dhondt:

> By a priori denying the Vlaams Blok the possibility to govern, they are offered the opportunity to express themselves in over-simplified and crude terms, without having to take into account that some day they might have to answer for it.[38]

## The neo-revisionism of the radical centre

Having outlined both the dominant political positions of the Vlaams Blok and the leading accounts for their electoral upsurge, along with the related strategies contrived to marginalize the party, I shall now elaborate on the concept of contemporary centre politics, in particular on the notion of a Third Way with which it is affiliated. The inadequacy of the current explanations can be traced back to their inability to understand the electoral success of the Vlaams Blok in the context of an emergent hegemonic consensus around the political centre. Yet, in order to elucidate this argument it is necessary to examine, to some extent, the genesis of contemporary centre politics and to problematize some of its distinguishing features.

Over the course of the last three decades, European social democratic parties (and by extension all parties that supported the Keynesian post-war settlement) have been confronted with a series of challenges that have had a serious impact upon their ideological orientation. From the late 1970s onwards, neoliberal ideology was increasingly adopted in virtually all European welfare states. The Keynesian national welfare state and the post-war consensus became subject to severe criticism from the so-called New Right. At that time, most of the social democratic parties – identifying themselves with the welfare state – often failed to provide an immediate and sufficient answer to the economic, political, and social crisis, either theoretically or in terms of government. The bankruptcy of the Keynesian orthodoxy, and by extension of the post-war settlement, has to be regarded as a dislocation.[39] As a result of the inability, at that time, to suture the dislocated structure, several social democratic parties lost office to conservative governments.

In the late 1980s, a crisis of social democracy was proclaimed. Until recently, the inevitable decline of social democracy was widely accepted. Social democratic parties throughout Europe were going through a period of severe depression, ideologically as well as in terms of electoral success. The collapse of communism further contributed to this climate of growing disorientation and despair. A number of reasons was put forward to explain this malaise. For example, it was argued that the redistributed prosperity that social democracy had achieved might have been the very reason for its decline, since large sections of the working class had been incorporated into a broad middle class. As a result, the social democratic electorate continuously changed and split up into various societal groups with particular interests and expectations towards social democracy.[40] The socio-economic conditions underlying the success of social democratic reformism gave way, from the mid-1980s onwards, to mass unemployment, a paradigm shift in economics resulting from the collapse of Keynesian orthodoxy, the crisis of Fordism, and so on. All this has put social democracy on the defensive. Concurrently, new themes, such as ecology and multiculturalism, and new 'postmaterial' values emerged and found their way onto the political agenda. And of course there was a severe attack on the post-war welfare consensus by the neoliberal offensive initiated by Thatcherism and Reagonomics.

Social democratic parties responded to this 'crisis of governability' by adjusting their ideological orientations and programmatic commitments. Almost all of Europe's social democratic parties have rearticulated their political position and identity. Meanwhile, we have witnessed a gradual withdrawal of state intervention from the economy, resulting from the rise of the neoliberal paradigm, as well as a general de-industrialization of society. Among other outcomes, the latter has resulted in a social structural modification within society, which has reduced the size of the electoral base of the traditional social democratic parties.[41] So, in order to maintain core support and to extend their appeal to new electoral divisions, which are predominantly middle class, social democrats were urged to reposition their parties.[42] From the late 1980s onwards we witnessed a clear move towards the centre by almost all social democratic parties in Europe. By then, most of them had gone through a series of drastic internal reorganizations and ideological and programmatic transformations. This primarily involved the rejection of remaining 'socialist' priorities or goals and the introduction of various elements of economic liberalism into their programmes, for example, New Labour's replacement of Clause IV of its constitution.

Towards the end of the nineties, it became obvious that social democrats had regained their confidence. By 1998, social democrats were in government in 13 of the 15 European member states. Since New Labour won the British general election in 1997, the notion of a 'Third Way' in politics has rapidly emerged throughout the member states of the European Union and elsewhere. According to its defenders, the Third Way is a modernized social democracy that aims to reconcile the neoliberal emphasis on economic efficiency and vitalism with the traditional leftist concern with equality and social cohesion.[43] It is an attempt to develop a left-of-centre political philosophy that responds to the major changes transforming our world: globalization, the rise of a knowledge economy, individualization, and so forth.

Within Third Way philosophy there is a dominant conviction that the old left/right distinction has become meaningless.[44] A broad consensus seems to have been established about the irrelevance of those categories.

> [T]he basic tenet of the third way ... asserts that, with the demise of communism and the transformation of society wrought by the information society and globalisation, the adversarial model of politics has become obsolete – that what we need is a politics 'beyond left and right', no longer structured around social division and without the us/them opposition.[45]

The current party leader of the Flemish social democrats, Steve Stevaert, in an interview with a Flemish newspaper:

> For me there are no left or right topics. There are no left or right solutions either – only good and bad ones. Like the Chinese say: what does it matter if a cat is black or white, as long as it is catching mice?[46]

Another leading SP-politician, Johan Vande Lannotte, addressing his party's congress in July 1999:

> We don't want to be only the Party of the weak, we also want to be the Party of the strong, of those who think that everybody deserves a just place in society. The SP does also appeal to those who are driving a big car, as long as they are willing to contribute to the mobility of those who don't have one.[47]

While accepting that there is no alternative to the neoliberal order, Third Way adherents have become convinced that 'unless [countries] can reach the standard of performance of its global competitors, in virtually every aspect of life, there is no hope of achieving lasting improvements in well-being... This frame of thinking is shaping most fields of government policy', says Rustin.[48] From this perspective, the key issue is how to create sustainable conditions for economic improvement in global markets without sacrificing the basic solidarity or cohesion of our society. Adaptation and reorientation are the order of the day.

> The most crucial step in constructing the logic of the 'Third Way' [says Fairclough] is the claim that, in a knowledge-based economy, the action that is needed to make Britain [or any other country for that matter] more competitive in the global market is also the action that is needed for greater social justice.[49]

Hence an approach that articulates neoliberal economic policy with social democratic social policy has been adopted, accepting the needs of global markets but adding key elements of social well-being. The following quote is from the leading Flemish social democrat Johan Vande Lanotte, and was articulated in the 1999 electoral platform 'The Third Contract':

> The Third Contract does not mean that we have to adjust our values, but that we have to reformulate them. Socialism is and will remain a permanent struggle for justice, life quality and social equality. Socialism is and will remain a form of resistance against all forms of social exclusion... [Yet] the socialism of the future must give the market a chance. Socialism without the market is no longer thinkable. It leads to an economy that is unable to provide for the basic needs of the people. A market without socialism is unfeasible as well. It leads to poverty and unrestrained competition...[50]

From the resolution of the 1998 ideological conference of the SP:

> We acknowledge the merits of market forces, it is one of the engines of economic development...An open and honest competition is essential for an effective market...Safeguarding free competition is an important European objective...Liberalisation is not synonymous with privatisation. Liberalisation means that the market is released, so that the benefits of free choice are put at work.[51]

## Politics without adversaries...and its threatening outside

According to Chantal Mouffe[52] we can comprehend the steady rise of contemporary rightist populist parties by examining them against the background of the emergence of the consensual politics of the centre. The urge of social democratic and other (left-wing) parties to position themselves at the political centre emerged during virtually the same period in which parties like the Vlaams Blok became increasingly successful. On the day that New Labour won the 1997 election in Britain, the Flemish television newscast (BRTN) asked the leaders of the traditional parties – the Christian democrats, the liberal democrats, and the social democrats – to comment on this event. All three of them independently declared that they were completely in line with Blair's political outlook and approach. By moving towards the political centre, Mouffe says, social democratic parties in particular have abandoned the struggle for equality, which has always been at the core of social democracy.[53] This view is shared by, among others, Joël Krieger, who argues that the politico-ideological project of the Third Way is distinctive in its rejection of the egalitarian tradition of the Old Left, reflected in their redistributive policies to counter socio-economic inequality.[54] According to Rustin, social democracy 'always had capitalism as one of its antagonists, and its task was to confront holistically the systemic problems of inequality and instability generated by capitalism'.[55] In the new consensual politics of the centre, however, every fundamental conflict of interest must give way to a confident belief in a politics without adversaries: there are hardly any conflicting interests that cannot be reconciled.[56] The following quote is from the German social democrat Bobo Hombach, Gerhard Schröder's former campaign manager:

> [T]he time of dogma and ideology is past... men and women who want practical solutions, are undogmatic and free from ideology.[57]

In the words of Blair and Schröder, two major advocates of the Third Way in Europe:

> In this newly emerging world people want politicians who approach issues without ideological preconceptions and who, applying their values and principles, search for practical solutions to their problems through honest, well-constructed and pragmatic policies.[58]

Rather than attempting to create an alternative hegemonic order and transform the relations of power, Third Way centre politics accepts that there is no alternative to free-market capitalism. In the words of Giddens:

> [One] can say that you can't do without a market economy. No one knows any other way of effectively organising an economy...[59]
>
> [This] is one of the defining views of the modernising Left: a positive attitude towards some core aspects of globalisation, including the global marketplace.[60]

According to Žižek, the Third Way is social democracy under the hegemony of liberal-democratic capitalism, for instance, 'deprived of its minimal subversive sting, excluding the last reference to anti-capitalism and class struggle'.[61]

In other words, the ideological struggle has been abandoned completely. Consequently, the so-called radical centre is a contradiction in terms: once beyond left and right, any social antagonism appears to dissolve and political solutions from which everybody seems to benefit come forth.[62] In the absence of a real ideological battle, the distinction between political parties is reduced to opposed cultural attitudes. '[T]he predominant form of politics in our post-political era, is the appearance of a choice where there is basically none', says Žižek.[63] There are no longer any clear issues which divide the established parties, no real political issue on which people can decide, since the policies of the mainstream parties became almost indistinguishable.

What is lacking, says Mouffe, is politics itself: the advocates of this radical centrism, in their attempt to circumvent fundamental social antagonisms permanently, refuse to draw clear political frontiers [64] Since there are no longer any conflicting interests that cannot be reconciled, we thus encounter a politics without adversaries. 'Third Way politics is one-nation politics', says Giddens.[65] Democratic politics is conceived as a dialogue, rather than as a confrontation:[66] 'conflicts... are reduced to a simple competition between interest which can be harmonized through dialogue', argues Mouffe. 'This is the typical liberal perspective that envisages democracy as a struggle among elites, taking place in a neutral terrain, thereby making adversary forces invisible and reducing politics to an exchange of arguments and the negotiation of compromises.'[67] Therefore, Mouffe continues, Third Way theorists are missing a crucial point about the primary reality of strife in social life, but also about the integrative role which conflict plays in modern democracy:

> The specificity of modern democracy lies in the recognition and the legitimation of conflict and the refusal to suppress it through the imposition of an authoritarian order... A democratic society must make room for the expression of conflicting interests and values.[68]

An important consequence of the blurring of the left/right division and the disappearance of antagonism is that it produces a significant democratic deficit:

> Major contemporary political passions cannot find an outlet within the democratic system as there is no debate about possible alternatives, no debate in which different forms of identification could be provided around which people could mobilize. We are therefore witnessing the growth of other forms of collective identification... that cannot easily be dealt with by the democratic system.[69]

So the problem is not merely that people want antagonism for the sake of it, but rather that the centre-drifting political parties, with their indistinguishable programmes, are not offering any radical, visionary, and antagonizing political alternatives on which people can decide, while at the same time numerous problems remain unsolved: for example, unemployment and job insecurity, falling welfare standards, inner city decay etc. It is precisely in this sense that the consensus politics of the centre is not addressing the 'real' problems of ordinary people. What they offer instead is a socially responsible, but nevertheless system-conforming adjustment to major social transformations such as globalization, the knowledge economy etc. In the absence of democratic channels through which a confrontation of values and interest can take place, extreme-right populism thus has been given the opportunity to win over a sector of the population whose demands have been ignored by the 'consensus at the centre'.[70] Given the lack of an alternative political discourse, the far right has been able to give a voice to the demands of those who could not find a place within the democratic space to express their different position. Parties such as the Vlaams Blok were the only ones offering an alternative through which antagonism could be voiced. The next quote is from the leading Vlaams Blok politician Filip Dewinter:

> More and more the Vlaams Blok has created a distinct profile for itself, as a party that differs from the others... It is offering an alternative for common people and workers in quarters where socialists no longer offer any solution for the problematic of foreigners and security. The Vlaams Blok also offers a straightforward alternative to the favouritism and the corruption of the other political parties...[71]

With the emergence of a Third Way, the new populist right thus seized the opportunity to occupy the terrain left vacant by the left. Today, right-wing populism is the only political force with serious weight that successfully exploits an anti-capitalist discourse. They present themselves as the only anti-establishment force that represents the will of the people. Unlike the adherents of a Third Way philosophy, right-wing populists are conscious of the fact that politics implies that political frontiers are drawn and that the enemy is named. According to Žižek, the triumph of right-wing parties across Europe is the price the left is paying for its renunciation of any radical political project and for accepting free-market capitalism as a 'fait accompli': right-wing populism is the negative common denominator of the entire centre-left liberal spectrum.[72]

## Conclusion

Returning to the present Belgian political situation where I began it seems that Mouffe's account succeeds where the others fail. It explains both why political dissatisfaction is translated into an electoral upsurge of right-wing parties and why the political developments in Flanders and Wallonia diverge. Indeed, while the Flemish social democrats gradually moved from a post-war state interventionism towards a market-oriented, left-of-centre party in the course of the last fifteen years, the Walloon Parti Socialiste maintained, to a remarkable extent – at least in comparison to its Flemish counterpart – its 'socialist' priorities and goals. In fact, the Parti Socialiste is still the biggest political party in Wallonia today, despite also being involved in political scandals. Moreover, exit polls conducted by Swyngedouw (KUB) clearly show that, particularly during the late 1980s and early 1990s, the Vlaams Blok initially recruited its voters among the electorate of the Flemish Socialist Party and among those who had cast invalid or blank ballots previously.[73] Here, discontent seems to be what both groups have in common. Besides, most observers will confirm that a similar observation can be made regarding the ecological parties in Flanders (Agalev) and Wallonia (Ecolo): Ecolo's political position, by comparison with that of Agalev, is situated more to the left, thereby providing more real political choices within the traditional democratic spectrum.

Mouffe's account also sheds a critical light on the major counter-strategy through which the mainstream parties have tried to marginalize the Vlaams Blok: for instance, the quarantine established by the cordon sanitaire. In Mouffe's line of reasoning, the political isolation of the Vlaams Blok might even have contributed to their electoral success, since it specifically confirmed that they are unacceptable. In the words of Žižek:

> They are the enemy whom we can all together properly hate, whom we can sacrifice – excommunicate – in order to demonstrate our democratic consensus. They are the excluded ones who, through this very exclusion (their unacceptability as a party of the government) provide the negative legitimacy of the liberal hegemony.[74]

The above quote of the former Government Commissioner Paula Dhondt confirms Žižek's conclusion altogether: the cordon sanitaire is condemning the Vlaams Blok to an underdog position from which it has prospered electorally.

Žižek refers to the Derridean notion of a constitutive outside, that is, a purely negative identity obstructing the identity of the inside, yet being a sine qua non for the construction of the identity of the inside. In the words of Torfing: '[T]he constitutive limits of a discourse are constructed in relation to the threatening outside.'[75] The entire spectrum of the legitimate democratic political parties, by excluding the Vlaams Blok, implicitly admitted time and again that the far right poses a real threat to them, thereby acknowledging the antagonistic response of 'us' against 'them', and actually encouraging those who wanted to reprimand the consensual politics of the centre by voting for this unacceptable party. To put it another way:

> The consensus at the centre which is supposed to include everybody in our so-called post-traditional societies cannot exist without the establishment of a frontier, because no consensus, or no common identity for that matter, can exist without drawing a frontier. There cannot be an 'us' without a 'them' and the very identity of any group depends on the existence of a 'constitutive outside'.[76]

This chapter is a spin-off of doctoral research on the ideological crisis and transformation of British and Flemish social democracy in the 1990s. In this research the question of the 'why' and 'how' of the democratic renewal process is focused on the (trans)formation of consensus among the social-democratic political elites. It was through this research that I became acquainted with the Mouffe/Žižek thesis. The literature and the research corpus (of political programmes and manifestos, campaign documents, records of conferences, articles, books, and interviews) that I was analysing at that time confirmed the thesis of the disappearance of antagonism from the discourse of contemporary social democrats. Still, the question was whether Mouffe's account of the rise of contemporary right-wing populism – initially articulated in more general, theoretical terms – would be applicable and appropriate to the Belgium case. In order to answer that question I first took a closer look at the dominant accounts offered in the 1990s, and problematized and related them to the strategies employed to marginalize the Vlaams Blok. I then collected a limited corpus of simular texts from the Vlaams Blok elite that enabled me to map the articulatory practices and to reconstruct concisely their main political positions for a non-Belgian audience that was not (too) familiar with the issue of the Vlaams Blok.

This chapter started from a concrete question that undoubtedly has puzzled many time and again: why is right-wing populism gaining ground election after election? First, I have tried to examine this matter in further detail by asking to what extent the democratic deficit revealed by their electoral upsurge can be related to the shortcomings of the responses of the political elites to this development and to the theoretical perspectives from which they depart. The approach of Chantal Mouffe in particular has shown that the terms in which we grasp right-wing populism in its contemporary context are as important as the phenomenon as such. Most of the work Mouffe has done since she wrote *Hegemony and Socialist Strategy* with Ernesto Laclau (1985) fits in with their conviction that it is urgent for political theory to provide an alternative framework that will enable us to come to terms with the conflictual nature of politics and the abiding nature of antagonism.[77] This, however, does not necessarily imply that we should discard all other theoretical frameworks at once. Instead, what it means is that we should determine the limits of these accounts.

After describing Mouffe's alternative account in some detail, I returned to the Belgian political situation, arguing from the conclusions of the analysis that her account succeeds where the mainstream explanations fall short. In this light, I also re-evaluated the major counter-strategy, the cordon sanitaire, which once again illustrates the constitutive logic of antagonistic articulation. It is by no means my intention to suggest that the Mouffe thesis is the only valid explanation of the phenomenon of the Vlaams Blok, but rather that a significantly different theory can be obtained from a deconstructive, discourse analytical approach, which is – at the very least – an enrichment of the debate.

## Notes

1. The author gratefully acknowledges the help of the European Union Social Science Information Research Facility (EUSSIRF), which enabled a research visit to The British Library of Political and Economics Science at the LSE.

2. *Immigratie: de tijdbom tikt!*, 2nd edn, 1996. This is the so-called '70-objectives strategy-plan', which bears a strong resemblance to the '50-demands platform' published by the French National Front in November 1991.
3. Institute of Social and Political Oppinion Research (ISPO)/*De Standaard*, 10 October 2000. Swyngedouw (Catholic University of Brussels (KUB)) has made similar observations for various previous elections; see: Swyngedouw, M., 'Het Vlaams Blok 1980–1991: opkomst, groei en doorbraak', in R. van Doorslaer and J. Gotovich (eds), *Herfsttij van de20ste eeuw: extreemrechts in Vlaanderen 1920–1990* (Leuven, Kritak, 1992), pp. 83–104.
4. University of Limburg (LUC)/*De Morgen*, 10 October 2000. This comparison, however, should be interpreted with caution. According to Jo Buelens (Free University of Brussels (VUB)), in 1994 the Vlaams Blok stood for election in 131 Flemish municipalities, while in 2000 this number increased to 180. This nevertheless reflects the Vlaams Blok's growing capacities to recruit militants and candidates, as well as the increased public acceptance of the party.
5. Spruyt, M. (2000) *Wat het Vlaams Blok verzwijgt* (Leuven, Van Halewyck), p. 69.
6. De Standaard Online: <http://www.standaard.be/extra/verkiezingen2003/ #uitslagen>.
7. Belgium is a federal state composed of three language communities (Dutch, French, and German-speaking) and three regions (Flanders, Wallonia, and a bilingual Brussels-Capital region): each of these entities has its own legislative assembly and government, although the parliament of Flanders and that of the Flemish community form a single body.
8. Vlaams Blok, *Een toekomst voor Vlaanderen: programma en standpunten van het Vlaams Blok* (Brussel: Vlaams Blok, 2003): <http://www.vlaams-blok.be> (author's translation).
9. Ibid.
10. Elbers, F., and Fennema, M. (1993) *Racistische partijen in West-Europa: tussen nationale traditie en Europese samenwerking* (Leiden, Stichting Burgerschapskunde), p. 92.
11. Torfing, J. (1999) *New Theories of Discourse: Laclau, Mouffe and Žižek* (Oxford, Blackwell), p. 301.
12. Howarth, D., and Stavrakakis, Y. (2000), 'Introducing Discourse Theory and Political Analysis', in D. Howarth, A. J. Norval, and Y. Stavrakakis (eds), *Discourse Theory and Political Analysis: Identities, Hegemonies and Social Change* (Manchester, Manchester University Press), p. 11.
13. De Smedt, D. (1997) 'Recht door zee!', *Vlaams Blok*, 21 (12): 10–11 (author's translation).
14. Vlaams Blok, *Wetgevende verkiezingen 1991: campagnestrategie* (Brussels, Vlaams Blok, 1991) (author's translation).
15. Verstraeten, G. (1998) 'Eigen Volk Eerst', *Vlaams Blok*, 1 (9): 4–5 (author's translation).
16. Dewinter, F. (1989) *Eigen volk eerst: antwoord op het vreemdelingenprobleem* (Brecht, De Roerdomp), p. 130 (author's translation).
17. Balibar, E., and Wallerstein, I. (1991) *Race, Nation, Class: Ambiguous Identities* (New York, Verso), p. 21.
18. Hossay, P. (1996) 'Our People First! Understanding the Resonance of the Vlaams Blok's Xenophobic Programme', *Social Identities*, 2 (3): 355.
19. Cited in Elbers and Fennema, *Racistische partijen in West-Europa*, p. 80 (author's translation).
20. Hossay, 'Our People First!', p. 355.
21. *De Morgen*, 24 November 1992, pp. 17–19.
22. Ibid.

23. Anastasakis, O. (2000) 'Extreme Right in Europe: a Comparative Study of Recent Trends', Discussion Paper no. 3, (London, The Hellenic Observatory/The European Institute-LSE), pp. 10–11.
24. See Betz, H. G. (1999) 'Contemporary Right-Wing Radicalism in Europe', *Contemporary European History*, 8 (2): 299–316; see also Swyngedouw, 'Het Vlaams Blok 1980–1991'; and Burghgraeve, P., Corijn, E., and Verbraeken, P. (2000) 'Vlaanderen: wat we zelf doen, doen we beter... niet': <http://www.antifa.com/afi/charta91/Charta91-2000txt.htm/>.
25. De Witte, H., and Scheepers, P. (1997) 'Twintig jaar Vlaams Blok', *Internationale Spectator*, 51: 7–8 , 420–8.
26. De Witte, H., Billiet, J., and Scheepers, P. (1994) 'Hoe zwart is Vlaanderen? Een exploratief onderzoek naar uiterst-rechtse denkbeelden in Vlaanderen in 1991', *Res Publica*, 36 (1): 85–102.
27. Eisinga, R., Lammers, J., Lubbers, M., and Scheepers, P. (1998) 'Het electoraat van extreem-rechtse partijen: individuele en contextuele kenmerken, 1982–1996', in J. van Holsteyn and C. Mudde, *Extreem-rechts in Nederland* (Den Haag, SDU), pp. 93–112.
28. Lipset, S. M. (1990 [1960]) *Political Man* (New Jersey, Doubleday).
29. See also Swyngedouw, 'Het Vlaamse Blok 1980–1991; Scheepers, P., Eisinga, R., and Felling, A., *Het electoraat van extreem-rechts: theoretische verklaringen, empirische bevindingen, conceptualiseringen en operationaliseringen. Bijdrage aan de studiedag over 'extreem-rechts'* (Voorburg, Centraal Bureau voor de Statistiek, 11 November 1994).
30. Anastasakis, 'Extreme Right in Europe', p. 12.
31. Hossay, 'Our People First!', p. 345.
32. See Anastasakis, 'Extreme Right in Europe', p. 14; see also Betz, 'Contemporary Right-Wing Radicalism', p. 41; see also de Witte, H. (1992) 'Racisten of apatici?', in E. Desle and A. Martens (eds), *Gezichten van hedendaags racisme* (Brussels, VUB Press): 190–1; see also Backes, U. (1990) 'Extremismus und Populismus van Rechts: ein Vergleich auf Europäische Ebene', in *Aus Politik und Zeitgeschichte*, B46–7/90: 3–14; see also Stouthuysen, P. (1996) 'Het cordon sanitaire is een blok aan het been', *Samenleving en Politiek*, 3 (3): 15–17.
33. See Elbers and Fennema, *Racistische partijen in West-Europa*, p. 82; see also Burghgraeve et al., *Vlaanderen: wat we zelf doen, doen we beter... niet*, see also, *The Economist*, 14 October 2000.
34. Vansevenant, J. (1994) *De Agusta-affaire: kroniek van een omstreden helikopteraankoop* (Antwerpen, Standaard Uitgeverij), pp. 31–6.
35. De Witte, H. (1997), 'Een overzicht en evaluatie van strategieën ter bestrijding van extreem-rechtse partijen', in H. De Witte (ed.), *Bestrijding van racisme en rechts-extremisme: wetenschappelijke bijdragen aan het maatschappelijk debat* (Leuven/Amersfoort, Acco).
36. Spruyt, *Wat het Vlaams Blok verzwijgt*, p. 42.
37. De Witte, H., and Scheepers, P. (1997) 'Twintig jaar Vlaams Blok: herkomst, evolutie en toekomst van partij en kiezers', *Internationale Spectator*, 51 (7/8): 421.
38. Dhondt, P., interviewed by Bert Decraene, 'Wereldbericht', VRT Radio 1, 14 October 2000, 10.00–11.00 a.m. (author's translation).
39. Torfing, *New Theories of Discourse*, pp. 225–41.
40. Cuperus, R., and Kandel, J. (1998) 'The Magical Return of Social Democracy: an Introduction', in R. Cuperus and J. Kandel (eds), *Transformation in Progress: European Social Democracy* (Freudenberg/Amsterdam, Friedrich Ebert Stiftung/Wiardi Beckman Stichting,).

41. Cuperus and Kandel, 'Magical Return', pp. 11–13.
42. Telò, M., 'Transformation of Programmatic Profiles', in Cuperus and Kandel (eds), *Transformation in Progress*.
43. Blair, T. (1998) *The Third Way: New Politics for the New Century* (London, Fabian Society); Giddens, A. (1998) *The Third Way: the Renewal of Social Democracy* (Cambridge, Polity Press); Hombach, B. (2000) *The Politics of the New Centre* (Cambridge, Polity Press).
44. Giddens, *Third Way*, pp. 37–46.
45. Mouffe, C (1999) '10 Years of False Starts', *New Times*, 9 November.
46. Stevaert, Steve, interviewed in: G. Roox, 'Het bruto nationaal geluk volgens Steve Stevaert: liefde moet van onderuit groeien', *De Standaard*, 14 October 2000, p. 13 (author's translation).
47. Vande Lanotte, J. (1999) cited in: P. Lambrechts, 'Belgische socialisten bewandelen al lang Derde Weg', *De Financieel-Economische Tijd*, 29 September (author's translation).
48. Rustin, M. (1998) 'The New Labour Project', *Soundings*, 8 Spring: 7–11.
49. Fairclough, N. (2000) *New Labour, New Language?* (London, Routledge), p. 43.
50. Vande Lanotte, J. (1999) *Het derde contract: de toekomst is van iedereen* (Antwerpen, Houtekiet), pp. 27–8 (author's translation).
51. Socialistische Partij (1998) *Het Toekomstcongres 1998* (Brussel, Socialistische Partij/SEVI).
52. Mouffe, C. (1993) *The Return of the Political* (London/New York, Verso); Mouffe (1995) 'The End of Politics and the Rise of the Radical Right', *Dissent*, pp. 498–502; Mouffe, 'The Radical Centre: a Politics without Adversary', *Soundings*, 9: 11–23; Mouffe, '10 Years of False Starts'; Mouffe (2000) *The Democratic Paradox* (London/New York, Verso).
53. Mouffe, '10 Years of False Starts'.
54. Krieger, J. (1999) *British Politics in the Global Age: Can Social Democracy Survive?* (Cambridge, Polity Press), p. 26.
55. Rustin, M. (1999) 'Editorial', *Soundings*, 11: Spring, p. 8.
56. Hall, S. (1998) 'The Great Moving Nowhere Show', *Marxism Today*, November–December: 9–14 (10).
57. Hombach, B. (ed.) (2000) *The Politics of the New Centre* (Cambridge: Polity Press, 2000), p. 66.
58. Blair, T., and Schröder, G. (1999) 'Europe: the Third Way/die Neue Mitte', reprinted in Hombach (ed.), *The Politics of the New Centre*.
59. Giddens, A. interviewed by J. P. Rondas, *Het wereldbeeld: interview Anthony Giddens*, Radio3/Klara, 30 April (2000), 11.00 a.m.–12.00 p.m.
60. Ibid.
61. Žižek, S. (2000) 'Why Do We All Love to Hate Haider?' <http://platon.ee.duth.gr/data/maillist-archives/cyberurbanity/msg00070.html>.
62. Mouffe, *Democratic Paradox*, p. 110.
63. Žižek, 'Why Do We All Love to Hate Haider?'
64. Bechler, R. (1998) 'The End of Politics?', *New Times*, 141.
65. Giddens, *Third Way*, p. 69.
66. Giddens, A. (1994) *Beyond Left and Right: the Future of Radical Politics* (Cambridge, Polity Press).
67. Mouffe, 'Radical Centre', p. 13; see also Mouffe, *Democratic Paradox*, pp. 110–11.
68. Mouffe, 'Radical Centre', p. 13.
69. Mouffe, '10 Years of False Starts'.

70. Mouffe, 'End of Politics', p. 500.
71. Dewinter, F., and Van Overmeire, K. (1993) *Een tegen allen: opkomst van het Vlaams Blok* (Antwerpen, TYR), p. 105.
72. Žižek, S. (2000) 'Wat is het fijn om tegen Haider te zijn', *Nieuw Wereldtijdschrift*, 17: 3, April, pp. 43–5.
73. Swyngedouw, 'Het Vlaams Blok 1980–1991', pp. 83–104.
74. Žižek, 'Why Do We All Love to Hate Haider?'.
75. Torfing, *New Theories of Discourse*, p. 299; see also Howarth, *Discourse*, pp. 106–7.
76. Mouffe, C. 'For an Agonistic Public Sphere', unpublished text (forthcoming), p. 12.
77. Mouffe, *Democratic Paradox*, pp. 110–11.

# 8
# Third Way Politics Today

*Steven Bastow and James Martin*

## Introduction

The 'Third Way' has come to symbolize the effort to revive European social democratic politics at the start of the twenty-first century. Having rejected old-style socialist statism and the free-market economics of the New Right, leading social democrats claim to have identified an alternative that cuts a path between state and market. Two of the major parties of the left in Europe – the British Labour Party under Tony Blair and the German Social Democrats under Gerhard Schröder – have heralded a Third Way or, in German, a 'new middle' (*Neue Mitte*), an ideology of the 'radical centre' (see Blair, 1998, 2001; Blair and Schröder, 1999). Instead of a confrontational leftism, doomed forever to protest and never govern, proponents of the Third Way have announced a politics that purports to move beyond the antagonism between left and right.

Not surprisingly, the proclamation of a Third Way in social democracy has initiated a vast debate over the policies, principles, and the future of the centre-left in Britain and Europe more widely (see Giddens, 2000, 2001). Increasingly, the contrasting meanings and implications of this Third Way are being debated in academic as well as party political discussions. However, absent in many of these discussions is an awareness of the variety of 'third way' ideologies that span the twentieth century and traverse the spectrum from left to right. Few commentators recognize that third ways proclaiming to have moved beyond established antagonisms have a steady lineage in European social and political thought in the twentieth century.

Our aim in this chapter is to grasp the specificity of Third Way politics today by elaborating the attributes of Third Way *discourse*. Understanding the Third Way as a discourse allows us to focus on the way its structuring principles open up a space for political intervention. In opposition to approaches that evaluate Third Way politics by reference to an 'objective' or 'external' referent, we look to the way its discourse helps construct its own objectivity and then poses itself as a response to these objective circumstances that other ideological positions have 'failed' to grasp. To do this, we shall sketch our analysis of the generic discursive 'repertoire' from which a variety of Third Way ideologies have drawn in the course of the twentieth century. This will enable us then to place the social democratic Third Way in a wider theoretical and ideological context. First, however, let us consider more closely some common approaches to the Third Way today.

## The Third Way: left, right, or centre?

The social democratic Third Way has been difficult to classify. This is partly because it deliberately evades the traditional categories of 'left' and 'right', and is positioned in a 'centre' or 'middle' that purports nevertheless to be 'radical' (See Driver and Martell, 2000; Giddens, 2000, 2001), but also because, at the same time, parties and advocates of the left who still claim to be working in that tradition have adopted it. At first glance, then, the Third Way is hard to locate in the received ideological spectrum because its proponents claim to move beyond its strictures while, in some way, remaining within them. This problem of classification pans out in more concrete terms, too. Social democrats of the Third Way repeatedly seek to dissolve or bridge certain policy choices and values: utilizing both state *and* market in a governing 'partnership', stressing rights *and* responsibilities in citizenship, individual *and* community as the basis of social order, and so on.

In abandoning a principled defence of one side of these oppositions over the other, the Third Way exhibits its central claim to have moved beyond antagonism. But moved where? What are the limits to the reliance on the market or the state? When do rights have precedence over responsibilities or vice versa? Can the needs of the individual be so simply reconciled with those of community? For many sympathizers and critics alike, it is not certain exactly whether there exists a new principle 'beyond' the traditional antagonisms that will enable the Third Way to answer such questions. In the absence of a clear point of reference many have accused the Third Way of being fundamentally 'vague and elusive' (White, 2001, p. 3), eclectically opportunist, or simply facile.

One response to this rather confused picture is to identify an underlying set of motivations that, for reasons of ideological immaturity or political expediency, are not always visible. If the Third Way can be shown to be intelligible by reference to an *objective* form of reasoning then, it is presumed, its true colours can be discerned. Interestingly, both proponents and critics alike share this approach.

In his important statement, *The Third Way* (1998), Anthony Giddens sets out his view of the Third Way as essentially a 'renewal' of the social democratic values of the left under new social conditions. Under these conditions – which include the development of the 'knowledge economy', the growing speed of telecommunications technology, and the increasing decline in traditional social identities and moral obligations – the traditional values of the left – equality of opportunity and social solidarity based around collective needs – are either hopelessly anachronistic or inadequately formulated as policy options. For Giddens, the Third Way represents a transformation of social democratic ideology which retains its essential guiding ambition: social equality. Globalization and the general trend towards a more pluralistic, non-traditional society disrupt the easy distinctions once grouped around the division between left and right (1998, pp. 37–46). Whereas traditional social democracy counterposed the state to the market, the Third Way dissolves the 'dogmatic' assumption of the state's moral and administrative superiority and looks to both the state *and* the market as institutional mechanisms for achieving equality. Equally, social democrats must grasp the emancipatory potential of, for example, voluntary organizations and civic activities, non-governmental organizations, proliferating differences in individual lifestyle, ecologism, and so forth. All the things that were dismissed or marginalized under old-style social democracy must be embraced in a 'more pragmatic attitude towards coping with change' (1998, p. 68). Underlying the apparent elasticity of the Third Way, then, is a positive evaluation of the possibilities for individual and social emancipation presented by global conditions.

By contrast, for many critics, especially those further to the left, the Third Way represents a capitulation to the demands of expanding global capitalist markets and US-driven policies promoting neoliberalism (see, for instance, Anderson, 2000). In his trenchant *Against the Third Way* (2001), Alex Callinicos provides an exemplary version of this critique. He disputes Giddens's account of globalization as a self-driven form of socio-economic transformation and points to the political and economic interests that actively guide it. New Labour's policies, and those of other Third Way adherents such as Schröder, and former US president Bill Clinton, are in his view little more than cynical rationalizations of a new stage of capitalist imperialism.

Despite appeals to a moderate pragmatism and sense of 'community', argues Callinicos, Blair and others are effectively seeking to introduce private companies into new areas of domestic public service provision and to impose neoliberal restructuring on the less developed countries as a quid pro quo for international aid. Tony Blair's appeal to ethical standards, therefore, represents 'a "caring" veneer pasted over the relentless commodification of the world that is the inner truth of the Third Way' (2001, p. 65). Rather than a policy of pragmatism, the Third Way expresses the 'sincere, indeed dogmatic, belief that private entrepreneurs just are better at running things than anyone else' (Ibid., p. 108). The consequence is not a renewal of left-wing aspiration to social justice and human emancipation but the further entrenchment of global inequalities and support for a chaotic and destructive economic system that rewards the few and exploits the many. Thus, in his view (and that of many other critics), the Third Way is essentially an ideology of the right whose underlying motivation is to conserve the power of capitalist interests: 'the Third Way is but an ideological façade behind which capitalism continues on its brutal and destructive way' (Ibid., p. 120).

Although they differ starkly in their evaluation, both Giddens and Callinicos explain the Third Way by reference to external (global) conditions that it more or less accurately represents. The truth and validity of the Third Way is a function therefore of the truth and validity of globalization. By consequence, different interpretations of globalization will produce different interpretations of the Third Way.

These interpretations provide a purportedly 'objective' grounding for a classification of the Third Way. What they miss, however, is the way the doctrine helps *constitute* the very objectivity of the world it is supposed to represent. The Third Way automatically positions itself as a *more objective* account of social conditions than the (first and second) partial views it claims to transcend. The latter can then be dismissed as insufficiently objective, one-sided and therefore limited. Thus the Third Way rhetorically invokes a 'clearing' between these one-sided views in which the full objectivity of social conditions can come into view. For Giddens and Callinicos, however, these social conditions are taken as *prior* to the analysis that the Third Way imposes. Whilst one accepts the analysis, the other rejects it. Yet both fail to see that the rhetoric of the Third Way is itself part of the politics its proponents seek to promote.

In our view, the Third Way represents a 'discourse' that functions to reset the horizons of social objectivity by claiming to transcend received ideological perspectives. In so doing, it resists easy classification along a left–right spectrum. Attempting to label the doctrine by reference to the analysis of pre-existing social conditions – however insightful these may be – rather misses the point. One key purpose of the Third Way is precisely to redefine the terms by which those conditions are understood and evaluated. This is not to accept the claim made by some proponents that the Third Way is in some way 'non-ideological'. Nor is it to deny that there are social conditions against which the claims of the Third Way ought to be challenged. Nevertheless, the nuances and tensions in the Third Way – and the third way tradition in general – are missed if we treat it simply as a set of postulates to be judged as either a true or false representation of the world and then classified according to a fixed ideological spectrum.

## Discourse theory and political ideology

If we are to conceive the Third Way as a type of discourse we first need to show the implications of discourse theory for understanding political ideology. As we have already noted, when conceived as an ideology both critics and proponents tend to miss the way the Third Way functions, in part, to constitute the conditions to which it purports to respond. They fail to notice the way the Third Way positions its audience in relation to these conditions by suggesting the partiality of the polarities it transcends. Discourse theory, however, helps us focus precisely on these peculiar attributes.

In recent years there has been wide and varied discussion of the nature of political ideologies and how they might be studied (see Freeden, 1996; Vincent, 1992; Norval, 2000). Political ideologies are commonly understood to be relatively stable, systematic bodies of concepts and analyses that express particular moral dispositions towards social and political arrangements and which define the range of legitimate choices available to individuals. Ideologies are typically expressed in generic form as 'isms': socialism, communism, liberalism, etc. They are distinguishable by the type of analysis of society that they make, the value commitments they express and the types of arrangements for reordering society that they propose. Of course, there are many different sub-groups of ideologies and even a considerable degree of overlapping between them. However, there is a recognizable set of conventionalized ideological 'families' that have come to define intellectual and theoretical traditions in modern society. Revival of interest in political ideologies turns on the recognition that, despite proclamations to the contrary in the 1960s, ideology has not come to an end (see Bell, 1988). Instead, the ideological frames through which people interpret and experience their world are recognized increasingly as an ever-present feature of modern social life.

A number of approaches to the analysis of ideology have pointed to the way in which the conceptual configurations of ideologies structure the universes of meaning which inform our everyday conduct, but are themselves hidden, or covered over, by the 'naturalizing' effect which ideologies confer upon this conduct (see Lefort, 1986). As such, ideologies are perceived to be rooted in social relations of power, and seek to legitimate existing social orders or delegitimize them in favour of another. With their partial and value-laden outlooks, ideologies continue to define the terrain of social and political practices.

There is certainly a considerable degree of convergence between ideologies and discourses. Both refer to relatively stable configurations of representations, concepts, and symbols that help construct social meanings. Both ideological and discursive configurations change over time and can be modified in a variety of ways. Both point to the way such meanings are often partial to specific values, and both are 'political' in as much as they seek to define the sources of social disorder so as to recommend a means of resolution.

However, there are a number of important differences that have methodological implications. First, ideologies are conceived in terms of a 'closure' in that they are often presented as being informed by some underlying, objective necessity that fixes their elements (for instance, its concepts and analyses) around a supposedly incontestable essence such as 'interests' or social structure which are purported to lie 'outside' ideology (see, for example, Mannheim, 1991; Eagleton, 1991). This has led to a 'totalizing' view of ideologies that stresses their fundamental coherence as paradigmatic doctrines. Discourse analysis, however, is focused on the contingent nature of meaning and demonstrates how essences are themselves intrinsically unstable and hence cannot be separated off from the realm of the discursive. Its anti-foundational approach means that it refuses any totalizing closure and emphasizes the temporary articulation of contingent and dissimilar elements.

Second, this refusal underlines a difference between the traditional study of political ideologies and discourse theory in practical analytical terms. As Norval (2000, p. 327) points out, the traditional study of ideologies has been focused primarily on the major political concepts and the complex formations of ideas formed around dominant political traditions. Such an approach accepts the divorce of 'ideas' from relations of power within society that is precisely an outcome of the naturalizing effect of ideology. Discourse theory, however, does not limit itself to dominant political traditions and complex theoretical arguments over the preferred social and political arrangements. On the contrary, it recognizes that the world is made meaningful not simply by expressly political concepts and ideals, but also by popular notions, 'common-sense' values and often quite irrational prejudices. As such, it is able to assess more adequately the extensive process whereby ideologies naturalize meaning.

Third, while the study of political ideologies is a highly formal conceptual analysis, discourse theory focuses less on the formal concepts and structure of ideologies than it does on the way this material functions to organize human experience. As Norval indicates, discourse theory is preoccupied with the way the subject is given coherence and meaning through discursive mechanisms and how this subjectivity is forged through relationships of power. Whereas studies of ideology consider the relatively stable frameworks that organize judgements about the world, studies of discourses focus on how symbolic frameworks get pieced together (or 'articulated') and enable certain types of agency and action, while marginalizing others.

Fourth, the study of political ideologies, by limiting the terms of the analysis to specifically delimitable ideologies (for instance, the 'isms'), often fails to examine the interrelationship *between* ideological formations. Discourse theory, in contrast, can examine patterns of thought and understanding shared across ideologies as well as within them. For instance, discourses of economic progress and rationality inform many socialist and liberal ideologies. Likewise, gendered and racialized discourses can be found within a variety of ideologies, often without being formally recognized as such. So, while we may consider discursive elements within political ideologies, we may also find them operating across ideologies, too.

Were we to treat the Third Way as a distinctive political ideology we might look for its recurrent concepts and analytical reference points, perhaps even consider these in relation to their 'parent' ideology, social democracy (see, for example, Driver and Martell, 1998, 2000). We could then proceed to break down the Third Way framework into its constituent elements, and review the policy outcomes delimited by such elements. While this approach may bring useful insights, it nevertheless remains limited. First, it overlooks the fact that the Third Way has never been presented as a fully coherent political ideology. Second, the approach neglects the deliberate effort by Third Way proponents to shake off the heritage of ideological continuity and steer a 'new path'.

In light of these difficulties, the methodological advantages of discourse theory for understanding the Third Way can be summarized as follows.

(a) Third ways can be conceived as innovative efforts to destabilize dominant ideological antagonisms, rearticulating in novel ways elements of preexisting political ideology around new concepts of difference and identity.
(b) Third ways deploy a range of common-sense ideas and not merely formal concepts to articulate their new path. These ideas will appeal to 'naturalized' social identities that are conceived as being inadequately served by existing ideological formations.
(c) Whatever their intellectual coherence, third ways can be understood as ways of shaping certain kinds of subjectivity around certain poles of identification that will supply them with political efficacy.
(d) Third ways are not exclusively of the left, right, or centre but can be found in a range of ideological formations. This suggests that we need to look across the ideological spectrum for 'family resemblances' if we are to properly understand the character of any one version.

With these advantages in mind, let us sketch some of the family resemblances in Third Way discourses (d), noting as we go the way they seek to rearticulate ideological elements (a), deploy common-sense concepts (b), and encourage certain kinds of subjectivity (c).

## The Third Way 'repertoire' in European ideology

New Labour's social democratic Third Way is part of a wider series of third ways enunciated from a variety of perspectives in the field of political ideology in the twentieth century. Considered together, this 'third tradition' exhibits a number of common features, or 'family resemblances', that centre around the motif of 'moving beyond' the established antagonism between left and right (see Bastow, Martin and Pels, 2002). That antagonism might be conceived in terms of opposed philosophical principles, models of social and political order, or competing policy options. Whichever forms they take, third ways are defined principally by the space they open up between preexisting alternatives, which they purport to both transcend and absorb into a new synthesis.

We have shown elsewhere how the innumerable third ways that have been proposed since the end of the nineteenth century are related to the crises of political ideology that have riven the twentieth century (see Bastow and Martin, 2003). These crises, themselves the condensation of a variety of social dislocations, mark a moment of rupture in the discursive fabric of social and political conflict in Europe, producing a fertile experimentation of ideas and ideological cross-overs that are not experienced at more stable moments, when the parameters of political debate are relatively fixed. While the twentieth century is plotted with numerous instances of ideological crisis of varying intensity, the most productive moments have been those in which a number of social and political dislocations converge. In Europe, such a conjuncture first occurred in the interwar period (1918–39) when third ways were developed from various quarters. A second, though perhaps less violently intense, series of dislocations occurs from the 1960s and culminates in the years after the end of the Cold War. In both periods, the settled parameters of conflict between left and right were disrupted and efforts were made to fashion a new politics that synthesized elements of each.

Common to all third ways is the claim to transcend the established antagonism between the 'left' and 'right' poles of the political spectrum, however these are defined in any particular instance. To go a *third* way is, by definition, to reject the first and second alternatives. But the third choice is not just one difference in a series (such as 1, 2, 3 . . .): typically it is presented as a transcendence of their mutually exclusive duality as the horizon of all ideological difference. The Third Way aims to define a new ideological space outside the traditional antagonism and, simultaneously, to absorb and reorder elements of those earlier ideologies, thereby creating a new synthesis superior to its predecessors. Whilst third ways differ markedly in content, their discursive form as the 'alternative to the alternatives' gives them a distinctive but ambiguous character: they are both outside established ideological discourse and yet inside it; they reject its duality but absorb elements of each in new ways. Thus third ways can be seen to emerge from within the left and right camps whilst often at the same time declaring themselves to be alternatives to that distinction.

We have analysed a range of texts from European political movements in the twentieth century from across the political spectrum, including works by conservatives, socialists and liberals, greens, and nationalists – in accordance with our view of the advantages of discourse theory for examining ideologies (noted above) – ranging from formal, academic texts of political thought and less formal manifestoes and political commentary by various radical movements. These texts were selected because of the explicit identification by most of their proponents with a discourse of the Third Way. In other cases, where there was no explicit reference, it is the homology between their analyses and the Third Way doctrines propounded by others that qualified them as contributions to the wider discursive field of Third Way discourse. As efforts to challenge dominant ideologies, Third Way doctrines would often have 'flanking' texts by supporters, in which aspects of political projects articulated through the notion of a third way were elaborated and defended. Key statements and flanking texts were found in a variety of documents such as official manifestoes as well as in day-to-day commentary in party journals and newspapers.

Rather than read these texts purely as abstract statements of principle (a difficult task given their often highly 'engaged' character) we conceived them as practico-theoretical efforts to modify the discursive field and deliberately open up political opportunities. Thus we contextualized each discourse in relation both to general displacements in the twentieth century between formations of state, economy, and social structure (Bastow and Martin, 2003, pp. 22–39), and to specific dislocations that problematized the reproduction of dominant ideological formations. Third Way discourses were then read as discursive interventions designed to have practical political effects by problematizing established ideological alternatives and rearticulating their elements into a new framework.

One problem with this approach, however, is that different social dislocations and ideological traditions promote radically different types of Third Way. Consequently, the precise content of Third Way doctrines differed starkly, some being focused primarily on issues of immigration, others on ecology or social justice. How, then, could we understand these discourses as having anything more than a passing resemblance? Our answer was to sketch a broad typology or 'repertoire' of common themes in Third Way discourses. These themes were more rhetorical than substantive, in so far as they indicate common reference points in the effort to move beyond a dominant antagonism of 'left vs. right'. How each discourse set about making this move was specific to its context and the ideological tradition from which it emerged.

The commonality of this rhetorical structure derives not from a transcendental origin but from the dissolution of the dominant ideological narratives inherited from the nineteenth century. These narratives (in particular liberalism and Marxism) had emphasized notions of historical progress or evolution, the objectively grounded character of human knowledge that would lead to universal emancipation, and the future reconciliation of social differences in a harmonized social order that would balance human freedom and communal identity.

The third ways of the twentieth century responded to the perceived exhaustion of these narratives by constructing their own narrative which would frame facts into a story about the objective world, its current condition, and the role of subjects in relation to it. The elements of the Third Way discursive repertoire that we brought to our reading of various texts included: the claim of 'crisis' in traditional antagonisms; an anti-materialism expressed in the appeal to ethics as the basis of social order; the promotion of a reconciled 'community'; and the designation of a key role for a specific agency (a vanguard or elite) to lead disaffected publics towards a new order. Let us examine these elements in turn.

### 1. Crisis

A crisis denotes a moment of rupture in which prevailing conditions are put in question and the possibility for a new order comes into view. Because they pit themselves against a dominant antagonism, third ways can only claim to transcend or move between that division if some space is opened up. The narrative of crisis is therefore designed to articulate the failure of a binary opposition and present the possibility for its supersession. Thus crisis involves two manoeuvres: the diagnosis of failure and the recommendation of intervention to resolve it.

In diagnosing failure, Third Way discourses bring together a number of dislocations and present them as moments in a generalized decline. A series of particular disappointments, short-term difficulties, and accumulated anxieties are metaphorically fused into a single argument pronouncing the total failure of existing institutions and options. These dislocations may include the experience of unemployment, the horrors and privations of war, forms of rapid and unregulated social change, environmental damage, the influx of immigrants, and so on. Taken by themselves these issues may constitute distinctive policy issues, but rolled together they symbolize a world increasingly out of control. Often, one problem alone is presented as symptomatic of a wider crisis. The dominant forces of politics are typically denounced as utterly unable to resolve this crisis adequately, being too complicit with the order that produced the problems in the first place.

To pose as a third option requires the other two to be conceived as limited or exhausted in some way. Third ways typically announce the historic end of a period of dominance by two opposed alternatives, which are often conceived in rather stereotypical terms. The crisis supposedly signals the exhaustion of these opposed options. The parties who embodied them no longer represent the experience of 'ordinary' people. Instead, they serve only specific, particular interests, not the interests of the people as a whole. It is in the space of crisis, therefore, that a Third Way becomes a plausible alternative.

New Labour's Third Way, for example, was announced in terms of a pervasive crisis of traditional party politics. Unable to grasp the logic of the new economy, it was commonly argued, both new right free-marketeers and old left statists had failed to seize the opportunities for enhancing both liberty and social justice by adapting to the global economy (see Blair, 1998, pp. 5–7; Giddens, 1994).

Other third ways, however, locate crisis elsewhere. European Greens, for example, have achieved significant success (especially in Germany) by alerting the public to a crisis supposedly threatening the very existence of humanity on the planet, the only solution to this crisis being the implementation of a sustainable economy. According to Greens, the problem is 'that there are natural limits to economic and population growth', because of the 'limited carrying capacity (for population), productive capacity (for resources of all types) and absorbent capacity (pollution)' of the Earth (Dobson, 2000, p. 15).

Neo-fascists, on the other hand, proclaim a crisis which comprises a generalized ethnic decline or degeneration whose markers are the triumph of global capitalism, the decline of the nation-state, decolonization, political corruption, the disempowerment of the 'people' by liberal democracy, and so on. Each of these results from the 'fact' that the people of Europe are being squeezed by the rampant materialism of both capitalism and communism.

### 2. Ethics and anti-materialism

Third ways commonly identify their goals in terms of a renewed ethics. The crisis of the old antagonism opens up a series of problems whose resolution can only be answered in terms of new ethical principles. This contrasts with the purported 'materialism' of earlier doctrines that appeal, for example, to class or individual 'interests' as the source of social order and improvement. Third ways reject this kind of materialism because it reduces humans to passive subjects of forces that seem to transcend them. In contrast, ethical principles imply a view of subjects as active and purposeful, consciously disciplining themselves to moral values that are authentically generated. It is this appeal to moral authenticity, a sense of genuine communal values in which the individual is aligned with the collective, that purportedly is lacking in older ideologies. By appealing to base instincts of class or individualism, they have lost touch with the moral bases of social life and are therefore responsible for 'decadent' and divisive behaviour.

In New Labour's discourse, the ethical imperative is defined in terms of a persistent appeal to 'values', in particular, liberal values of tolerance, opportunity, responsibility, and so forth (see Blair, 1998, pp. 3–4). Neither market nor state can of themselves motivate individuals. The traditional left, for example, 'mistakenly believed that somehow the actions of the state can fill this gap in values and attitudes among the least well-off in society. But it can't' (Mandelson, 2002, p. xxxi). Likewise, the right sought to make up for the failures of the market with an anachronistic moralism. For New Labour, however, the needs of social justice and the liberty of the individual are to be expressed in terms of an ethical relationship between individuals. This relationship is often summed up in terms of a conjoining of 'rights and responsibilities' (Giddens, 1998, pp. 36–7, 65–6; Blair, 1996, p. 298).

Again, however, other third ways construct the ethical imperative differently. Green discourse, for instance, seeks to bring about a new form of ethics – born from a complete reworking of the relationship between humankind and nature, as well as a stress on the ethical demand of our relationship as humans living in a community – and they challenge our commitment to material wealth on this basis. Neo-fascists, however, understand ethics in terms of the spiritual values of a 'natural' ethnic community, rooted either in the nation or in wider ethnic groupings (white European, for instance), which take the form of an ethics of action and militant engagement.

### 3. Community

This emphasis on ethics is typically accompanied by an appeal to 'community' as an absent order that needs to be made present. Third ways often identify community – a practically cohesive moral order – as something that has been disrupted by the invidious presence of the materialism of earlier doctrines. Of course, all ideologies make an appeal to community of some kind as a future reconciliation of individual and society (see Little, 2002a; Finlayson, 2002). Third ways follow this tradition but make a distinctive appeal to community as dependent primarily on an ethical transformation in subjects rather than a structural change to socio-economic institutions (although these are often involved). For third ways, the community is first and foremost an ethical ideal.

The specific content of the community may be defined in various ways but, as with all notions of community, it is premised on a sense of a common identity. The communal identity may be a racial or ethnic group, it may be a community of socially minded individuals or ecologically aware citizens. Whatever the content, the community is typically represented as what Laclau calls an 'absent presence' (see Laclau, 1996). That is, its presence in the discourse is as something that has 'declined' or has been undermined or blocked by certain contingent factors (the arrival of 'foreigners', the misdeeds of a political elite, and so on). Laclau argues that it is precisely this absence or blockage that heightens the sense of the community as a common identity. Discourses of community function through their symbolization of a deferred presence. That way, the differentiated components of this community are abstractly related, as their individual gripes and issues are symbolically blurred into a generalized claim to sameness.

The Third Way discourse proffered by the radical right, for example, articulates an organic, biologistic notion of the community to be reborn. Thus the French radical right movement L'Œuvre Français proclaimed the existence of 'a natural community', articulating links with all those rooted in the French nation through blood, a common Celtic ancestry and productive activity (see Le Goff, 1968). Such forms of community are also expressed by 'ecofascist' forms of ecologism.

Whilst these appeals to community often invoke a homogenous and deep sense of collective solidarity, New Labour's discourse is slightly different. It does make a very noticeable appeal to the ideal of community, but it typically does so in a more liberal vein, highlighting not ethnic bonds but looser connections such as 'partnerships' between businesses and localities, or the ongoing responsibilities of individuals to their families, or of the state to the socially excluded (see Blair, 1996, pp. 215–22, 297–309; Mandelson and

Liddle, 1996, pp. 19–21; Giddens, 1998, pp. 78–98). However, community is nevertheless conceived in often contradictory ways (see Hughes and Little, 1999): it is both the solid foundation of family life and the source for individuals to realize themselves in the market. The need for community as the central source of social life paradoxically demands strong government action to enforce individual responsibilities both to their families and to others.

## 4. Agency

Finally, third ways tend to associate the emergence of their new order with the agency of a particular group, individual or elite. While they need not be *elitist* in the sense of asserting the absolute superiority of particular individuals over others, nevertheless third way discourse gives a certain priority to a creative person or people. This elite is deemed to represent or have a particular understanding of the moment of crisis opened up by the failure of the old antagonism. Because third ways predicate their argument on a notion of ethical, as opposed to material, transformation, proper intervention in the crisis will occur not as a spontaneous movement of impersonal forces (for example, Marxism's 'dialectical laws', or the 'hidden hand' of the free market), but through a full comprehension of the situation and the audacity to challenge the old order.

This elitism is often complemented by optimism about the historical force of ideas and the mission of 'intellectual' politicians, and the style of a new generational or 'young' politics. Both of these elements point to a further feature of third way ideologies, namely, that they tend to come to prominence during periods of crisis in which traditional ideas of left and right no longer seem adequately to apply. This partly explains the missionary status of those preaching a third way doctrine. It ties in with a common emphasis on a 'new generation', 'new order', and youth that is a recurrent feature of third way ideologies. It is precisely because they have no roots in the order which has been dislocated that third way activists can stress their novelty, and claim to offer a way out from the problems caused by decaying doctrines.

The elitism found in Green politics, for instance, takes different forms depending on whether the ideology in question is egalitarian and decentralized or authoritarian. In terms of the former, one finds an emphasis on a 'new' – in this case 'postmaterialist' – generation, as analysed in the work of Inglehart (see Inglehart, 1977, 1990). Such arguments clearly display optimism about the historical force of ideas and the mission of 'intellectual' politicians. In terms of the latter, the hierarchical, organic forms of community that they advocate obviously lend themselves to the notion that an elite exists which symbolizes the form of society to come, and has the will to bring it about.

Similar variations and contradictions can be found in other third way discourses. Whilst neo-fascists often claim to speak for a repressed national community, they claim at the same time that this ethnic community will be deliberately (re)created through historical intervention. As such, they often attach great significance to leaders and to youth organizations that are deemed to represent that community. The French National Revolutionary grouping, Jeune Nation (JN), for example, claim that history 'has always been written by small minorities', and positively cite the statement by José-Antonio Primo de Riveira that 'the revolution is the work of a minority which is inaccessible to discouragement' (Benedetti, n.d.).

New Labour, whilst accepting the parameters of party politics, has nevertheless self-consciously marketed itself as the agency of radical change and social renewal. Few slogans express this better than 'New Labour, New Britain'. As an agency of modernization, Labour's newness was to become Britain's newness. Thus, like other third ways, the movement comes to incarnate the ideals it represents (see Blair, 1996, pp. 35–50). In his 1995 speech to the Labour Party conference Tony Blair invoked the classic image of 'youth' as the symbol of a reinvigorated unity and purpose: 'I want us to be a young country again. With a common purpose. With ideals we cherish and live up to. Not resting on past glories' (Ibid, p. 46).

While New Labour avoids the openly authoritarian emphasis on charisma or vanguardism of other third ways, nevertheless, like other proponents of third ways, it sees itself as more than just a party: it is the living symbol of the change it wishes to bring about. While this has led to accusations of excessive media manipulation ('spin'), insensitivity to the party's democratic traditions, and even presidentialism, in many respects it tallies with an assumption common to third ways, that the agent of change to a certain extent incarnates the order it seeks to bring about.

## Embracing antagonism: radical democracy and the Third Way

The semantic structure of the Third Way, we have suggested, is itself part of the politics it promotes. Third ways, however they are constructed, direct us to the exhaustion of dominant forms of ideological thought; they make explicit the failure of ideologies to dominate fully the field of dislocated subjects and social antagonisms. However, in looking 'beyond' antagonism, third ways run the danger of seeking to eradicate antagonism altogether. Let us consider the possibilities signalled by third way discourses and the problems these raise in relation to New Labour.

As forms of practico-theoretical intervention, third ways acknowledge the possibility for reassembling political ideas and practices in novel ways, for refashioning the hierarchies of principles and values that other systems of belief appear to set in stone. They do this with an emphasis on developing new types of ethical subjectivity, on forging social order from within the authentic experience of social subjects themselves. In many respects, New Labour's success as a leading social democratic force in Europe lies precisely in its promise to revive the left's role as a source of progressive change against conservatism and as a mobilizer of popular sentiment. It addresses individuals as social subjects, not as atomistic individuals or passive bearers of class interests, but as conscious agents of a better society to come.

However, this opening to the contingency of ideological structures and the active role of subjects is often strikingly limited by a further appeal to essentialist principles aimed at grounding the Third Way in some kind of 'necessity'. This essentialism is often visible in the notions of community that we have argued are key to third way discourses, and it is visible in New Labour's discourse, too. Third ways typically point to notions of communal solidarity, not on the basis of rational choices of individuals but on that of a spiritual bond, which ties people together at a pre-rational level. This bond – expressed in terms of ethnic or national identity, a common link to nature, or a shared sense of 'risk' in a global society, for example – is typically presented as forming a necessary part of subjective identity. That is, it is a bond that is not open to contest but precedes the subject as a natural, or nature-like, condition.

Essentialist principles, however, effectively close down the space for rearticulating ideological elements. Indeed, some notions of community achieve this closure retroactively by positing the community as an already given identity, not one that is itself forged contingently (see Finlayson, 1998). While New Labour's invocation of community certainly does not resemble the far right's aspiration to return to an authentic community lost in the empty decadence of the modern age, it remains problematic, as New Labour's essentialism lies in its effort to ground community in the underlying necessity of globalization. As various commentators have indicated, a central plank of New Labour's political discourse is its acceptance of globalization as a 'fact' to be accommodated through strategies of modernization (similar to Giddens's argument, mentioned above. See Hay, 1999). While there are many separate strands in New Labour's idea of community (such as liberal meritocracy, the struggle against anti-social behaviour, support for civic associations) a dominant theme is its view of political economy – propounded now in governmental documents and legislative proposals – being driven by the global demand for greater competition, increased flexibility, and the need for a highly skilled labour force (see Raco, 2002).

One of New Labour's great novelties has been its ability to make this purportedly objective condition the unifying centre of its vision of a renewed civic life. Thus the 'need' for skills, retraining ('education, education, education') and entrepreneurial common sense to adapt the workforce to a 'post-Fordist' capitalism has underscored key aspects of public policy (see Finlayson, 2003; Rose, 1999). While this competitive ethic differs from neo-fascist or Green third ways in that it renounces any essential cultural, ethnic, or natural bond, the effect is similar: the unifying principle of community is conceived as fundamentally incontestable. Alternative forms of economic activity and association – and different ways of construing globalization itself – are ruled out as legitimate options.

It is the tendency towards essentialist closure that makes the third way claim to move beyond the antagonism of left and right tend towards a claim to move beyond *all* antagonisms. This explains a common orientation towards various levels of authoritarianism. It is because the essential unity of society has been grasped as the ethical basis of social order that its institutional form does not need to be open to contest. The economic plan, the party, the social reformer, and so on are too often conceived as being beyond reproach, and any difference in opinion over their functioning is assumed to be neutralized by the wider ethical unity that legitimates them. Thus, while third ways may be more or less democratic in their organization, the limits of democracy are often placed around the conditions that give rise to the community itself. In New Labour's case, the claim to represent a 'radical centre' based on 'consensus' has been seen by some as potentially authoritarian in that it fails to acknowledge openly relations of power and hence the potential for antagonism that its programme might encounter (see Mouffe, 2000, ch. 5). Paradoxically, unlike many other radical right- and left-wing third ways – which have engaged in various kinds of antagonistic conflicts with their opponents – New Labour treats overcoming antagonism as a form of governing practice and not just a future ideal.

Third ways, then, typically promise a genuine, radical change and yet often limit this change within an essentialist discourse that restricts political conflict (that is, contest over the boundaries and needs of the community) by disguising its own contingency. But does this, admittedly sweeping, characterization limit the radical potential of third way discourses?

We want, briefly, to suggest here that radical democratic theory might itself be understood as a third way discourse. However, what is distinctive about radical democracy – built, as it is, on the anti-essentialism of discourse theory – is its refusal of any final closure on the idea of community, and the impossibility of eradicating antagonism. Radical democrats seek to extend democracy to struggles and subjects usually excluded from parliamentary politics, but they do so without losing sight of the contingency and conflict that such an extension implies. Certainly, this requires a politics that is quite different from that of New Labour and other social democratic third ways. But it is no less an effort to reorient political life away from established antagonisms of left and right and towards a new sense of ethics and community.

Let us think about radical democracy in relation to the elements of the repertoire outlined above. First of all, radical democracy is conceived as a response to a crisis within the left between its revolutionary and reformist wings, and within the political spectrum as a whole. Like contemporary third ways of the centre-left, it recognizes the failure of parliamentary politics to respond effectively to the rise of new social movements and forms of antagonism beyond the interest groups of capital and labour. Unlike the centre-left, however, the failures of traditional politics are not regarded as an opportunity to reinvent the centre-ground of pragmatic liberal reformism.

Instead, radical democrats promote a *post-liberal* form of politics, one that recognizes the intrinsic plurality of social identities and the role of power and conflict in producing them (see Mouffe, 1992; 1993; 2000). This places them on the left, but not in any exclusive or rigid sense. Whilst emerging from the Marxist tradition, Laclau and Mouffe have drawn upon insights from both Gramsci and right-wing thinkers such as Carl Schmitt (see Laclau and Mouffe, 2001; Mouffe, 2000, ch. 2).

Secondly, radical democracy renounces efforts to tie the revival of political life to material interests, particularly those of class. This reflects a wider rejection of any rationalism that might bind together the future political community and it opens up radical democracy to the terrain of ethics, that is, the contingent agreement between subjects as to how to live together. But if political association cannot be founded on any rational principle then all order is ultimately grounded on contingent hegemonic practices that stabilize social relations. As Mouffe argues, this rules out any appeal to consensus as the ultimate basis of ethical life. All association will be marked by the limited, partial, and antagonistic experiences and dislocations that generate social identities. All that we may expect is a temporary 'conflictual consensus' about the proper parameters of public concern and forms of inclusion and exclusion it entails (2000, p. 103). Indeed, who 'we' are can only be specified by excluding those we are not. However, the absence of a final foundation upon which to regulate social differences and collective concerns opens up opportunities for new and diverse identities to assert themselves. Mouffe suggests that this requires an 'ethics of democracy', one in which different subjects are encouraged to accept that their conflictual relationship with others need not impede their own or others' participation in social and political life (Ibid., pp. 129–40).

Thirdly, radical democrats accept the multiplicity of forms communities may take and renounce the idea of a politics limited exclusively to communities. However, this need not imply a rejection of the idea of community per se. Instead, a radical democratic politics promotes a notion of political community as a loose form of identification, but one that is more than a shared set of legal entitlements. While this community lacks any substantive sense of the Common Good, it remains a 'form of life' united through a shared 'language of civil intercourse' (see Mouffe, 1993, pp. 66–73) promoting the expansion of liberty and equality for all. Thus it is possible to conceive of political community neither as an exclusive ethnic group nor as an association of atomized individuals (see Little, 2002a; 2002b).

Finally, radical democracy's emphasis on hegemony raises the question of agency. Unlike most third ways, radical democrats avoid privileging any social group, individual, or institutional model as the incarnation of the future order. Indeed, it is precisely because there is no final order that reconciles social differences that such an idea of agency is inconceivable. Here, then, radical democracy departs significantly from most third way discourses.

Instead, we might conceive radical democracy as being in a permanent 'war of position', constantly looking to different sites and innovative forms of struggle and representation that might further the effort to expand the presence of democratic subjects. These might involve, for example, new forms of democratic governance or deliberative assemblies, as well as dialogues and confrontations with groups typically excluded from liberal democratic politics.

## Conclusion

Let us sum up our argument. Methodologically speaking, discourse theory involves an anti-essentialist approach to the interpretation of ideological formations. Rather than look for a stable, objective point of reference – such as 'globalization' – with which to evaluate the Third Way, we need to consider the contingent articulation of its diverse elements. This indicates a number of things. The Third Way is partly involved in constructing its own objective reality. It is less a response to certain social conditions than a way of framing social change in a way that positions us as certain kinds of subjects. To offer, as Callinicos does, an alternative (and opposed) reading of that reality does not in itself address how the Third Way works (although this point does not invalidate his remarks). We, however, have tried to unravel the discursive elements that structure third way ideologies. While these differ starkly in their analysis and substantive concerns, an approach based in discourse analysis enables us to show how third ways are built around the claim to move beyond a dominant ideological antagonism that inhibits the resolution of crisis. This discourse addresses its audience as ethical subjects in need of a communal reunification that is not provided by existing political traditions. Thus it is third way discourse itself that performatively opens a space for political intervention with a distinctive ethical and communitarian appeal, not just New Labour's Third Way.

While third ways have been forged on the left, right, and centre of the political spectrum, they need not all be authoritarian, reactionary, or complicit with global capitalism. The Third Way admits of a variety of different possibilities; its ambiguity is in many respects its advantage, since it opens a space for a creative reformulation of political possibilities. Indeed, we might consider, as we have suggested, the possibility that there can be a radical democratic third way. Of course, the condition of this third way would be that the left–right antagonism isn't abandoned altogether. Rather, a radical democratic third way would have to accept the ineradicable nature of antagonism in social life, and yet be prepared to move beyond the stale alternatives offered up by traditional political ideologies. While there are many plausible reasons for radical democrats to reject New Labour's project, discourse theory permits us to think that there remains scope for radicalism in third way politics today.

## Bibliography


Anderson, P. (2000) 'Renewals', *New Left Review*, (II), 1: 5–24.

Bastow, S., and Martin, J. (2003) *Third Way Discourse: European Ideologies in the Twentieth Century* (Edinburgh, Edinburgh University Press).

Bastow, S., Martin, J., and Pels, D. (eds) (2002) *Third Way Ideologies*, special Issue of the *Journal of Political Ideologies*, vol. 7 (3).

Bell, D. (1988) *The End of Ideology: On the Exhaustion of Political Ideas in the Fifties* (Cambridge, Mass., Harvard University Press).

Benedetti, J.-Y. (n.d.) 'Le Front national et nous', editorial, *Jeune Nation*, 17.

Blair, T. (1996) *New Britain: My Vision of a Young Country* (London, Fourth Estate).

Blair, T. (1998) *The Third Way: New Politics for the New Century* (London, Fabian Society).

Blair, T. (2001) 'Third Way, Phase Two', *Prospect*, March: 10–13.

Blair, T., and Schröder, G. (1999) *Europe: the Third Way/die Neue Mitte* (London, Labour Party).

Callinicos, A. (2001) *Against the Third Way* (Cambridge, Polity).

Dobson, A. (2000) *Green Political Thought: an Introduction* (3rd edn) (London, Routledge).

Driver, S., and Martell, L. (1998) *New Labour: Politics after Thatcherism* (Cambridge, Polity).

Driver, S., and Martell, L. (2000) 'Left, Right and the Third Way', *Policy & Politics*, vol. 28 (2): 147–61.

Eagleton, T. (1991) *Ideology: an Introduction* (London, Verso).

Finlayson, A. (1998) 'Ideology, Discourse and Nationalism', *Journal of Political Ideologies*, vol. 3 (1): 99–118.

Finlayson, A. (2002), 'The Horizon of Community', in A. Finlayson and J. Valentine (eds), *Politics and Post-structuralism: an Introduction* (Edinburgh, Edinburgh University Press).

Finlayson, A. (2003) *Making Sense of New Labour* (London, Lawrence and Wishart).

Freeden, M. (1996) *Ideologies and Political Theory: a Conceptual Approach* (Oxford, Clarendon).

Giddens, A. (1994) *Beyond Left and Right: the Future of Radical Politics* (Cambridge, Polity).

Giddens, A. (1998) *The Third Way: the Renewal of Social Democracy* (Cambridge, Polity).

Giddens, A. (2000) *The Third Way and Its Critics* (Cambridge, Polity).

Giddens, A. (ed.) (2001) *The Global Third Way Debate* (Cambridge, Polity).

Hay, C. (1999) *The Political Economy of New Labour: Labouring under False Pretences* (Manchester, Manchester University Press).

Hughes, G., and Little, A. (1999) 'The Contradictions of New Labour's Communitarianism', *Imprints*, vol. 4, (1): 37–62.

Inglehart, R. (1977) *The Silent Revolution: Changing Values and Political Styles among Western Publics* (Princeton, N. J., Princeton University Press).

Inglehart, R. (1990) *Culture Shift in Advanced Society* (Princeton, N. J., Princeton University Press).

Laclau, E. (1996) *Emancipation(s)* (London, Verso).

Laclau, E., and Mouffe, C. (2001) *Hegemony and Socialist Strategy: Towards a Radical Democratic Politics* (2nd edn) (London, Verso).

Le Goff, J.-C. (1968) 'Le Nationalisme', *Le Soleil*, 6–12 November.

Lefort, C. (1986) *The Political Forms of Modern Society: Bureaucracy, Democracy, Totalitarianism* (Cambridge, Polity).

Little, A. (2002a) *The Politics of Community: Theory and Practice* (Edinburgh, Edinburgh University Press).

Little, A. (2002b), 'Community and Radical Democracy', in Bastow, Martin, and Pels (2002), *Third Way Ideologies*.
Mandelson, P. (2002), 'Introduction', *The Blair Revolution Revisited* (London, Politico's).
Mandelson, P., and Liddle, R. (1996) *The Blair Revolution* (London, Politico's); re-issued in 2002 as Mandelson, P., *The Blair Revolution Revisited* (London, Politico's).
Mannheim, K. (1991) *Ideology and Utopia: an Introduction to the Sociology of Knowledge* (London, Routledge).
Mouffe, C. (ed.) (1992) *Dimensions of Radical Democracy: Pluralism, Citizenship, Community* (London, Verso).
Mouffe, C. (1993) *The Return of the Political* (London, Verso).
Mouffe, C. (2000) *The Democratic Paradox* (London, Verso).
Norval, A. (2000) 'Review Article: the Things We Do with Words – Contemporary Approaches to the Analysis of Ideology', *British Journal of Political Science*, 30: 313–46.
Raco, M. (2002) 'Risk, Fear and Control: Deconstructing the Discourses of New Labour's Economic Policy', *Space and Polity*, col. 6 (1): 25–47.
Rose, N. (1999) 'Inventiveness in Politics', *Economy and Society*, vol. 28 (3): 467–93.
Vincent, A. (1992) *Modern Political Ideologies* (Oxford, Blackwell).
White, S. (2001) 'The Ambiguities of the Third Way', in S. White (ed.), *New Labour: the Progressive Future?* (Basingstoke, Palgrave Macmillan).

# 9

# New Labour's Politics of the Hard-working Family

*Oscar Reyes*

This chapter uses the case of New Labour's family politics to investigate the general claim that the party rejects a social democratic politics 'grounded in collective agency, attachments, and interests' (Krieger, 1999, p. 19).[1] It argues that New Labour has not abandoned the attempt to construct political subjects, as its politics both presupposes the existence of bonds of community and seeks to strengthen them. This is, in fact, the core of Blair's 'social-ism': an ethical judgement that individuals are socially interdependent human beings who owe a duty to one another and to a broader society (Blair, 1994, p. 4). But does the displacement from class to the notoriously slippery concept of community leave the meaning of this collectivity radically unspecified, and therefore incapable of constituting lasting attachments (Krieger, 1999, p. 160)? I argue that it does not, because the particular case of the 'hard-working family' is promulgated as typical of the universal notion of community, providing it with a concrete representation. My main thesis, then, is that the 'hard-working family' has emerged as the principle subject posited by New Labour politics. This marks the abandonment of the working man (and his dependants) as Labourism's historical subject. As Mandelson and Liddle put it, 'Whereas the old left saw its job as to represent trade unions, pressure groups and the "working class" . . . New Labour stands for the ordinary families who work hard and play by the rules' (1996, p. 18).

This also allows for a new perspective on the debates within social policy, which have concentrated on the tensions and contradictions between New Labour's politics of the family and its welfare policies that emphasize work (for example, Levitas, 1998; Driver and Martell, 2002). There is general agreement that these positions conflict, although the degree to which this is the case is a matter of some continuing controversy. What this debate overlooks, however, is an understanding of how these 'obvious' contradictions are experienced as coherent parts of the same New Labour project, tied together by the notion of the 'hard-working family'. This can, in part, be explained by the nature of political discourses themselves – which can tolerate high levels of logical inconsistency in terms of both their conceptual morphology and the types of subject they promote (Freeden, 1996, p. 71; Laclau, 1977, p. 104). It also points to a significant change in the way that policy is now formulated: 'New Labour is perhaps the first government genuinely committed to the view that presentation is part of the process of policy formation' (Franklin, 1998, p. 4; Fairclough, 2000, p. 122). This dimension should not be ignored, because it impacts upon the quality of the contribution policy scholars can make.

The chapter begins with an analysis of the dislocation of Labour and European social democracy, and its impact upon the class-based agency that the parties of the West European left traditionally privileged. The aim is to show how an analysis of structures and institutions can provide political discourse analysts with a useful resource for identifying points of discursive concentration. This is also, implicitly, a response to the accusation that discourse analysis is 'subjectivist' and privileges agency over structure (for example, Dallmayr, 1989, p. 131).[2]

What such an analysis cannot offer, however, is an understanding of how these changes have been interpreted by the main thinkers who have influenced New Labour. From the outset, New Labour has drawn upon and articulated two conflicting analyses of family change: the social conservatism associated with Etzioni and the notion of the post-traditionalist (or 'democratic') family that informs reflexive sociology (Deacon and Mann, 1997, 1999). New Labour in general, and Blair in particular, are usually seen as being closer to Etzioni on this point, viewing the family as a *counterbalance* to flexibility and change rather than an *expression* of it (Driver and Martell, 2002, p. 48).

The analysis of these tensions within New Labour discourse is now well advanced in the social policy literature. What is so far lacking, however, is an appreciation of how these divergent strands come to be represented as part of the same political project. It is at this point that I introduce the notion of the 'hard-working family' as the nodal point which organizes New Labour's discourse on work and the family, as well as holding together the contending strands of New Labour's communitarian values, as mapped on a liberal-authoritarian dimension.[3]

Broadly speaking, the tensions that arise at the level of public philosophy and sociological analysis[4] are reconciled at the level of popular discourse. The 'hard-working family' entered New Labour discourse via its political marketing operation, but moves to integrate presentation into the political process have resulted in its holding an important role in organizing New Labour discourse. In particular, I show how the hard-working family gives substance to the empty signifier of 'community', and serves as an important locus for New Labour's development of a 'value'-driven rather than 'class'-driven politics.

## The dislocation of Labour's traditional appeal: a European perspective

The British Labour Party in particular, and European social democracy in general, has traditionally grounded its politics on a claim to represent the material interests of the manual working class. Without debating the finer details of what this appeal to 'the working class' actually meant, a number of relatively uncontroversial aspects of its meaning can be clearly discerned. The working class was principally defined in terms of *male* workers in the *industrial* sector, and each social democratic party drew the boundaries of this constituency within the borders of a single *nation-state*. If the British Labour Party is the exception to the rule of European social democracy – as orthodox interpretations insist – then it is partly because it exemplified this model of distributive politics rather too well. Where other social democratic parties were established to achieve the transformation of capitalism into a socialism based on the common ownership of the means of production, Labour emerged 'from the bowels of the trade union movement' to promote legislation 'in the direct interests of labour' (cited in Pelling, 1965, p. 209).[5] Yet, in common with other European social democrats, the rationale underpinning Labour's demands was ultimately universalistic, with its 'socialism' emphasizing 'not class consciousness, but community consciousness' (Ramsay MacDonald, cited in Panitch, 1972, p. 190). That is, the particular interests of the manual working class were advanced insofar as they could be made to coincide with the purported aims of the national community, to which they were ultimately subordinated (Panitch, 1972). Revisionism did not mark a break with this model but further embedded it. In its 1950s variant, it continued the 'de-proletarianization' of social democracy, which had accompanied the steady march from anti-system force to electoral reformism (Sassoon, 1996, pp. 25–53). While the British Labour Party failed to match the symbolism of the German SPD, whose Bad Godesberg programme of 1959 announced its transformation from 'a party of the workers' into a 'party of the people', it nevertheless followed a similar trajectory. The articulation between the working class and 'the people' gradually gave way to the displacement of the former by the latter.

A similar story can be told regarding the rise of the welfare state. The Labour Party of the 1930s had favoured a tax-financed system of subsistence payments, a set of proposals 'overwhelmingly based on a *class* analysis of the structure of national wealth' (Harris, 1996, p. 128, italics in original). By contrast, the central planks of the post-war welfare state were 'universal' in their aspiration: full male employment and the setting of a national minimum provision for dependants and non-insured workers (Glennester, 2000, pp. 4–5). Yet the limits of this universalism were quickly reached, since the adopted system of contributory insurance accorded full citizenship to paid workers only. So the division between the worker and his dependants was a telling one – as it had been for Beveridge, who firmly believed in 'the household of man, wife and children maintained by the earnings of the first alone' (cited Glennester, 2000, p. 32). The 1945 Labour government adopted a system of contributory insurance based on paid work which effectively marginalized anyone outside the labour market. In practice, this affected women most sharply.

Finally, it is worth considering the economic conditions under which this settlement was established. In common with their continental counterparts, Labour governments have relied on market-led growth to improve basic social conditions, while at the same time seeking to mitigate the worst inequalities generated by capitalism.[6] In its various forms, the welfare state became the institutional lynchpin of post-war settlements across Europe. This was rendered possible by the Fordist organization of the means of production – or, rather, a 'flawed Fordism' (Jessop, 1994, p. 28). But it was also sustained by the persistence of the 'traditional' family (Esping-Andersen, 1999, p. 15). Whether we talk in terms of three (or more) worlds of welfare capitalism, most post-war welfare states assumed a division between a world of paid work, in which male breadwinners predominated, and a private domain of the family, where women were dependants (J. Lewis, 1997, p. 167).[7]

What this brief survey shows is that the organization of Labour's popular appeal and the principle institution with which it sought to associate itself (the welfare state) assumed a particular mode of production (Fordism) and typical subjectivity (the male manual worker). The resonance of this appeal was guaranteed by its universalist pretensions, although 'the disparity between the professed goals and the stipulated means was palpable' (Elliott, 1993, p. 161). A similar set of assumptions and limitations was, to a greater and lesser extent, common to post-war social democrats across Europe. The crisis that has affected the Labour Party and its European counterparts from the mid-1970s is, to a great extent, a product of the fact that these assumptions no longer hold. As a result, social democratic parties across Europe have sought to embody the 'universality' of their demands in different ways. It is my argument, in what follows, that the British Labour Party has done this by appealing to the 'hard-working family', which embodies and represents the universal notion of community. But, before we analyse the emergence of this, it is first necessary to examine in more detail the emergence of a post-industrial society, and its dislocatory impact upon the British and European left.

## Post-industrial society

In Western Europe, recent decades have seen the arrival of a 'post-industrial' society. This term is effectively a shorthand for the relative decline of manufacturing industry in Western economies and its replacement by a mode of production in which no single form of work is dominant (Sassoon, 1996, p. 654).

For Daniel Bell, who, in 1976, theorized 'The coming of postindustrial society' in a book of that name, this should have resulted in a benign new world, where technicians and professionals predominate, and affluent consumers' appetites are met by a service economy. This is not far removed from the gleaming future projected by today's new economists, whose vision of an emerging knowledge economy has heavily influenced New Labour (for example, Leadbeater, 2000).[8] Its modernization agenda has emphasized the development of human capital, equipping individuals to meet the needs of the 'knowledge based service economy of the future' (Blair and Schroeder, 1999, p. 5). Like much of New Labour's economic policy, this is presented as a logical response to changed circumstances – in this case, the undeniable fact that Western economies (including Britain) have shifted away from industrial employment and that the service sector now predominates. Yet this dislocation has not been sufficient to secure the progressive outcome that New Labour ideologues would claim for it. Why not? Discourse analysis offers one theoretical reason: dislocation is not explanatory, so the shift from one form of capitalism to another is, in itself, insufficient grounds for progress. Empirical analysis of economic and social trends provides another, which is that technological futurism of the sort New Labour has espoused underestimates the continued reliance on labour-intensive, low-skilled employment – today's low-status 'McJobs' (Ritzer, 1993, p. 153).[9]

This is not to deny that under the label of post-industrialism lie some real processes of employment change, including the widespread entry of women into the labour market and the rise of 'flexible labour' (part-time and short-term jobs). These changes have served to fragment working-class associations, the former by dislocating the predominant, traditional image of the 'worker', the latter by reducing job security and weakening unions. Moreover, these changes (which are not merely economic, but also cultural and political) have attenuated workplace solidarities by individualizing industrial relations. This is a process to which British trade unions, as well as the Thatcher government, have also contributed (Krieger, 1999, pp. 60, 73). Britain has unenviably led the way, but the pattern here is consistent with Europe-wide trends, which have arguably contributed to a convergence of parties of the left (Vanderbrouke, 1999, p. 37).

Yet the social changes that have both produced the post-industrial condition and, to a large extent, driven it do not stop at the doors of the labour market. As Esping-Andersen has recently argued, 'the household economy is *alpha and omega* to any resolution of the main postindustrial dilemmas, perhaps the single most important "social foundation" of postindustrial economies' (1999, p. 6). At the heart of this economy lies the institution of the family, which is one of the main sites at which the advance of post-industrial society has been 'experienced'. These changes have given rise to two main contradictions. First, the rise in women's labour market participation has generated tension between the commitment to paid work and the continuing (male) assumption that women bear the brunt of unpaid care work:

> although women are in the labour force on this massive scale, society as a whole has not really accepted this fact of life: the domestic sphere, the world of work, the welfare state are all organized as if women were continuing a traditional role. (A. Sassoon, cited Krieger, 1999, p. 97)

Secondly, although the emergent post-industrial society has resulted in the feminization of the labour force, it has not eroded the gendered division of labour that was a defining characteristic of the prior, Fordist work regime. What has happened, rather, is that the division between male and female work has been redrawn *within* the world of paid work. This is not altogether surprising, since the growth of the service sector is premised on the purchase of personal services formerly provided by household labour: 'women's work', to borrow a sociologically accurate but sexist terminology. A new dualistic structure has emerged, consisting of a stagnant or declining full-time sector of mainly male employees and a growing sector of predominantly female part-time workers (Sassoon, 1996, p. 659). The impact of this flexibility has been felt most sharply by women workers (Krieger, 1999, p. 85).

To conclude: post-industrialism and the reorganization of family life have served both to loosen traditional attachments to the Labour Party and dislocate the model of the 'worker' on which its politics had traditionally been grounded. These changes form the backdrop for the emergence of New Labour, which can justly claim that its freedom of political movement is checked by new structural constraints that exceed the boundaries of the British state within which it operates. Yet alterations in the mode of production in no way determine the direction that New Labour has, in fact, taken – as its more fervent apologists sometimes assume.[10] If 'the world has changed' (Blair, 1998, p. iv), then it remains very much a matter of political judgement as to how these changes are interpreted, and what ideological directions are followed in response. In the discourse of New Labour, they are interpreted in terms of the rise of a knowledge-based service economy, which is thought to have permanently altered the relationship between work and the family. But it can be argued that New Labour's preoccupation with the work–family nexus – such as its programmes for family friendly employment, childcare, and a working families tax credit – emerges on the site of a structural tension that it never really resolves (except by definitional fiat). It is my thesis that the emergence of the 'hard-working family' as the privileged subject organizes New Labour discourse in such a way as to cover over the contradictions that these structural changes generate. It also offers a way for Labour's championing of family values *and* its emphasis on the moral good of paid work to be thought of as part of the same project (Beck-Gersheim, 2002, p. x). In the long term, the material effects of these contradictions threaten to destabilize

New Labour discourse and weaken its grip – not least because the emerging assumption of dual-earning families rather than a male breadwinner model ignores the persistence of a gendered division of labour in the spheres of both paid and unpaid work (J. Lewis, 2002, p. 56). For the analysis of New Labour discourse as it is now, however, the importance of the work–family nexus lies elsewhere: a structural analysis of its centrality has helped to reveal the *articulation* between work and family.

What this analysis of structural change cannot offer, however, is an understanding of the specific meanings accorded to the hard-working family (and the policies and ideas relating to it) in New Labour discourse. To discern these meanings, we first need to look at the *interpretations* of these changes by the main thinkers who have influenced New Labour, before turning our focus to the development of the 'hard-working family' as a nodal point organizing New Labour discourse.

## The contradictions of New Labour discourse

New Labour articulates two contradictory responses to the structural and institutional changes outlined in the first part of this paper: the conservative communitarianism associated with Etzioni and the post-traditionalist family of reflexive sociology (especially Giddens).

New Labour's emphasis on 'community', and the stress upon 'rights and responsibilities' at the heart of its discourse, are predominantly advanced to counterbalance the new insecurities, which the emergence of a post-industrial society is seen to generate. This is the Etzioni side of New Labour discourse. The rise of individualism (of both Left and Right)[11] is held to have undermined the moral foundations of society. If left unchecked, this 'anarchic drift' can encourage the rise of right-wing authoritarianism (Etzioni, 1995, p. 6). Progressive politicians should therefore seek to reverse the 'imbalance' between rights and responsibilities and work towards a moral revival, encouraging the development of stable families as the means to reinforce communities: 'To shore up the moral foundations of our society, we start with the family. The family was always entrusted with laying the foundations of moral education' (Etzioni, 1995, p. 248). A new emphasis on 'parental responsibility' is central to this task, and this is set in the context of a defence of the nuclear family (Etzioni, 1995, pp. 54, 72–3, and ch. 2).

Giddens is rather more relaxed about the form that the family might take – a point that is well illustrated by his attitude to marriage. For Giddens it is the stability of relationships – rather than marriage itself – which serves as the main normative ideal. The family is not what it once was, and this is in many ways a good thing. Inequality between men and women was intrinsic to the traditional family; women and children lacked rights; and sexuality was dominated by reproduction (1999, pp. 55–6). This old pattern was undesirable, and is in any case unsustainable in the late-modern world.

The economic basis of marriage and family life has been displaced – initially by romantic love, and more recently by an intimate 'coupledom' bonded by trust. Sexuality is no longer reducible to reproduction, and need not be heterosexual. Moreover, the transformation of women's 'roles' in recent decades has reshaped the internal dynamics of family life in a democratic direction. All of these developments are to be encouraged.

The fundamental ethical principle animating Giddens's new model family – which reflects these changes in family life rather than seeking to hold them in check – is the need to form intimate relationships. Such relationships are built around an ideal of emotional communication, which requires equality between partners if it is to succeed in developing a bond of trust. As a result, 'marriage is no longer the chief defining basis of coupledom' (1999, p. 60). In fact the reverse is true. The meaning of marriage, for Giddens, is that it is the predominant form of stable relationship. Stability is based on the ideal of emotional communication and trust, and marriage is valuable only insofar as it can live up to that ideal: 'Marriage signifies that a couple is in a stable relationship, and may indeed promote that stability' (ibid.).

This emphasis on stability comes through strongly in New Labour's discourse on the family, and lies at the heart of the proposals outlined in the *Supporting Families* Green Paper (Home Office, 1998b). Yet this same document is also riddled with contradictory messages: the government is both laissez-faire and interventionist on the family, the government wants to *strengthen* (heterosexual) marriage but claims not to stigmatize other stable relationships; and the emphasis on unpaid parenting contradicts Labour's zeal for paid work (a point I return to below) (see Fox-Harding, 2000).

In addition, there are two main contradictions between the Etzioni and Giddens accounts. Etzioni sees family change – and in particular the abdication of parental responsibility – as a cause of decline rather than as an effect of globalization, which is how Giddens would view it. This leads into the second point, which is that the outer limits of Etzioni's communitarianism are 'the reinvention of American Society', as the subtitle of his book *The Spirit of Community* suggests. The result is that his account largely overlooks the impact of globalization. By contrast, Giddens sees globalization as the driving force behind family change. Both accounts are evident within New Labour's discourse on family change. The predominant account, however, is one that tries to square the circle by setting up parental responsibility and the stable family as the basis of community (the Etzioni side) and then projects globalization as a benign development (the Giddens side) whose meaning is defined by a doctrine of international community (a novel product of the articulation of these two strands). The space between the two accounts is further covered over by the fact that the Third Way, as understood by Tony Blair, is *itself* a form of communitarianism with a commitment to rights and responsibilities at its heart (Blair, 1998, p. 4).

One can note further contradictions between New Labour's 'communitarian' attitudes to work and the family. New Labour's discourse on social inclusion[12] emphasizes paid work as the primary means of access to social integration, status, and self-esteem. Parenting is played up politically (and morally) while it is simultaneously talked down economically (Levitas, 1998, p. 28). This entails an ambiguous recognition of unpaid domestic work. Parenting, for example, is recognized as socially necessary but is referred to as 'responsibility' rather than work. When Gordon Brown dealt with child-care in his first budget, for example, he argued that it was a necessary precursor to women's entry into the labour market. The underlying assumption was therefore that women's 'unpaid work did not itself constitute an economic contribution' (Levitas, 1998, p. 146). Work performed within the family can only generate a proxy inclusion, therefore: 'Social inclusion cannot be performed within the family, so unpaid work in the private sphere does not count' (Levitas, 1998, p. 158). The contradiction is particularly acute in the case of New Labour's treatment of lone parents (J. Lewis, 1998).[13] Moreover, New Deal schemes and tax credits create an incentive structure that prioritizes the move into paid work, while failing to account for the fact that 'women themselves [often] continue to put caring responsibilities first' (J. Lewis, 2002, p. 55).

Similar arguments have been made by a number of social policy scholars, sociologists, and journalists (for example, Franks, 1999, p. 211; Beck-Gernsheim, 2002, pp. x–xi). More recently, Driver and Martell have offered some dissenting voices. They point out that New Labour's 'pragmatic combination of agendas' is not necessarily incoherent and contradictory. Unpaid work is *valued* by New Labour, but in terms that are not always economic and which focus on the inclusion of the child as much as the parent.[14] Yet even they are forced to admit that 'There *is* a tension between . . . the communitarianism of inclusion through work and the moral communitarianism of strengthening family life' (2002, p. 57).

What none of these appraisals can account for, however, is the way in which such 'obvious' contradictions are experienced as coherent parts of the same New Labour project. This is what a discourse analytic approach to the same problem allows us to do. The study of political subjectivity can shed some light on how discourses cohere. It also allows us to delve into the taken-for-granted assumptions that inform political decisions. When applied to the analysis of New Labour, we find that the 'hard-working family' acts as a nodal point which organizes its discourse and reconciles its conflictual strands as part of the same political project – as I shall now show.

## The hard-working family: ignoble beginnings

As early as 1987, the Shadow Communications Agency – arguably the birthplace of the Blairite brand of modernization – had emphasized the 'aspirational classes' as Labour's key target group (Gould, 1998, p. 122; Anderson and Mann, 1997, p. 19). The construction of this term drew on the work of Stanley Greenberg, President Bill Clinton's personal pollster and a close associate of Philip Gould, who played an equivalent role in the Blair team. For Greenberg,

> The new popular progressive majority will be built broadly among working middle-class families, shaped by the new task of helping people of ordinary luck to achieve a better life in a world of unimagined changes and of growing economic and family pressures. (Greenberg cited in Gould, 1998, p. 420)

This new constituency of aspirant working middle-class families, to which Greenberg tailored the campaign efforts of the US Democrats, was the same group to which New Labour sought to appeal. As Gould and Hewitt (both ex-SCA) wrote in the pages of *Renewal* in January 1993: 'Most poor people also work, or want to work, and identify strongly with middle-class aspirations of security and upward mobility' (1993, p. 174).

At around the same time (January 1993), Blair and Brown were in Washington taking lessons directly from Clinton's advisers. The solution that the Clinton team came up with, and which New Labour seems to have accepted, was that it was necessary to reclaim conservative social values based on individual responsibility, the family and community, and take a 'tough' stance on crime. In the words of Blair's biographer,

> Blair's four days in America marked a turning-point in his development as a politician. He had at last found a populist language in which to express the ethical socialist ideas which had formed his political convictions. (Rentoul, 2001, p. 198)

This new stance was reflected in Blair's 'tough' message on crime, the family, and the importance of 'duty' during his time as Shadow Home Secretary. In his February 1993 Wellingborough speech, for example, Blair placed a strong emphasis on family values at the heart of community values (cf. Gould, 1998, pp. 234–5; Rentoul, 2001, p. 200). In a speech in Alloa on 25 June 1993 he went even further:

> It is largely from family discipline that social discipline and a sense of responsibility is learnt. A modern notion of society – where rights and responsibilities go together – requires responsibility to be nurtured. Out of a family grows the sense of community. The family is the starting place. (Blair, cited in Rentoul, 2001, p. 207)

The same theme was taken up in the immediate aftermath of Blair's successful bid for the Labour leadership. In an ITV interview with Brian Walden, he claimed that two-parent families were better than one, stressed responsibility as the core of both the family and the community, and enforced this message with the moral communitarian claim that 'The family is important because it is the social unit where people learn the boundaries of decent conduct and behaviour and where people are brought up' (cited in the *Daily Mail*, 25 July 1994).

The combination of marketing advice and Blair's political 'instincts' continued to drive the notion of the hard-working family forward. At a brainstorming session at Chewton Glen Hotel in September 1994, Labour's marketing strategists Colin Fisher and Philip Gould suggested to several key Labour modernizers[15] that the party capitalize on the national mood of anxiety by appealing to middle-class voters from aspirational, working families (Macintyre, 2000, p. 312; Gould, 1998, pp. 216–18). The prognosis was largely Gould's, who since the beginning of Blair's leadership bid had been bombarding Blair with memos advocating

> Populism, which means Labour becoming once again the instrument through which ordinary people believe they can achieve their aspirations. We have to make it clear to working people that we understand their aspirations and that we want to make them better off; that we are against taxation for its own sake; that we are tough on crime; that we stress individual responsibility. (Gould, 1998, p. 201)

This message does not seem to have been lost on Blair – despite his distaste for Gould's rambling memos. In his speech to the 1995 Labour Conference, for example, Blair decontested the notion of the hard-working family while claiming that 'we all want ordinary hard-working families to pay less tax' (1996, p. 64).[16] A similar line was also taken up by Gordon Brown, who launched the party's welfare-to-work policy in the following defensive terms: 'This is not a lurch to the right. It is the Labour Party stating the values of decent hard-working people in this country – that in a modern society rights are matched by responsibilities' (*Financial Times*, 10 November 1995).

## The hard-working family: identifying a nodal point

While the preceding section has given a flavour of the importance of the rhetoric surrounding the hard-working family, and traced its emergence at the intersection between US-style political marketing and Blair's own political 'instincts', it has not yet revealed the hard-working family to be a nodal point organizing New Labour discourse. What I hope to have shown so far is that the emergence of a new articulating principle is a necessary condition for the 'coherence' of New Labour discourse – first, by identifying the dislocatory impact of the post-industrial society on traditional family ties and work relations, and second, by showing how New Labour's response has been informed by two contending analyses (Giddens/Etzioni) which inform two important policy strands (work and family). In this section I shall demonstrate, from a number of different angles, how the 'hard-working family' has emerged as the nodal point of New Labour discourse, and how it has come to embody the empty signifier of 'community'.

If a nodal point is the site of a particular discursive concentration – the point at which several associative chains are condensed – then it is more likely to be apparent in a series of similar terms rather than the recurrent use of a single term. In a discourse on education, for example, a stress on 'parental responsibility' can represent the wider notion of the 'hard-working family' insofar as it can be shown to stand in a metonymic relationship to it. In looking for a nodal point, then, we should look for signs of over-wording – a proliferation of different words with roughly similar meanings which extend across a wide range of policy fields (Fairclough, 2000, p. 163). Looking back at the examples identified in the extracts above, we find that the hard-working family is also the 'ordinary people', 'aspirational classes', 'working middle-class', 'stable families', 'responsible parents', and 'poor people who want to work'. It is also the 'aspirational' home owners of 'Middle England' and those who engage in 'flexible working, most typically women doing shift work in a call centre to fit round family commitments' (Keeble, 1999, p. 264). Plenty more examples could also be cited to suggest that it is a central aspect in establishing the meaning of what Tony Blair has called 'Middle income, Middle Britain'.

The hard-working family, and variants upon it, also proliferate across a wide range of policy fields and genres (draft bills, newspaper articles, etc.) through which the Labour Party gives voice to its world-view. As well as the specific terrain of welfare and family policy, the hard-working family crops up in numerous articles by Ministers and more wide-ranging political announcements. In March 2000, the Labour spin machine busily promoted a 'Budget for hard-working families', a phrase which appeared in several press reports at the time. The pre-election Budget of 2001 followed a similar tack, as Gordon Brown proclaimed 'a Budget that puts families first'. His Budget speech reaffirmed this impression, with the words 'family', 'families', and 'children' mentioned an impressive 93 times, compared with only 27 mentions of 'invest' or 'investment', which was the next most popular key word (*Guardian*, 7 March 2001). The phrase 'hard-working family' itself also recurs frequently in the 2001 Labour Manifesto, and is particularly prevalent in the prime minister's Introduction.

On other indicators, such as those measuring the material impact of Labour's policies, the picture is more mixed. The Institute for Fiscal Studies, for example, has concluded that Labour's tax and benefit reforms have mainly benefited the poorest families, although this is offset by the wider economic climate which has seen the stabilization of inequalities between rich and poor, but not their reduction (Clark, Myck, and Wakefield 2001, p. 14).

In general, however, families with children have been rewarded most generously. The introduction of Children's Tax Credits, alongside the abandonment of the Married Couples Allowance, suggests a child-centred policy more in line with Giddens's (and Third-Way Demos pamphleteer Helen Wilkinson's) vision of a post-traditional family than that of the Conservative traditionalists who still set the tone in that party during Labour's first term (Wilkinson, 2000; Durham, 2001).

The policy implications of New Labour's welfare-to-work drive also reinforce the view that it is targeting hard-working families – though, again, with some qualifications. The main thrust of the government's tax and benefits reforms has been to shift the balance towards means-tested and in-work benefits in the form of tax credits.[17] This is clearly a manifestation of the government's wider welfare-to-work strategy, although its willingness to increase the levels of out-of-work benefits, even for lone parents, means that it avoids the punitive consequences of the welfare-to-work reforms instigated by the Clinton administration: 'the UK's approach to families with children has been about promoting work as well as supporting those who are not working – welfare and work, perhaps' (Brewer, Clark, and Wakefield, 2001, p. 43). Further changes announced in the 2000 Budget are only just being implemented at the time of writing so it is too soon to measure their effects, but the ostensible purpose of these reforms fits closely the picture I have presented:

> supporting families with children, recognising the responsibilities that come with parenthood; tackling child poverty by offering the greatest help to those most in need, such as low income families; and helping to make sure that work pays more than welfare and that people have incentives to move up the earnings ladder. (HM Treasury, 2002, p. 3).

It should be noted, however, that the importance of the hard-working family cannot ultimately be proved (or disproved) by a straightforward test of the material effects of government policy upon the appropriate 'referent'. From a discourse theory perspective, the analysis of the material impact of policy remains *internal* to the frame of 'discourse' itself, which encompasses the totality of meaningful elements and not simply the linguistic ones. Economic measures are not privileged, or conceived as the material basis upon which these superstructural political changes proceed. Indeed, as we have seen, New Labour's rhetorical focus on families with children provides the framework within which its tax credits policy can emerge. It should also be pointed out that economic measures are, by definition, mediated and understood in terms of the ideational and rhetorical frameworks in which they exist. 'The *pianissimo* pedal applied to the spinning of some of [the government's] tax-benefit policies' might be said to reflect its own perception of the electorate in general and especially those in Middle Britain, and the main measure of how such voters think appears to be the editorial column of the *Daily Mail* (Lister, 2001, p. 67). Moreover, the political impact of Labour's focus on the hard-working family has as much to do with its ability to forge an 'imaginary community' around its project as it does with the immediate material effect of its policies. This symbolic majority would include those who identify ideologically with the party's vision of the future, and who imagine themselves as the likely beneficiaries of it (Hall, 1988, p. 262). Again, New Labour itself has proven highly sensitive to this, and it is not by accident that the party's 2001 election manifesto was entitled *Ambitions for Britain*. The virtue of ambition is also central to Blair's own vision of

> a new, larger, more meritocratic middle class... A middle class that will include millions of people who traditionally may see themselves as working class, but whose ambitions are far broader than those of their parents and grandparents[18] ... and expanded middle class, with ladders of opportunity for those from all backgrounds. (Blair, 14 January 1999)

Indeed, the more recent manifestations of the hard-working family have stressed the need for 'real upward mobility', and, in the run up to the 2001 general election, Blair reaffirmed his emphasis on 'middle and lower income families' and 'work for those who can', the overall aim of which was 'to improve the lives of the vast majority of the British people' (Blair, 8 February 2001).

## Community as an empty signifier

The presentation of such families as forming the vast majority is not arbitrary either, insofar as the hard-working family is promulgated as the 'typical' subject position from which New Labour discourse should (ideally) be viewed. It is the embodiment of the universal 'community' and 'the people', providing a concrete representation of those otherwise vague terms. More precisely, my argument is that the hard-working family fleshes out the empty signifier 'community', which lies at the heart of New Labour discourse.

In order to establish the validity of this claim it is first necessary to show that 'community' functions as an empty signifier – meaning that it promotes a particular and ideologically loaded notion as a universal panacea to the fundamental lack that prevents society from achieving its full realization (Laclau, 1996). To start with, we can note the importance that several of the key figures behind the New Labour project attach to it. Tony Blair has often claimed that 'At the heart of all my beliefs is the idea of community' and, more generally, he has suggested that 'community is the governing idea of modern social democracy' (Blair, 2000; 2002a, p. 9; 2002b). He is not alone in this view. Peter Mandelson has claimed that 'New Labour's distinctive emphasis is on its concept of community', and Gordon Brown has also stressed its centrality (Mandelson and Liddle, 1996, p. 19; Brown, 1994). These claims are important because they are voiced by New Labour's 'founders of discursivity' – those who produce 'the possibilities and the rules for the formation of other texts' (Foucault, 1984, p. 114). New Labour has even institutionalized these rules of formation by changing Clause IV of the party's constitution to set down its fundamental principles in communitarian terms. Blair summarized the new clause as follows:

> The central belief of the Labour Party is in social cohesion...the basic principle is solidarity, that people can achieve much more by acting together than by acting alone. I think that all this is best represented by the idea of community, in which each person has the rights and duties which go with community. (Blair, cited in *The Guardian*, 13 March 1995)

In a quite literal sense, then, 'community' functions as an empty signifier because it suggests that lack can be eliminated and social cohesion can be brought about.

Beyond this, 'community' plays a role in organizing the discourse of New Labour. It is what distinguishes New Labour from *both* 'Old Labour' *and* Thatcherism, and so gives meaning to the political frontier that the modernizers seek to establish against their precursors (Driver and Martell, 1997, pp. 27–8).[19] The coherence of 'New' Labour, in other words, rests upon its ability to distinguish itself from the 'Old', which is why Blair propagates the myth that 'Old Labour' and Thatcherism are in some sense equivalent 'forces of conservatism' (Blair, 1999).[20] There is an attempt here to determine retroactively the meaning of 'Old Labour' and Thatcherism as hostile to the demands of the 'community' – the former being insufficiently moral and the latter overly individualistic. This is rather ironic, given that Labour's policies on crime and the family, which are central to its communitarian agenda, 'acted as lines of continuity with the neo-conservative strand of new right politics under Thatcher, but also harked back to an older, paternalistic form of Labourism evident in the concept of "ethical socialism"' (Newman, 2001, p. 148). But it may also be a measure of what the New Labour myth has achieved – organizing a discourse around the empty signifier 'community' and thereby rearticulating several 'Old' elements in a way that makes them seem New.

It might reasonably be objected, however, that the politics of New Labour are not coherent at all, but are an 'ideologically eclectic' mixture of liberal, social democratic, and conservative traditions (Freeden, 1999a, p. 43). Indeed, this chapter has already shown that New Labour's political sociology is an uneasy mix of Giddens and Etzioni, overdetermined by the influence of the US New Democrats, Blair's personal vision, and the heightened moral climate of the early 1990s.[21] The sheer variety of these influences makes it unsurprising that 'community' has no steady or generally agreed upon meaning. It is multifaceted at best and contradictory or vacuous at worst (Driver and

Martell, 1997; Hughes and Little, 1999). Yet this eclecticism is a precondition for the emergence of an empty signifier, which is one that condenses various meanings under a single term. 'Community has a multi-faceted appeal precisely because it draws on diverse sets of images, not all of them compatible' (Newman, 2001, p. 147). In fact, the point is not just that 'community' draws on diverse images but that it draws them together as part of the same discourse. The *intellectual incoherence* of New Labour's conception of community contributes to the *discursive (or ideological) coherence* of its politics.

The empty signifier 'community' is not sufficient to bind New Labour discourse together in its own right, however. It helps us to understand how that discourse is organized, but this formal arrangement doesn't explain how people come to identify with it. To do that, New Labour must (as with every discourse) establish a position from which it might ideally be viewed, from which it makes sense. In the critical idiom of discourse theory this is called a subject position, and in this chapter I have argued that the 'hard-working family' performs this role.

## New Labour's political subject

In place of a conclusion, I want to show why it is the hard-working family in particular that has emerged as New Labour's political subject. This returns us to the point at which we began, since it is closely linked to the way in which New Labour accounts for the dislocation of traditional working-class subjectivity. It is not enough to claim, as some recent analysts have done, that New Labour simply sought an alternative social base to the working class and found it by appealing to a 'middle Britain' whose interests coincide with those of capital (Crouch, 1999, pp. 78, 80). Labour's social base (especially when the party has been in government) has always been wider than that of the one class; and its political appeal has, in any case, remained universalistic in its rationale, if not in its effect. The specificity of the New Labour project cannot, therefore, be realized by treating the matter in strictly class terms. Correspondingly, the 'hard-working family' is not simply an alternative interest-formation. Blair seeks 'a basis of support that is "value"-based, not simply "class"-based' (Blair, 1996, p. 221). He wants to replace a socialism based on class, and an appeal to interests and economics, with a 'value-driven' politics (social-ism). Community is the core value of this new politics and the family is presented as the basis of community, 'the essential bedrock of society' (Blair, *Daily Mail*, 17 April 1998).

It is also clear that New Labour's sociology has more strings to its bow than class alone. From the report of the Commission on Social Justice onwards, the party leadership has been attentive to 'a revolution of women's life-chances, of family structures and of demography' with important implications for employment (1994, pp. 3, 77–84). It has accounted for the dislocatory effect of post-industrialism in terms of a narrative of women's entry into paid work, in relation to which 'work' and the 'family' are logically adjacent.[22] This articulation is well illustrated by Blair's Foreword to the 1998 Green Paper on Welfare:

> the system must change because the world has changed, beyond the recognition of Beveridge's generation. The world of work has altered – people no longer expect a job for life; traditional industries have declined; new technologies have taken their place. There is a premium on skills and re-skilling throughout life. The role of women has been transformed. Family structures are different. We live longer, but work for fewer years. (Home Office, 1998a, p. iv).

What this shows, moreover, is that the narrative of a change in women's working patterns is overdetermined by a more general account of industrial and technological transformation. This is unsurprising, since 'change' is roughly synonymous with globalization in the discourse of New Labour (for example, Blair, 1996, p. 31).[23] Here, as elsewhere, Blair assumes that the mere fact of change is sufficient justification for the particular type of change he advocates – as though New Labour's policy prescriptions follow effortlessly from a sober look at how the world actually is (Finlayson, 2003, p. 136).

In practice, this sociological framework is far from neutral and is overlain by a communitarianism whose source is more immediately political. The point is nicely (and inadvertently) illustrated by Mandelson and Liddle, who affirm that 'When Blair talks about the importance of strong families, it is because he regards them as the foundation of a cohesive society and of strong communities' (1996, p. 47). They go on to ascribe this emphasis to Blair's frustration at 'the left's uninterest in social order' and its 'disregard for moral structures' (ibid.). As we have seen, this is one side of Labour's modernizing narrative – which emphasizes community as a counter to the Old Left (as well as Thatcherism). In this way, Blair's potentially progressive articulation of work and the family, which celebrates women's entry into the labour market, is overlaid by a conservative communitarianism that stresses personal morality. Whilst I would not want to give the impression that New Labour's chief protagonists (let alone the members of the party as a whole) are univocal in their understanding of the hard-working family, this nevertheless shows how the meaning ascribed to it has become conservative and exclusionary.[24]

The organization of New Labour discourse around the empty signifier 'community' and its incarnation in the shape of the hard-working family is galvanized by these exclusions, which take a variety of forms.[25] We can, for example, note a consistent defence of the family and community as an antidote to criminality: 'the best two crime prevention policies are a job and a stable family' (Blair, 1996, p. 68).[26] In some cases, whole sectors of the population are targeted. Asylum seekers (who are presumed to be illegal immigrants) are multiply and rather crudely excluded, since they are banned from working, as well as falling foul of the national criteria that New Labour draws around 'community'. The homeless also have a tough time, redefined as 'rough sleepers' or 'beggars', and subjected to new regimes of containment and control (Newman, 2001, p. 159). Rather more typical, though, is the seeming 'inclusion' of marginalized groups (sexual and ethnic minorities, the disabled, etc.) under the banner of tolerance and diversity, and their simultaneous exclusion by means of a narrowly drawn and conservative conception of the British people (Lewis, 2000; Newman, 2001, p. 157).

New Labour's conception of the people is ostensibly inclusive, of course. It promises to 'govern in the interest of the many, the broad majority of people who work hard, play by the rules, pay their dues', in the words of its 1997 General Election Manifesto. But as Michael Freeden has pointed out,

> The sub-text of this passage, borne out in other utterances, is that there may also be others, on the marginalized outreaches of society, who do not – in the language of socialist expectations – work hard, who do not – in the language of conservative conventionalism – play by the rules, and who do not – in the language of liberal contractarianism – pay their dues. Communal membership is not ascribed, but earned; it is not a status but an activity. (Freeden, 1999b, pp. 161–2)

As we have seen, the 'other utterances' to which Freeden refers tend to articulate 'working hard' to the family. The passage cited above, for example, merely echoes Mandelson and Liddle's claim that 'New Labour stands for the ordinary families who work hard and play by the rules' (1996, p. 18). In these and other cases, the remarks are animated by a conception of citizenship (or communal membership) which sees it not as a right but as *a status that is conditional upon personal moral responsibility* (Newman, 2001, p. 149). The family is doubly important here, as both the place where responsibility is learnt and one of the places where it is enacted in the form of parental obligation. Work is important too, as the New Labour subject is expected to be employable (though not necessarily employed) if he or she is to cope with the challenges of globalization. Work and the family are articulated by means of a causal link: a stable *family* life breeds *responsibility* which manifests itself in the desire to *work*. Yet, as these different aspects become more closely articulated, the reasoning becomes obscured, or rather, the interconnections make it possible for these terms to be expressed in virtually any order. Sometimes, morality comes first: 'Ours is a moral cause, best expressed through how we see our families and children.' At other times the community is what makes both possible: 'we cannot resolve the issues of work and family without addressing the issue of community – of the creation of strong social ties and structures within which families and individuals can flourish' (Blair, 1996, p. 151). In these shifting patterns of justification, in which premises and conclusions swap places and mutually protect each other, we can find a clear sign that the articulation of the hard-working family as the embodiment of community has become an important part of New Labour's 'common sense' (Billig, 1998, p. 51).

## Notes

1. I would like to thank the ESRC for the funding that enabled me to carry out this research.
2. As Laclau and Mouffe put it, 'the practice of articulation, as fixation/dislocation of a system of differences, cannot consist of purely linguistic phenomena; but must instead pierce the entire material density of the multifarious institutions, rituals and practices through which a discursive formation is structure' (1985, p. 109).
3. As Giddens rightly notes: 'The family is a site for the struggles between tradition and modernity, but also a metaphor for them' (1999, p. 53).
4. While New Labour pragmatism often boils down to the legitimation of policy on the basis of certain social facts (Finlayson, 1999, p. 271), these are nevertheless constructed in terms of the normative principles of the sociologists and political scientists it chooses to trust.
5. The first quotation here is from Ernest Bevin. The second is from Keir Hardie.
6. This is the main thesis of Donald Sassoon's (1996) work.
7. France provides the main exception here: 'while British welfare policies reflected a "male breadwinner" logic, those of France expressed a "parental" logic' (Sassoon, 1996, p. 142). For a more detailed discussion of this, see Pedersen (1993).
8. Charles Leadbeater was one of the principal authors of the New Times Manifesto, whose relation to New Labour is judiciously explored by Finlayson (1999, pp. 84–92, 119–24). He was also responsible for drafting the Government's Knowledge Economy White Paper.
9. The twist in the tale is that New Labour's interpretation of these economic changes grew out of the New Times thesis, which explicitly cautioned that the reorganization of work around new technology was promoting 'far more savage forms of polarisation' (Manifesto for New Times, 1989, p. 34).
10. As Gareth Stedman-Jones puts it: 'Changes in the social realm form a large part of the raw material out of which different political languages and practices may be forged or reforged. But such changes are not bearers of essential political meaning in themselves. They are only endowed with political meanings so far as they are effectively articulated through specific forms of political discourse and practice' (1983, p. 242).
11. New Labour contests what it sees as the libertarian individualism of the left, which focused on rights *at the expense of* responsibilities, and refused to deal with crime or the family because they were seen as 'right-wing' issues. It is also against 'me-first' Thatcherite individualism. 'Communitarianism' is New Labour's rebuff to both (Driver and Martell, 1998, p. 29). The interpretation of left-libertarianism is borrowed from Etzioni's emphasis on 'rebalancing' rights and responsibilities without regard to the relative weakness of human rights discourse and left-libertarianism within British politics. As a result, it offers a facile and historically inaccurate account of an 'Old Left' which 'appeared indifferent to the family and individual responsibility' (Blair, 1996, p. 206; Levitas, 1998, p. 113; Driver and Martell, 2002, p. 48). The New Labour account of Thatcherism, while not simply

wrong, remains incomplete because it underplays the persistence of *conservative* elements within a project that was never simply neoliberal (Levitas, 1998, p. 103).

12. Somewhere between social-integrationist and moral-underclass discourse, according to Levitas.
13. Ann Orloff (1991) points out that 'what the state does in respect of one-parent families is analytically strategic for assessing the relationship between policy and gender equality' (cited J. Lewis, 1993, p. 12).
14. The latter point about parenting is well taken, but to reconcile unpaid and paid work on the basis of the non-economic value of the former is to miss Levitas's point. As shown above, Levitas *does* recognize that New Labour values unpaid work (especially parenting) by talking up its *moral* worth (parenting as a 'responsibility'). Her point, rather, is that this moral worth is pretty *worthless* to women who are left juggling work and family responsibilities – the former having been made a necessary prerequisite to the acquisition of full citizenship rights, the latter being a product of the general failure of men when it comes to taking a fair share of unpaid domestic labour.
15. Including Tony Blair, Gordon Brown, Peter Mandelson, and Alistair Campbell.
16. 'Decontestation' is the name given to any operation that limits the scope of political disputes by normalizing and generalizing a particular arrangement of meanings and concepts (Freeden, 1996, pp. 76, 82).
17. Such schemes were not altogether new: the Working Families Tax Credit (WFTC), for example, is basically a more generous and more widely available version of the old Family Credit.
18. It is worth noting the unstated assumptions about the procreative family that permeate this statement.
19. For examples of this, see Blair (1996), Mandelson and Liddle (1996), and Brown (1994, p. 118).
20. In discourse theory, myths involve the formation of 'a new objectivity by means of the rearticulation of the dislocated elements' within any given situation (Laclau, 1990, p. 61). The task of the critical researcher is not so much to show that a myth is *untrue*, but rather to reveal the hegemonic moves through which a mythic construction *presents itself as true*. This does not mean that we should ignore the historically dubious nature of New Labour's account of itself – which has been ably rebuffed by Eric Shaw (1996).
21. Most notably, the murder of James Bulger in February 1993 resulted in a media-fuelled moral panic to which the Prime Minister John Major responded with the notorious soundbite that 'We must condemn a little more, and understand a little less.' The case brought together concerns about crime, education, and the family – the same combination of issues underlying Major's ill-fated 'Back to Basics' crusade, which was launched at the Conservative Party Conference in October that year. As Shadow Home Secretary, Blair was the architect of Labour's response to these issues. His 1993 speeches at Wellingborough and Alloa emphasized the moral value of community, with family as the starting place (Rentoul, 2001, pp. 200–1).
22. For a theoretical account of 'logical adjacency', which I am treating as a distinctive variant of articulation, see Freeden (1996, pp. 68–71).
23. Colin Hay's work provides the best analysis of New Labour and globalization – a good recent example being Hay and Watson (2003).
24. Although the meaning of the hard-working family is contested and subject to several differences of emphasis, it is not arbitrary. In a widely publicized case, Foreign Office minister Peter Hain was quickly and resoundingly rebuffed when

he advocated raising the top rate of income tax in the interests of 'hard-working middle-income families', suggesting that the New Labour definition of the term conceives of those families as allergic to progressive tax rises (see 'Blair slaps down Hain on tax', http://news.bbc.co.uk/1/hi/uk_politics/3005496.stm).

25. Chantal Mouffe has argued that all political discourses are 'attempts to create specific forms of unity among different interests by relating them to a common project *and by establishing a frontier to define the forces to be opposed, the "enemy"*' (1993, p. 50, my emphasis). In these terms, the critique of New Labour would not be that it makes exclusions, but rather that its exclusions are reactionary and anti-pluralistic.
26. This juxtaposition emerged in the speeches of Tony Blair when he was Shadow Home Secretary, and has continued to structure New Labour discourse since that time. In his 1993 speech to the Labour Party conference, for example, Blair noted (in quick succession) that 'Labour is the Party of strong communities... the Party of law and order... tough on crime'. This articulation presupposes many aspects of an 'underclass' analysis – linking crime, family breakdown, teenage pregnancy, etc. – even though Blair did not fully accept that analysis.

    More recently, the opposition between community and criminality has been rearticulated in the domain of international politics, culminating in Blair's evangelical desire to set 'the moral power of a world acting as a community' against the evils of terrorism (see Blair, 2001).

## Bibliography


Anderson, P., and Mann, N. (1997) *The Making of New Labour* (London, Granta).

Beck-Gernsheim, E. (2002 [1998]) *Reinventing the Family* (Cambridge, Polity).

Billig, M. (1998) *Talking of the Royal Family* (London, Routledge).

Blair, T. (1994) *Socialism* (London, Fabian Society).

Blair, T. (1996) *New Britain: My Vision of a Young Country* (London, Fourth Estate).

Blair, T. (1998) *The Third Way: New Politics for the New Century* (London, Fabian Society).

Blair, T. (1999) Speech to Labour Party Conference, 28 September.

Blair, T. (2000) Speech to the Women's Institutes' Triennial General Meeting, 7 June.

Blair, T. (2001) 'The Power of Community Can Change the World', Speech to the Labour Party Conference, 3 October.

Blair, T. (2002a) 'New Labour and Community', *Renewal*, 10.2: 9–14.

Blair, T. (2002b) Tony Blair talks to *Newsnight*, 14 May http:/ /news.bbc.co.uk/2/hi/programmes/newsnight/1985222.stm.

Blair, T., and Schröder, G. (1999) *Europe: the Third Way/die Neue Mitte* (London, The Labour Party and SPD).

Brewer, M., Clark, T., and Wakefield, M. (2001) *Social Security under New Labour: What Did the Third Way Mean for Welfare Reform?* (London, Institute for Fiscal Studies).

Brown, G. (1994) 'The Politics of Potential', in D. Miliband (ed.), *Reinventing the Left* (London, Polity).

Clark, T., Myck, M., and Smith, Z. (2001) *Fiscal Reform affecting Households, 1997–2001* (London, Institute for Fiscal Studies).

Commission on Social Justice (1994) *Social Justice: Strategies for National Renewal* (London, Random House).

Crouch, C. (1999), 'The Parabola of Working Class Politics', in A. Gamble and T. Wright, *The New Social Democracy* (Oxford, Blackwell).

Dallmayr, F. (1988) 'Hegemony and Democracy: On Laclau and Mouffe', *Strategies*, 1: 29–49.

Deacon, A., and Mann, K. (1997) 'Moralism and Modernity: the Paradox of New Labour Thinking on Welfare', *Benefits*, 20: 2–6.

Deacon, A., and Mann, K. (1999) 'Agency, modernity and social policy, *Journal of Social Policy*, 28: 3: 413–35.

Department of Social Security (1998) *New Ambitions for Our Country: a New Contract for Welfare*, Cm. 3805 (London, The Stationery Office).

Driver, S., and Martell, L. (1997) 'New Labour's Communitarians', *Critical Social Policy*, 17.3: 27–46.

Driver, S., and Martell, L. (1998) *New Labour: Politics after Thatcherism* (Cambridge, Polity Press).

Driver, S., and Martell, L. (2002) 'New Labour, Work and the Family', *Social Policy & Administration*, 36.1: 46–61.

Durham, M. (2001) 'The Conservative Party, New Labour and the Politics of the Family', *Parliamentary Affairs*, 54: 459–74.

Elliott, G. (1993) *Labourism and the English Genius* (London, Verso).

Esping-Andersen, G. (1999) *Social Foundations of Postindustrial Economies* (Oxford, Oxford University Press).

Etzioni, A. (1995) *The Spirit of Community: Rights, Responsibilities and the Communitarian Agenda* (London, Fontana).

Fairclough, N. (2000) *New Labour, New Language?* (London, Routledge).

Finlayson, A. (1999) 'Third Way Theory', *Political Quarterly*: 271–9.

Finlayson, A. (2003) *Making Sense of New Labour* (London, Lawrence and Wishart).

Foucault, M. (1984), 'What Is an Author?', in P. Rabinow (ed.), *The Foucault Reader* (Harmondsworth, Penguin).

Fox-Harding, L. (2000) *Supporting Families/Controlling Families? Towards a Characterisation of New Labour's Family Policy*, Working Paper no. 21 (Centre for Research on Family, Kinship and Childhood, University of Leeds).

Francis, M. (2000), 'Labour and Gender', in D. Tanner, P. Thane, and N. Tiratsoo, *Labour's First Century* (Cambridge, Cambridge University Press).

Franklin, B. (1998) *Tough on Soundbites, Tough on the Causes of Soundbites: New Labour and News Management*, Cataylst Paper 3 (London, Catalyst Trust).

Franks, S. (1999) *Having None of It: Women, Men and the Future of Work* (London, Granta).

Frazer, E. (1999), 'Unpicking Political Communitarianism: a Critique of "the Communitarian Family"', in G. Jagger and C. Wright (eds), *Changing Family Values* (London, Routledge).

Freeden, M. (1996) *Ideologies and Political Theory* (Oxford, Oxford University Press).

Freeden, M. (1999a) 'The Ideology of New Labour', *Political Quarterly*, 70.1: 42–51.

Freeden, M. (1999b), 'True Blood or False Genealogy: New Labour and British Social Democratic Thought', in A. Gamble and T. Wright (eds), *The New Social Democracy* (Oxford, Blackwell).

Giddens, A. (1999) *Runaway World* (London, Profile Books).

Glennester, H. (2000) *British Social Policy since 1945*, 2nd edn (Oxford, Blackwell).

Gould, P. (1999) *The Unfinished Revolution* (London, Little, Brown).

Gould, P., and Hewitt, P. (1993) 'Lessons from America', *Renewal* January.

Hall, S. (1988) *The Hard Road to Renewal* (London, Verso).

Harris, J. (1996), '"Contract" and "Citizenship"', in D. Marquand and A. Seldon (eds), *The Ideas That Shaped Post-war Britain* (London, Fontana).

Hay C., and Watson, M. (2003) 'The Discourse of Globalisation and the Logic of No Alternative: Rendering the Contingent Necessary in the Political Economy of New Labour', *Policy and Politics*, 31: 3: 289–305.

HM Treasury (2002) *The Child and Working Tax Credits: the Modernisation of Britain's Tax and Benefit System* (London, HM Treasury).

Home Office (1998a) *New Ambitions for Our Country: a New Contract for Welfare* (London, The Stationery Office).

Home Office (1998b) *Supporting Families: a Consultation Document* (London, The Stationery Office).

Hughes, G., and Little, A. (1999) 'The Contradictions of New Labour's Communitarianism', *Imprints*, 4: 1: 37–62.

Jessop, B. (1994), 'The Transition to Post-Fordism and the Schumpeterian Workfare State', in R. Burrows and B. Loader (eds), *Towards a Post-Fordist Welfare State?* (London, Routledge).

Keeble, S. (1999), 'Middle England', in M. Linton, K. Raymond, and A. Whitehead (eds), *Beyond 2002: Long-term Policies for Labour* (London, Profile Books).

Krieger, J. (1999) *British Politics in the Global Age: Can Social Democracy Survive?* (Cambridge, Polity).

Laclau, E. (1977) *Politics and Ideology in Marxist Theory* (London, Verso).

Laclau, E. (1990) *New Reflections on the Revolution of Our Time* (London, Verso)

Laclau, E. (1996) *Emancipation(s)* (London, Verso).

Laclau, E., and Mouffe, C. (1985) *Hegemony and Socialist Strategy* (London, Verso).

Leadbeater, C. (2000) *Living on Thin Air: the New Economy* (Harmondsworth, Penguin).

Levitas, R. (1998) *The Inclusive Society? Social Exclusion and New Labour* (Basingstoke, Palgrave Macmillan).

Lewis, G. (2000), 'Discursive Histories, the Pursuit of Multiculturalism and Social Policy', in G. Lewis, S. Gewirtz, and J. Clarke (eds), *Rethinking Social Policy* (London, Sage).

Lewis, J. (1993), 'Introduction: Women, Work, Family and Social Policies in Europe', in J. Lewis (ed.), *Women and Social Policies in Europe* (London, Edward Elgar).

Lewis, J. (1997) 'Gender and Welfare Regimes: Further Thoughts', *Social Politics*, 4: 2 (Summer): 160–77.

Lewis, J. (1998). 'Work, Welfare and Lone Mothers', *Political Quarterly*, 69: 4–13.

Lewis, J. (2002), 'Individualisation, Assumptions about the Existence of an Adult Worker Model and the Shift towards Contractualism', in A. Carling, S. Duncan, and E. Edwards (eds), *Analysing Families: Morality and Rationality in Policy and Practice* (London, Routledge).

Lister, R. (2001) 'Doing Good by Stealth: the Politics of Poverty and Inequality under New Labour', *New Economy*, 65–70

Macintyre, D. (2000) *Mandelson* (London, Harper Collins).

Mandelson, P., and Liddle, R. (1996) *The Blair Revolution: Can New Labour Deliver?* (London, Faber & Faber).

Manifesto for New Times (1989) 'The New Times', in S. Hall and M. Jacques (eds), *New Times: the Changing Face of Politics in the 1990s* (London, Lawrence and Wishart).

Mouffe, C. (1993) *Return of the Political* (London, Verso).

Newman, J. (2001) *Modernising Governance: New Labour, Policy and Society* (London, Sage).

Panitch, L. (1972) 'Ideology and Integration: the Case of the British Labour Party', *Political Studies*, 19: 2: 184–200.

Pedersen, S. (1993) *Family, Dependence and the Origins of the Welfare State* (Cambridge, Cambridge University Press).

Pelling, H. (1965) *The Origins of the Labour Party 1880–1900* (Oxford, Oxford University Press).
Rentoul, J. (2001) *Tony Blair* (London, Warner Books).
Ritzer, G. (1993) *The McDonaldisation of Society* (Thousand Oaks, CA, Pine Forge Press).
Sassoon, D. (1996) *One Hundred Years of Socialism* (London, Fontana).
Shaw, E. (1996) *The Labour Party since 1945* (Oxford, Blackwell).
Stedman Jones, G. (1983) *Languages of Class* (Cambridge, Cambridge University Press).
Vanderbrouke, F. (1999), 'European Social Democracy', in A. Gamble and T. Wright (eds), *The New Social Democracy* (Oxford, Blackwell).
Wilkinson, H. (ed.) (2000) *Family Business* (London, Demos).

# 10
# From Welfare to Social Exclusion: Eugenic Social Policies and the Swiss National Order

*Véronique Mottier*

## Introduction[1]

This chapter aims to provide an analysis of the role eugenic expert discourses played in the construction of the Swiss welfare state, as well as their effects on Swiss national identity. It explores the influence of eugenics on Swiss social policies, and shows how eugenic ideas and policy practices formed the basis for mechanisms of exclusion, from the Swiss national order, of categories of citizens deemed 'unfit'. The science of eugenics emerged during the second half of the nineteenth century, with the aim of assisting nation-states to formulate social policies which would improve the 'quality' of the population. The emergence of modern techniques of government, including the growth of health and social policies from the turn of the twentieth century, provided the institutional conditions for translating the eugenic rhetoric into a concrete policy programme. The Swiss case is interesting in that it pioneered a number of eugenic ideas and policies in Europe, some of which continued until well into the post-war period. Swiss eugenic policies were mostly articulated from within a social-democratic perspective. They were closely bound up with the emerging welfare system and shaped by the specific Swiss political institutions, in particular federalism.

While focusing on the specific forms of social exclusion that resulted from the eugenic policy experience in Switzerland, this study is intended to raise wider critical questions concerning modern welfare. Adopting Foucault's notion of a 'history of the present', the aim is thus not so much to increase our historical knowledge of the Swiss experience with eugenics, but, rather, to bring a different perspective to current debates on the nature of the welfare state.

The opening sections of this chapter explore the use of a Foucauldian theoretical framework for analysing the formation of national identity in the context of eugenicist 'science' and social policies, and for conceptualizing the nature of the forms of power and techniques of government involved in the modern welfare state. The second part of the chapter shows how eugenicist expert discourses shaped a number of social policies in pre- and post-war Switzerland, explores resulting mechanisms of exclusion from the national order, and examines the implications for wider debates concerning the welfare state.

## Method: Foucauldian discourse analysis

As Torfing explains in the introduction to this volume, discourse analysis has been used principally within political research to study the construction of political identities. In contrast to mainstream political approaches to collective identities, which have typically concentrated on the political role of 'preexisting' identities, discourse theory has shifted the focus to an increasing emphasis on the ways in which political identities and 'difference' are in fact both shaped and challenged by political actors, on local as well as global levels (see also Mottier, 2002). In addition, discourse analysis has also been used to conceptualize the policy-making process in discursive terms. Following Hajer's influential work (1995), policy discourses are thus seen as the outcome of joint productions of meanings among various policy actors. The meanings that underlie and emerge from specific public policies are analysed at the interactive level of policy-making and policy-implementation (for example, Litfin, 1994; Stone, 1997).

The analytical strategy in this chapter is to link the application of discourse analysis of public policy discourses with the analysis of identity constructions. In other words, I shall shift the focus from a concern with the actual process of policy-making or policy-implementation to the social and political identities that are being articulated and produced through public policy discourses.[2] In doing so, I shall draw upon Foucauldian strands of discourse analysis, which use the term 'discourses' to refer to the 'macro-level' of structural orders of discourse (Foucault, 1971): broad historical systems of meaning including meaningful political practices (referred to as *discursive practices*), which are relatively stable over time. However, in light of the genealogical method developed in Foucault's later writings, it is important to emphasize that identity is constructed not only in the context of relations of meaning but also within institutionalized relations of power. Discourses around, for example, national identity, sexuality, and gender or race are not autonomous systems but operate in the context of the institutional supports and practices that they rely upon (see also Mottier, 2000).

Consequently, the main aim of Foucauldian discourse analysis is not to reveal how specific discursive constructions result from the mere play of free-floating signifiers (in contrast to postmodern approaches, especially Derridian deconstruction), or from unconscious desires (in contrast to psychoanalytic approaches). Instead, it explores how specific discourses reproduce or transform relations of power as well as relations of meaning. As such, Foucauldian versions of discourse analysis also differ from approaches developed by social linguists such as Van Dijk, social psychologists such as Potter and Wetherell, or ethnomethodological conversation analysts, which focus on the micro-level of communicative interactions. In contrast, Foucauldian understandings of discourse refer to two aspects of discursive practices. First, to a set of *language games*, statements or constructions of meaning, and, secondly, to a set of *strategic games*, exploring the ways in which these constructions of meaning produce, reproduce, sustain, or subvert relations of social and political power.

The theorization of power and its links to truth and meaning within Foucauldian discourse theory contrasts in particular with Marxist perspectives. First, Foucauldians take issue with Marxism for its structural theorization of power as a substance that is concentrated in a specific site (social class or state), and the attendant reduction of politics to class struggle. Foucauldian discourse theory instead develops a relational understanding of power as a more diffuse network that cannot be reduced to the state alone, but pervades all areas of social life, and sees politics as a struggle over meanings and identities. The conceptual tools, which theorize power in the context of social relations outside the state – including the family and intimate relationships – have made Foucault very appealing to social movement researchers and feminist theorists. Secondly, in contrast to the Marxist concept of ideology, which focuses on the study of ideological 'distortions' of reality and truth, the Foucauldian notion of discourse centres on the study of discursive strategies, without assuming an essential preexisting truth. Instead, each society is thought to have its own 'truth regime', its own contingent rules that define what is 'true' or 'false' at given moments in history.

Drawing on the Foucauldian framework, the following sections analyse the intersections between Swiss eugenic policies and the construction of Swiss national identity. The focus will be both on the social meanings and scientific 'truths' that formed the basis for eugenic policy discourses and practices (language games) and on the role that these played regarding wider relations of social and political power (strategic games). Finally, in addition to the analytical focus on the Swiss state, the study will also include more diffuse para-state actors such as psychiatric institutions or scientific experts, who had at their disposal important powers within the context of eugenic practices.

Empirically, my study is based on an analysis of Swiss eugenic practices from the start of the twentieth century up to the 1960s and on a textual corpus[3] that includes historical documents collected through archival research. These include relevant legal codes, policy documents, and the writings of key eugenic scientists. Eugenic scientific discourse constituted an extensive field in Switzerland, covering a number of disciplines and authors, so I shall not present an exhaustive analysis. Instead, I shall focus in particular on the writings of Auguste Forel, who was a socialist reformer and one of the most prominent eugenic scientists in Switzerland, and whom I consider paradigmatic of the eugenic scientific rhetoric. In other words, my empirical data are representative rather than exhaustive. With regard to Forel's writings, however, I have based my study on the entirety of his oeuvre, rather than only selected key texts.

## Governmentality, pastoral power, and national identity

The term 'eugenics' was coined by Sir Francis Galton in 1883, to refer to the genetic improvement of the national 'stock' on the basis of the scientific study of 'all influences that tend in however remote a degree to give to the more suitable races or strains of blood a better chance of prevailing speedily over the less suitable than they otherwise would have had' (Galton, 1883, p. 25). Galton regarded the evolutionary processes described by his cousin Charles Darwin, in particular natural selection and the idea of the survival of the fittest,[4] as too slow and uncertain for modern needs. The complexities of modern scientific and cultural developments, he argued, put particularly high demands on political and other elites, whose intellectual capacities he deemed insufficiently evolved. Galton saw an urgent need for managing the consequences of modernity. The dominance of Western nation-states seemed in danger and his theories were formulated in response to this threat.

The new science of eugenics aimed at assisting governments to implement social policies that would improve the national 'breed'. Hostile to the laissez-faire of political liberalism, eugenics advocated active social engineering. The individual had a patriotic duty to contribute to the improvement of the national community through what Galton's student and successor Karl Pearson (1909, p. 170) called a 'conscious race-culture'. From the beginning, therefore, eugenics was deeply intertwined with social and political aims. It emerged as both a science and a social movement, with the term catching on rapidly as numerous eugenics societies were established, in Great Britain and elsewhere, followed by the creation of International and World Leagues (see Kühl, 1997). Through such social reform societies, as well as various scientific disciplines such as psychiatry, anthropology, biology, and sexology, eugenicist discourses acquired institutional support.

During the second half of the nineteenth century, eugenics remained mostly a rhetoric with political implications. But the growth of social policies implemented by nation-states around the turn of the twentieth century provided opportunities for translating the rhetoric into practice. The eugenicist concern for improving the population through the regulation of reproductive sexuality chimed with a new-found preoccupation of Western industrializing nation-states with the health and size of their populations. In the context of accelerating industrialization and urbanization, the rapidly growing urban population appeared as potentially destabilizing to public order, while an orderly, healthy, and prolific population came to be seen as a source of wealth for expanding nation-states (Nye, 1999). The modern state thus combined the exercise of disciplinary power with that of pastoral power. On one hand, modern disciplinary techniques, including mechanisms of surveillance and normalization within state and para-state institutions, such as educational establishments and prisons, aimed to produce orderly and docile subjects. On the other hand, the population was cared for and protected by the new welfare policies, which in turn involved both relations of care and exposing them to further mechanisms of scrutiny, surveillance, and discipline (Foucault, 1979; 1983). These modern techniques of government, which Foucault calls 'governmentality', were not limited to governmental action by the state, but included more diffuse ways of directing and regulating the conduct of citizens (Foucault 1991; see also Dean 1999).

Citizens' bodies are central targets in pastoral relations of care and discipline. This bodily aspect of modern power is expressed in Foucault's concept of 'bio-power' (Foucault 1990). Bio-power includes, first, disciplinarization of the movements, capacities, and behaviours of individual bodies. Secondly, it refers to the regulation, by state policies, of the welfare, health, and education of the collective national body (see also Sawicki, 1991, p. 67). The control of conduct involved in these practices of bio-power and governmentality, such as the eugenic regulation of the reproductive sexuality of the national body, is dependent upon the constitution of a body of expert knowledge, produced through careful observation and classification. In eugenics, Switzerland was at the forefront of both. Swiss scientists made significant contributions to the international scientific discourse of eugenics, while important eugenicist practices and policies were pioneered and implemented in Switzerland, as will be shown below.

The practices of care and normalization involved in pastoral power are internalized by individuals, as contributing to the common good. In this respect, pastoral power also involves a normative articulation of collective identity. The national order of the welfare state is discursively constructed as founded on the notions of community and solidarity – even though entitlement to welfare provisions has always been conditional, and was in fact restricted to a very limited number of specific categories of the population at its historical beginnings. Pastoral power thus contributes to the discourse of national identity.

From a discourse-analytic perspective, national identity is not seen as a 'given' natural entity but as an 'imagined community' (Anderson, 1983) which is constructed through 'narration' (Bhabha, 1990), 'foundational fictions' (Sommer, 1990), and 'invented traditions' (Hobsbawm, 1983). Discourses of national identity are reproduced (as well as transformed) by specific individual and collective *narratives*. Narratives are variously defined as 'a story with a beginning, middle and end that reveals someone's experiences' (Manning and Cullum-Swan, 1998); 'an original state of affairs, an action, or an event, and the consequent state of events' (Czarniawska, 1998); 'any form of communication' (Barthes, 1974); or 'the main mode of human knowledge' (Bruner, 1986). Whereas some uses of the term narrative, such as Barthes's or Bruner's, suggest no difference between narrative and discourse, I consider narratives in the more limited sense, as *stories*. As such, narratives are possible forms of discourse, while discourses include (but are not reduced to) narratives. Specific narratives of the nation such as historical accounts, myths, or metaphors are important narrative forms that contribute to broader discourses of national identity (see also Mottier, 2000). From this perspective, my focus will be on the type of narrative of the national community that eugenic scientific and policy narratives tell.

Much narrative analysis is concerned with the formal properties of narratives or 'stories', such as 'act, scene, agent, agency and purpose' (Burke, 1945); 'building the "and, and, and" connections between action and events' (Czarniawska, 1998); or 'temporal sequence' (Propp, 1928). However, following Plummer (1995, p. 19), my concern here is not with the structural aspects of eugenic narratives, but with their social and political role.

Collective identities are continuously reconstituted in both individual and collective narratives. Borrowing both from Austin's speech act theory and Goffman's theatrical model of identity, I want to emphasize the *performative* nature of collective identity narratives (Austin, 1962; Goffman, 1959). Narratives do not simply express a pre-given national identity but function as *performatives: speech acts* which bring into being that which they name. Narratives both enact and perform the nation. Historical accounts, myths of origin (which may or may not be based on historical 'fact'), or policy texts can all be read as examples of narrative enactment and performance of national identity. National identities thus tend to draw upon elements from many different domains. Adopting Hajer's concept, these can be usefully analysed in terms of their storylines, that is, 'the narratives on social reality through which elements from many different domains are combined and that provide actors with a set of symbolic references that suggest a common understanding' (Hajer, 1995, p. 62).

Identity formation involves the formulation of specific forms of narrative, which constitute commonalties and differences between self and others (Yuval-Davis, 1997, p. 43). As Plummer (1995, p. 19) puts it: 'stories mark out identities; identities mark out differences; differences define "the other"; and "the other" helps structure the moral life of culture, group, and individual'.

Consequently, of central importance to processes of identity formation are what I propose to call discursive mechanisms of *boundary-drawing, boundary-maintenance, ordering,* and *othering*. National identities are built on storylines which are concerned with the drawing and maintenance of boundaries between 'us' and 'them', between members of the national order and non-members. This construction of the nation as an ordered system of exclusion and disciplinary regulation is central to the workings of modern welfare and the formation of national identity. As Bauman argues (1989; 1991), the modern nation-state has emerged through a 'quest for order': its aim was to create an orderly society through the twin reigns of Science and Reason. Hobbes's discovery that order was not natural led to the idea that the social and political order needs to be constructed through the design, engineering, and management of existence, combined with the mastery and subordination of nature (Bauman, 1991, p. 7). Under conditions of modernity, old certainties and identities disappeared in the context of rapid social and political change. As a consequence, the concern with boundary-drawing and boundary-maintenance as mechanisms for reducing ambivalence and constructing the social and political order became intense. 'Whatever remained of old boundaries needed desperate defence', Bauman (1991, p. 40) writes, 'and new boundaries had to be built around new identities'.

Discursive mechanisms of *othering*, of constructing specific groups of people *as* other, as fundamentally 'different', are a politically important aspect of identity narratives and, consequently, particularly crucial in modernity. They allow for the self-affirmation of inherently fragile modern identities, including national identities. As Connolly points out: 'Identity requires difference in order to be, and it conveys difference into otherness in order to secure its own self-certainty' (Connolly, 1991, p. 64).

Sexuality is an important site of othering mechanisms in modernity, as well as a central dimension of national identity. The connections between power and sexuality are all the more important because our relation to ourselves as sexual beings constitutes such a central component of modern self-identity. At the collective level, it is through reproductive sexuality that the nation is biologically reproduced, which makes it a concern of the state. As Foucault puts it, 'Sexuality has always been the site where the future of our species, and at the same time our truth as human subjects, is formed' (Foucault, 1994, p. 257; my translation). Consequently, sexuality is the prime target of 'bio-power' and fundamental to processes of disciplinarization, normalization and marginalization of individuals (Foucault, 1990).

Narratives of sexual purity and danger are central to the policing of the boundaries of the national order. They constitute an important dimension in the making of the nation, though by no means the only one. Adapting Yuval-Davis's terminology (1997, pp. 21–2), three major types of narratives of national identity can be distinguished: *Kulturnation narratives*, which construct language, religion, traditions, or customs as the essential 'stuff' of the nation; *Staatnation narratives*, which privilege political institutions, citizenship rights, and access to state territory; and *Volksnation narratives* which centre on notions of the origin of the people or race (see also Mottier, 2000). Though all three dimensions have contributed to the making of the Swiss nation, the focus of this text is on the *Volksnation* dimension of national identity. While I do not claim that the *Volksnation* narrative has been the only, or even the most important, basis for Swiss national identity, it has nevertheless formed a crucial dimension of the construction of the national order. *Staatnation*-centred analyses, as we have seen above, claim that the exclusionary aspects of Swissness centre on the *othering* of foreign people and nations, conflating identity boundaries with national borders. My argument is that the boundaries drawn within *Volksnation* narratives have also structured the order of the nation *within* the national borders, through specific mechanisms of inclusion and exclusion, ordering, and othering.

*Volksnation* narratives, as I have noted, are concerned with the origins of the people or race. Reproductive sexuality is therefore central to *Volksnation* narratives. Genealogical stories about the 'purity' of the race are deeply intertwined with the regulation of sexuality. Given that female identity has been traditionally tied up with women's reproductive roles, as the biological producers of the members of the nation, this is a particular concern of *Volksnation* narratives. Female bodies and 'respectable' female sexuality become the 'gate-keepers' of the moral as well as biological boundaries of the national community (Yuval-Davis, 1997, p. 106). In the Swiss context, *Volksnation* narratives have mostly taken the form of eugenics. Eugenicist discourses were highly influential in Switzerland from the end of the nineteenth century up to the end of the Second World War; concomitant with the construction of national identity. Eugenics has consequently made a particularly important contribution to the construction of the *Volksnation* dimension of Swiss national identity.

I now move on to focus on the discursive mechanisms of *boundary-drawing, boundary-maintenance, ordering,* and *othering* within eugenic scientific and policy narratives, which enact and perform Swiss national identity.

## Tales of heredity and degeneration

Eugenic versions of *Volksnation* narratives sprang up in various forms and from multiple sites and were articulated from within opposite political projects. Nowadays, eugenics has become associated with the politics of the extreme right, especially with the large-scale social experiments of forced sterilization and 'euthanasia' of 'unfit' persons by Nazi Germany during the Second World War. However, eugenic concerns were in fact found across the political spectrum and included socialist and anarchist thinkers. Feminists were found on opposite sides – supporting and opposing eugenics, while most opposition came from liberal parties, who rejected state intervention in private life, and churches – particularly the Roman Catholic Church. This was also the case in Switzerland.

Eugenics initially emerged in the form of scientific narratives. In the Swiss context, the terms racial hygiene and eugenics were used interchangeably, the former concept being the most widely used (Schwank, 1996). The most important sites of racial hygiene discourse in Switzerland were the emerging disciplines of psychiatry and sexology. In the course of the nineteenth century, psychiatry and sexology emerged from the field of medical science as autonomous disciplines with a specific focus on sexuality. Among the most important Swiss 'degeneracy experts' (Aeschbacher, 1998, p. 291) were the psychiatrist and sexologist Auguste Forel (1848–1931) and the psychiatrist Eugen Bleuler (1857–1939).

The psychiatrist Auguste Forel was one of the leading sexologists of his time. At the Sex Reform Congress in London in 1929, Forel was cited as one of the founding fathers of sexology, along with the British sexologist Havelock Ellis and the German doctor Iwan Bloch (see Bland, 1998, p. 13). He was a particularly influential pioneer of eugenics both nationally and internationally. His most important book, *La question sexuelle* (1906), was translated into numerous languages. He was elected Member of the Advisory Board of the International Federation of Eugenic Organisations (see Keller, 1995) and Honorary President of the World League of Sexual Reform in 1930. His enduring prestige within Switzerland is reflected by the place of honour accorded to his portrait, which until recently graced 1,000 francs bills.

Forel's promotion of the eugenic project was made from a socialist perspective. In addition to his psychiatric and sexologist activities, he was a social reformer and member of the Swiss social-democrat party from 1916. His progressive campaigns included calls for sexual education in schools, women's voting rights, abstinence from alcoholic drinks and other 'poisons', pacifism, etc. The science of eugenics would provide the impetus for social, moral, and racial purification, he argued. Rejecting the 'false patriotism' of militaristic capitalist nationalism (Forel, 1925, p. 15), Forel promoted the construction of a social and national order based on the scientific management of reproduction by the welfare state, as a moral duty to the future national community.

> The regulation of procreation through appropriated means is a moral task. It is necessary to the hygiene of our race. Only this, combined with the elimination of narcotic poisons, will be able to block the increasing degeneration of our race, and bring us a better future. We owe this to the progress, happiness and health of the future generations, for whose quality we are responsible. (Forel, 1916, p. 12, my transl.)

The discursive mechanisms of *boundary-drawing, boundary-maintenance, othering*, and *ordering* of the nation in Forel's writings were based upon a narrative of heredity and degeneration. The nation was at risk, Forel's narrative suggested, from the hereditary degeneration of the race which was not only physical but also moral. In this story of danger and decay, individuals with flawed hereditary dispositions were attributed roles as victims as well as agents of degeneration. Indeed, for Forel, it was unfair to hold people responsible for having flawed hereditary dispositions. The construction of the social order should therefore not centre on the management of deviants, but rather on the eugenic prevention of degeneracy, an argument articulated in *The True*

*Socialism of the Future* (Forel, 1925, p. 23). Consequently, the worst enemies of eugenics were war (which selects the best to be killed) and alcoholic drinks and other 'narcotic poisons' which damage the mind as well as the body (Forel, 1925).

The central storyline of Forel's eugenic narrative draws together the story of a social order based on hereditary dispositions and currently under threat, with the traditional social-democratic narrative of the redeeming powers of education (Forel, 1910). While 'only a healthy selection of the race' could improve the former, this sexual selection should be combined with active education campaigns based on science and reason: 'Let Science enlighten our sexual life freely and openly; then, the hypocrisy of normal people will cease, and that of abnormal people can be recognized on time and damage be prevented' (Forel, 1916, p. 14 my transl.). Given the importance of sexual selection for the regulation of procreation, sexual education policies were strongly promoted within Forel's narrative. It was through selective, scientifically-informed reproductive sexuality that the boundaries around the national order were to be established and maintained. It was crucial, he argued, to teach young people about the consequences of having sexual relations with 'inferior' partners, and about the corresponding necessity to gather information on the hereditary background of the potential spouse. 'Each fiancee has the right and, in the interest of the future children, the holy duty, to know the sexual antecedents of their future spouse' (Forel, 1916, p. 12; my transl.).

In Forel's imagination of the social order, women constitute a site of narrative ambivalence. On the one hand, he discursively positioned women as political subjects, promoting political equality between the genders and especially women's voting rights – a progressive view in a nation that only awarded voting rights to women in 1971. On the other hand, the reproductive bodies of women were a particular source of narrative anxiety. Given their reproductive responsibilities to the nation, women were seen as particularly important targets for the eugenic education and regulation of sexuality by the state that was called for. 'Well-informed and superior women will be the ones, I expect, who will participate most energetically and most successfully in human selection' (Forel, 1906, p. 575; my transl.). Women's bodily 'instincts of procreation', which he considered 'much stronger in woman than in man', were combined with the will to 'give herself passively', to be 'conquered, mastered and subjugated' (Forel, [1906] 1998, p. 29). In Forel's narratives, female identity is thus ambivalently performed. Women are both political subjects and sexual objects in the social order.

The mechanisms of *othering* within the eugenic narrative centre on different categories that are seen to form hereditary 'threats' to the nation: criminals, prostitutes, alcoholics, immoral people, the mentally ill, haemophiliacs, people with tuberculosis, drug addicts, gypsies, vagrants...Strong boundaries are drawn between the national, white race and the 'inferior races' such as

Jews, 'Negroes', the Chinese. 'How is our Aryan race and its civilisation to guard against the danger of being passively invaded and exterminated by the alarming fecundity of other human races?' Forel wrote.

> One must be blind not to recognize this danger... Up to what point can the Mongolian, and even the Jewish race, become mixed with our Aryan or Indo-Germanic races without gradually supplanting them and causing them to disappear?... The connection of this with the sexual question is not difficult to understand. (Forel, 1906, pp. 222–3)

Indeed, in accordance with conventional views among sexologists at the time, 'sexual drives' of other 'races' were discursively constructed as less constrained by civilization and therefore as more intense than the white race. For example, according to Forel, the 'mental inferiority' of 'Negroes' was combined with 'intense, unbridled sexual passion'.

Different categories of sexual 'perversion' such as sadism or masochism formed another important strand of the eugenic storyline, and were similarly *othered* within Forel's eugenic narrative. Homosexuality was a particular preoccupation to sexologists at the time. Most considered homosexuality as a pathology, although some sexologists such as Magnus Hirschfeld considered homosexuals as 'a variant of normal human beings'. In contrast to other eugenicists, however, Forel was little worried by the sexually 'inverted' or 'urnings' (homosexuals). He considered them to be 'abnormal', 'psychopaths', and 'neurotics', whose sexual drive, similar to that of other 'races', 'is not only abnormal but also, in general, higher'. But, they would not reproduce anyway and therefore posed not much of a threat towards the national 'breed', even though sexual perversions were considered to be hereditarily transmissible.

> As long as homosexual love does not implicate minors, or the feeble-minded, it remains rather innocent, because it does not produce any offspring and will therefore become extinguished automatically through the process of selection. When two individuals are adult and consenting, it is certainly less harmful than prostitution, which is legally protected. (Forel, 1906, p. 270, my transl.)

The sharpest identity boundaries were drawn through eugenic sterilization discourses and practices. Sterilization practices constitute radical mechanisms of inclusion and exclusion of the national community. On the level of discourse, Forel constantly called for the sterilization of the above-mentioned 'degenerate' categories of the population by the state, as a rational measure to prevent their reproduction – a task which was all the more urgent as he considered these sexualized 'others' such as other 'races' and sexual 'perverts' (as well as women in general) as 'more sexual', as we have seen. Having become the director of the world-renowned psychiatric clinic Burghölzli in Zürich from 1879, he put his ideas into practice by pioneering the very first sterilizations without consent within German-speaking nations in 1892 (Aeschbacher, 1998, p. 286).

Forel's successor as director of the Burghölzli Clinic from 1898 to 1927 was his student Eugen Bleuler. In contrast to Forel, the psychiatrist Bleuler was politically rather conservative though also less politically active than Forel. His main narrative focus was the degeneration of the nation through mental illness, which he interpreted as a symptom of diseased modern society and considered to be hereditarily transmissible. The concept of schizophrenia – narrated as the illness of civilization par excellence – was invented at the Burghölzli, and Bleuler developed a highly influential theory of schizophrenia in his widely used classic textbook on psychiatry, published in 1916.[5] Bleuler's version of the eugenic narrative emphasized the threat of *Volksdegeneration* (degeneration of the population) through hereditarily transmissible mental illness, especially in Jews, deemed 'particularly predisposed to mental illnesses: manic depression and psycho-neuroses' in his book *Geborene Verbrecher* (Born Criminals) (see Wottreng 1999).

Both Bleuler's and Forel's storylines drew together a narrative of degeneracy with a narrative on the nature of modern civilization. As Forel put it,

> In the past, in the good old days, incapable and inadequate persons were treated differently from today. Enormous numbers of pathological brains, which damaged society, were simply executed, hanged or beheaded; the process was short and insofar successful, as these people could no longer reproduce or spoil society with their degenerate germs. (Forel, 1906, p. 226)

Forel's narrative tells us the story of the modern national order characterized by the absence of natural selection through fighting and execution of degenerate individuals. Consequently, Forel called for 'artificial sterilization' by the welfare state to 'decrease the numbers of inferior individuals'.

## Eugenics and social policies

Eugenic storylines of degeneration and racial hygiene provided an important framework for the specific mechanisms of boundary-drawing, boundary-maintenance, ordering, and othering that characterized the construction of Swiss national identity. Eugenic narratives express the nation in sharply exclusionary terms. They construct a national order based on sexual, racial, and gendered boundaries. Through the exclusion of 'degenerate' categories both outside and within the national borders, they narratively perform a racially, morally, and socially regenerated *Volk*. As Yuval-Davis points out, 'the myth of common origin or shared blood/genes tends to construct the most exclusionary/homogeneous visions of "the nation"' (Yuval-Davis, 1997, p. 21).

Thus, the construction of Swiss national identity was at least partly founded on what I have termed elsewhere the Swiss 'dream of order' (Mottier, 2000). The social and political order was seen to be 'troubled' by various categories of 'unorderly' (*unordentlich*) citizens and non-citizens, such as Jews, 'vagrants' such as Jenitsch and other 'travellers', the mentally ill, the physically handicapped, unmarried mothers, homosexuals, etc. The eugenic imagination of the national order was concerned with the elimination of such 'troubles'. The rational management of reproductive sexuality by the state was a central mechanism for doing so.

The emerging welfare state provided the means to translate eugenic narratives of the nation into large-scale social experiments. It also added an additional motive to that of preventing degeneracy: limiting public expenditure. Indeed, the 'inferior' categories of the national population were soon to become the main recipients of the expanding welfare institutions. Limiting their numbers appeared as a rational means of reducing costs. The fact that, in the Swiss federal state, local authorities and not the federal state carry the financial burden of supporting 'indigent' members of local communities may also have increased the appeal of the argument of cost-reduction. The eugenic experiments in social engineering were thus shaped by specific Swiss political institutions and federalism, in particular. Federalism led to important cantonal differences in policy frameworks and practices. The main dividing line here seems to have been religion: while Protestant cantons tended to adopt for example sterilization policies, Catholic cantons did not, reflecting the differences in attitudes towards poverty, illness, and disability among Protestant and Catholic doctrines.

Eugenicist narratives of the nation, often drawing on organic metaphors, called for scientifically founded state intervention to prevent further degeneration of the diseased national body. Forel, for example, called for an 'intelligent, scientific (not dogmatic) social-democracy' in order to 'solve the eugenic problem' (Forel, 1910). The newly emerging disciplines of psychiatry and sexology played a pivotal role in providing institutional supports to eugenic discourse. Their scientific expertise was used to legitimize eugenicist policies, in turn legitimizing their own emergence as autonomous disciplines. 'Degeneracy experts' were actively involved in the process of policy-making, for example, through their routine inclusion in expert committees. Psychiatrists also played an important role in the policy implementation. For example, cantons such as Basel introduced an examination by a psychiatric expert of candidates for the acquisition of Swiss citizenship, with the aim of detecting hereditarily transmissable degenerate features.

Thus, eugenic ideas were influential on a number of Swiss pre-war and post-war[6] health and social policies. Such policies included forced sterilization practices, legitimized by the subordination of individual interests to the collective interest of the nation, but also education programmes, non-voluntary incarceration in psychiatric clinics, as well as other measures targeting specifically vagrants, Jenitsch (gypsies), and Jews. World-wide, the first eugenic sterilization law was introduced in Indiana in 1907 and by the 1930s almost two-thirds of US states had similar legislation targeting, in particular, institutionalized individuals such as criminals and those labelled as mentally ill. In 1912, Switzerland was the first European country to introduce eugenically motivated marriage interdiction legislation targeting the mentally ill (see Wecker, 1998, p. 169). In 1928, the Swiss canton of Vaud, influenced by Forel's ideas, adopted the first eugenic sterilization law in Europe (followed by Denmark in 1929, Germany in 1933, Sweden and Norway in 1934, and Finland in 1935).

The law in the canton of Vaud targeted in particular the mentally ill, stating:

> When it is likely that a person who has a mental illness or a mental defect, which is proven to be incurable, will have degenerate offspring,[7] medical measures may be applied to this person in order to prevent the birth of offspring.[8]

It should be noted, however, that the label of mentally ill was a rather loose category which could include vagrants, people of 'weak morals', delinquents, unmarried mothers, etc. The Vaud law existed from 1928 to 1985 and was applied to 187 individuals during these 57 years. Though only a handful of eugenic sterilizations took place in the post-war period in Vaud, the last case took place only 25 years ago: in 1977 (see Jeanmonod and Heller, 2000).

Reflecting the eugenicist focus on female bodies as the reproducers of the nation, the sterilization of 'inferior' categories of the population was a strongly gendered practice. An early evaluation of the application of this law in the canton of Vaud carried out in 1944 reported that nine out of ten eugenic sterilizations were carried out on women (see Ehrenström, 1991, p. 74). Similarly, data on Zürich show that from 1929 to 1931, eugenic sterilizations were carried out on 480 women (in conjuction with abortion) and 15 men, while Runcis (1998) reports that almost 95 per cent of the Swedish sterilizations were carried out on women. As Jeanmonod and Heller (2000) note, the majority of legal sterilizations in the canton of Vaud were applied to young female social deviants: women who were deemed 'maladapted', living in poor conditions, mostly unmarried, and were judged to have 'low intelligence'. The policing of respectable female sexuality appears as a central motive, since 'loose morals', 'uninhibited' female sexuality, or 'nymphomania' were frequently used as arguments for forced sterilization.

Exact figures on the number of sterilizations in other Swiss cantons are not yet available to date. Historians agree, however, that the practice became relatively widespread in Switzerland, especially among individuals who were already institutionalized in those psychiatric clinics that were the playgrounds of the eugenicist ideologues. When Vaud introduced legislation permitting sterilization of the mentally ill without consent, this allowed already existing sterilization practices belatedly to acquire a legal basis – an argument which was in fact used to promote this legislation. It has also been argued that the introduction of the legislation in fact restricted a previously less regulated and more widespread practice (Aeschbacher, 1998, p. 299). While sterilization policies were the most extreme form of eugenic regulation of reproductive sexuality by the welfare state, these practices of bio-power were complemented by 'preventive' education policies. Following Forel's and other campaigners' insistance on the necessity for eugenicist sexual education and marriage advice, eugenics entered the education curriculum. For example, an information brochure was produced and distributed to Swiss schoolchildren in 1939. The brochure educated children about the dangers of reproducing with degenerate others, and pointed out their patriotic duty to the national collective. Schoolchildren were encouraged to: 'Choose your spouse from a physically and morally healthy, mentally superior family! You owe this to your offspring and to the Nation' (Schmid, 1939, p. 44).[9] A 'Central Agency for Marriage and Sex Advice' was founded in 1932, and organized exhibitions and conferences on themes such as 'hereditary responsibility' and 'psychiatric-eugenic advice on marital candidates' (1930s), or 'prevention of hereditarily diseased offspring' (1949).

Other mechanisms of inclusion and exclusion in the national community through practices with eugenic overtones included the notorious policy of the removal of Jenitsch, 'vagrant' or 'traveller' children from their parents, to be raised in state orphanages. The policy operated from 1926 until 1973 and was implemented by the Federal agency titled Pro Juventute, Hilfswerk fuer die Kinder der Landstrasse (Aid agency for children of travellers) which has since been disbanded as a result of later controversies around the policy. Although, strictly speaking, this policy seems somewhat contradictory with eugenic doctrines, demonstrating that the social meanings around policies are not necessarily always coherent, it reflected the views of eugenicist scientists such as Forel and Bleuler, who considered travellers to be hereditarily flawed, and was legitimized on the basis of eugenicist degeneracy narratives. Eugenicist practices towards gypsies were intertwined with disciplinary policies that targeted marginalized categories of the population more generally, including the economic underclass and social deviants.

Overall, the eugenic technologies of power in the Swiss welfare state were characterized by a mix of (relatively low levels of) intervention by the Federal State, such as through Pro Juventute and through federal legislation prohibiting marriage for mentally ill persons or Jews, and high levels of intervention through legislation and administrative measures by communal and cantonal authorities as well as para-state actors such as institutional psychiatry. Psychiatric institutions, especially the university clinics in Zürich, Basel and Lausanne, offered practical opportunities for developing eugenicist ideas and technologies on a population which was most often already under tutelage. While eugenic ideas were articulated within opposite political projects, these projects shared a common call for interventionist state policies in this domain. Eugenicist versions of *Volksnation* narratives provided the ideological basis for the Swiss 'Gardening State', concerned with eliminating the 'weeds' from the national garden.[10]

## Concluding remarks

Mainstream political science analysis of the Swiss political institutions of direct democracy and federalism usually presents these as mechanisms of national integration which allow for the expression of cultural 'difference' and for feelings of national unity and common national identity, despite the linguistic and religious diversity that characterizes the Swiss nation.[11] Although this account of Switzerland is not, in itself, inaccurate, its overemphasis on cohesion leaves us without conceptual tools for explaining how sharply exclusionary practices such as the eugenic policy experiments could have been possible in such an integrative community. In this chapter, I have proposed an alternative account of the construction of Swiss national identity. While not denying the importance of political institutions for the construction of Swiss national identity, I argue that the focus on the institutionalized expression of 'difference' fails to take into account other important historical discourses and practices, which have been concerned not with respect for diversity but with the (relative) eradication of some 'differences': those deemed 'degenerate' or 'un-Swiss'. The analysis of eugenic discourses demonstrates that these have played an important role, not only as symbolic constructions of Swiss nationhood but also as the foundation of social policies which aimed to eradicate the 'weeds' from the Swiss garden. Whereas Swiss immigration and foreign policies have been traditionally concerned with propping up the boundaries against foreign 'outsiders', eugenic policies involved social exclusion of 'internal outsiders' to the national community. As such, the pastoral relations of power embedded in the modern welfare state contributed both to the care and protection of some categories of the population, and to the construction of a sharply exclusionary national order, based on the othering of 'inferior' categories. As we have seen, this exclusionary dimension of welfare policies was strongly supported by the argument of rational reduction of the cost of caring for hereditarily flawed categories of the population – interestingly, an argument that is similarly central to modern debates on the future of welfare.

The use of Foucauldian discourse theory has primarily allowed me to question traditional understandings of power by revealing the central role of relations of bio-power in the modern welfare state. Secondly, in contrast to conventional approaches to state power, it has shifted the focus away from a purely state-centred analysis, to explore instead the multiple sites of bio-power in relation to the eugenic experience. As we have seen, many of the eugenic practices such as forced sterilization of (mainly) women's bodies were not carried out by the central state, but through local legislation and administrative measures implemented by local authorities and para-state actors such as psychiatric clinics. The scientific narratives of heredity and degeneration articulated most prominently within the disciplines of sexology and psychiatry played a key role in serving as institutional supports and as strategies of legitimization for these eugenic practices of bio-power, while schools were instrumental in diffusing eugenic knowledge to the future generations of the nation. Thirdly, in contrast to the conventional history of ideas, this analysis has not centred primarily on the study of the underlying representations of heredity and degeneracy that have guided past behaviours. Rather, it has sought to develop a genealogical analysis exploring the ways in which a historical regime of truth around eugenics was constructed, its institutional supports, and most importantly its connections to modern relations of power.

Moving away from a focus on institutions as privileged by mainstream political analysis toward a concern with practices of bio-power and governmentality in the area of eugenics, shows us the central role that the eugenic regulation of the national body has played in the policing of the social order. The underlying aim of the analysis has been to adopt the view of a history of the present: to look from a different angle at Swiss national identity, usually presented as inclusive, in order to examine its concomittant exclusionary tendencies; but also to interrogate modern welfare practices, by exploring implications of the eugenic experience for our understanding of the nature of modern welfare, care, and power. With respect to the latter, we need to ask whether Switzerland was possibly a special (or especially extreme) case with regard to eugenic practices of bio-power? I do not believe so. Whereas Switzerland and the Scandinavian countries were pioneers of eugenicist discourses and policies in the European context, other countries were soon to follow. Eugenic discourses were scientific orthodoxy in pre-war Europe and their respectability was little called into question at the time. I therefore suggest that the Swiss eugenic practices of biopower constitute a paradigmatic rather than a special case. They reflect the core of the modern welfare state, where regulation, policing and disciplinarization are intertwined with care and protection.

## Notes

1. Many thanks for helpful suggestions to Olaf Corry, Natalia Gerodetti, Jens Henrik Haahr, David Howarth, Lea Sgier, and Jacob Torfing; for archival research to Brigitte Schwab and Natalia Gerodetti; and for linguistic corrections to Emma Broadbent. Deep gratitude is also due to the Swiss National Science Foundation for funding this research (Grant 61-66003.01), to the Fondation Chalumeau (Geneva) for financing a small preparatory archival study, and to the IEPI, University of Lausanne, and Jesus College, Cambridge, for institutional support.

2. Other studies that similarly explore the different ways in which politics shapes identities associated with language, ethnicity, sexuality, or gender are, for example, Weeks (1989), Carver and Mottier (1998), Bacchi (1999), Mottier (2000).
3. The term 'corpus' conventionally refers to the textual material on which the discourse analysis is performed.
4. Darwin adopted the latter idea from Herbert Spencer in 1868.
5. The textbook (Bleuler, 1916) is still influential today, though it has since been purged of its eugenic passages by Bleuler's son.
6. Such distinctions being of somewhat less symbolic importance in Switzerland, which had remained neutral during the Second World War, compared to other European countries.
7. The original phrasing is 'une descendance tarée'.
8. Recueils des lois et décrets du Canton de Vaud, Lausanne, September 1928; quoted in Ehrenström, 1991, my transl.
9. Also quoted in Kreis (1992: 184); my transl.
10. I borrow the term 'Gardening State' from Bauman (1989).
11. Switzerland has four national languages and two main religions.

## Bibliogaphy


Aeschbacher, U. (1998), 'Psychiatrie und Rassenhygiene', in A. Mattioli (ed.), *Antisemitismus in der Schweiz 1948–1960* (Zürich, Orell Füssli Verlag).

Anderson, B. (1991) (1st edn 1983) *Imagined Communities* (London, Verso).

Austin, J. L. (1962) *How to Do Things with Words* (London, Oxford University Press).

Bacchi, C. L. (1999) *Women, Policy and Politics: the Construction of Policy Problems* (London, Sage).

Barthes, R. (1974) *Introduction to the Structural Analysis of the Narrative* (New York, Hill and Wang).

Bauman, Z. (1989) *Modernity and the Holocaust* (Cambridge, Polity Press).

Bauman, Z. (1991) *Modernity and Ambivalence* (Cambridge, Polity Press).

Bhabha, H. (1990), 'Narrating the Nation', in H. Bhabha (ed.), *Nation and Narration*, (London, Routledge).

Bland, L. (1998) 'Introduction', in L. Bland and L. Doan (eds), *Sexology Uncensored: the Documents of Sexual Science* (Cambridge, Polity).

Bleuler, E. (1916) *Lehrbuch der Psychiatrie* (Berlin, Julius Springer).

Bruner, J. (1986) *Actual Minds, Possible Worlds* (Cambridge, MA, Harvard University Press).

Burke, K. (1945) *A Grammar of Motives* (New York, Prentice-Hall).

Carver, T., and Mottier, V. (eds) (1998) *Politics of Sexuality: Identity, Gender, Citizenship* (London, Routledge).

Connolly, W. (1991) *Identity/Difference: Democratic Negotiations of Political Paradox* (Ithaca, N.Y., Cornell University Press).

Czarniawska, B. (1998) *A Narrative Approach to Organization Studies* (Thousand Oaks, Sage).

Dean, M. (1999) *Governmentality: Power and Rule in Modern Society* (London, Sage).

Ehrenström, P. (1991) 'Eugénisme et politique: réflexions sur une étude de cas', *Les Annuelles 2* (Lausanne, Université de Lausanne).

Forel, A. (1906) *La question sexuelle exposée aux adultes cultivés* (Paris, Steinheil).

Forel, A. ([1906] 1998), 'The Sexual Question', in L. Bland and L. Doan (eds), *Sexology Uncensored: the Documents of Sexual Science* (Cambridge, Polity).

Forel, A. (1910) *La Morale en soi* (Lausanne, Administration de la libre pensée).
Forel, A. (1916) *Le Rôle de l'hypocrisie, de la bêtise et de l'ignorance dans la morale contemporaine* (Lausanne, Libre Pensée Internationale).
Forel, A. (1925) *Le Vrai Socialisme de l'avenir* (Lausanne, Imprimerie populaire).
Foucault, M. (1971) *L'Ordre du discours* (Paris, Gallimard).
Foucault, M. (1979) *Discipline and Punish* (New York, Vintage Books).
Foucault, M. (1983), 'The Subject and Power', in P. Rabinow and H. Dreyfus (eds), *Michel Foucault: Beyond Structuralism and Hermeneutics* (Chicago, The University of Chicago Press).
Foucault, M. (1990) *The History of Sexuality, Volume 1: An Introduction* (New York, Random House).
Foucault, M. (1991), 'Governmentality', in G. Burchell, C. Gordon, and P. Miller (eds), *The Foucault Effect: Studies in Governmentality* (London, Harvester Wheatsheaf).
Foucault, M. (1994), 'Non au sexe roi', in D. Defert and E. Ewald (eds), *Dits et ecrits 1954–1988 par Michel Foucault*, Vol. 3 (Paris, Gallimard), pp. 256–69.
Galton, F. (1883) *Inquiries into Human Faculty and Its Development* (London, Macmillan).
Goffman, E. (1959) *The Presentation of Self in Everyday Life* (London, Penguin).
Hajer, M. (1995) *The Politics of Environmental Discourse* (Oxford, Oxford University Press).
Hobsbawm, E. (1983), 'Inventing Traditions', in E. Hobsbawm and T. Ranger (eds), *The Invention of Tradition* (Cambridge, CUP)
Jeanmonod, G., and Heller, G. (2000) 'Eugenisme et contexte socio-politique: l'exemple de l'adoption d'une loi sur la stérilisation des handicapés et malades mentaux dans le canton de Vaud en 1928', *Revue d'histoire suisse*, Vol. 50: 20–44.
Keller, C. (1995) *Der Schädelvermesser: Otto Schlaginhaufen – Anthropologe und Rassenhygieniker: eine biographische Reportage* (Zürich, Limmat Verlag).
Kreis, G. (1992), 'Der "Homo Alpinus Helveticus": Zum schweizerischen Rassendiskurs der 30er Jahre', in G. Marchal and A. Mattioli (eds), *Erfundene Schweiz: Konstruktionen nationaler Identität* (Zürich, Chronos Verlag).
Kühl, S. (1997) *Die Internationale der Rassisten: Aufstieg und Niedergang der internationalen Bewegung für Eugenik und Rassenhygiene im 20. Jahrhundert* (Frankfurt, Campus Verlag).
Litfin, K. (1994) *Ozone Discourses: Science and Politics in Global Environmental Cooperation* (New York, Columbia University Press).
Manning, P., and Cullum-Swan, B. (1998), 'Narrative, Content, and Semiotic Analysis', in N. Denzin and Y. Lincoln (eds) *Collecting and Interpreting Qualitative Materials* (Thousand Oaks, Sage).
Mottier, V. (2000) 'Narratives of National Identity Sexuality, Race, and the Swiss "Dream of Order"', *Swiss Journal of Sociology*, Vol. 26: 533–56.
Mottier, V. (2002) 'Discourse Analysis and the Politics of Identity/Difference', *European Political Science*, 2.1 (autumn): 57–60.
Nye, R. A. (1999), 'The Discovery of "Sexuality" at the Turn of the Century', in R. Nye (ed.), *Sexuality* (Oxford, OUP).
Pearson, K. ([1909] 1998), 'The Scope and Importance to the State of the Science of National Eugenics', in L. Bland and L. Doan (eds), *Sexology Uncensored: the Documents of Sexual Science* (Cambridge, Polity).
Plummer, K. (1995) *Telling Sexual Stories: Power, Change and Social Worlds* (London, Routledge).
Propp, V. ([1928] 1968), *Morphology of the Folktale* (Austin, University of Texas Press).
Runcis, M. (1998) 'Sterilization in the Swedish Welfare State', English summary of doctoral thesis, University of Stockholm.

Sawicki, J. (1991) *Disciplining Foucault: Feminism, Power, and the Body* (New York, Routledge).
Schmid, W. (1939) *Jung-Schweizer! Jung-Schweizerinnen! Das Schicksal des Vaterlandes ruht in Euch!* (Erlenbach, Rotapfel Verlag).
Schwank, A. (1996), 'Der rassenhygienische (bzw. eugenische) Diskurs in der schweizerischen Medizin des 20. Jahrhunderts', in S. Weigel and B. Erdle (eds), *Fünfzig Jahre danach: Zur Nachgeschichte des Nationalsozialismus* (Zürich, Hochschulverlag ETH).
Sommer, D. (1990), 'Irresistible Romance: the Foundational Fictions of Latin America', in H. Bhabha (ed.), *Nation and Narration* (London, Routledge).
Stone, D. (1997) *Policy Paradox: the Art of Policy Decision Making* (New York, Norton).
Wecker, R. (1998), 'Eugenik – individueller Ausschluss und nationaler Konsens', in S. Guex et al. (eds), *Krisen und Stabilisierung: die Schweiz in der Zwischenkriegszeit* (Zürich, Chronos).
Weeks, J. (1989) *Sex, Politics and Society: the Regulation of Sexuality since 1800* (London, Longman).
Wottreng, W. (1999) *Hirnriss: Wie die Irrenarzte August Forel and Eugen Bleuler das Menschengeschlecht retten wollten* (Zürich, Weltwoche-Verlag).
Yuval-Davis, N. (1997) *Gender & Nation* (London, Sage).
Yuval-Davis, N., and Anthias, F. (eds) (1989) *Woman–Nation–State* (London, Macmillan).

# 11
# Media Discourse and the Public Sphere

*Lilie Chouliaraki*

This piece of research belongs to a tradition in media and cultural studies which treats television as text. The goal is to understand how our experience of the media and particularly of television is produced in meaning. Making sense of media texts primarily involves treating television talk and images as practices of representation, situated in specific political and cultural contexts. Earlier interpretative projects involved a preoccupation with the gap between the real world and the meanings disseminated through the media as well as with the ideological effects that media have on contemporary culture. More recently, post-structuralist theories of meaning have shifted the emphasis away from 'hidden' meanings towards the articulations of meaning and power in television texts, which themselves produce specific 'reality effects' – rather than reflecting or distorting a reality 'out there'.[1]

My focus in this paper falls on the meaning-power articulations in a specific television genre, that of public debate. My assumption is that public debate involves primarily the establishment of a meaning horizon which delimits what can be said and known, and which authorizes as true certain meanings and knowledges at the expense of others. Put differently, there is a *politics of truth* at play in every mediated debate, which is central to the constitution of the debate as a public sphere. It is this 'politics' that I want to examine below.

## The significance of trivia

The 'politics of truth' question becomes more prominent when the debate concerns not the 'legitimate' politics of, say, the Middle East, but the 'royal fairy-tale' in *Billed Bladet* (*BB*), a local weekly offering of spicy celebrity gossip for domestic consumption. Following Silverstone, I suggest that, though media analysis often makes 'worthy' matters its object of inquiry, it is actually on the mundane, the 'non-political', and yet the intensely politicized, that the media operates most significantly:

> [The media] filter and frame everyday realities through their singular and multiple representations, producing touchstones, references, for the conduct of everyday life, for the production and maintainance of common sense. And it is here, *in what passes for common sense,* that we have to ground the study of the media. (Silverstone, 1999, p. 6, emphasis added)

It is precisely this emphasis on how common sense is imperceptibly reproduced in the media, and so reappears as yet another resource for the conduct of everyday life, that the focus on the politics of truth in the debate explores. How is a particular story, devoid of political content in itself, construed as relevant for public debate in television? Which meanings on truth and ethics does the story's focus on gossip and trivia entail? And to what effect?[2]

## Media in the media

In October 1998, the Danish celebrity magazine *Billed Bladet* came out with the headline 'Crack in the Marriage' – a provocative claim. The claim referred to the marriage of Prince Joakim with Princess Alexandra; the evidence provided for the claim was two pictures from the Royal Theatre of Copenhagen, where the couple appeared to look each their own way. 'There is something terribly wrong in this marriage', commented the text, racketting sales to over one and a half million. There is nothing unusual about celebrity magazines printing such stories. They are trivial and fleeting, perhaps, but spicy enough to satisfy popular voyeurism – hence the label 'trashy'. Yet, on that particular occasion, there was a reaction. A royal representative bemoaned the excesses of the celebrity press ('this has gone too far'), the issue made national news, and the prime-time debate shows on Danish television made it that week's topic. On Wednesday 21 and on Thursday 22 October, an average of 600,000 viewers watched heated discussions on the right of the royals to privacy and on the role of celebrity magazines in public life.

It is the first of these two television debates that is the subject of this article. What I find interesting in it is the way in which one mass medium, television, reflects upon another, the press (or a section of it). There is an element of reflexivity in television's attempt to deal with journalistic practice. Questions of truth and ethics, which are raised with respect to the celebrity magazine, reflect the guiding assumptions of mediated debates themselves. This, in turn, throws into relief significant aspects of the function of this television genre as a public sphere.[3] How is the televised debate constituted as a public space? What are the communicative practices which confer upon this genre the legitimacy of public debate? What are the principles by which communication is regulated? What domains of knowledge are construed as legitimate by this regulation? And what is the potential for democratic deliberation released in these domains?

## The debate as government

There is, of course, a close link between the politics of truth and the democratic potential of televised debate. If the politics of truth authorizes the meaning horizon within which the topic of debate is understood, then it is by assessing the contours of this horizon, what it includes and what it excludes as possible knowledge, that we also assess the capacity of the debate to deliberate. That is, the capacity of the debate to subject its topic to rational critique, by opening up to scrutinity the partiality of *all* relevant knowledge, irrespective of its status or power.[4]

This, in turn, pressuposes a modest view of democracy, away from the 'grand politics' of the state, the parliament or the party, nonetheless equally tied to institutions and to power. It presupposes a 'local' view of democracy as a practice which activates minor and often invisible relations of power, so as to act upon the detail of individual conduct, to increase its 'good order', and maximize its freedom. This is a view of democracy that Rose refers to as 'government' (1999, p. 6) and which Hall also applies to the media as 'government by culture' (1997, pp. 227–8).

From this point of view, the televised debate can be seen as a minor device of government, a mode of ruling through *showing how* we should think and act under certain norms of civility – it is rule by 'the conduct of conduct', to use Rose's words again (1999, p. 21). Conceptually speaking, the government perspective helps us approach the television debate as a *practice of discourse* – as a local game of power which involves the mediazation of meaning resources (Thompson, 1995, pp. 3–4, for the term 'mediazation'). That such resources are indeterminably appropriated by audiences is clear; the key issue here is that televised debate does suggest which meanings are relevant for public dialogue, and does enact certain practices of communication as the most appropriate for civic behaviour – it is not and could not have been an 'everything goes' practice.[5] The focus on the politics of truth captures just that aspect of government where competing discourses struggle for hegemony – for authorizing their version of truth as 'the' true discourse in the debate.

### The methodology of Critical Discourse Analysis (CDA)

The analytical task is then an enquiry 'into the instabilities and flux of meanings and into their transformations, but also into the politics of their fixing' (Silverstone, 1999, p. 16). This calls for a Critical Discourse Analytic methodology (Fairclough, 1992, 1995; Chouliaraki and Fairclough, 1999). CDA rejects the dominant view of language as primarily a referential system and theorizes language both as practice itself (in its pragmatic or 'performative' dimension) and as representation of practice (in its semantic dimension). Language in this double capacity is discourse – the constitutive power of signification. CDA's claim is, therefore, that forms of knowledge and social identity are produced and transformed within and through discourse, in a range of social practices. The methodological assumption of CDA rests on the constructivist view of language and text as a social semiotic (Halliday, 1978, 1985). Specifically, this systemic-functional view of language entails the claim that three major types of processes are always at play in semiotic practices: the construction of reality, the enactment of social relations and identities, and the construction of text itself (respectively the 'ideational', 'interpersonal', and 'textual' metafunctions of language). The textual metafunction, text-making, is the specifically semiotic facet of the production of social life in social practices; and people only engage with reality and with each other semiotically through text-making. Text, therefore, holds a privileged position in the methodological apparatus of CDA, in that it provides a link between concrete meaning-making processes (including identity-making) and the conditions of possibility (the discursive horizon) that meaning-making draws upon. The CDA methodology treats the linguistic and visual resources of the text as subtle indicators of the struggle over truth, and of the social positions from which truth is spoken. So, the following discourse analysis is a kind of 'magnifying glass' upon the debate, where the object, the word choice, and the mode of address are instruments strategically (though not necessarily consciously) mobilized in a play of power.[6]

Specifically, the analysis of this television text posed two main procedural issues. First, how to analyse the dialogic flow from the perspective of discursive regulation, that is, with a view to examining the establishment of a normative discourse in the debate. Second, how to account for the two distinct semiotic modalities that coexist in the course of the television debate, the linguistic and the visual, each modality playing its part in the construction of normative discourse.

Obviously, the first issue, the matter of discursive regulation requires a concrete analytical vocabulary capable of conceptualizing the dialogue in terms of specific moves of power. I elaborate on this analytical vocabulary in a moment (the debate as an articulation of universal and particular meanings). For now, it suffices to say that, in order to redescribe the dialogue in terms of two rival fields of meaning that the participants bring into confrontation with one another, I used a technique that we may call *sequence condensation*. This means that I picked out and condensed all of the host's questions to his guest as well as the ways in which he treated his interlocutor's responses – respectively, the sections where *Truth was made universal* and where *Truth was kept particular*. Sequence condensation enabled me to show how the host's positional power turned into a local form of control in the interactional flow and, at the same time, to show how this local form of control restricted and shaped the guest's responses, so that they were never given the chance to become normative.

The second procedural issue, the issue of the visual-verbal on-screen relationship, requires an understanding of the visual semiotic, not as merely 'reflecting' the material environment of the debate, its theatrical set-up for instance, but as actively participating in the politics of truth of the debate and, therefore, on the construction of normative meanings. In order to establish the centrality of the visual semiotic in the play of power enacted in this dialogue, I decided to examine the presence of the *objects-on-display* in it. These objects were a number of celebrity magazine issues that were recurrently flagged by the host and zoomed in upon by the television camera. In the analysis, I focused on the regular insertion of these objects into the flow of the debate and I studied how this insertion was articulated with and framed by linguistic commentary. As we shall see, the visual presence of objects in the debate brings with it a degree of factuality and fixity that is hard to establish by linguistic argument alone; this is because images have, in Latour's words, a *globalizing* effect upon meaning and, thus, enable the consolidation and legitimation of discourses of truth in a subtler and less visible manner than language. In focusing upon the visual semiotic then, I was able to establish the instrumental role that the presence of physical objects played in the establishment of normative truth in this debate.

## The debate as an articulation of universal and particular meanings

Which *analytical concepts* can best describe the operation whereby a normative discourse is imposed over other meaning possibilities in a debate? This question is best approached via the categories of *universal and particular* (Laclau, 1996). The particular refers to here-and-now meaning, to situated and embodied practice, to the concrete event, whereas the universal refers to meaning abstracted from the here-and-now, to a meaning horizon that contextualizes and evaluates the particular, to a normative ideal. The disjunction between the two is misleading, though. No particular can claim an identity without simultaneously evoking, implictly or explicitly, some horizon for its contextualization – a horizon which, at the same time, dissolves the particular by subsuming it in the universal body. By the same token, no universal can be postulated without the simultaneous evocation of a particular identity that 'grounds' and legitimates it. The two are co-emergent. Caught in this double-bind, any claim to identity is constantly undermined by the very movement which makes it possible: 'the particular exists only in the contradictory movement of asserting at the same time a differential identity and cancelling it through its subsumption in the non-differential medium [the universal]' (Laclau, 1996, p. 28). Even if the negotiation of this double is unresolvable at the epistemic level, however, it is always temporarily settled in specific discursive practices (Jørgensen, 2002).

The televised debate is an exemplary illustration of this process – it is anchored upon particulars in order to evoke and establish universals. If 'the universal is no more than a particular that at some moment has become dominant' (Laclau, 1996, p. 26), then the analytical task is to establish *the process* by which this hegemonic operation is accomplished discursively. Indeed, the search for a universal is not a search for a fixed discourse evoked once and for all. The universal is best conceptualized as a *principle* that controls the signifying process by which, theoretically, any discourse can assign to a particular the function of universal representation. Yet, even though the universal does not have a neccesary content, it would be misleading to assume that it is in constant flux. Which discourse acts as universal, at any specific moment, depends upon the power relations and institutional logics of the social practice within which it is embedded. Though Laclau recognizes this, he does not empirically investigate the process by which specific institutional logics stabilize the contingency of discourse towards certain articulations of the universal over others (Bernstein, 1990, 1996; Chouliaraki and Fairclough, 1999; Chouliaraki, 2001). Analysing the televised debate as an institutional practice means, therefore, paying attention to the ways in which the structuring of power within this genre regulates the dialogic flow so as to enable certain discourses only to act as normative horizons.

Following the above, the issues I address in the analysis are: (a) how the particulars are formulated from specific social positions; (b) how a dominant discourse on truth is established as universal in the debate (in the sections 'Truth in objects' and 'The opening sequence. Truth-for-truth's-sake'). The power and interests of the host and his guest are both a condition and a stake in the 'ultimate' fixing of a certain universal. This, in turn, leads me to comment on the politics of truth in this part of the debate: (c) a discussion of the principle of 'Universal articulations in the debate' and; (d) the potential effects of its politics of truth in the 'Debate as public sphere'.

## The debate: 'Fingers off Frederic', *Reimer Bo* 21 October 1998

On the occasion of *Billed Bladet*'s 'crack in the marriage' story, referring to the most popular royal couple in Denmark, the weekly debate programme *Reimer Bo* (named after its host) came out with the title 'Fingers off Frederik'.[7] The reference to Crown Prince Frederik broadens the focus beyond the actual issue of Joakim and Alexandra's marriage towards the general issue of when the private turns public. Other cases of publicity are also brought into the discussion, yet the royalist perspective is clear. The debate is formulated in the specific terms of the royals' right to privacy, thus harmonizing with the concerns expressed by the royal house (though, as I shall argue, the stronger the royalist perspective, the less it is discussed). The discussion opens with a confrontation between Bo and his main guest, the chief editor of *Billed Bladet*, Anders Thisted. 'It was basically you who started the whole story', says Reimer Bo, casting Thisted as protagonist as well as 'accused'. Thisted sits facing the host, and both of them are surrounded by the audience. It is this opening sequence with Thisted that is the focus of my analysis. It is only at the end of the interview that the host leaves his seat and moves among the audience to ask further questions.

Throughout the host's interactions with his guests, continuity and coherence are established through five magazine articles which, one after the other, structure separate but interrelated sequences of exchange. Each sequence takes up the debate topic by reference to a specific celebrity magazine story.[8] Thus, issues on the truth and ethics of press journalism, universal meanings which underpin the topic, emerge in the course of local talk about these specific stories, these particulars. The point about the truth claims and ethical values of journalism is that their content is not settled but is precisely the bone of contention. Following Laclau and Mouffe, truth and ethics are *empty signifiers* in this discursive practice. Dispersed and disconnected as they are in the flow of language, they do not form a readily available and coherent principle for explaining the particular – they rather 'await' fixation by their multiple and differential references to this particular. The articulation of the particular and the universalizing and particularizing of normative horizons of meaning are the main moves that constitute the discursive field of the debate. My analysis below focuses on two aspects of these universal/particular moves: first, the use of celebrity magazines as objects in the programme (Truth in objects) and second, the management of the argumentative dynamics in Reimer Bo's confrontation with Anders Thisted (Truth in language).

## Truth in objects

Celebrity magazines are not only talked about in the programme. They are also shown, touched, and read in the programme. Their material nature as tangible objects is drawn into the debate at strategic points. Every time a particular story is introduced, Reimer Bo holds the relevant magazine issue in his hands and, whilst the camera zooms onto it, he reads from it or describes the pictures within.

As mentioned, the magazines function as a cohesive device, in that they structure the five sequential units of the debate. They embody the particular, the here-and-now meanings of celebrity journalism, upon which a concrete discussion on the how and why of each story rests. As such, the magazines function as points of reference with respect to which more abstract meanings are articulated – the universals of the truth and ethics of this journalism. Let me sum up the specific contribution the magazines as objects make to the establishment of universal meanings.

First, the presence of magazines also relates journalists to the particular. All the journalists in the programme are introduced through their relationship to a specific celebrity story, they are held responsible for it, and are expected to defend it. As a consequence, *their* space of argumentation is considerably reduced – their ability to move from the particular story to a universal argument on, say, journalistic ethics is seriously restricted. For example, a *Her og Nu* journalist was called to order thus: Journalist: 'but it's quite impressive that you had to go so far back to find a spectacular front page'; Reimer Bo: 'You should respond to what you have been asked' – (laughter).

Second, the magazines function as factual evidence. *All* Reimer Bo's questions to these journalists begin (and usually end) with *a claim to truth*, a cross-check between the magazine's story and the real events. For example, this is how Reimer Bo ridicules the claim of a 1997 *Her og Nu* issue that Alexandra was pregnant – a claim predating Alexandra's pregnancy by two years. He flags the magazine issue, gives time details (10 April 1997) and a direct quote ('Alexandra pregnant'), and while the camera zooms on the magazine's cover, he asks: 'how's the child?' – sharp sarcasm. The presence of the object as evidence of Reimer Bo's truth claim works to produce authenticity and convince the audience. Compare the advantages of this confrontation based on the force of the magazine's photo and layout with a hypothetical confrontation based on, say, Reimer Bo's own recollections of the publication – 'I remember last year you came out with a solo story on your front page where...'.

The presence of the celebrity magazine as object in this programme can be seen as one technique through which a universal truth is implicitly established – a technique of 'globalizing' meanings (Latour, 1996). Globalizing refers precisely to the *effect of fixity* conferred upon meanings by the physical materiality of objects. The immediacy of the pictures, the detail of the layout, the specificity of time details, the association with concrete people physically present in the programme (the journalists), all combine together to endow celebrity journalism with facticity and authenticity. Each time a story is challenged, the magazine issue in question is flagged as evidence of fraud.

In this way, the presence of the magazine becomes instrumental in a specific truth operation: *the recovery of facts*. In a first move, the magazine's truth claim is measured against reality, a reality evoked either by Reimer Bo's reference to external events or by insiders' own accounts. In a second move, the magazine's truth claim is proclaimed invalid precisely because it has failed to relate to the world of facts. In this operation, the assessment of celebrity journalism, the 'accused' in this programme, seems to take place within a discourse of legal positivism: questions of the multiple values (and therefore of competing truths) involved in the representations of public personalities in the media are kept separate from questions of fact. The latter are recoverable as such (Goodrich, 1994, p. 328). Though this truth operation is part of a broader mechanism for the establishment of a truth regime in the debate, it is the only one which systematically reappears throughout the programme, thus establishing the criteria by which truth is assessed.

The politics of truth enacted by the celebrity magazine as object can be summed up in the phrase 'globalize the particular to universalize'. This implies that the insertion of the celebrity magazine as an object in the debate works to keep one semiotic form, the visual, constantly in the service of one universal. Irrespective of the linguistic struggles to impose different truth interests on this class of press, the object itself speaks one truth: the celebrity press is unequivocally dishonest and untrustworthy. Because this modality is not centrally perceived as creating meaning (objects are usually taken as 'givens' rather than as semiotic resources), its effect in fixing meaning becomes even stronger.

As a consequence, the possibility of discussing the celebrity press as something else than just 'the village's fool' spreading rumours, as Reimer Bo put it, is considerably reduced. Let us now move to the linguistic representations of truth in the opening sequence of the programme.

**Truth in language**

* what are you grounding this on [Pause] break in the marriage
* have these six journalists written all they knew I see two pictures and I see a text where they somehow speculate that the marriage is in trouble (2/7–9)
* now when you have . . . when you now have a story like this which you think is really good and you have six really really smart journalists did you ring to the interested parties before you published this story

*Truth made universal*

These are Reimer Bo's first three questions. Each refers to a particular, to a specific operation of the *Billet Bladet* text, in order to 'dig out' the premise on which each operation is grounded. But, although each question evokes a certain particular, altogether they establish *a chain of equivalential demands* (Laclau, 1996) – a field of meanings within which these particulars are placed. Thus, each question contributes to building up a discursive horizon in which the truth and validity of journalistic practice are construed and understood. It is within this regime of truth that a certain epistemology of representation is made universal in the debate. Specifically, all three questions address the claims to truth in *BB*'s text: evidence status ('what are you grounding this on?'); evidence adequacy ('I see two pictures and I see a text'); evidence validity ('did you ring to the interested parties before you published the story?').

The first question undermines the very status of evidence provided by the magazine to support the claim 'crack in the marriage' – that is two photographs of the royal couple at the Royal Theatre, each looking their own way. The *what* in Reimer Bo's initial question '**what** are you grounding this on [Pause] break in the marriage?' begs for a specification of the source of information itself. In so doing, the question implies that the photographic material of the reportage cannot be taken as a given piece of evidence. Reimer Bo's next question casts double doubt upon the adequacy of the magazine's evidence. First, it casts doubt upon the journalists as legitimate sources of information, suggesting that there may be more to reality than what they write about: 'have these six journalists written **all** they knew?'. Second, it casts doubt on the photographic material of the reporting, suggesting that it is poor evidence of reality: 'I see two pictures and I see a text where they somehow speculate that the marriage is in trouble'. In insisting on what he sees ('I see', twice, a perception rather than a cognitive process – compare to 'understand' or 'get to know') Reimer Bo destabilizes the automatic interpretative link readers usually establish between picture and text in order to make sense of a story – what Barthes calls the 'anchoring' of the picture onto text. Separating the two ('two pictures... a text'), leaves the coherence of the story suspended. In Reimer Bo's talk, the interpretative link ('crack in the marriage') is thus attributed solely to the story writers themselves ('where **they** somehow **speculate**' – compare to a potential use of a perception process such as 'show' or 'demonstrate'). In both cases, the doubt about journalists and the doubt about photographic evidence, it is implied that there is a dislocation between the truth claimed in the story and the truth outside the story. On these grounds, Reimer Bo discredits *Billed Bladet*'s credibility. But he does not abandon truth claims as such. For Reimer Bo, truth exists outside its narrative form and it is possible to recover it. His third question, on validation procedures, suggests such a possible locus for truth: the testimony of the 'protagonists' of the story, in this case the royal environment ('Did you ring to **the interested parties** before you published the story?').

The universal can be described as a move from the particular, that is, Reimer Bo's questions and other relevant references to the 'marriage troubles' text, to the formulation of a normative discourse on truth that informs journalistic practice. This universal posits an external reality that it is possible to recover accurately. Truth is verifiable-falsifiable by a procedure of matching locution, the text, to this reality. Such evidence is provided through insider's knowledge, the testimony of those 'within'. The journalism of this universal establishes facts. A story has to be based on hard data rather than speculative evaluations and, on the basis of this criterion, *Billed Bladet*'s photographs are relativized as contingent and partial. A story also has to be cross-checked through contact with the parties involved and, in failing to follow this procedure, *Billed Bladet* leaves the truthfulness of its claims suspended.

What appears as a universal in this text is a specific discourse on truth, what I earlier referred to as a discourse of legal positivism, which frames and evaluates the particulars of the *Billed Bladet* story. This discourse is based upon a radical split between fact and evaluation – it selectively elevates some elements as crucial in the pronouncement of truth (facts), whereas others are construed as subjective speculation (evaluations). The ethical 'moment' of the discourse is precisely the moment of the recovery of truth, of factualizing reality. It does so, via the positivist operation of privileging one locus of truth over others: insiders have direct access to reality, they know best. However, in positing an external reality, the discourse obscures the ways in which language always already participates in defining what a fact is before it 'recovers' it. The regime of truth which makes this epistemological operation possible simultaneously denies its own partiality, its own politics of representation. On the one hand, *Billed Bladet*'s 'fact' of a conflict between the royal couple – itself established by force through the photographic image (and the powerful visual 'I-see-therefore-I-believe' epistemology) – is made relative as 'evaluation'. On the other hand, insiders' accounts are elevated to privileged validity criteria for truth, though one might wonder if such participants do not inevitably provide interested and thus partial accounts of events.

> what are you grounding this on [Pause] break in the marriage. To this question, Anders Thisted responds as follows: well we're grounding it of course on the research we did [Pause] I have six journalists who work on the royal family domain and it's clear that they should report on what they experience you can't just say send six journalists out in the field and tell them well you must come back and write about everything that's good and glamorous but if you see some who are in trouble some who can't make it please tell your colleagues in the canteen but the readers (Reimer Bo: have they written) they can just be fooled... (Reimer Bo: have these six journalists written **all** they knew)

*Truth kept particular*

The direct response to Reimer Bo comes in the first two lines of Anders Thisted's turn: 'well we're grounding it of course on the research we did [Pause] I have six journalists who work on the royal family domain...' Notice here the choice of the word 'research' that denotes thorough investigation, the choice of a numerative ('six') to specify the precise number of journalists, and the choice of expressions like field work ('out in the field') and subject-matter area ('domain') to specify the procedure and subjects under research. The field of meanings concentrated in this brief sentence construes truth as a product of specialized, quasi-scientific work. Research, fieldwork, subject-matter area, professional expertise, collective enterprise, all contribute to injecting celebrity journalism with authority and credibility.

Further, the discourse categorically ('it's clear') construes truth as the journalist's own experience ('what they experience') of an external reality, 'in the field' – compare this to Reimer Bo's locus of truth which is 'protagonists' or insiders rather than journalists themselves. Reality is construed as an object of direct perception – vision ('but if **you see**'; and again in the claim that readers 'can be fooled'). It is disconnected from the process of representative-journalistic writing. This belongs to a distinct sphere – the office or 'home' (notice the 'come back' expression in the quote) It is the process of representation 'back home' that is subject to manipulation. How the journalistic 'gaze' is produced as public text is a question of ethics.

Indeed, by the use of deontic modality ('you can't just say...'), Anders Thisted spells out an ethics that guides the representation of the real world:

transparency. The journalists mediate between the real and the readers under the obligation ('they should report on') that they make visible 'everything' they see, not only the positive ('everything that's good...') but also the negative sides of reality ('some who are in trouble...') – the metaphor for the latter is the 'backside' as Anders Thisted puts it later on. Like Reimer Bo, Anders Thisted's discourse on truth posits an objective reality existing independently of particular interests – specifically, here, the interests of the royal family. Unlike Reimer Bo, the 'moment' of ethics in this discourse lies in the manner of mediation – not as a recovery of facts, but as an extension of the field of public visibility. The committment is to the readers, the public – that some topics may be kept 'between us' ('tell your colleagues in the canteen') constitutes deception: the readers 'can just be fooled'.

We saw that Anders Thisted's direct response to 'what are you grounding it on?' was the construal of *Billed Bladet*'s journalism as the collective research of professionals in their expert area, coupled with a universal on journalistic truth as a matter of transparency. In the argumentative dynamics of the interaction, this elaborate response is left suspended. The host cuts Anders Thisted off to come back on track: 'have these six journalists written all they knew I see two pictures and I see a text where they somehow speculate that the marriage is in trouble'. Anders Thisted is pushed to respond to the specifics of the story's validity. His discourse is kept particular. His answer, though, 'deviates' towards another universal:

> Well we say yes it's obvious there is a crack in the marriage **because** [Pause] **it's not it's just not easy** to be [Pause] let me tell you **it's just not easy for a foreigner to move to Denmark** it sounds so great that you can move from one culture to the other ( ... ) **but it's not that easy to manage in Denmark** we are not that tolerant and [Pause] that easy to socialize with ( ... ) and it's clear that for Alexandra the conditions are more or less the same as for other people [Pause] and **like I said if you want to tell the positive sides you're also obliged to engage with the 'backside' of it** (Reimer Bo: when you now have) **it's no publicity** (2/13–24).

Here, Anders Thisted draws on a discourse of cultural mismatch, which foregrounds the difficulties of adaptation that foreigners face in the country: 'it's just not easy for a foreigner to move to Denmark; it's not that easy to manage in Denmark'. This is a popular discourse on immigrant relations in Denmark. In this environment, the discourse acts as a meaning horizon contextualizing a certain class of particulars, intercultural marriages – including the supposed conflict between the royal couple (as Alexandra comes from Hong Kong). Notice how the discourse lifts the royal member out of her particularity and aligns her with foreigners as a universal class: 'foreigner'; 'for Alexandra the conditions are more or less the same as **for other people**'. What this discourse universalizes is one explanatory version which could lend legitimacy to *Billed Bladet*'s own truth claim – cultural mismatch leads to marital conflicts. It is activated at this point to provide that interpretative link between the photographic material and the 'marriage troubles' text which Reimer Bo had skillfully rendered arbitrary (above): 'I see two pictures and I see a text'. But once such a dislocation has taken place and *Billed Bladet*'s own interpretation loses its 'natural' force, any universal that 'comes to the rescue' equally runs the risk of exposing its own arbitrariness. Any explanation would do as well as that of the cultural mismatch – perhaps even better.

It is in order to strengthen his argumentative position that Anders Thisted seeks further support from his epistemological universal which he has already introduced: such as 'I said if you want to tell the positive sides you're also obliged to engage with the "backside" of it (Reimer Bo: when you now have) it's no publicity'. If the discourse of cultural mismatch cannot validate the story, then the discourse on truth as transparency would. Here, modality construes journalistic practice as a matter of volition ('will'), a wish to recount a positive reality, *and* as obligation ('you're also obliged to'), a duty to attend to its 'backside' – two distinct modes of attachment to the journalistic task. But, at the same time, these modes of attachment are structured in a conditional clause, 'if you', which *subordinates wish to obligation* and construes the journalistic ethic again as committment to transparency (if you want *plus*, then you are also obliged to *minus*). Notice here the contrast of this ethics with advertising, a practice which operates exclusively on the wish to make visible the positive without a conditional obligation: *it's not publicity*. The effect is that Anders Thisted distances himself from an ethic that would subordinate transparency of vested interests; in this case advertising for the royals.

This univeralizing attempt again remains suspended. As before, Reimer Bo interrupts Anders Thisted's talk to ask another question:

> Anders Thisted: *you're also obliged to engage with the 'backside' of it* – Reimer Bo: **now when you have** – Anders Thisted: this is not publicity ... Reimer Bo: now when you have ( ... ) when you now have a story like this which you think is really good and you have six really really smart journalists did you then ring to the interested parties before you published this story

Reimer Bo's intervention particularizes. Present tense 'now when you have ( ... ) when you now have', the use of 'now, twice, as well as the and-links connecting all processes, construe story-writing as a step-by-step process in a here-and-now context. Once established as the particular relevant for discussion, story-writing is then approached from the temporal perspective of the debate – there is a shift to past tense in 'did you then ring ...'.

The qualifiers of amount, 'six', and nature, 'really really smart journalists', echo Anders Thisted's earlier argument on the professionalism of *Billet Bladet*'s research (notice the repetition of the numerical, 'six', and the double use of qualifier of manner, 'really'). This intertextual weaving of Anders Thisted's discourse in Reimer Bo's current narrative has a certain effect: irony. This is based on the contrast between the journalists' deliberately emphasized competence and their failure to follow the professional norm (cross-checking information). A failure anticipated in Reimer Bo's question and confirmed in Anders Thisted's negative response: 'no we just can't... we just can't come to talk with the interested parties but it's clear that we talk with the royal sphere we do that **to a great extent**'.

Notice, again, Anders Thisted's move away from the particular and towards a universal. First, his negative response is qualified by a present tense modal ('can't') which de-temporalizes possibility and construes Reimer Bo's suggestion as impossible not because of specific circumstances but because of general conditions: journalists do not have direct access to the royal family, the 'protagonists' of the story. This implication is rather off the point (everybody knows that journalists don't just ring up the prince), but it offers Anders Thisted the rhetorical advantage of moderating his negative response with some degree of plausibility. His second responsive move, addressing (more to the point) contact with the 'royal sphere', still continues to steer away from the particular case: 'but it's clear that we talk with the royal sphere we do that to a great extent'.

Present tense, 'we talk', and a frequency adverb, 'to a great extent', again project a general, de-temporalized state of affairs rather than a circumstance. This insistence upon the general invites yet another temporalized question from Reimer Bo, 'did you ring', and a specific, 'this story'.

The host's cornering strategy does not give Anders Thisted enough space to move to another universal without the cost of appearing suspiciously to evade the question. His next and final turn is a direct answer to Reimer Bo's question 'did you ring the interested parties...'. He manages, however, to evade the question's topical focus: 'hm yes P I can't just sit here and tell you which sources em all journalists have and who they contacted and why and how I don't know but...' First, Anders Thisted substitutes the 'royal sphere' with 'sources', turning a specific into a general category. Then, he lines up 'sources' in a long chain of multiple topical specifications (all wh-constructions demanding new information): '**wh**ich sources em all journalists have and **wh**o they contacted and **wh**y and **h**ow'. Parataxis (the use of and-links) has two interrelated effects. On the one hand, not only is the who-specification kept abstract ('who'), but it is further diffused and defocused among others. On the other hand, the cumulative effect of parataxis is that of an information overload. Reimer Bo 'asks-for-too-much' and this makes it possible for Anders Thisted's to claim ignorance, 'I don't know', and to avoid responding again.

'But', an adversative conjunction, allows Anders Thisted to move quickly away from this particular and refocus upon the meaning horizon in which his story is most convincingly legitimated. The rest of his talk can be seen as consisting of four related intertexts, which cumulatively build up Anders Thisted's preferred universal: the quasi-scientific discourse of journalistic professionalism ('but it's smart people we're talking about') and the discourse on truth as transparency with its concomitant obligation to attend to the 'naturally right' (deontic modality: '**cannot; is obliged to** engage with what happens to be right'). In the final turn, the 'naturally right' is established by reference to external reality ('and we are in contact with reality'), which enables Anders Thisted to reassert the validity of his story ('and it's correct what stands in the story') – notice that the use of the semi-scientific 'correct' suggests that the truth of the story is accurately recoverable.

With the exception of this last clause, Anders Thisted's talk operates exclusively on universal meanings – discourses on professional competence and truth, in which the particular, the story, is contextualized. These meanings are linked together paratactically (with and-links) rather than hypotactically (with because of; despite of; as a result of etc. links). In this way, Anders Thisted's text both avoids argumentative depth, in that there are no references to reasons or effects, and obstructs linkages to real-time-and-place accounts. His text excludes the particular.

Reimer Bo leaves the dialogue with Anders Thisted here and turns to Søren Haslund Christiansen, the royal representative. The shift is timely. An insider is drawn into the debate precisely at the moment when his 'voice' is shown to have been excluded from *Billed Bladet*. The move sets up a contrast between celebrity journalism and the TV journalism of Reimer Bo. Enacting the principle of involving interested parties adds to the ethical aura of the latter, whilst it further exposes the ethical 'nakedness' of the former. At the same time, from an argumentative point of view. Reimer Bo appears to have rested his case. Concerning the truth claims of the case under debate, his interlocutor has failed. Anders Thisted consistently avoided giving precise responses to the host's persistent questioning – rather than defending his argument with concrete documentation, he is responding with 'hot air'.

## The politics of truth in the debate

The opening sequence can be summed up in terms of two different positions in the field of meanings available in the debate. Each offers a distinct norm of truth. Though both share an objectivist epistemology in appealing to external reality, they differ in the procedures of validating truth and, therefore, in the ethics of representation each validity procedure implies. Reimer Bo posits a discourse on truth as the establishment of facts, and its ethics 'oblige' the journalistic text to maintain a tight match between fact and locution. Anders Thisted posits a discourse on truth as transparency of representation, and its ethics 'obliges' the text to encompass an ever-broadened field of visibility. Whereas the first makes a commitment to truth-as-an-end-in-itself, the latter makes a commitment to the social body the readers. Of the two, it is the first discourse which acquires the status of the universal, the natural meaning horizon which contextualizes and evaluates other discourses. As mentioned, it is the host, Reimer Bo, who is the bearer of this discourse. This is by virtue of his structural positioning in the practice of the debate and, specifically, by virtue of his control over who participates, as well as over turn-taking and topic-shifts – including his right to interrupt, reformulate, and recoup.

It appears that the organizing principle in debating truth is 'keep particular'. We saw that the discursive practice begins and ends with specific references to one publication of *Billed Bladet*. Its status, adequacy, and validity is systematically tied down to the language, the pictures, and the step-by-step actions of the journalists. These references to the particular accumulate a set of equivalential meanings on what is evidence, what is adequacy of evidence, and what is validation of truth and how it is accomplished. Dispersed as they are, these constitute a powerful discursive field. We could claim that the discourse on truth as the establishment of facts is construed in the course of the practice of questioning, its linguistic detail, and interactional set-up. This means that the universal is activated as *a mode of control*, a mode best described as 'individuating' a rationality: singling out the epistemological properties of the publication and getting down to its nitty-gritty details so as to disprove it (Rose, 1999, p. 275). This mode of control is strategic in constituting the debate as a public sphere: the rational, detached examination of a class of social practices, celebrity press, in a public forum. Indeed, it is precisely the capacity of a collective space *to assume an aperspectival objectivity*, a perspective from nowhere, which confers on this space the political legitimacy of a public sphere – a legitimacy also conferred on the host as impartial spectator committed to the truth and only to that (Boltanski, 1999, p. 32; see also Bourdieu, 1992).[9]

By the same token, the mode of control of the practice affords only one position for Anders Thisted, that of keeping to the particular also. This proved to be effective for Reimer Bo in that he managed to catch Anders Thisted in a double bind. On the one hand, had he kept to the particular, Anders Thisted would have run the risk of getting nailed down. Indeed, he did not appear in a position to give concrete details of the story. Concerning the status of his evidence, the sociological discourse of cultural mismatch sounded like a rather long shot as a legitimate explanation of two pictures of the royal couple not looking at each other. Concerning the validation of his evidence, that is, contact with the parties involved, his evasive responses discredited his appeal to truth. On the other hand, Anders Thisted's preferred defence strategy, to make available a competing discourse on truth, also proved to be ineffective. Unlike Reimer Bo's implicit universal, this counter-universal took the form of explicit expositions which connected to the particular, the story, either very loosely or not at all. Such contributions were construed as irrelevant to the pragmatics of the interaction. They made claims to appropriateness, the social norms and values that guide journalistic practice, rather than addressing the claims to truth, the validity criteria of the specific publication, as Reimer Bo had it. As a consequence, they were ignored. Anders Thisted's insistence on the ethics of journalism as transparency was, thus, deprived of the legitimacy to act as a contextualizing frame for the particular – it was denied the capacity to become universal. More specifically, now, the politics of truth during this sequence of the debate can be summed up as 'keep particular to universalize'. The power to universalize truth, in other words, does not lie in being able to articulate a set of meanings explicitly, to make the discourse visible. On the contrary, the power to universalize truth lies in embedding the discourse as a presupposition in a specific procedure of questioning. Indeed, the more Anders Thisted keeps producing universal statements (statements disconnected from the specifics of the case) the more his responses are controlled to remain particular. The more Reimer Bo's questions 'hammer upon' the particular, the more universal validity they acquire. It is precisely its status as a non-discourse that enables Reimer Bo's truth to work as a material technique of government, a technique for regulating the debate as a public sphere so that certain things only can be constituted as truthful and legitimate, as universal (Rose, 1999, pp. 36–7). Universalizing is indeed inevitable in public debate. How else can a group of people deliberate unless on a ground of common understandings? But the question is which interest is kept suppressed by this specific operation of rendering hegemonic one discourse on truth over another? The relentless questioning in this sequence construed the *Billed Bladet* story *as fiction rather than fact*, and so implictly privileged a certain truth: the supposed conflict between the royal couple *did not* take place. This is, of course, a truth which upholds the royal family's positive image: royals don't fight – at least in public – an interest already evident in the title and choice of story. Prioritizing this truth at this early point in the debate quickly does away with the doubt concerning the incident itself and facilitates the move on to a debate proper of the 'real' issue – privacy and the ethics of the celebrity press.

In this sense, the universalizing of a legal positivist discourse on truth carries the cost of a displacement: in the course of debating, *the royalist interest is construed under the guise of aperspectival objectivity*, and therefore as *beyond discussion*. Thus, the restoration of the royal family's integrity becomes an implicit subtext upon which discourses of truth and ethics of journalism are convincingly articulated.

## The debate as public sphere

In this article, I followed the process by which a legal positivist discourse on truth acquired universal validity in a television debate on the celebrity press and the public personalities' right to privacy. I exemplified two aspects of this universalizing process. First, the insertion of the celebrity magazine as an object in a procedure of recovering the truth. Second, the linguistic procedure of questioning the truth claims of a specific celebrity press publication. The first, the use of objects, universalizes by 'globalizing' meaning, that is, by fixing the meaning of the celebrity press as untruthful journalism and by evoking this meaning throughout the television programme being studied. The second, the procedure of questioning, universalizes by keeping the interaction particular, that is by focusing exclusively on the details of the publication – evidence status, adequacy, and validity.

Via this double truth operation, the debate programme is construed in terms of an aperspectival objectivity – a perspective from nowhere which pursues truth-for-truth's-sake. Aperspectival objectivity manages to confer upon the debate the legitimacy of the public sphere as the collective endeavour of an unbiased search for truth. At the same time, it manages to render normative the royalist interest which underpins this search for truth and which informs the ethical and aesthetic norms of the debate overall.

At the beginning of this article, I postulated that the democratic function of the mediated debate is to be assessed by the way it construes its dialogic space – by universalizing, that is, by rendering normative, the specific discourses on truth and ethics, and by particularizing, that is, by denying authority to other discourses that do not 'fit' its regulative logic. This debate is subject to the critique of failing to fulfil its democratic function, insofar as it renders normative, and therefore avoids discussing, a certain interest – the royalist interest. The point is not that the royal family is not victimized by a mercilessly avid celebrity press. It is. The 'gaze' of the celebrity press constitutes probably one of the most powerful fields of discipline for the conduct, both public and private, of royalty and that should be held in check. However, the position of the royal family in the institutional landscape of the country is complex. For one thing, the rare privileges of the royal family do come with the obligation of heightened visibility, vis-à-vis ordinary citizens. Furthermore, the royal family's own performance is itself situated at a cross-section between the private and the public, with often fuzzy lines between the two. The royal theatre appearance is only a small example of this fuzziness. Do the royals attend a public event as private individuals or do they do so as institutional representatives of the nation? Such issues do raise the question of individual sovereignty for the members of the royal family. Where does their privacy stop and the public's begin?

But who decides, and under what circumstances, where the borders of individual sovereignty lie is not an easy matter. It is perhaps the most fundamental controversy in contemporary democracies (Held, 1993, pp. 303–4). In this mediated debate, what is itself at stake in the discussion was construed as beyond discussion – it was already precluded in its discourse. Ironically, perhaps, these are some of the issues Anders Thisted tried to put on the agenda.

Two consequences follow from this premature closure. First, the right to privacy, essentially the issue of the borders of individual sovereingty, is cast throughout the debate as an issue of truth vs. lies – the right to privacy is activated when the celebrity press's lies and rumours begin. This is a circular argument, insofar as the question of truth is itself open to multiple interpretations. What is truth is embedded in different logics of representation, as the Reimer Bo–Anders Thisted exchange made clear. There is an inherent relativism in this argument, which can only be anchored on a normative principle when the competing interests of *both* sides are put explicitly on the agenda and discussed as such. Selectively suppressing one of them leads to argumentative circularity – a reproduction of common sense, as Silverstone has put it. How to decide when the right to privacy clashes with the right to inform is primarily a question of ethics. Interestingly, throughout the debate, every time Anders Thisted put forward an ethical claim (of the 'readers-need-to-know' type), he was confronted with a truth claim. But how did ethics figure in this programme?

This brings me to the second consequence of aperspectival objectivity in the debate. Ethics, as I mentioned, does not figure as a practice of juxtaposing rationalities and their interests. It rather takes the form of a *code of conduct*, a model of acting for the good citizen. Truth is implicated in this code in two ways. First, there is a prescription for acting truthfully which is directed to the celebrity press, and specifically to *Billed Bladet* The magazine should come out with a correction and an apology for its improper publication – this is an explicit formulation of the code. Second, there is a systematic undermining of the celebrity press as journalism proper, which turns its untruthfulness into a marker of (low) ethical and aesthetic status. We should keep a distance from celebrity magazines because they are 'the village's fool', telling absurd lies and spreading rumours. This is an implicit formulation of the code which addresses the television audience and attempts to moralize its consumption practices – thus again reproducing a commonsensical judgement of taste, the low aesthetics of trash media.

## Conclusion

In this article, I have written of the way in which a television debate enacts public dialogue: how it mobilizes a certain politics of truth to confer legitimacy upon itself by thematizing a non-political issue in a celebrity magazine. The public sphere function of this debate can be summed up as a governmental act of etho-politics. It is an attempt to regulate self-conduct by imposing certain norms of civility and ethics (as well as aesthetics) under the guise of objective rationality. Drawing on Rose (1999, pp. 192–3), this is a specification of etho-politics gravitating towards the 'pole of morality', a *prescriptive* code of conduct.One question for the critical analysis of television debate is, therefore, that of seeking an alternative set of norms for the government of conduct, which moves away from prescriptive morality. That would involve a debate practice in which the politics of truth 'validates diverse ethical criteria','minimizes codification and maximizes debate' – what Rose (ibid.) calls the 'pole of ethics' rather than morality. The contrastive analysis of *Reimer Bo* with *Rigets Tilstand* points to such alternatives, without suggesting that the latter is the more desirable genre.

Another issue for the critical analysis of television debate would be to take seriously what, at face value, appear to be trivial affairs. Just as celebrity gossip is not outside the domain of the political (and indeed, as *Reimer Bo* showed, it is a deeply politicized matter), so debate shows should not be rejected as argument sacrificed for entertainment, pure spectacle. Rather the task is to complement the study of the debate's politics of truth, what Silverstone calls the 'rhetoric' of television, with a study of its politics of pleasure, what he names the 'erotic' aspect of television. This erotic element, how television grants its audience the pleasure of watching, is not a trivial matter – it is a constitutive part of it. The significance of trivia seems to me to be more significant than we take it to be. They may help us understand better what is happening to democratic debate when television claims to seek the truth. They may also help us rethink how meaning can be rearticulated in the same media under a different politics of truth with hopefully different effects.

## Notes

1. For an overview of the debate see Hall, 1985/1996, pp. 11–34; Poster, 1990, pp. 1–20; Thompson, 1990, pp. 264–271; Gibbins and Reimer, 1999, pp. 37–53.
2. Yet, there is another side to this argument: that television debate is not real debate and, therefore, it should not be taken at face value. Indeed, televised debate has been strongly challenged as a public sphere genre (for an overview see Livingstone and Lunt 1994, pp. 9–23, also Habermas, 1989/1997, and Bourdieu, 1998). Moreover, the Danish daily press has criticized the programme I analyse here on the grounds that what it promises as debate is a 'circus' – argument sacrificed for the sake of entertainment. I would like to take this argument seriously. In fact, I agree that the debate is not a simulation of the public sphere alone. The self-reflexivity of television I referred to above is also a device for the spectators' play of imagination. Television's fascination with itself and its fascination with another medium, the celebrity press, address not so much common sense as *the desire* of the audience for pleasure. But instead of subscribing to either of the two poles of the argument (debate as either public sphere or circus), I elsewhere take a dual analytical focus on the debate so as to identify the points where its politics of truth articulate with a different kind of politics, the politics of pleasure (Chouliaraki, forthcoming).
3. For literature on the function of televised debate as a democratic forum where people deliberate collectively over issues of common interest, see Scannel, 1989, pp. 135–66; J. B. Thompson, 1995, pp. 100–9; Livingstone and Lunt, 1994, pp. 9–35; Wodak and Wetter, 1997, pp. 209–37. For the debate genre in Denmark, see Bruun, 1998, 2000, pp. 237–60.
4. See Held, 1993, Laclau, 1996, for this view of democratic deliberation; Livingstone and Lunt, 1994, p. 35, for a similar norm on televised debates.

5. For the ground norms of televised public debate and their appropriation by audiences, see Livingstone and Lunt, 1994, ch. 6.
6. For a discussion on the relationship between systemic-functional semiotics and CDA see Chouliaraki and Fairclough, 1999, ch. 7; for applications of CDA analysis specifically on television texts see Fairclough, 1995; Madsen and Andersen, 1998; Phillips, 1999; Chouliaraki, 2000; for a broader discursive perspective on media texts see Hall, 1997, pp. 208–36.
7. Denmark's national TV channel's (DR) debate programme *Reimer Bo* was on every Wednesday, from 8 to 8.40 p.m., for 16 weeks in the period 2 September to 2 December 1998. Its host, Reimer Bo Christensen, earlier hosting another successful debate programme (*Rigets Tilstand*, March–June 1998), is a well-reputed actuality and debate tv personality, managing an average audience rate of 500,000 people every week. His programme competed with TV2's debate programme, his previous *Rigets Tilstand*, now hosted by Trine Gregorius. *Rigets Tilstand* ran every Thursday at 8 o'clock, managing a slightly higher audience rate.
8. Apart from the main story in *Billed Bladet*, the programme also introduces the following celebrity stories: 'Her og Nu': speculative story on Alexandra's pregnancy; 'Ekstra Bladet': a story on Frederik's night-life in Paris; 'Kig Ind': famous comedian accused as a car thief; 'Alt for Damerne': a female politician takes part in car advertising and models for a fashion shoot in a lifestyle women's magazine.
9. 'The constitution of a public sphere and a definition of political legitimacy based on a conception of objectivity that emphasizes the possibility of an observation without any particular perspective are strictly interdependent' (Boltanski, 1999, p. 24).

## Bibliography


Bernstein, B. (1990) *Class Codes & Control Vol. IV. The Structuring of Pedagogic Discourse* (London, Routledge).

Bernstein, B. (1996) *Pedagogy, Symbolic Control & Identity* (London, Taylor & Francis).

Boltanski, L. (1999) *Distant Suffering: Politics, Morality & the Media* (Cambridge, Cambridge University Press).

Bourdieu P. (1992) *Language and Symbolic Power* (Cambridge, Polity).

Bourdieu P. (1998) *On Television* (New York, New Press).

Bruun H. (1998) 'Talkshowet som tv-genre', *Kvan* (50).

Bruun H. (2000), 'Eleva2ren – TV2 og Talkshowet', in H. Bruun, K. Frandsen, and H. Søndergaard (eds), *TV2 på Skærmen: Analyser af TV2's programvirksomhed* (Copenhagen, Samfundslitteratur).

Chouliaraki, L. (2000) 'Political Discourse in the News: Democratising Responsibility or Aestheticizing Politics', *Discourse & Society*, Vol. 11 (3).

Chouliaraki, L. (2001), 'Pædagogikens Sociale Logik', in L. Chouliaraki and M. Bayer (eds), *B. Bernstein: Pædagogik, Diskurs, Magt* (Copenhagen, Akademisk Forlag).

Chouliaraki, L. (forthcoming) *Discourse & Culture* (London, Sage).

Chouliaraki, L., and Fairclough, N. (1999) *Discourse in Late Modernity* (Edinburgh, Edinburgh University Press).

Fairclough, N. (1992) *Discourse & Social Change* (Cambridge, Polity).

Fairclough, N. (1995) *Media Discourse* (London, E. Arnold).

Gibbins, J., and Reimer, B. (1999) *The Politics of Postmodernity* (London, Sage).

Goodrich, P. (1994) 'Legal Studies' entry in *The Blackwell's Dictionary of Social Thought* (London, Blackwell).

Habermas, J. (1989/1997), 'The Public Sphere', in P. Marris and S. Thornham (eds), *Media Studies: a Reader* (Edinburgh, Edinburgh University Press).
Hall S. (1985/1996), 'Signification, Representation, Ideology: Althusser and the Post-structuralist Debate', in J. Curran, David Morley, and Valerie Walkerdine (eds), *Cultural Studies and Communications* (London, E. Arnold).
Hall S. (1997) *Representation: Cultural Representations and Signifying Practices* (London, Sage and Oxford University Press).
Held, D. (1993) *Models of Democracy* (Cambridge, Polity).
Jørgensen, W. M. (2002), 'The Cogito and the Unthought: Foucault's Doubles in Social Scientific Discourse', in R. Wodak and G. Weiss (eds), *Theory and Interdisciplinarity* (Basingstoke, Palgrave Macmillan).
Laclau, E. (1996), 'Universalism, Particularism and the Question of Identity', in E. Laclau, *Emancipations* (London, Verso).
Latour, B. (1996) 'On Interobjectivity', *Mind, Culture and Activity*, Vol. 3 (4).
Livingstone, S., and Lunt, P. (1994) *Talk on Television* (London, Routledge).
Madsen L. H., and Andersen, J. E. (1998), 'Publikum til Pynt?', in I. Poulsen and H. Søndergaard (eds), *Mediebilleder: Studier i Mediernes Udtryksformer* (Borgen, Media).
Phillips, L. (1999) 'Media Discourse and the Danish Monarchy: Reconciling Egalitarianism and Royalism', *Media, Culture & Society*, Vol. 21, pp. 221–45.
Poster, M. (1990) *The Mode of Information: Poststructuralism and Social Context* (Cambridge, Polity).
Rose, N. (1999) *Powers of Freedom: Reframing Political Thought* (Cambridge, Cambridge University Press).
Scannel, P. (1989) *Broadcast Talk* (London, Sage).
Silverstone, R. (1999) *Why Study the Media* (London, Routledge).
Thompson, J. (1990) *Ideology and Modern Culture* (Cambridge, Polity).
Thompson J. B. (1995) *The Media and Modernity* (Cambridge, Polity).
Wodak, R., and Wetter, E. (1997) *Competing Professions in Times of Change: the Discursive Construction of Professional Identities in TV Talk-Shows*, research report, Department of Linguistics and Department of Sociology, University of Vienna.

# 12

# Coalitions, Practices, and Meaning in Environmental Politics: From Acid Rain to BSE

*Maarten A. Hajer*

In the late 1980s, I studied developments in environmental politics, a field that I had, until then, not examined in any detail. Given my background studying social movements and political institutions, I was intrigued by the 'career' of the environmental movement. In twenty years, it had transformed from a counter-cultural movement, practising the symbolic politics of street demonstrations, lifestyle choices, and alternative consumption (expressed in an elaborate and very visible urban circuit encompassing bookshops, wholemeal food stores, dress codes, communal households, and so on) to a more mainstream political force, seeking representation and influence through 'green' parties and professional lobbying (see Hajer, 1995). Upon reflection, it seemed obvious that much more was going on in environmental politics than fighting 'environmental degradation'. The differences in style, both in terms of ways of life and of conducting politics, signalled that environmental politics was in fact a field of profound 'cultural politics'. Environmental politics appeared to be a stage at which society reflected on its record: values were at risk, moral commitments were contested and the very form of conducting politics was questioned (Hajer, 1996).

How were we to make sense of environmental politics? If environmental politics was not simply about who gets what, when, and why, how were we to analyse these political processes? Indeed, what was the environmental conflict about? Moreover, what was the influence of the change in style of conducting politics? Did it make any difference if environmental issues were addressed via a counter-cultural protest or via the slick media-oriented campaigns made famous by Greenpeace?

As it is quite impossible to study such complex conflicts 'in the round', an empirical focus was needed. Reflecting on the content of environmental discourse, I was struck by the dominant role of acid rain at the time. Could it be that we used this topic as a vehicle to discuss the environmental crisis? There were, of course, documents that discussed the 'environmental problematic' in the round. The report, *Limits to Growth* (1972), made such an attempt, as did the *World Conservation Strategy* (1980). Examining environmental discourse in the 1980s, it was clearly acid rain that captured the minds of policy-makers, politicians, the media, and indeed the public. It occurred to me that this issue seemed *emblematic* of the bigger 'problematic' or, more precisely, for *understanding* that problematic at the time. Focusing my empirical research on acid rain, I could perhaps gain meaningful insights on what was going on in environmental discourse. I examined the acid rain controversy in two countries: Great Britain and the Netherlands.

The study, which eventually became *The Politics of Environmental Discourse*, was first of all a critique of the prevailing 'realist' way of analysing environmental problems. Realism here refers to the fact that the definition of the problem was taken for granted: the analysis focused on the *why* and *what sort* of action was taken, explaining these dynamics in terms of the 'interests' and 'power' of the parties involved. The prevailing method of analysis was to illuminate the 'rhetoric' that kept the government from acting. Whereas activists argued that government was 'doing too little, too late', academics framed the problem as one of (governmental) 'rhetoric' versus (environmental) 'reality' (Park, 1987). In this way, the whole dimension of the meaning of politics and political actions was lost. The take on the position of the British government was particularly illuminating. The acid rain controversy had earned Britain the label of 'the dirty man of Europe'. Britain was notoriously stubborn in denying accusations that the sulphur dioxide ($SO_2$) and nitrogen oxide (NO) emissions of its coal-fired power stations caused environmental damage abroad. Analysts pointed out the 'conflict of interest' as the reason for Britain's failure to deal with the problem. Britain's unwillingness to act was interpreted as 'governmental delaying tactics', while the government's reference to scientific uncertainty was criticized as using science as a 'fig leaf' for policy (Boehmer-Christiansen, 1988; Boehmer-Christiansen and Skea, 1991). Hence, inaction was explained in terms of the conscious exercise of power by key actors.

Such an account in terms of strategic behaviour and conflicting interest always has an obvious sense of truth to it. From a discourse-analytical perspective the argument was not, however, that there was no strategic behaviour as such (which would have been an odd position to take for a political scientist, anyway), rather that the political conflict that was played out in the acid rain controversy *transcended* a simple conflict of interest. I was intrigued by the way in which institutions were implicated. Was the acid rain conflict perhaps such a controversy because it suggested that the established institutional way of conducting environmental policy-making had failed? Was there some double-play, in which actors within the acid rain controversy drew on particular institutional positions; while others criticized those positions with other arguments from the acid rain case?

An analysis of the actual discourse – that is, the examination of argumentative structure in documents and other written or spoken statements, as well as the practices through which these utterances were made – illuminated this new dimension of the environmental conflict. Using discourse analysis, the acid rain controversy could be understood in terms of two distinct approaches to pollution that competed for dominance in the realm of British environmental politics. First, a 'traditional-pragmatist' approach, well established in the British institutional arrangements of pollution control. Secondly, a rival discourse of 'ecological modernization', initiated not only by environmentalists who had swapped the streets for direct lobbying of governments but also by some leading industrialists (arguing that 'pollution prevention paid') and critical scientists. Illuminating this latter discourse led to a markedly different *interpretation* of both natural and socio-political phenomena.

## Discourse-coalitions in politics

The alternative to the realist analysis of the acid rain controversy was to examine how the definition of a political problem relates to the particular narrative in which it is discussed. In the case of acid rain, large groups of dead trees are, of course, not a social construct; the point is how one *makes sense* of dead trees. In this respect there are many possible (political) realities. One may see dead trees as the product of 'natural stress' caused by drought, cold, or wind, or one may see them as victims of 'pollution'. Pollution can thus be seen as an ordering concept, a 'way of seeing', or interpreting a given phenomenon. 'Acid rain' might be constructed as an element of a narrative on industrial society and pollution. It then labels the dead trees as victims of pollution, and thus the sight or, more indirectly, the report of 'dead trees' might acquire a different meaning. Instead of approaching them as a 'natural' phenomenon they now potentially become a political problem. Or, to put it differently, a narrative *constructs* a particular problem: dead trees become 'victims' and, as where there are 'victims' there are 'perpetrators', that should be corrected. Framed according to the pollution narrative, dead trees are no longer 'an incident' but signify a 'structural problem'.

Here the *metaphor* of 'acid rain' (scientifically one would speak of 'acid precipitation') also facilitates this new understanding: 'rain' is no longer natural; it kills life instead of nourishing it. So a pollution narrative and the metaphor of 'acid rain' facilitate seeing dead trees as an indicator, a sign, a piece of evidence, of a broader crisis of industrial society.

Thus, discourse seems to matter. If all political actors began to talk about dead trees in these terms a different set of questions would open up. For example, are there no policies that are meant to avoid this sort of degradation? Or, more fundamentally, what kind of society tolerates dying forests?

Language has the capacity to make politics, to create signs and symbols that can shift power-balances and impact on institutions and policy-making. It can render events harmless, but it can also create political conflicts. It can suggest we should discuss the problem in terms of operational solutions, but it might also suggest that this is meaningless, as solutions would require substantial institutional or cultural change.

The analysis of discursive constructions such as narratives, story lines or metaphors is especially powerful when done in the context of the study of the social-historical conditions in which the statements were produced and received. Discourse analysis then opens up methodologically sound ways to combine the analysis of the discursive production of meaning with the analysis of the socio-political practices from which social constructs emerge and in which the actors that make these statements engage. Metaphors, narrative, and story lines are three concepts that help illuminate distinct features of discourse. Before we proceed, we will clarify these key concepts and a fourth, discourse-coalitions.

**Discourse**

Discourse is defined here as an ensemble of ideas, concepts, and categories through which meaning is given to social and physical phenomena, and which is produced and reproduced through an identifiable set of practices. So, for instance, in the case of acid rain, discourse can refer to a particular tradition in dealing with environmental problems, with its particular ideas about the role of a pollution inspectorate, and particular notions of what industries should do in response to pollution (some examples follow below). It is important to point out that discourse, thus understood, is *not* synonymous with discussion: a discourse refers to a set of concepts that structure the contributions of participants to a discussion. For example, a discourse analysis would illuminate a particular *discursive structure* in the discussion of the policy towards, say, immigration in the European Union. Here a discourse analysis would bring out a certain regularity in the particular ideas, concepts, and categories *in which terms* immigration is discussed. In addition, it identifies the practices in which this discourse gets reproduced.

One recurring problem with discourse analysis is deciding at what level one defines a discourse. Inevitably, one will find that, upon closer examination, many statements are based on more than one discourse: when talking about pollution one easily draws on discourses deriving from biology or chemistry (to state what causes trees to die), engineering (to show what could be done), and public policy (to see how the government might respond). One could, of course, try in a hermeneutic fashion to recover all the roots of the utterances. Yet my 'argumentative discourse analysis' suggests one might find more analytical power in focusing on the way in which the social interaction evolves via the exchange of linguistic and symbolic utterances. For instance, in very institutionalized settings, such as a court of law, one will find that legal discourse, with its own well-defined concepts and categorizations, dominates the exchange. Indeed, there a judge can 'rule out' certain utterances if they do not meet the preconceived discursive rules that lawyers are supposed to respect. It is important to carefully consider the *site* at which one conducts a discourse analysis. If this is a court, then it is crucial to examine those instances in which some contributions are ruled out, as that is a moment in which it becomes obvious how institutionalized discourse helps construct a problem in a particular way. One might also look at a broader spectrum and compare the different ways in which a court or, for instance, a parliamentary enquiry 'talk' environmental politics. In that way, one can come to meaningful findings regarding the interaction of discourse and practice.

Illuminating discourse(s) allows for a better understanding of controversies, not in terms of rational argumentation, but in terms of the argumentative rationality that people bring to a discussion. Hence, discourse should be distinguished analytically from discussion, so as to allow for the differentiation of plural discourses. Discourses consist of structures embedded in language. They are therefore 'found' or traced by the analyst. Discourses might not be immediately obvious to the people that utter them, although respondents should recognize a discourse when it is pointed out to them by the analyst.

**Metaphor**

We can refer to acid rain as a *metaphor* – it stands for something else. 'The essence of metaphor is understanding and experiencing one kind of thing in terms of another', wrote Lakoff and Johnson in their classic *Metaphors We Live By* (1980). In the most immediate way, this is the case as the biological phenomenon of 'acid precipitation' is reduced to 'acid rain'. The significance of this is shown by a Dutch controversy involving dead trees where, for a long time, policy-makers and activists conceived of the problem in terms of 'acid rain'. Only years later did the Dutch discover that the problem was caused by the ammonia emissions from nearby pig farms. A second way in which metaphor helped our understanding of environmental politics was by showing how the 'environmental crisis' was constantly experienced through the acid rain problem. People would argue that the emergence of acid rain was indicative of how industrial society produced welfare at the cost of an environmental crisis. This was an important linkage as it explains the central role that the acid rain controversy fulfilled in environmental politics (more on this below).

**Story line**

During the analysis, one examines statements. These often have the form of a narrative: people convey facts in story form. One quickly realizes that in any field there are a couple of such stories, which fulfil an especially important role. For instance, there is often a particular way to describe acid rain by positioning it historically. I employ the concept of *story line* to refer to a condensed form of narrative in which metaphors are used. Identifying story lines in the acid rain example reveals that people actually *do something with acid rain* when talking about it, rather than referring to a problem with a fixed identity.

The essence of a story is that it has a beginning, a middle, and an end. Yet, one will find that people often have their own versions of a particular story. Acid rain, for instance, is rather complex to understand so mostly people do not tell the whole story but use short cues. People frequently use the words 'acid rain' *assuming the hearer will know what he/she means*. In other words, we are used to assuming that the more complex narrative of acid rain is available in the mind of the receiver and can be activated by giving a cue ('you know what I mean'). Yet, this is where interesting social effects start to occur. Very often, it is assumed that the meaning that the receiver 'reads' into a message is the same as the sender intended to put into the message. This assumption of *mutual understanding* is false. Discourse analysis brings out, time and again, that people often speak at cross-purposes. Interestingly, however, this can be quite instrumental towards creating a political coalition.

My argumentative discourse analysis does not start from the assumption of coherence or full understanding. I suggest that much communication is in fact based on interpretive readings, on mulling over and measuring statements in terms of whether they 'sound right'. That is why the concept of *story line* is important. A story line is a condensed statement summarizing complex narratives, used by people as 'short hand' in discussions. An example is the 'summary' of the phenomenon of acidification in the suggestion that 'sulphur dioxide ($SO_2$) emissions from British coal-fired power stations lead to acidification of Swedish lakes'; that 'what goes up, must come down'. Emphasizing the role of metaphors and story lines should not be regarded as a totally pessimistic approach. It can be shown that people who *can be proven not to understand one another fully*, nevertheless together produce meaningful political interventions.

### Discourse-coalition

A discourse-coalition refers to a group of actors that, *in the context of an identifiable set of practices*, shares the usage of a particular set of story lines over a particular period of time. It is important to take into account the particular situations in which story lines are uttered and discourses are drawn upon. For this purpose we use the concept of *practice*: embedded routines and mutually understood rules and norms that provide coherence to social life. Hence, we can think of going to church as a practice or writing articles for academic journals as a practice characteristic of the life world of university professors. A key point coming out of the Wittgensteinian philosophy of language is that linguistic utterances cannot usefully be understood outside the practices in which they are uttered. Similarly, discourse should always be conceived of in interrelation with the practices in which it is produced, reproduced, and transformed. Consequently, we can refine the definition of discourse given above to include practice. *Discourse* therefore is defined as an ensemble of ideas, concepts, and categories through which meaning is given to phenomena, and which is produced and reproduced through an identifiable set of practices.

So a discourse-coalition is not so much connected to a particular person (as if such a person would have a coherent set of ideas and beliefs that were not context specific), but is related to practices in the context in which actors employ story lines and (re)produce and transform particular discourses. Thus, it becomes possible to come to terms with the fact that some actors might utter contradictory statements, or indeed help reproduce different discourse coalitions (for a more detailed account, see Hajer, 1995, ch. 2, for empirical examples, ch. 4).

To apply this whole vocabulary to politics one should also be able to link discourse to power and dominance. It should be possible not only to identify discourses but also to assess their influence as well. Two terms facilitate this: *discourse structuration* occurs when a discourse starts to dominate the way a given social unit (a policy domain, a firm, a society – all depending on the research question) conceptualizes the world. If a discourse solidifies in particular institutional arrangements, say a measuring system for air pollution, then we speak of *discourse institutionalization*. We thus have a simple two-step procedure for measuring the influence of a discourse: if many people use it to conceptualize the world we may speak of discourse structuration. If it solidifies into institutions and organizational practices we may call this discourse institutionalization. If both criteria are fulfilled we argue that a particular discourse is dominant.

The acid rain case helps illustrate this. Acid rain is, of course, a metaphor that does something: first of all with the discussion of air pollution, but also with the institutional response to air pollution. During the 1950s and 1960s, air pollution was discussed in terms of 'urban smog'. Not only did most people conceive of air pollution in these terms, but it also structured institutional practices. The monitoring of air quality was, for instance, concentrated in cities. After all, why monitor the countryside if smog is an urban problem? Of course, discourse institutionalization facilitates the reproduction of a given discourse. Moreover, actors who have been socialized to work within the frame of such an institutionalized discourse will (often unwittingly) use their positions to persuade or force others to interpret and approach reality according to their own routinized institutionalized insights and convictions. Hence, one of the highest forms of discourse-institutionalization occurs if things appear as 'traditional', 'natural', or 'normal' ways of reasoning, or are even seen as 'natural social facts'. Similarly, getting acid rain on the agenda was difficult, as one needed to break the 'structured way of seeing' air pollution as an urban problem (not one of the countryside) and cope with the institutionalized nature of that urban definition. For a long time there simply were no 'data' available to prove that air pollution affected the countryside and lakes.

In politics we characteristically deal with mixes of elements drawn from various discourses. In most cases we do not find one simple discourse that structures the utterances of all contributors to a given political discussion. Yet, there often is a discourse with a particular claim to power. In the debates on the welfare state, neoliberal economics fulfils a key role and, in the case of environmental politics, the natural sciences constitute a particularly powerful and legitimate form of discourse. Ultimately, the political debate draws on many different discourses. Still, the remarkable fact that people from widely varying backgrounds seem to find ways to communicate receives little attention in policy analysis.

The concept of story lines helps to explain this 'communicative miracle'. After all, the different discursive elements are mostly presented via story lines, in which elements of the various discourses are combined into a more or less coherent whole and the discursive complexity is thus concealed. Nobody in politics knows the details of the economic models that neoliberal economists draw upon to underpin their claims (indeed, it is argued that they do not understand these models themselves any longer), and the science of environmental problems is notoriously complex. Hence, even experts draw on story lines to convey meaning. In most cases many of the actors involved are *experts of some sort*, yet they still depend on other experts for a full understanding. Story lines thus have tremendous importance for organizing social interaction.

A second way of explaining coherence or understanding is via the concept of *discursive affinity*: arguments may vary in origin but share a similar way of conceptualizing the world. An important example from pollution politics is the discursive affinity shared by the moral argument that nature should be respected, the scientific argument that nature is to be seen as a complex ecosystem (which we will *never* fully understand), and the economic idea that pollution prevention is actually the most efficient mode of production (this is the core of the discourse of sustainable development). The arguments are different but similar: from each of the positions the other arguments 'sound right'. The task of the analyst is to expose such discursive affinities.

A discourse coalition can be defined then as an ensemble of story lines, the actors that utter these story lines, and the practices through which these story lines are expressed. The discourse-coalition approach suggests that politics is a process in which different actors from various backgrounds form specific coalitions around specific story lines. Story lines are the medium through which actors try to impose their view of reality on others, suggest certain social positions and practices, and criticize alternative social arrangements.

For instance, the reemergence of environmentalism in the late 1960s was not just a protest against the perceived risks associated with new large-scale technological projects. It was also a celebration of the virtues and morality of unspoiled nature and a call to change the conceptual framework and start thinking about nature in terms of beauty and as necessary to life, instead of in terms of domination and as a system of cause-and-effect relationships. This also implied a critique of the positions and practices that accompanied the prevailing scientific mode of thinking (expert decision-making, quantification of damage, and so on).

New story lines can become a popular way of conceptualizing the world, but for a discourse coalition to become dominant in a given political realm two conditions must be fulfilled: (1) central actors should be forced to accept the rhetorical power of a new discourse (discourse structuration); and (2) the new discourse should be reflected in the institutional practices of that political domain, that is, that the actual policy process is conducted according to the ideas of a given discourse (discourse institutionalization).

To summarize, the politics of discourse is best seen as a continuous process of giving meaning to the vague and ambiguous socio-physical world by means of story lines and the subsequent structuration of experience through the various social practices that can be found in a given field. The discourse-coalition approach thus has three advantages. First, it analyses strategic action in the context of specific socio-historical discourses and institutional practices and provides the conceptual tools to analyse controversies over individual issues in their wider political context. Secondly, it takes the explanation beyond mere reference to interests, analysing how interests are played out in the context of specific discourses and organizational practices. Thirdly, it illuminates how different actors and organizational practices help to reproduce or fight a given bias without necessarily orchestrating or coordinating their actions and without necessarily sharing deep values.

## Argumentative Discourse Analysis

Key to Argumentative Discourse Analysis (ADA) is the examination of what is being said to whom, and in what context. The axiom is that, in uttering statements, people react to one another and thus produce meaning interactively. This emphasis on *argumentation* as interplay in the context of practices puts methodological constraints on the way in which data can be interpreted and indeed accessed. Ideally, an argumentative discourse analysis is based on the detailed analysis of accounts of these interactions. This is why we now work with video-recordings of policy deliberations and newly emerging forms of governance to create the high quality data required. In such cases one can, first of all, transcribe interactions in a very detailed manner, taking into account not only what is said, but also *how* it is said, to whom and to what *effect*. Secondly, one might be able to consider the effect of the setting in which some things are said. While language philosophy and the discourse-analytical literature manifest a strong awareness that people do things with words (Austin, 1955), we sometimes forget that settings do things with people, too. A discussion is not merely talk; it is an act as well. And every act takes place in a particular 'contexture' (Lynch, 1991) that influences the quality of that act. Elsewhere, I have introduced the concepts of 'setting' and 'staging' to analyse precisely that (Hajer, 2004).

Obviously, one is not always in the position to do video-monitoring of political processes. In most cases one has limited access to such rich material. A very useful source is an inquiry in which a variety of actors can present written evidence, be examined, and can respond to various other contributions. A committee hearing can be equally useful. Yet, here one has to take into account that, in some cases, the *way in which arguments have to be presented* exerts an influence on what can be said meaningfully. For instance, the judicial format of many Anglo-American inquiries put a premium on legalistic reasoning, a mode of expression that excludes some other contributions. Similarly, the current move to discuss complex questions relating to biotechnology in 'ethics commissions' privileges ethical reasoning over other possible concerns.

In all, there are some 10 steps that will always be part of the analysis:

1. Desk research: a general survey of the documents and positions in a given field; newspaper analysis and analysis of news sections in relevant journals. This all goes to make up an initial chronology and provide a first reading of events.
2. 'Helicopter interviews': interviews with three or four actors ('helicopters') who are chosen because they have an overview of the field, if from different positions. They might comprise a well-informed journalist, a key advisor to the government, and an expert policy-maker.
3. Document analysis: analysing documents for structuring concepts, ideas, and categorizations; employment of story lines, metaphors, and so on. This should result in a first attempt at defining structuring discourses in the discussion. At this stage one would get a basic notion of the process of events as well as the sites of discursive production.
4. Interviews with key players: on the basis of the preceding steps, interviews can be conducted with central actors in the political process. These interviews can be used to generate more information on causal chains ('which led to what'). Participants will always assume this is the central purpose of the meeting but the interviews might also be used to get a better understanding of the meaning of particular events for the interviewees. It then becomes a 'focused interview' (Flick, 1998). How did they interpret a particular event? In doing this, one aims to reconstruct the discourse from which an actor approached the situation. We can also analyse how a particular cognitive shift came about. What led to the actual 'reframing'? Was it reading a report (which is not very likely)? Was it a meeting? Or was it a confrontation with a question to which the

actor did not have an answer? It might also be possible to use an interview to find out what made a person recognize another perspective as valuable. What was the shift about? Was it about learning that people uttered a particular point of view? Did it concern a practice in which people engaged (Forester, 1999)?

5. Sites of argumentation: searching for data, not simply to reconstruct the arguments used, but to account for the *argumentative exchange*. Examples might be parliamentary debates, minutes of inquiries (a very rich source), presentation and interpretation of evidence presented to a particular research commission, and panel discussions at conferences.
6. Analyse for positioning effects: actors can get 'caught up' in an interplay. They might force others to take up a particular role, but, once others are aware of what is going on, they might also try to refuse it (indicators: 'No, that is not what I meant', 'That is not what it is about at all'). This positioning not only occurs on the level of persons but can, of course, also be found among institutions or even nation-states.
7. Identification of key incidents: this would lead to the identification of key incidents that are essential to understand the discursive dynamics in the chosen case. As much as possible, these key incidents are then transcribed in more detail allowing for more insights, through which their political effects are determined.
8. Analysis of practices in particular cases of argumentation: rather than assuming coherence on the part of particular actors, at this stage one goes back to the data to see if the meaning of what is being said can be related to the practices in which it was said.
9. Interpretation: on this basis one may find a discursive order that governed a particular domain at a particular time. Ideally, one should come up with an account of the discursive structures within a given discussion, as well as an interpretation of the practices, and the sites of production that were of importance in explaining a particular course of events.
10. Second visit to key actors: discourses are inferred from reality by the analyst. Yet when respondents are confronted with the findings, they should at least recognize some of the hidden structures in language. Hence, to revisit some key actors is a way of determining if the analysis of the discursive space made sense.

### The question of 'detail versus relevance'

A recurring discussion among discourse analysts is the question of what detail of analysis one needs. Of course, this is more generally the case for interpretive social science. So there are some who would argue for an extremely detailed analysis and also suggest that the data set can only be very limited and that the researchable questions should be similarly restricted. Others would argue that politics requires contextualization and would insist on showing connections between different utterances, practices, and periods. Some discursive psychologists would nowadays defend one end of the spectrum, while Foucault is still the unrivalled master of sweeping statements over periods of a hundred years or more.

How one puts into operation discourse analysis, of course, depends very much on the type of questions one has. So, if one is interested in interpersonal dynamics it makes sense to search for data that do indeed derive from a carefully selected exchange. If one is interested in the discourse of the World Bank, documents and evaluation studies might be a useful starting point.

In many cases, however, the opposition between detail and relevance is a false one. It is, after all, a matter of research design. Altruism is an unwieldy topic, but if one wants to study it one can argue that interviewing blood donors in a setting in which one is not paid for it can help provide understanding.

In my case, I tend to apply discourse analysis to the study of policy-making and politics to see how discourse, cognition, strategic behaviour, and institutional patterns interrelate and how political change occurs. That still leaves a wide range of choices. As I am interested in European environmental politics (among other topics), I keep an eye on the change occurring in that domain. Yet, it is clear that this is unwieldy, so one needs a sharper focus. To overcome the false dichotomy of detail versus relevance I focus on 'emblematic issues'. To conclude, I will elaborate on this and show how I recently gained an interest in British environmental politics.

Looking at environmental discourse in Britain over the last twenty-five years, we can see that some of the conceptual innovations that were first discussed in the context of the acid rain controversy are, after two decades, still struggling to become institutionalized. Here, the scientific establishment proved particularly resistant. Below, we examine how science was called upon either to legitimate inaction or to help resolve essentially political choices.

## Acid rain as emblematic issue

Above, we argued that the acid rain controversy was not merely about dead fish and trees, but was also very much a matter of institutional politics. An important point that came out of the study of the acid rain controversy was the essential role of acid rain as an 'emblematic issue', in terms of which a general understanding of what environmental problems were about was constructed. As an emblem, it had a central role in facilitating much more than a 'mere' change in policy: it brought about a larger conceptual shift. This was evident, for instance, in the constant reference of White Papers and reports of advisory councils, such as the Royal Commission on Environmental Pollution, to acid rain when they were really addressing the ways in which to combat the ecological crisis (Southwood, 1984). Theoretically, this underlines the importance of identifying such emblematic issues for understanding political discourse. In environmental politics issues like acid rain come and go but what remains is the emblematic level. Urban air pollution, acid rain, global warming, BSE: altogether they constitute a 'premier league' of issues within the environmental domain. As such, these emblematic issues play a key role in the definition of solutions to the ecological crisis at large and, more generally, seem to play a key role in shifts in policy discourse.

The concept of emblematic issues suggests that some issues fulfil a key role in institutional change. Yet, by no means, does it follow that the actors involved are themselves always aware of their key role in institutional politics. On the contrary, the post-structuralist background of a discourse-analytical approach does not assume coherent and concerted political action. Politics is better understood in terms of the various practices of 'micro-power': many, often seemingly trivial, mechanisms influenced the way in which ecological modernization was interpreted, so as to make acid rain manageable for the structures of industrial society. A discourse analysis would try and find these mechanisms, and would attempt to show how they together can produce certain effects.

A key moment in the British acid rain controversy was the 1984 inquiry into acid rain undertaken by the House of Commons Select Committee for the Environment, whose hearings clearly indicated the polarized nature of the debate. A majority of the experts who gave evidence argued that enough was known about acid rain to warrant action. Yet a small but influential group argued that 'policy was in danger of running ahead of science', as Minister of the Environment Patrick Jenkin put it. The Select Committee report, however, argued that enough was known and urged the government to join the '30 per cent club' (30 per cent reduction of $So_2$ emissions by 1993). In December 1984 the government responded with a proposal that aimed for a reduction in $So_2$ emissions of 30 per cent by the end of the 1990s but did not accept the necessity of installing expensive FGD scrubbers.[1] Then, in September 1986, on the basis of new scientific evidence, the government suddenly proposed to install FGD equipment in all new coal-fired power stations. The government also announced plans to retrofit 3 of its 12 large coal-fired power stations with FGD equipment at a total cost of about £600 million.

Looking at the terms in which the actors expressed themselves over the period 1979–89, we can see a slow shift in the terms used to discuss air pollution, which might help explain this change of heart. I labelled these 'traditional-pragmatist' and 'eco-modernist'. Understanding the acid rain controversy in terms of these two competing discourses created a new perspective. It illuminated the wider picture: if acid rain was a real problem, British institutional practices were implicated.

Now, the interesting effect was that, *through the controversy over acid rain,* actors were actually fighting a more complex political battle. Here the same piece of evidence was interpreted differently, depending on the actors.

Some, metaphors legitimized inaction, other metaphors warned against complacency. Some saw acid rain as an isolated phenomenon; others argued it was an illustration of a structural mismatch. So, looking at the texts and utterances, we saw two reasonably coherent discourses slowly emerge, which structured the controversy. The discourses took markedly different positions on such themes as the meaning of acid rain as a policy issue, the consequences of acid rain for the institutionalized way of making policy, and the role of science and expertise and the future of environmental regulation.

The first discourse was 'traditional pragmatism'. Here, acid rain was seen as a problem primarily related to the $So_2$ emissions of big coal-fired power stations. Damage was seen as a foreign affair. Acid rain was seen as an 'incident' and was understood against the British government's endlessly reiterated 'proud record' of pollution abatement. Consequently, those who suggested otherwise were labelled 'irresponsible scaremongers'. In the inquiry and policy documents one could often read that pollution should be seen as acceptable, unless damage was scientifically proven (for details and references see Hajer, 1995, ch. 4).

The rival discourse of 'ecological modernization' interpreted acid rain in a markedly different fashion. The claim of a 'proud record' was placed within an international context: the UK as the 'dirty man of Europe' that exported its pollution. Moreover, acid rain caused domestic damage, too. The 'proud record' was an anachronism. The regulation of new problems like acid rain required institutional change.

So, where the traditional-pragmatists argued that, because of Britain's 'proud record', there was no need for a new policy regime; the eco-modernists suggested that the seriousness of the problem called for a reversal of the burden of proof. Pollution was in principle undesirable and, from now on, the new 'precautionary principle' (better safe than sorry) should guide policy-making.

Behind these two positions on acid rain we can discern a profound difference as to the role of science and expertise in policy-making. Within the traditional-pragmatist discourse, which used the distinguished Royal Society as the norm of proper science (standing above the sphere of pressure group politics), it was argued that 'policy was in danger of running ahead of science'. Conversely, eco-modernists argued that we 'cannot wait until all evidence is in' and challenged the idea that the Royal Society could be taken as a standard for the mundane and complex field of 'pollution science'. The former group emphasized the need for the precise study of cause–effect relationships; the latter introduced a whole new vocabulary with terms like 'multiple stress', 'critical load', and 'precaution' and emphasized investment in R&D solutions, rather than spending on 'fundamental' research. It put forward the Royal Commission on Environmental Pollution as a respectable mediator of public concerns (was the Chairman not a respected member of the Royal Society?).

The two discourses also differed in terms of the principles of environmental regulation. Whereas the traditional-pragmatists saw the environment as a subordinate sectoral concern that should lead to policy-making if, and only if, experts showed it would solve real environmental problems in an effective and economically feasible way, eco-modernists argued for an 'integrated approach'. They wanted to internalize costs, implement 'obvious' solutions, abate the largest emissions, remove the obsolete bar on disclosure of information, and take the public seriously. Moreover, based on the dictum that 'pollution prevention pays', they argued that investing in research on new equipment to abate pollution could make environmental care a 'positive sum game'.

**From acid rain to BSE**

Despite the empirical evidence that ecological modernization caught on in Britain, the discourse never institutionalized. For example, the new ideas about science and the suggestion that it would be wiser to adopt the 'precautionary approach' in cases of complex environmental problems never really became the British position. So until the mid-1990s the idea that 'science determines policy' remained in place and the idea was that all is safe until scientists tell us otherwise. The occurrence of Bovine Spongiform Encephalopathy (BSE) and the subsequent BSE crisis struck another blow against this deeply embedded institutional commitment.

BSE or 'mad cow disease' first emerged in 1985 and over fifteen years developed from a local British problem of animal health into a major issue of food safety. It started with the inexplicable death of a British cow in 1985. Scientists found evidence of a new animal disease, which they called Bovine Spongiform Encephalopathy. The government sought to contain this new and ill-understood disease, including preventing BSE from spreading via meat and bone meal (MBM) from possibly sick slaughtered animals. It became a hot political issue only in the mid-1990s when it became public that BSE could be related to the variant Creutzfeldt-Jacob Disease (vCJD), which affected humans. The first known victim of vCJD died on 21 May 1995. On 20 March 1996 the UK Health Secretary officially announced a 'probable link' between BSE and vCJD (Dressel, 2002; Oosterveer, 2002). The announcement led to an international 'food scare' that resulted in a sharp fall in the consumption of beef. More importantly here, however, was that it also led to a fundamental loss of trust in institutional safe guards.

BSE quickly became the 'emblematic' issue for the institutional crisis in the broader field of environmental politics. Like acid rain in the 1980s, it fulfilled a key role in rethinking or reordering the rules of politics in their particular domain. This time, the traditional-pragmatist view could no longer be employed legitimately. The double responsibility of the Ministry of Agriculture, Fisheries, and Food (MAFF), combining the task of protecting the public health throughout the food chain (using a science-based policy approach) alongside its role in promoting the economic interests of the food industries, was seen as one of the key failures within the system. In studying the acid rain controversy one could examine to what extend the debate on acid rain indeed impacted on the rules of the game. In the end, the British acid rain controversy was regulated by a wide recognition of the new 'eco-modernist' perspective but without an institutionalization of the new principles. Acid rain was more or less resolved but that had more to do with the usage of low-sulphur coal than with a cognitive shift. One of the key discursive principles that were first discussed in the acid rain controversy in Britain, however, was the so called 'precautionary principle'. The British establishment was very reluctant to accept this concept, as it ran against its long-standing commitment to an empiricist orientation. Interestingly, this debate resurfaced in the 1990s with BSE.

For the British government, the issue with BSE was how to contain the crisis and how to restructure the institutional regime in such a way that: (a) consumers regained confidence in beef; (b) producers would not again fall victim to a similar crisis; and (c) the idea of science-based policy-making would not be lost entirely. This time the issue achieved immediate European dimensions, as the European Commission closed the borders on British beef. Behind this was a wider debate on cultures of regulation, which had been taking place for a much longer period of time but which was now acted out over the BSE case, once more proving that this was an emblematic issue.

In the end, the British government created the Food Standards Agency (FSA) in April 2000. The FSA was created in the wake of the 'food scares' and was supposed to 'protect the public and restore public confidence in the way food safety decisions are made' (FSA, 2002) As with acid rain, with BSE the role of scientific advice was crucial. It was not merely a response to a sectoral crisis, though, as it also featured in the Labour Party's commitment to reform the civil service. The creation of a Food Standards Agency was a Labour Party manifesto commitment, which recognized the strategic importance of protecting consumer health and food safety.[2]

The British acid rain controversy had not led to the widespread restructuring of the science–politics interface (for example, via the discourse institutionalization of the precautionary principle). At that time, the British government held on to its principle that nothing was pollution unless it was scientifically proven. With hindsight, it is clear that this institutional commitment was a parent to the BSE disaster. Although the government had been warned many times that something *might* be wrong, it insisted for more than ten years that there were no significant risks of spreading the disease to humans. In March 1996, however, the UK Health Secretary had to admit that there was possibly a link between BSE and Creutzfeldt-Jacob and five years later there were 95 confirmed human deaths from it in the UK (Oosterveer, 2002).

Elsewhere, I employ discourse analysis to examine how the Food Standards Agency acted upon the complex situation. From its inception, the FSA was very clear about its commitment to basing its decisions on scientific facts. Yet, it combined this with a pledge to 'be honest about uncertainty' (FSA, 2002) and introduced a policy of transparency to back this up. One of the key organizational practices that it introduced was the 'Open Board meeting'. This implied that the decisions of the governing board would be taken in public and based on argumentative exchanges that took place in public as well. By examining how this new agency performs, we hope to understand more about the process in which new rules get established and trust can be regained.

Here is an excerpt of one of the meetings:

1. Good morning board members and uhhm good morning <members of the
2. audience.>
3. Uhmm (.) I would like to uhmm (.) kick off by uhh just saying a few words
4. to uhh those of you who are here as *observers* before we get on with our
5. business *meeting*.
6. Uhmm as you kno:w the Board of the Agency *always* uhmm *decides* and
7. discusses its policies in *public* >in a forum like this< and *your presence* and
8. *your participation* as an audience is a is a ((gesture with the hand)) very *key* part of
9. our commitment to >openness and transparency.<
10. >So thank you very much for *coming* to attend.<
11. Uhh we *also* uhh make a point of travelling *around* the United Kingdom to
12. different *parts* so that uhh not only those in London and the major
13. capitols can uhh see us at work and take part but also those in other parts
14. of the country, >and we are particularly pleased to be here in Armagh
15. City.<
16. uhhm (.) once we start the Board meeting we will carry on as though the
17. audience didn't exist.
18. *But* when we get to the en:d at around quarter to one uhh I will hand over to
19. Suzy Leather the Deputy Chair who will chair a question and answer
20. session, at which point *you* as members of the audience will have an
21. opportunity to (.) *make* comments, *ask* questions, *either* on the issues we've
22. discussed *today* >and we have a very full agenda< or on other items that
23. *may* uhh may occur to you.

Here, we see how discourse analysis can bring out the struggle of redefining the rules of the game.[3] Although it is not the first time that the board meets, its chairman, Sir John Krebs, clearly is very much aware of the need to explain precisely the rules and, in trying to show how the FSA responds to the BSE crisis, has learned from it, and is determined to continue learning from it. He reinforces the differentiation between the groups suggested by the staging and assigns roles to each, though the implications of these roles are not yet felt. Members of the audience have been given limited cues on what they're supposed to do in an immediate sense: 'observe – as if they didn't exist – until a quarter to one'. The 'key part' they will play in the 'commitment to openness and transparency' remains opaque, however. The role of the board seated around the table is presumably to make good on this commitment, but what they will do to accomplish this is not clear.

The point here is not to go into the details of this research. Rather, it is important that one can overcome the opposition between detail and relevance if one employs a research format that relates a complex question to a particular choice of empirical material. Having identified BSE as an emblematic issue and having identified the FSA as the institutional response, the meetings of that agency are obviously central for a discourse analysis of environmental politics. The fragment also shows that transcribing the text allows for a much more detailed analysis than the straightforward notation of what people said.

Discourse analysis is not one coherent method, but a wide family of approaches. This brief chapter showed how it allows for new ways of analysing policy-making processes, bringing in new sites of politics and showing new dynamics.

## Transcription conventions

| | |
|---|---|
| (.) | Pause |
| <word> | Relatively slowly uttered |
| >word< | Relatively quickly uttered |
| *word* | Uttered with emphasis |
| woo:rd | lengthened sound |
| woor- | interrupted utterance (for example, in case of interruption or slip of the tongue) |
| ( ) | Unclear from tape |
| ((remark)) | Observation of nonverbal act |
| ! | Marking an animated, empathic tone |
| . | Logical end of sentence |
| , | Marking intonation indented continuation |
| X: word | |
| L: word | Simultaneously expressed statements |

## Notes

1. Select Committee on Agriculture, *Fourth Report*, 22/04/98, § 5; http://www.publications.parliament.uk/pa/cm199798/cmselect/cmagric/331iv/ag0403.htm.
2. Ibid.
3. For transcription conventions, see the end of the article.

## Bibliography

Austin, J. L. (1975 [1955]) *How to Do Things with Words* (Oxford, Oxford University Press).

Boehmer-Christiansen, S. (1988). 'Black Mist and the Acid Rain: Science as a Figleaf of Policy', *Political Quarterly*, 59 (2): 145–160.

Boehmer-Christiansen, S., and Skea, J. (1991) *Acid Politics: Environmental and Energy Politics in Britain and Germany* (London, Belhaven Press).

Dressel, K. (2002) *BSE – the New Dimension of Uncertainty: the Cultural Politics of Science and Decision-making* (Berlin, Ed. Sigma).

Financial Services Agency (2002) *The Food Standards Agency – the First Two Years* (London, FSA).

Flick, U. (1998) *Qualitative Forschung: Theorie, Methoden, Anwendung in Psychologie und Sozialwissenschaften* (Reinbek bei Hamburg, Rowohlts Enzyklopadie).

Forester, J. (1999) *The Deliberative Practitioner: Encouraging Participatory Planning Processes* (Cambridge, Massachusetts, The MIT Press).

Hajer, M. A. (1995) *The Politics of Environmental Discourse: Ecological Modernization and the Policy Process* (Oxford, Clarendon Press).

Hajer, M. A. (1996) 'Ecological Modernisation as Cultural Politics', in Lash, S., Szerszynski, B., and Wynne, B. (eds), *Risk, Environment & Modernity: Towards a New Ecology* (London, Sage).

Hajer, M. A. (2004) 'Setting the Stage: a Dramaturgy of Policy Making', *Administration and Society*, forthcoming.

Lakoff, G., and Johnson, M. (1980) *Metaphors We Live By* (Chicago, Chicago University Press).

Lynch, M. (1991) 'Laboratory Space and the Technological Complex: an Investigation of Topical Contextures', *Science in Context*, 4 (1): 51–78.

Oosterveer, P. (2002) 'Reinventing Risk Politics: Reflexive Modernity and the European BSE Crisis', *Environmental Policy & Planning*, 4 (3): 215–30.

Park, C. (1987) *Acid Rain: Rhetoric and Reality* (London, Methuen).

Southwood, R. (1984) *Tenth Report – Tackling Pollution – Experience and Prospects* (London, Royal Commission on Environmental Pollution).

# Applying Discourse Theory: the Method of Articulation[1]

*David Howarth*

Methodological questions play something of a Cinderella role in discourse theory. Although discourse theorists attack mainstream approaches from an alternative epistemological and methodological standpoint – a stance that embodies a particular conception of social science – there are very few explicit theoretical statements of it. For the most part, such statements are either pitched at a high level of abstraction – dealing mainly with the formal ontological assumptions of discourse theory – or exist in what might be termed a practical state, that is, they are present in the outcomes of empirical research, but remain theoretically latent. This chapter begins the process of rectifying this 'methodological deficit' by focusing on the way discourse theory is applied to empirical objects of investigation. By reflecting upon existing research in the field and drawing upon the practice of conducting empirical research in discourse theory, especially with respect to protest movements in Britain and South Africa, I elaborate a method of articulatory practice that avoids the difficulties surrounding the mechanical application of 'formal-abstract' theory to 'real-concrete' events and processes. This involves a logic of explanation that brings together and transforms a plurality of formal social logics, together with the political logics that constitute and contest the latter, in order to elucidate a carefully problematized instance of research.

In developing this approach, the first half of the chapter sets out the basic characteristics and purposes of discourse theory, together with some preliminary remarks about the role of method. I then locate the emergence of the 'application problem' within the methodology of the social sciences, and in discourse theory more specifically. The principal aim is to show how the question of method ought to be conceived within the latter. The second half of the chapter endeavours to put this approach into practice by developing an appropriate set of research strategies, techniques, and methods of discourse analysis, while also considering the status and generation of the empirical data used in discourse theory.

## Discourse theory and the question of method

Post-Marxist discourse theory is best understood as a research programme or paradigm, and not just an empirical theory in the narrow sense of the term. It thus consists of a system of ontological assumptions, theoretical concepts and methodological precepts, and not just a set of falsifiable propositions designed to explain and predict phenomena such as the behaviour of the capitalist state, or different forms and logics of collective action. The kernel of this research programme centres on the idea that all objects and practices are meaningful, and that social meanings are contextual, relational, and contingent. In addition, it asserts that all systems of meaningful practice – or discourses – rely upon discursive exteriors that partially constitute such orders, while potentially subverting them. A little less abstractly, social relations exhibit four properties – contingency, historicity, power, and the primacy of politics (Laclau, 1990, pp. 31–6) – while the identities of social agents are constituted within structures of articulatory practice, and political subjects arise when agents are identified anew under conditions of dislocation. At most, such assumptions represent the formal ontological presuppositions of discourse theory. A fuller expression would require the introduction of further concepts and logics pertaining to the constitution and dissolution of political identities, the processes of hegemonic construction, the structuring of social spaces, and so forth (see Howarth, 2000a, pp. 101–25; 2005; Torfing, 1999, pp. 81–131). However, along with normative and ethical considerations, these issues are beyond the scope of this chapter.[2] To the extent that they are addressed, they will be discussed in conjunction with issues directly connected to epistemological and methodological concerns.

Turning to the latter, discourse theorists oppose the balkanization and reification of methodology. Method is not synonymous with a free-standing and neutral set of rules and techniques that can be applied mechanically to all empirical objects. Instead, while discourse theorists ought to reflect upon and theorize the ways they conduct research, these questions are always understood within a wider set of ontological and epistemological postulates, and in relation to particular problems. The problem of method in discourse theory is thus closer to Durkheim's conception – 'primarily an exercise in the clarification of logical issues' (cited in Giddens, 1976, p. 8) – or Weber's suggestion that it should be conceived as 'the reflective understanding of the means which have already demonstrated their value in practice by raising them to the level of explicit consciousness' (Weber, 1949, p. 115). In short, methodological concerns turn on questions concerning the appropriate relationship between description, understanding and explanation, the role (if any) of causal explanation, the place of critique and normative evaluation, the problems surrounding appropriate research design, and so on.

This contrast can be sharpened if we distinguish between discourse theory and discourse analysis. In our view, the former does not strictly overlap with the different varieties of 'discourse analysis' – argumentative discourse analysis, critical discourse analysis, and so forth – which have emerged and flourished in recent times (see Jaworski and Coupland, 1999; van Dijk, 1997b; Wodak and Meyer, 2001). More precisely, it is not just a toolkit designed to analyse 'language in use', where attention is focused on 'talk and text in context' (van Dijk, 1997a, p. 3), as the conduct of discourse analysis is only meaningful within a particular social and political theory, alongside its core ontological assumptions and overall political purposes. At most, therefore, the various tools of discourse analysis constitute one particular set of techniques that can help us to understand and explain empirical phenomena which have already been constituted as meaningful objects of analysis. They do not exhaust the concept of discourse theory itself.

Finally, it is important to stress that discourse theory is best seen as a version of 'problem-driven' rather than 'method-' or 'theory-driven' research. Method-driven approaches are animated by the techniques of data-gathering and analysis, rather than the empirical phenomena under investigation, while theory-driven research aims 'to vindicate a particular theory', rather than 'illuminate a problem that is specified independently of the theory' (Shapiro, 2002, p. 601). The latter is driven by the desire to confirm a 'particular theoretical outlook', rather than an exploration of 'what is actually going on in the world'. It thus runs the risk of detaching itself from social reality and atrophying (Shapiro, 2002, p. 601). Equally, problem-driven research should not be confused with 'problem-solving theory', as advocated *inter alia* by Popper and opposed by Oakeshott.[3] Indeed, the former is clarified in opposition to the latter for, as Robert Cox (1981, pp. 129–30) insists, problem-solving theory generally takes existing social structures as a given, as well as the assumptions of the dominant theories of such reality, and then addresses anomalies that arise *within* such frameworks.

By contrast, the problem-driven approach advocated here is more akin to Foucault's technique of problematization in that it begins with a set of pressing political and ethical problems in the present, before seeking to analyse the historical and structural conditions which gave rise to them, while furnishing the means for their critique and transgression. As Foucault (1985, pp. 11–12) puts it, this method is not simply a matter of analysing 'behaviour or ideas, nor societies and their "ideologies", but the *problematizations* through which being offers itself to be, necessarily, thought – and the *practices* on the basis of which these problematizations are formed'. In so doing, Foucault synthesizes his archaeological and genealogical moments of analysis, in which the former makes possible the examination of 'forms themselves', while the latter accounts for their contingent emergence and production. For instance, by describing the rules that condition the elements of a particular discourse – its objects, subjects, concepts, and strategies – in a given period, say the discourse of 'madness' or 'illness' in the nineteenth century, archaeology provides the means to delimit research objects, while genealogy analyses their constitution by recounting the historical practices from which they were constructed. The latter enables research to show the contingency of identities and practices and foreground possibilities foreclosed by the dominant logics.

In short, problem-driven discourse theory not only constitutes new objects of inquiry through interrogating particular phenomena, in which it seeks to challenge existing accounts and the theoretical frameworks that engender them, but, most importantly, it begins with and challenges the political circumstances within which such theories emerge and operate. Finally, while the focus of research is the interrogation of a specific problematized phenomenon, it is important to stress that these problems are not specified in a completely independent and atheoretical fashion. On the contrary, as against empiricism or rationalism, the emergence and constitution of research problems always presupposes the ontological assumptions and categories of discourse theory for their initial discernment and description.

## Discourse theory and hermeneutics

The way such problems are constructed and analysed is constrained by the overall *purposes* of discourse theory and the epistemological *ideals* such purposes harbour. In this regard, post-Marxist discourse theory locates itself within the hermeneutical branch of the social sciences. In general, this means that it seeks *inter alia* to provide second-order interpretations of social actors' own self-understandings and interpretations of their situations and practices (see Heidegger, 1962, pp. 32–5). This in turn presumes that institutions and practices are partly constituted by the beliefs and desires of social actors; that there is an internal relation between subjective meanings and actions; and that the understanding of meaning presupposes a set of shared, background practices. Consequently, a key objective of discourse theory is to elucidate carefully problematized objects of study by seeking their description, understanding, and interpretation (see Taylor, 1971; Winch, 1990). Without going into detail at this stage, this conception effectively bypasses law-like models of explanation and prediction put forward by positivists and naturalists, as the latter are apt to bracket-out subjective meanings, intentions, and interpretations either by denying an internal link between actions and meanings, or by viewing the latter as dispositions to behave, or by treating meanings and shared background practices themselves as the objects of law-like generalization (see Connolly, 1981, pp. 23–8; Howarth, 2002; 2004).

Nonetheless, a couple of immediate caveats are in order. For a start, the hermeneutic enterprise involves practices of characterization and explanation that *require* the application of theoretical concepts and logics, along with their concomitant value commitments (both of which cannot be derived from a purely ethnographic or descriptive social science). This is not to make explanation synonymous with furnishing causal accounts, nor are explanations – when construed in causal or statistical terms – the ground upon which description and interpretation function. Instead, the task of explanation is relative to the practice of elucidation in that some kind of intelligibility is presupposed for it to take hold, and is only called upon where 'there is, or at least thought to be, a deficiency in understanding' (Winch, 1990, p. x). In short, from a hermeneutic point of view, researchers use their initially blurred and cloudy understandings as yardsticks to assess the degree to which understanding has been advanced in the process of articulating a new characterization and theoretical explanation.

Despite these caveats, however, the traditional hermeneutical starting point falls short on at least three counts. First, even if one overlooks the ontological deficit among many hermeneutical approaches – the failure, that is, to elaborate logics and concepts that can assist in the explanation of practice – it is not sufficient on epistemological grounds to rely upon actors' self-interpretations, as perspicuous understandings of social practice frequently require an external vantage point to detect partialities and distortions. This usually involves the location of their interpretations in a broader historical perspective by employing theoretical concepts and logics not readily available to social actors themselves.[4] Secondly, while hermeneuticists such as Charles Taylor correctly understand language to be a constitutive medium for the articulation of meanings, moods, and feelings, they are overly optimistic about its capacity to *express* our inner thoughts and desires, thereby enriching our own self-understandings and enabling their 'attunement' with higher-order goals (see Connolly, 1987, pp. 146–52; Taylor, 1981, pp. 207–11). By contrast, post-structuralists focus on the polysemic and distorting effects of language, which weakens both its capacity to express our innermost thoughts and experiences, as well as the constitutive sovereignty of a subjectivity that pre-exists language in some way (see Derrida, 1982, p. 313; Lacan, 2002, pp. 138–68). A third difficulty arises from the presumption that social meanings and background understandings are implicit in the social practices of specific 'forms of life', which are taken to be homogenous and coherent entities, whose underlying logic can be uncovered and described. This idealization is empirically problematic because the social worlds we inhabit are for the most part inherently multiple and heterogeneous (Tully, 1995, pp. 106–7) and it is also ontologically flawed because – as discourse theorists insist – the construction of any 'form of life' is predicated upon a relation to a 'constitutive outside' which problematizes any internal purity (see Staten, 1984, pp. 16–17; Derrida, 1976, pp. 44–65; Said, 1995).

These reservations demonstrate the complex relationship between post-Marxist discourse theory and the hermeneutical tradition of inquiry. On a more positive note, however, they give rise to a more concrete understanding of discourse theory. To begin with, it should be (re-)emphasized that the main aim of discourse theory is not merely to provide novel descriptions or facts about specific objects of investigation, but to produce new *interpretations* either by rendering visible phenomena previously undetected by dominant theoretical approaches, or by problematizing existing accounts and articulating alternative interpretations.[5] For instance, Edward Said's (1995) interpretation of Orientalist discourse disclosed a whole new set of identities and phenomena for analysis, thus helping to constitute the field of subaltern studies. By contrast, Anna Marie Smith's (1994) account of New Right discourse elaborates an alternative interpretation of Thatcherism in Britain, which challenges mainstream positivist and Marxist accounts by focusing specifically on its changing discourses about sexuality and its 'racialized others' (for other examples see Griggs and Howarth, 2002; Howarth, 1997; Norval, 1996). When translated into the language of discourse theory, this means that facts have to be situated within wider fields of social meaning or discourses, that their interpretation relies upon the theoretical concepts and logics furnished by its social ontology, and that the resulting interpretations are contingent and contestable. The latter condition reflects not only the contingency of all ontological platforms but also the contestability of particular interpretations, which represent only one possible way of ordering the facts and descriptions.

Given these premises, it would be contradictory to enumerate all possible problems within discourse theory in an a priori fashion. Nonetheless, as the latter is not a totalizing approach that can be applied to *all* problems, it is possible to demarcate a legitimate range of research objects. In general, these include the constitution of political identities; the practices of hegemonic articulation among particular discourses and subjectivities; the construction of social antagonisms and the establishment of political frontiers; the ways subjects are 'gripped' by certain discourses and not others; and the social fantasies which sustain such identifications and the 'enjoyment' thereby procured. The analysis of these issues means that discourse theorists are also concerned with a set of cognate topics, such as the changing character of public policy-making in today's condition of multi-level governance; the practices of groups and social movements; the role of the mass media; and the dislocatory effects of economic change, commodification, and bureaucratization on the fabric of social life. The process of applying discourse theory to this diverse set of empirical problems, the problems this practice engenders, and the solutions which might be proffered are now addressed.

## Application, articulation, and explanation

As intimated, the employment of discourse theory in concrete empirical research centres on the 'problem of application'. This problem names a set of dangers which emanate from separating a theoretical approach from its object of study, and positing or assuming what Althusser (1990, p. 49) calls 'a relation of exteriority' between the two levels. A first danger arises from treating the 'real-concrete' as the raw material which forms the essential starting point of theoretical and empirical analysis. This *empiricist* conception suggests an unmediated access to the 'real-concrete', in which abstraction consists in the knowing subject isolating and extracting the essence from the real, and/or generalizing in an inductive fashion from a number of empirical observations. The opposite danger is a *theoreticism* which either logically derives the explanations of concrete phenomena from the abstract concepts of a general theory, or subsumes particular events and processes under empirically verified laws. Such theoreticism is evident, for example, in both Marxist and positivist accounts of phenomena. In the former it normally takes the form of deducing the concrete from the simple abstractions of dialectical and historical materialism, while for the latter it consists in subsuming particular events and their variable initial conditions, under causal laws, which are usually taken to be the product of well-founded empirical generalizations.

As against empiricism, discourse theorists maintain that there can be no unmediated access to the real-concrete. Indeed, the very idea of 'accessing' the real-concrete presupposes a gulf between the subject and object of knowledge, which objective knowledge somehow bridges. Instead, following Heidegger's critique of classical epistemology, it is better to conceive of the subject as 'always already' within a world of meaningful objects and practices, and to conceive of the norms of that world as providing the criteria for subjects to identify objects in the first place (Heidegger, 1962, pp. 88–90). In contrast, in order to counter the problems of logical derivation or theoretical subsumption, the employment of abstract tools to explain concrete objects requires a work of theoretical elaboration that *articulates* concepts and logics which are, initially at least, located at different levels of abstraction, focused on different levels of analysis, and drawn from a variety of theoretical problematics.

## Logics

Having introduced the general idea of an articulatory practice and its relation to method, more needs to be said about the basic unit of explanation in discourse theory – the notion of a logic – as well as the character of the articulatory practice that combines different logics together in any given explanation. To begin negatively, the concept of a logic in discourse theory does not refer to the formal analysis of propositions so as to determine their validity or truth. Equally, it is important to stress that the general notion of a logic in discourse theory is not a law as in 'Duverger's law' or Marx's 'general law of capital accumulation'. To take the latter for example, even though Marx (1976, p. 798) concedes that laws are 'modified in [their] working by many circumstances', his notion of 'natural laws of capitalist production... working themselves out with iron necessity' (Marx, 1976, p. 91) is too strong and deterministic to be compatible with the ontological presuppositions of discourse theory. Nor for that matter are logics synonymous with tendencies, such as Marx's 'tendency of the rate of profit to fall', which are more akin to empirical generalizations that may or may not occur, and which generally presuppose more determining laws at higher levels of abstraction.

Instead, at the most general and abstract level, a logic refers, first, to the rules governing a practice, institution or system of relations between objects and, secondly, to the kinds of entities (and their relations) presupposed by the operation of such rules (cf. Laclau, 2000, pp. 282–3). For example, 'the logic of the market' comprises a particular set of rules governing the arrangements bringing together buyers and sellers of commodities. Importantly, the organization of such interactions via the price mechanism presupposes a set of entities that make possible the operation of such rules. Hence the logic of the market presupposes a particular set of subjects (buyers, sellers), objects (commodities, means of exchange) and a system of relations between subjects and objects (exchange). More concretely, it is important to distinguish between social and political logics within post-Marxist discourse theory. Whereas social logics are conditional and historically specific systems of sedimented practice, such as 'the logic of the market', 'the logic of bureaucracy' or 'the logic of apartheid', political logics refer to special kinds of practice that *constitute* and *contest* these social logics. Political logics thus fulfil a role analogous to 'fundamental ontology' in Heidegger's philosophy, as they condition the emergence and character of the rules governing any particular social logic. Thus, for example, the (social) logic of apartheid was formed, instituted and later challenged by precise political logics. In other words, the 'system of differences' through which particular ethnic and national groups were allocated separate and formally equal institutions and territorial spaces wherein they could exercise their legitimate 'demands' for political and cultural self-determination was a product of the intersecting logics of equivalence and difference that divided and structured social space in South Africa, as different political forces competed for hegemony.

The characteristics of political logics are captured by the ontological structure of discourse theory itself. As I have suggested, political practices are not reducible to individual intentions or actions, nor to the mechanical and deterministic operation of social structures. Instead, the practices governed by the logic of politics erupt when there is a *failure* or *impossibility* of an existing social structure, and when subjects are literally 'forced' to act and identify anew. Thus political practices both condition and stand at the limit of any social practice. Of central importance in this regard is the logic of hegemony. This logic is designed to elucidate the practice of constructing political alliances and coalitions between differently positioned social actors. It captures the process by which actors link together a disparate set of particular demands in a common discourse so as to construct a more universal political project. The logic of hegemony, together with the grammar of related concepts and conditions that make it possible, furnishes a language of description for the analysis of political phenomena. More specifically, the operation of a hegemonic logic presupposes the existence of a social field criss-crossed by social antagonisms and the availability of contingent ideological elements – or 'floating signifiers' – that can be articulated by opposed political projects striving to confer meaning to them (Howarth, 2000, p. 110). Importantly, these concepts and their logical relations are underpinned by the ontological assumptions of discourse theory – the contingency of all objects and identities, the subject as lack, and so on – which together constitute their conditions of possibility.

Consider, for instance, the way this logic can help to investigate the Black Consciousness Movement (BCM) in South Africa. This movement, which challenged the logic of apartheid during the 1960s and 1970s, was formed in July 1967 at Rhodes University after black students attending a supposedly non-racial student congress were prevented from occupying 'whites only' residences. The dislocatory effects of this rebuttal led students to form an alternative student organization in 1968 – the South African Students Organization (SASO) – which spearheaded the campaigns of the BCM. During the 1970s Black Consciousness intellectuals and activists aimed to construct oppositional chains of equivalence linking all blacks against white racists, 'non-whites' (that is, those blacks who did not identify as blacks) and the system of 'separate development' as a whole. They did this by seeking to engineer a new black/not-black division of the social that cut across the existing logic of apartheid. In order to construct this new political frontier, the leaders of SASO, most notably activists like Steven Biko, Barney Pityana, and Harry Nengwekhulu, took up and instigated demands in a variety of contiguous spheres and sites – the workplace, black townships, rural areas, and ethnically segregated institutions such as universities and colleges – in an effort to hegemonize popular demands and struggles against the apartheid state. They did this by articulating and reiterating a discourse of Black Consciousness that valorized black identity and culture, while negating white racism in its various guises (see Howarth, 1997).

I come now to the key aspect of the movement I want to focus upon here. How can we explain the *failure* of the movement to achieve its goals in the wake of the Soweto uprising of 1976, the conjuncture which simultaneously represented the apogee and nadir of the BCM. The logic of hegemony discloses a number of potential factors that can account for this *explanandum*, whereupon empirical inquiry is required to determine which factors, or which combination of factors, actually explain the dissolution of the movement. On the one hand, potential explanations need to centre on whether or not the *structural conditions* for a hegemonic practice were propitious for the construction of a viable hegemonic project. On the other hand, attention must focus on the character of the *subjective practices* of the movement itself. Any fully-fledged account of the particular instance would consist of a particular combination of these different empirical aspects.

In the case of the BCM, it is evident that up until 1976 the structural conditions for constructing a viable hegemony were not propitious. The discourse of apartheid in its 'separate development' form had been imposed upon and largely internalized by a compliant black majority. At the same time, the coercive power and ideological unity of the South African state prevented any meaningful resistance. This is not to imply that the effects of the BCM during this period were negligible, as the BCM instilled a new consciousness of self-assertion and confidence amongst its supporters, and the movement contributed to a climate of defiance that would later manifest itself in the Soweto uprisings. In short, however, during these conditions social antagonisms were relegated to the margins of society and the availability of floating signifiers was minimal.

The events leading up to the Soweto uprisings, and the rebellion itself, changed these conditions. The events destabilized the existing apartheid order, led to the eruption of widespread antagonism and conflict, and provoked a process of 'reform from above'. These dislocatory events provoked a crisis of the regime and saw an unfixing of the dominant signifiers. 'Apartheid', 'separate development', 'independent, self-governing homelands' and the other signifiers of white domination were now the objects of political contestation, and new signifiers such as 'black power!', 'freedom' and 'Amandla!' ('Power!') were in the air. And yet in this new context of ideological fluidity and protest the BCM was still not able to capitalize fully on the organic crisis engendered by the uprising.

How are we to explain this failure? First, the institutions of the South African state were still capable of repressing the movement through a combination of violence, detention and threat, thus managing to reproduce the logic of apartheid. This forced many BC activists to flee the country, exit the political struggle altogether, or reorient their political practices. Secondly, with respect to the BCM, a number of internal failings showed themselves. On the one hand, the inadequacies of its inconsistent political strategy together with its weakly rooted organizational structure made it vulnerable to state repression. This resulted in the rapid disintegration of the movement in the immediate aftermath of Soweto (Howarth, 1995; 2000b). On the other hand, the limits of its language of protest, especially the role of 'blackness' as an empty signifier that could hold together an opposition coalition, was also thrown into relief. This was particularly evident in the period of realignment following the Soweto uprising, when competing ideological traditions and movements ranging from the Charterist language of democratic, non-racialism to the more socialist discourses of the independent trade union movement jostled for hegemony. And by the mid-1980s, with the formation of the UDF and COSATU, together with their growing cooperation, Black Consciousness had lost the ideological struggle. Indeed, many former Black Consciousness activists and supporters shifted to these competing ideological traditions and became leading figures in the UDF, the ANC, or the trade union movement. In short, the dislocatory impact of the Soweto uprisings not only destabilized white minority rule, but it also revealed weaknesses in the practices of the BCM. This led ultimately to the collapse of the movement and its ideology. In addition, this structural void was soon to be filled by the emergence and reactivation of other ideological traditions, which would prove better able to articulate the proliferation of demands in the country. Thus by the mid-1980s it was the discourse of 'non-racial democracy' which was destined to lay the foundations for the emergence of the 'Rainbow nation' of the 1990s.

The above discussion of Black Consciousness represents no more than an explanatory sketch. Much more empirical material needs to be presented to vindicate the claims that are made. Nevertheless, I do believe it goes some way in showing the way political and social logics can account for the failure of this movement to hegemonize a particular field of signifiers in a given historical conjuncture. In sum, the BCM embodied a political logic that contested the logic of apartheid; the dislocatory events of the Soweto uprisings destabilized both the South African regime and the BCM; and the failure of the latter to elaborate a credible empty signifier that would grip possible supporters resulted in its replacement by better positioned and more believable political forces and movements.

**Articulatory practice**

The preceding example shows the way in which a discourse theoretical approach can explain events and processes. It is evident, however, that any fully fledged *explanans* contains a *plurality* of different *kinds* of logics and concepts. These are likely to include theoretical logics and concepts such as the Lacanian logic of fantasy or the Derridean concept of iterability; more concrete social logics, whether they be the logics of apartheid or the market, which have to be constructed in order to account for a particular set of sedimented practices; as well as the political logics that have been involved in constituting and contesting the social logics and phenomena under investigation. As already suggested, the problem in this regard concerns the conditions under which it is possible to bring together these heterogeneous theoretical and empirical elements into an explanatory chain without reducing or subsuming those elements to higher-order laws or abstractions, and without giving way to an eclecticism in which incompatible logics and concepts hold sway in an inconsistent fashion.

The solution put forward here harnesses the concept of an articulatory practice alongside a fullyfledged logic of formalization. In order to specify the concept of an articulatory practice, let us begin by recalling Laclau and Mouffe's definition of the term. For them, an articulatory practice is 'any practice establishing a relation among elements such that their identity is modified as a result of the articulatory practice' (Laclau and Mouffe, 1985, p. 105). (It goes without saying that these practices are only possible given the ontological assumptions of discourse theory – the 'openness of the social', the interweaving of necessity and contingency, the subversion of any identity by a constitutive exterior, and so forth – which I have outlined earlier in the first part of the chapter.) In an analogous fashion, the application of various theoretical and social logics to account for a particular problem involves *a mutual modification of the logics and concepts articulated together in the process of explaining each particular instance of research*. This is because different concepts have to be rendered compatible with one another, and with the underlying ontological assumptions of discourse theory, and both modifications only take place within the particular context of understanding and explaining the particular object investigated. Without such modification, the separations between different logics and concepts, and between those logics and the empirical problems investigated, would remain in place.

What are the precise conditions of possibility for an articulatory practice of this sort? First, the *theoretical* logics and concepts employed in any putative explanans must be consistent and compatible with the underlying ontological assumptions of discourse theory. In order to specify the conditions under which this is possible, I need to say something about the logic of formalization. This practice avoids the positing of a hierarchy of different levels of abstraction, or giving in to an empiricist epistemology, by seeking to construct purely formal theoretical logics and concepts drawn from a plurality of theoretical problematics. These can then be articulated together in conjunction with the relevant empirical raw materials to produce a coherent explanatory chain.

There are four related aspects to this logic of formalization. These are the processes of reactivation, deconstruction, abstraction, and 'commensuration', each of which requires some discussion. Drawing on Husserl's phenomenological method, the *reactivation* of concepts and logics returns us back to the precise problems which were originally addressed in the constitution of a particular theory, together with the structuring assumptions that enabled the production of its concepts. The main point of the exercise is to lay bare the sedimented questions and presuppositions that led to the production of a particular concept or logic. This makes possible the *deconstruction* of those essentialist or deterministic aspects that make them incompatible with discourse theory (cf. Norval, 2000). The practices of *abstraction* and *commensuration* consist in the elaboration of purely formal concepts and logics which are compatible with the underlying assumptions of discourse theory. This consists in producing logics that are appropriate to the object (and the level of abstraction) being explored, and which have been purified of those traces of particularity that may preclude their being applied to a variety of commensurate problems and questions. These modular elements constitute the theoretical raw materials for the construction of any putative *explanans*. It is then left to the method of articulation to bring these elements together, along with the appropriate empirical raw materials, to produce an explanation consisting of 'a concentration of many determinations' (Marx, 1973, p. 100).

In a similar vein, the more concrete *social* logics that are constructed to explain particular conjunctures and events must be compatible with the underlying assumptions of discourse theory. Thus, for instance, they must not be predicated on essentialist or deterministic accounts of social practices. Naturally, they must also provide a perspicuous representation or interpretation of the practices described. Finally, as I have suggested, the *political* logics employed occupy what might be called a quasi-transcendental role in explaining events and processes. As they are integral to the construction and contestation of social relations and practices, they function as both the latter's condition of possibility and impossibility. Moreover, although political logics *qua* political logics are substantively empty in that they do not determine in an a priori fashion the *content* of particular social logics or formations, they are at the root 'cause' of all social practices given that the latter are ultimately the product of the operation of the former. In short, discourse theoretical explanations give primacy to the role of political practices – understood via the logic of hegemony – in the concrete explanation of social practices, though such explanations must draw upon and articulate a variety of theoretical and social logics in order to constitute satisfactory accounts.

### Verification

The task of corroborating the data gleaned from empirical research, whether in the form of qualitative interviews or documentary evidence, will be considered en passant in my discussion of appropriate research strategies and techniques in discourse theory. However, to conclude this section on the method of articulatory practice, it is necessary to say something about the status of the claims and explanations proposed by discourse theorists. Of course, this topic raises immense questions about the nature of truth and validity, and the following remarks constitute little more than an outline in search of further elaboration. Nevertheless, in line with much contemporary philosophy of science, whether inspired by Popper (1989) or Kuhn (1970), discourse theorists reject notions of directly accessing a final or absolute truth (via scientific propositions, for example), and problematize oversimplified correspondence theories that compare propositions with existing states of affairs. Equally, however, they distance themselves from truth as a kind of 'subjective imposition', which theorists such as Habermas and Taylor often accuse Nietzsche and Foucault of asserting (see Habermas, 1987, pp. 95–7; Taylor, 1985, pp. 174–84). In discourse theory, truth and knowledge are not reducible or equivalent to power.

By contrast, discourse-theoretical interpretations can only count as 'candidates for truth or falsity', that is, can be regarded as potentially true, if they first accord with the social ontologies and 'regimes of truth' within which they are generated. In addition, they must also constitute warranted interpretations of the new phenomena they purport to understand and explain, or at least plausibly contest and refute accepted interpretations. They are thus subject to the usual burdens of reliable evidence, objectivity, and internal consistency consonant with the prevalent regimes of truth (although it goes without saying that discourse theorists challenge and in certain respects seek to extend the character and parameters of these regimes). In Popperian terms, interpretations that successfully pass this double threshold of acceptability are held to be true until decisively refuted or surpassed by other interpretations.

## Research strategies

This chapter has thus far examined the conditions under which empirical research can fruitfully be undertaken in discourse theory. It now turns to more concrete questions about the conduct of research. These concern the choice and character of appropriate *research strategies*, the *generation* of empirical data, and the different ways of *analysing texts*. It is important to stress at the outset that the choice of appropriate research strategies or the different techniques of textual analysis depend upon the underlying principles of method already elucidated. Thus, for instance, the decision as to whether or not to focus on one or many case studies, or whether or not to engage in comparative research, is determined by the process of problematization, the questions that need to be addressed, and the hypotheses that are being investigated. It also depends on the kind and quality of available data and the depth of analysis required. Similarly, whether or not one chooses to focus on the rhetorical or narrative structures of texts – or both – is relative to the kinds of research questions one asks. The purpose of these reflections is thus not so much to delineate the practical skills and procedures required by these research strategies but to clarify their point and purpose, to reflect upon the theoretical issues they engender, and to establish the proper limits of their employment. Bearing these qualifications in mind, I begin by considering two central research strategies in discourse theory, namely, the use of case studies and the comparative method

### Case studies

Much of the empirical research conducted in the name of discourse theory is case based. Thus, while the method of articulation has weakened the strong separation of theoretical discourse and empirical objects, more specific questions need to be examined about the precise role of case studies within discourse theory. How are they selected? What is their status within our overall research objectives? What are the limits, if any, of employing the case study method? How do case studies connect organically to theoretical discourse both in terms of 'the logic of discovery' and 'the logics of presentation and validation'? What wider set of inferences or generalizations, if any, can legitimately be drawn from single or multiple case studies? In order to address these issues, it is instructive to begin by challenging a pervasive view of this research strategy.

There is a widespread misconception among many social scientists that case studies are at best a limited tool for producing knowledge, or at worst misleading and ultimately dispensable. In *Making Social Science Matter*, Bent Flyvbjerg (2001, pp. 66–87) has identified five common misunderstandings. They are (a) that general and theoretical (that is, context-independent) knowledge is more valuable for social science than the concrete, practical (that is, context-dependent) knowledge associated with case studies; (b) that one ought not to generalize on the basis of individual cases, thereby implying that the case study method contributes little to scientific development; (c) that the case study is most useful for generating hypotheses, but other methods (usually quantitative) are more suitable for testing hypotheses and theory building; (d) that the case study method is biased towards a particular conception of verification, that is, the tendency to confirm the researcher's preconceived notions, and thus not conducive to scientific testing (as is the case with the method of falsification, for instance); and (e) that it is often difficult to establish general propositions and theories on the basis of specific case studies.

This picture is an anathema to discourse theorists. With respect to (a), the search for universal and closed explanatory theories that exhibit complete predictive power is an unobtainable ideal in the human sciences. Discourse theory focuses instead on the interpretation of singularly problematized phenomena and the critique of sedimented and exclusionary practices. In both respects, the case study represents an ideal vehicle for achieving these ends. Indeed, the task of analysing various in-depth cases not only develops a researcher's skills and intuitions, but is crucial in enabling students to learn the grammar of discourse theory, while sensitizing the researcher to the complexity and nuances of social reality itself. As Dreyfus (1986, pp. 11–13) and Flyvbjerg (2001, pp. 69–71) correctly argue, the search for context-independent knowledge that is not grounded in particular cases ultimately obstructs learning; in a practice-based model one requires the other.

Misunderstandings (b) and (c) homogenize the different types of case study and their multiple usages. As Flyvbjerg suggests, following Popper, case studies can be used as 'critical cases' to falsify or confirm theories, and are thus important means of testing and building theory. In fact, it is possible to outline at least four types of case study alongside their method of selection. At the outset, *extreme* or *deviant* cases can serve to highlight particular phenomena in a dramatic fashion. In *Discipline and Punish*, for instance, Foucault (1977, pp. 3–16) describes the gory execution of 'Damiens the regicide' in 1757, followed by the intensely invasive 'rules for the House of young prisoners in Paris' some eighty years later, a juxtaposition which heightens our sense of discontinuity, while underlining the contingency of different modes of punishment. *Critical* cases, by contrast, can be selected to prove or disprove theories or hypotheses. These cases allow logical deductions of the form 'if this is (not) valid for this case, then it applies to all (no) cases' (Flyvbjerg, 2001, p. 79). In this regard, it is useful to distinguish between 'least likely' or 'most likely' cases, as they afford the opportunity to confirm or refute hypotheses or hunches. If 'least likely' cases are shown to refute or confirm a hypothesis, then it plausibly holds for other more likely cases. In contrast, if 'most likely' cases do not confirm a proposition, then it is unlikely to hold for less likely cases.

Thirdly, *maximum variation* cases might be chosen precisely because they are as different from each other as possible, thus enabling researchers 'to obtain information about the significance of various circumstances for case process and outcome' (p. 79). For example, a small number of cases might be selected because they are very different in particular respects: size, form of organization, geographical location, historical background, and so forth. It is then possible to assess to what extent these variables affect particular outcomes. Finally, *paradigmatic* cases can be selected and used to provide an accurate representation of a wider field of phenomena (p. 80). These cases often function as exemplars or metaphors for an entire society. As Foucault (1977, pp. 200–9) insists, for example, Jeremy Bentham's 'Panopticon' crystallized an entire system of disciplinary and surveillance mechanisms, thus constituting an exemplary embodiment of what he calls disciplinary society.

This typology of case studies provides ammunition to dispel misunderstanding (d). For a start, the various ways in which case studies can be employed problematizes a supposed bias towards verification, which is only one specific use. Indeed, critical cases tend to display a greater bias towards falsification than other methods. Moreover, those who engage in thorough and in-depth case studies commonly report that their preconceptions and assumptions are challenged by their work, possibly to a far greater extent than methods that remain more removed from their object of enquiry. Finally, with respect to (e), it is important to make the sceptical point that for discourse theorists an overhasty and unreflective tendency to generalize *is* an inaccurate way of depicting, explaining, and intervening in social reality. From this perspective, one of the virtues of the case study method – its greater attention to detail and its closer proximity to the object of study – is to reveal this inadequacy. For discourse theorists, this is not a failing of the case study approach, but arguably its greatest benefit.

By unpicking the misconceptions surrounding the role and purposes of the case study method, I have shown how the analysis of single or multiple cases is essential to the conduct of empirical research in discourse theory. Not only does this research strategy furnish the means to condense a number of theoretical and empirical elements in order to elucidate a singular practice or phenomenon, but it can also be articulated, if necessary, with other research strategies to achieve this goal. For example, when harnessed alongside the comparative method, a knowledge of 'extreme cases' can serve to shed light on our taken-for-granted practices, just as 'anomalous' or 'peripheral' cases can disclose something unexpected and invisible in apparently more 'normal' cases. In contrast, the invention and discovery of what Wittgenstein (Wittgenstein, 1953, # 122) calls 'intermediate cases' can help to form a bridge between those practices (we think) we understand and those which we do not. In addition, the description of 'maximum variation' cases can be useful in establishing the conditions under which certain practices emerge and develop (and others do not), as well as identifying the presence or absence of certain factors in the constitution and reproduction of particular phenomena. These remarks bring us to the role of comparative research in discourse theory.

**Comparative research**

Implicitly or explicitly discourse theorists often employ the comparative method. Some of the chapters in this volume compare different cases in order to clarify their understandings of particular phenomena, or use their interpretations to cast light on similar or different phenomena. However, as with many more narrowly defined methodological questions, there is very little direct reflection about the comparative perspective in discourse theory. To begin with, as with the case study method, the practice of comparison needs to be related to the practice of interpreting problematized phenomena. This means that a comparative perspective in discourse theory has to be detached from purely positivistic and quantitative stances. More precisely, whereas discourse theorists can go along with tasks such as 'contextual description' or the 'classification of empirical phenomena into distinct categories with shared characteristics', they balk at the way political scientists regard these 'lower level' objectives as merely precursory moments in the desire to explain via the testing of hypotheses (usually but not exclusively using quantitative data) and to predict via the use of lawlike theories (see Landman, 2000, pp. 4–10).

Instead, two conditions must be satisfied for comparative research to be undertaken in discourse theory. First, it is necessary to specify the problems and questions to be addressed, as mainstream comparative approaches in the social sciences are strong candidates for method-driven research. For discourse theorists, by contrast, the practice of comparison is always relative to the specific problems addressed and tackled. The second condition is that comparative research in discourse theory cannot short-circuit its focus on historical context and concrete specificity. The basis for comparison must comprise thick descriptive interpretations of particular empirical phenomena (despite being able to discern important similarities and resemblances among a group or class of phenomenona). In short, the use of a comparative method to explain why similar logics give rise to different logics, or why different systems produce similar effects, ought to be both problem-driven and grounded on the interpretation of particular cases. This rules out 'large-n' comparisons involving quantitative data as the end-point of research from a discursive point of view. While such data may be useful for other purposes – establishing overall patterns to assist in hypothesis formation, for example – they cannot provide the basis for comparisons and overall interpretations.

Discourse theorists thus need to draw on different theoretical resources to develop an appropriate perspective on comparative research. Fortunately, these resources are available among the philosophical traditions and thinkers which discourse theory draws upon.[6] For the purposes of this chapter I shall principally draw upon the writings of the later Wittgenstein to set out five general reasons why discourse theorists ought to engage in comparative research and how they might proceed in so doing. First, the description and introduction of comparative cases is important to render phenomena more intelligible. Consider the way Wittgenstein uses 'intermediate cases' to illuminate 'alien' practices which are prone to be misinterpreted either because they are too easily assimilated into our dominant, parochial understandings, or because they are conceded an 'unintelligible otherness'. In his critical remarks on James Frazer's *The Golden Bough*, for instance, Wittgenstein (1979, p. 64) describes the way American pilots during World War Two 'kiss[ed] the pictures' of their loved ones before embarking on a mission, thus drawing attention to the expressive, rather than functional or instrumental, character of certain human actions. He then shows how this particular 'complex of actions' helps us to understand that so-called 'primitive practices' in 'traditional societies' should be first viewed as internally related to the customs and rituals of these forms of life, and not automatically as implausible proto-scientific beliefs about the efficacy of their actions. This quintessentially hermeneutical operation seeks to clarify and understand sets of beliefs and practices that may initially appear strange, or even 'barbaric', by connecting them to behaviour that is at once intelligible to us (Wittgenstein, 1979, pp. 61–81; see also Cioffi, 1988). Questions of explanation and evaluation may then follow.

A second reason is precisely to *desediment* and *defamiliarize* our normal understandings of phenomena by drawing attention to their contingent peculiarity. Again the later Wittgenstein is helpful here. His desire for *übersicht* – finding the correct overview or perspective on the meanings of our words and practices (Wittgenstein, 1953, # 122) – endeavours to reorganize our existing empirical knowledge in order to cast new light on our objects of investigation. For instance, his understanding of certain primitive practices relativizes and 'decentres' sedimented beliefs about the universal superiority of scientific reasoning, which we assume to be natural and normal. He also employs comparative 'language games' that accentuate normalized understandings so as to demystify misleading conceptions of language use. For instance, in the opening pages of the *Philosophical Investigations*, his example of two persons building a wall draws our attention to the fact that we do not just use words to denote objects in the world, as the Augustinian picture of language suggests. When 'A' shouts out the words 'block', 'pillar', 'slab', and 'beam', and 'B' passes the block, pillar, slab, or beam, he is not pointing out the objects to which these words refer; rather, he is using words to communicate with 'B' in order to perform the task of building the wall. In this way,

Wittgenstein draws attention to the way in which words and actions are interwoven in a particular language game and are not separate forms (Wittgenstein, 1953, # 2, 6–8). Wittgenstein also invents unfamiliar practices to show the contingency and strangeness of that which we take for granted. For instance, he asks us to imagine pupils that diverge 'irrationally' from conventional modes of rule-following in order to clarify conventional ways of learning and following rules.

A third reason to engage in comparative research centres on the pinpointing of *decisive factors* in understanding and explaining phenomena. When allied to the case study method, especially extreme or maximum variation cases, comparative research can help to highlight a crucial aspect that is either present or absent in the phenomenon. This technique can both enhance understanding while pointing out further areas of investigation. For instance, we may wish to know why and how some hegemonic projects or social movements reproduce themselves while others do not, or we may wish to understand why certain societies with similar historical starting points evolved in very different ways. Comparative research of a few carefully selected case studies, focusing on a key set of variables, is essential for delimiting which factors explain such differential outcomes. However, it is important to dispel one possible misunderstanding in this regard. Even though we are interested in why and how one set of patterns exists rather than another, comparative research in discourse theory does not involve the comparison of identical practices or institutions which are treated as purely equivalent units. Instead we compare practices and objects which share certain family resemblances, rather than essences. It is for this reason that the interpretation of particular phenomena necessarily precedes the comparative dimension.

A fourth reason centres on the continuous interplay between universality and particularity, necessity and contingency. As Slavoj Žižek (1994, pp. 1–3) suggests, a central ideological trope involves the continuous inversion of these dialectical oppositions. For instance, whereas thirty or forty years ago capitalism was understood as one form of productive relations amongst others, and our relationships to nature were seen as fixed and constant, our contemporary world assumes capitalism to be a necessary and universal horizon which allows no escape, while our recent preoccupations with 'environmental catastrophe' and the 'breakdown of nature' show the contingency of human/nature relationships and have evoked a plurality of political imaginaries aimed at their rethinking. By describing and displaying a range of comparative cases, we can thus explore these dialectical shifts, track the ideological mechanisms which generate them, and engage in the task of 'ideology critique' by unpicking and reinscribing the logics we detect.

Finally, a comparative ethos in discourse theory may involve *projecting* 'ideals' into the phenomena we wish to explain and evaluate. This move is typical in Wittgenstein's texts where he often injects 'ideals' into his discussions of linguistic phenomena so as 'to teach us something about the actual use' of language (Wittgenstein, 1977, # 35). 'Ideals' here do not 'mean something specially good, but only something carried to extremes', and they function as '*objects of comparison* which are meant to throw light on the facts of our language by way not only of similarities, but also of dissimilarities' (Wittgenstein, 1953, # 130). The 'clear and simple language games' he invents are thus held up as a comparative 'model' or 'measuring-rod', and 'not as a preconceived idea to which reality *must* correspond' (Wittgenstein, 1953, # 131). Not only is this comparative device useful in explaining phenomena by allowing us to focus attention on absences and presences in the object of investigation, but it also enables the project of evaluation and critique by providing ethical levers to detect divergences between the ideals and phenomena explored. In the field of political theory, for instance, William Connolly employs this technique in his project of onto-political interpretation. Overcoming the 'negative dialectic' of much contemporary post-structuralism, he argues for a mode of interpretation that explicitly projects 'ontopolitical presumptions . . . into detailed interpretations of actuality', thereby 'acknowledging that your implicit projections surely exceed explicit formulation of them and that your formulations exceed your capacity to demonstrate their truth'. The aim is 'to challenge closure' in the dominant theoretical and political matrices 'by affirming the contestable character of your own projections, by offering readings of contemporary life that compete with alternative accounts, and by moving back and forth between these two levels' (Connolly, 1995, p. 36).

## Data as text, text as data

The consideration of case studies and comparative research presupposed the generation and analysis of a wide range of empirical data. Primary documents, in-depth interviews, newspaper reports, observed and unobserved social practices, images, quantitative data, even buildings and historical monuments, are grist to the mill of problem-driven discourse theory. More systematically, it is possible to distinguish between linguistic and non-linguistic, reactive and non-reactive data (as I have done in Figure 1), although these distinctions are pragmatic, rather than ontological. This means that the

| | Linguistic | Non-linguistic |
|---|---|---|
| Reactive | Interviews | Participant observation, action research |
| Non-reactive | Documents | Images, constructs, architectures |

*Figure 1*

distinction between the linguistic and the non-linguistic does not strictly overlap with the discursive/non-discursive or the verbal/non-verbal divisions, as both are internal components of the concept of discourse itself. In the language of semiotics and structural linguistics, an anti-war march or a prison modelled on Jeremy Bentham's (in)famous Panopticon are both differential signifiers of a discourse, as their identities are determined by their differences with and oppositions to other signifiers. Similarly, it is useful to distinguish between reactive and non-reactive sources, that is, those sources that presuppose an element of inter-subjectivity for their generation and those that do not, because they enable us to disclose different theoretical difficulties and questions. Again, however, this division is not synonymous with a sharp subject/object distinction, as both reactive and non-reactive sources have to be viewed within the meaningful systems which confer their identity and meaning; they thus both presuppose a passage through subjectivity.

In this sense, it is possible to treat *all data as text* (as Derrida does when he infamously claimed that '*[t]here is nothing outside the text*' (Derrida, 1976, p. 158, emphasis in the original). However, an important word of caution and clarification is required in this regard. Discourse theory needs, on the one hand, to guard against charges of linguistic reductionism, in which practices are merely the effects of texts, while on the other hand it must not conceive texts as purely epiphenomenal – as the effects of more objective and deeply rooted logics. Discourse theorists need in short to deal with texts at the appropriate levels of abstraction. Let us begin in this regard by reiterating the distinction between discourse analysis and discourse theory, in which the former consists of a range of techniques to analyse 'talk and text in context', while the latter provides the underlying assumptions for their appropriate employment. To rephrase the contrast in Heideggerian terms, discourse theory corresponds to the ontological level, where the concept of discourse specifies the necessary presuppositions of *any* inquiry into the nature of objects and social relations, while discourse analysis operates at the ontical level, and is concerned to analyse the particular objects specified by one's ontological presuppositions (Heidegger, 1962, pp. 31–5; see Mulhall, 1996, p. 4). More concretely, discourse in the first usage is an ontological category that specifies the interweaving of words and actions into practices, the contingency of all identity, the primacy of politics, and so forth, whereas in the second usage it is understood more narrowly as a set of symbolic representations and practices embodied in a range of texts, speeches and signifying sequences of all sorts. I turn now to a consideration of three issues that arise about the generation of textual data.

## The archive

The first concerns the construction of a documentary archive. Do we have to collect all possible documents or can we rely on a representative sample?

What are the criteria for selection? What are the problems in analysing documents and how can they be handled? In line with my methodological principles, there are very few general answers to these questions, as they can only be addressed in the light of the specific *problem* investigated. Whether or not we need to collect an exhaustive corpus of primary documents, or can rely on a representative sample, or even exemplary documents, will depend on the specification of the problem, as it is the latter which strongly determines the appropriate context and limits of a particular research project. A narrowly defined project focusing on a few texts may make an exhaustive archive feasible, indeed necessary, while a more extensive and open-ended research project usually excludes such an option. More open-ended research, which is characteristic of much discourse theory, raises questions about defining the appropriate context of study, as well as the criteria for selecting documents. With respect to the former, it is evident that the macroscopic nature of many discourse theoretical studies means that the researcher has to deal with multiple and overlapping contexts, as well as the infinite task of contextualizing the problem under consideration; as Derrida suggests there are no fully saturated contexts, as the traces of signifiers are always detectable in innumerable other contexts. Instead, the researcher is compelled to make decisions about the appropriate level and degree of contextualization and must establish the limits of any particular project. The key principles underpinning these decisions are that they must be explicit, consistent, and justified.

As to the criteria governing the selection of documents, they are similarly multiple and similarly constrained, as their choice is shaped by the purposes and methods of research. Take for instance a study into the character and evolution of a party's political ideology. Such research may combine quantitative methods designed to provide an initial picture of the overall patterns of discourse, while registering the presence of overwording, unusual collocations, and specific rhetorical figures. This may require a consistent and narrowly construed selection of documents, such as party manifestos or leaders' speeches in specific forums. Alongside this quantitative approach, the discursive analysis of a looser selection of pamphlets, politicians' writings, qualitative interviews, and so on may aim to uncover aspects surrounding the meaning, genesis, and dissemination of ideas, which are not easily detectable by quantitative methods. The texts selected in the latter case will be more the result of the researcher's intuitive judgements about their significance and meaning, rather than the more objective criteria of the former. Again, the principles of these multiple selection criteria are relative to the research problems and questions pursued, as well as the principles of publicity, consistency, and justifiability. The central injunction governing these reflections is not to give in to an unobtainable scientism, while simultaneously guarding against the usual positivist allegations that discourse theory relies upon anecdotal evidence and arbitrary choices of source.

### Qualitative interviews

The second issue concerns the role of qualitative interviewing (and ethnographic methods more generally) in generating data, and the problems associated with this practice. For an approach that stresses the importance of subjectivity in explaining social reality, and which seeks to provide 'thick descriptions' of events and processes, which are not readily achievable from a purely positivistic point of view, in-depth qualitative interviewing is an important means of generating primary texts. As with some other topics addressed in this section, a number of issues raised by the conduct and analysis of interview material has been covered by several contributors to the volume (see the chapters by Griggs, and Hansen and Sørenson in this volume). My discussion thus brackets questions about the selection of interviewees, the representativeness of their accounts, and the multiple functions they perform in executing research projects. It focuses instead on three important aspects relating to the position of the interviewee and her discourse (the object of the research); the role of the interviewer (the subject conducting research); and the complex relationships that arise between the object and subject of the interview process.

Let us begin with the series of issues that crystallize around the role and position of the interviewee.[7] Consider questions arising from interviews conducted with members of protest movements. They include, first, the problem of 'retrospective rationalizations' in which interviewees articulate well-rehearsed storylines that conform to the 'official versions' of the movement or oppositional group. For instance, it is well-known that participants in successful movements often erase difficulties and complexities in the name of seamless, teleological narratives that culminate in the realization of clearly defined goals, while activists in failed campaigns and movements are prone to stories of 'heroic failure' or 'leadership betrayal'. A second difficulty concerns hyperbolic representations of events and processes, in which the past or present is depicted too glowingly or too pessimistically, and where the role and contribution of the interviewee is often over-exaggerated or underplayed depending on the prevalent circumstances of the interview. A third difficulty centres on layers of potential information and discourse that often remain inaccessible to the interviewee. James Scott, for instance, draws attention to the existence of 'hidden transcripts' of resistance functioning beyond the 'direct observation' of 'powerholders', which consist of 'offstage speeches, gestures, and practices that confirm, contradict, or inflect what appears in the public transcript' (Scott, 1990, pp. 5–6). And although his empirical research skilfully endeavours to examine the *discrepancy* between the hidden and public discourses, he acknowledges the methodological difficulties of accessing and charting 'the entire concealed transcript' of resistance practices (Scott, 1985, p. 288).

In short, and generalizing from this example, we are confronted with the difficulty of validating and corroborating what is said in interviews, of analysing information which we believe either to be true or false, and of accessing information that remains deliberately or unintentionally hidden. There are a number of techniques and strategies that can potentially offset these problems. The technique of *triangulation* – comparing different sorts of data (quantitative or qualitative, primary and secondary) and different types of method (for example, interviews and textual analysis) to see whether they support one another – is useful in validating evidence obtained during interviews. Moreover, material which is shown to be false, distorted, or partial can and ought to be analysed precisely *because* of their inaccuracies and concealments. In other words, rather than being discarded or discounted they may themselves constitute important windows into actors' understandings and interpretations of events. Hyperbolic representations, omissions, over-wording, slips and unusual collocations thus constitute valuable points of condensation in an interview, which require closer inspection and analysis (see the chapters by Reyes and Stavrakakis in this volume). It goes without saying that psychoanalytic categories are extremely important in analysing such overdetermined symptoms. Finally, it is important to acknowledge the limits of the information gleaned from interviews, especially in cases where there are significant asymmetries of power, or where 'hidden transcripts' are more to the fore, and thus to supplement interview data with other sources such as primary documents (pamphlets, minutes of meetings, and so on), secondary interpretations, interviews from different places of enunciation, and so on.

A key issue with respect to the interviewer (or the subject conducting research) centres on 'the problem of preexisting paradigms', that is, the temptation to impose our own views on the interviewee in the form of leading questions designed to confirm our intuitions and hypotheses, assumptions that lead to infelicitous questions, or categories that result in the misinterpretation of the information gleaned. In this respect, Quentin Skinner (1969) has examined the deleterious effects of the myths of 'coherence' or 'prolepsis' where we are inclined to impute a false consistency onto the texts of political philosophy, or in this case the interviewee's discourse, or where we anticipate what is being said in ways that are congenial to our hypotheses and research designs. Instead, a critical reflexivity about one's theoretical assumptions and research project, while adopting an 'ethos of openness' to the other, are useful ways of guarding against the temptation to reduce the other's discourse to familiar and self-serving purposes. In short, it is to view the dialogical relationship between interviewer and interviewee not as a species of Habermas's 'ideal speech situation' designed to encounter irreducible asymmetries of power but an encounter in language with all the attendant difficulties post-structuralists have noted about communication in general.

**Non-linguistic data**

The final issue concerns the place of non-linguistic data within discourse theory. What are the principles and methods informing the selection and interpretation of observed actions, institutions, images, and physical objects? It is important to begin by recalling the claim that discourse theory regards all such data as internal components of a discourse. To use Heidegger's terms, they are elements of 'the worlds' in which the subjects of our research – and we as researchers – partake (Heidegger, 1962, pp. 91–5). This means that a 'thick description' of a practice or action, a strategy of participant observation, or an indepth interview occurs within such meaningful contexts, and the process of understanding and interpretation will be marked by their complex relationships to the objects of such worlds. As with other sorts of data discussed so far, our concern with such non-linguistic, non-reactive objects is by definition problem-dependent. This means that the selection of an image or building, as well as the point and purpose of interpreting such objects, is relative to the problems and research strategies employed.

In general, however, it is possible to specify two main types of research object in this regard. First, such objects can be viewed as essential components of the situation under analysis. For instance, a study of deliberative policy-making may pay special attention to the precise physical configurations of the rooms or places within which such deliberations take place, as they may disclose the latent or overt relations of power exercised by experts and officials over ordinary citizens. This is because the precise spatial positionings of the chair vis-à-vis expert witnesses, citizens, and public are the physical embodiments of the different 'places of enunciation' involved, and these spatial distributions are not neutral.

Secondly, such objects may be the principal objects of research themselves. For instance, in defending her claim that the organization of urban space into racially segregated living areas was critical to the reproduction of the racial state in South Africa, Jenny Robinson (1996) takes the layout and physical positioning of the African 'townships' or 'locations' surrounding Port Elizabeth as the principal objects of study. Drawing on Foucault's investigations into the spatial configurations of prisons, asylums, and hospitals in modern society, she shows how these physical manifestations of spatial ordering are deeply enmeshed in the dominant relations of power and discourse in South African society (Robinson, 1996, pp. 19–20). She concludes by demonstrating how the ordering of urban space in South Africa was intimately connected to the extension of surveillance, control and enhanced administrative capacity of the regime (Robinson, 1996, p. 63; see also Mitchell, 1991, pp. 63–94; Scott, 1998). The same may be true of other images, caricatures, buildings, and so on, which are either essential ingredients of a discursive ensemble or independently significant objects in their own right.

## Analysing text

Having clarified the way discourse theorists generate and conceive of empirical data in textual analysis, we can turn to the point and purpose of such analysis, as well as it is practised. As it has been repeatedly stressed, the practice of textual analysis cannot take place in the abstract, but is related to the specific instance of research undertaken. Nevertheless, it is possible to pinpoint three forms of textual analysis that are commonly employed by discourse theorists. These concern the analysis of meaning in texts (semantics), the role of rhetoric in bringing about certain effects, and the construction and role of subjectivity (pragmatics). I shall consider each in turn.

### The analysis of meaning

A central aim of textual analysis in discourse theory is to locate and analyse the mechanisms by which meaning is produced, fixed, contested, and subverted within particular texts. Many of these logics and mechanisms – logics of equivalence and difference, the production of floating and empty signifiers, iterability, and so forth – have already been discussed in earlier examples of analysis, and more attention will be paid to them in my discussion of subjectivity and rhetoric below. Hence it is not necessary to examine them again in this section. Instead, I want to concentrate on the legitimate and illegitimate employment of such logics in conducting textual analysis within the overall project of developing discourse-theoretical accounts.

Consider for instance a description that appears in an official South African Department of Information book that was published in 1973:

> In a nutshell, the inescapable feature of the South African situation is that South Africa is a country of many nations: Four million whites of European origin, four million Zulu, two million Tswana, two million Sotho and so on. Each group is a minority – there is in fact no single majority group.
>
> Each of the different black nations in South Africa, we believe, should have the opportunity to exercise its basic right to determine for itself its own future. Nothing should prevent each of these black nations from becoming independent in the fullest sense. They are being helped to reach that objective. (South African Department of Information, 1973, pp. 29–30)

This description of a country of many qualitatively different nations, and not a society divided along racial and class lines, or a single nation composed of internal differences, crystallizes the particular logics of difference and equivalence at play in South Africa during the 1960s and 1970s. That is to say, it points to the process by which the governing National Party had successfully managed to disarticulate the equivalent chains of protest established by the African National Congress during the 1950s and early 1960s, while spelling out the alternative ideology of ethnic and national particularity which characterized the 'separate development' ideal (see Norval, 1996). In representing the 'absent fullness' of South African society – what it lacked and how this lack was to be filled – terms such as 'apartheid', 'separate development', and 'self-determination' functioned as empty signifiers, which bound white South Africans together in opposition to the demands of African nationalism. In short, such statements are both exemplary representations of the macro-logic of 'Grand Apartheid', while constituting one local instance of its creation, and a close analysis of such texts enables the researcher to tease out the meaning and logic of the discourse under investigation.

Nonetheless, it is imperative *not* to conflate such paradigmatic representations of 'Grand Apartheid' with the system of practices – both 'micro' and 'macro' – that created such political frontiers and social spaces in the first place. Nor should these statements be seen to exhaust such political practices for this would be to assume that textual condensations are synonymous with the dense practices of identity formation and frontier creation, thus reducing practices to linguistic traces. Instead, a fully fledged analysis would have to describe and analyse the array of micro- and macro-practices – both 'linguistic' and 'non-linguistic' – that produced such divisions and conflicts, in which the textual analysis constitutes an internal component of the wider enterprise. In short, the narrow textual analysis of official documents, public statements, newspaper reports, party political manifestos, and so on constitutes only one aspect of a fully fledged discursive analysis. It needs always to be supplemented with indepth interviews, thick descriptions of practices and institutions, historical reconstructions of phenomena drawing on a range of empirical data, and so forth.

## Rhetoric

A related set of prefatory remarks is helpful in understanding the way rhetorical categories are used to analyse texts. On the one hand, rhetorical categories are an important means of fleshing out the ontology of discourse theory. On the other hand, they also constitute an important set of tools for analysing the construction and subversion of meaning. With respect to the former, for instance, the concept of a hegemonic practice is conceived as a *metonymical* operation in which a particular group or movement takes up demands articulated by contiguous groups (for example, a student movement begins to organize and address workers' demands), or extends one set of demands into adjacent spheres (workers' struggles come to symbolize the demands of an entire nation). By contrast, attention to the role of specific tropes such as metonyms or metaphors in a rhetorical analysis of politicians' speeches – for example, the usage of terms such as 'New Labour' and 'Labour' by Tony Blair and Gordon Brown respectively in their struggle to lead the Labour Party – operates at the ontical level and presumes the basic categories of discourse theory for its analysis.

At the ontical level, and so long as they are commensurate with its ontological assumptions, discourse theorists can draw freely upon a range of figures and devices to analyse texts and practices. For instance, discourse theorists can profit from Quentin Skinner's reactivation of Quintilian's technique of rhetorical redescription (*paradiastole*) to analyse struggles for hegemony. Skinner elaborates upon Quintilian's advice to those charged with presenting factual narratives to persuade a court of law, for example. The technique involves restating facts 'but not all in the same way', as the rhetorician 'must assign different causes, a different state of mind and a different motive for what was done' (Quintilian, cited in Skinner, 2002, p. 183). Of particular interest for discourse theorists is the substitution of a rival – yet neighbouring – evaluative term 'that serves to picture an action no less plausibly, but serves at the same time to place it in a contrasting light' (p. 183). Thus 'prodigality must be more leniently redescribed as liberality, avarice as carefulness, negligence as simplicity of mind' (Quintilian, cited in Skinner, 2002, p. 183). The logic of rhetorical redescription is thus useful to discourse theorists who wish to examine the way in which hegemonic battles involve constant endeavours to reframe issues and processes in ways that are conducive to a particular project.

## The construction of subjectivity

An important aspect of discourse theory concerns the way in which subjectivities are constructed in and through texts. In this regard, there are many compatible – or at least potentially compatible – theoretical language games that can assist in analysing the subjective dimension of discourse. At the outset, following post-structuralist conceptions of language elaborated by theorists such as Roland Barthes and Lacan, a useful heuristic distinction can be drawn between the statement (*énoncé*) and the act of saying or the enunciation (*énonciation*). This contrast allows us to focus either on what is said or written, in which the 'the subject of the enunciation' is treated as a finished product through which language speaks, or on the acts of saying or writing, in which the subject is constituted or subverted by the act itself.

The first focus is evident in Foucault's *Archaeology of Knowledge*, where he sets out a project for describing the statements of discourse at the level of 'things said' (Foucault, 1991, p. 63). Here Foucault isolates what he calls the 'enunciative modality' of a discursive formation – those conditions and rules that must be satisfied in a given order of discourse for a statement to qualify as meaningful and thus to constitute a candidate for truth and falsity. Take, for instance, the case of a text or statement produced by an academic expert for a public inquiry. In this regard, the conditions and rules of the enunciative modality centre on the subject's recognized training and specialization (Is she a properly trained and authorized scientist?), the 'institutional sites' from which she speaks (Does she speak from a legitimately constituted institution of learning?), and the 'subject position' from which appropriate and binding statements are made (Does she properly occupy the 'empty place' of 'the professor'?). For purposes of textual analysis, such an approach leads the researcher to inquire into the conditions under which subjects speak or write, the specific constraints to which they are subjected, the limit points which determine what can and cannot be said, as well as the different positions from which a subject can speak. Such an investigation enables the researcher to clarify what a subject means when she utters a statement, while also seeking to determine the available positions from which a subject can speak.

The second focus concerns the *act* of enunciating. With respect to this aspect of subjectivity in textual analysis, at least two fruitful avenues of research are opened up. On the one hand, research can centre on the *intentions* of those making or uttering statements. For example, Quentin Skinner's critique and reworking of traditional histories of ideas stresses the inadequacy of concentrating solely on the meaning of what a writer *said* about a particular doctrine or topic, by concentrating on 'the intended force with which the utterance is issued' (Skinner, 2002, p. 82). Borrowing from J. L. Austin's theory of speech acts, Skinner not only examines what writers say in a text, but investigates what they are *doing in* saying it. This task requires an analysis of the historical contexts within which such illocutionary acts take place, so as to reconstruct the background conventions and conditions against which the utterances can be interpreted. For discourse theorists, Skinner's focus is important in understanding the pragmatic dimension of language – what a subject is doing when saying something – and it is also useful in establishing and corroborating the meaning of what a subject says.

Equally, but from a different vantage point, a concern with what is said in a statement or political speech may blind us to the different ways in which certain speech acts are taken-up, 'lived-out', and acted upon by those who are addressed. That is to say, the actual words and meanings of a political address may be much less significant than *where* and *how* they are delivered, as well as their hidden surmises and cues. The latter aspect focuses on the place from which the addressee inscribes the enunciation, and he is led to ask: 'Why did the speaker say that to me?' 'What did she mean by it?' In short, the very enunciative act of a political leader addressing a deprived social group, or an embattled national minority, may produce effects that far exceed the actual content of the message delivered, as those addressed are moved more by the appeal than its meaning. Take for example a couple of statements made by Slobodan Milošević shortly after coming to power in Serbia in 1986. One of his first speeches was delivered at Kosovo Polje, a small village near Pristina, which is the actual site of the Battle of Kosovo, where the Serbs were defeated by the Turks in 1389. As is well documented, standing on a balcony and pointing to the Field of Blackbirds, Milošević addressed an angry crowd of Serbs with the words: 'Nobody, either now or in the future, has the right to beat you' (cited in Campbell, 1999, p. 152). He was later to state that 'My foot shall not touch the Kosovo ground as long as Kosovo is not free' (cited in Salecl, 1994, p. 217). The circumstances surrounding these apparently neutral and innocuous statements, and the hidden surmise of such enunciations, carried a clear political message for the embattled Serbians: 'liberate Kosovo from the Albanians by any means' (Salecl, 1994, p. 217). Indeed, one of the effects of such enunciating acts was the terrifying mobilization of a latent Serbian nationalism that few could have anticipated or planned in the 1980s and 1990s.

On the other hand, from a more fully fledged post-structuralist perspective, analysis can explore the character of subjectivity itself. Here attention is concentrated on the *difference* between what is said – the content of the text – and the act of saying itself, between what is called 'the subject of the enunciation' and 'the enunciating subject'. This is especially relevant from a psychoanalytic perspective, where an important research goal is to examine the way in which unconscious desires – in the form of slips, lapses, gaps, elisions, jokes, and so on – manifest themselves in, or interrupt, what is said. At the level of the said, these interruptions may be meaningless, but when interpreted they may divulge aspects of subjectivity concealed or disguised by the apparent meaning, or intended force, of a given speech act. From another perspective, a concern with the acting subject may transform the way we understand the meaning of what is said, thus making possible a new interpretation of a text. For instance, the very act of remembering past events by the subject in an indepth interview may alter both the subject of the enunciation and the previous content of the interview. Paying attention to patterns and instances of 'overwording', symbolic condensations and displacements, unusual expressions and lacunae in texts can thus lead to the uncovering of unconscious investments, surmises, or enjoyments not easily detectable by simply inspecting what is said in a speech, document, or interview. In short, by simply focusing on what is said in a text or speech – the presences or absences that might lack any immediate sense or meaning – or just endeavouring to work out a subject's intentions, the researcher can be blinded to the tensions, contradictions, and enjoyments at work in the subject itself.

## Conclusion

This chapter addresses a wide range of issues raised by methodological questions in discourse theory. More particularly, it pinpoints the problem of application in discourse theoretical studies, and elaborates a method of articulatory practice. The temptation in tackling such a vast topic is to say too much, and end up saying too little. There is also the trap of falling between those critics who view any reflection on method as complicit with positivism and method-driven research more generally, and those who see such reflections as insufficiently scientific and prescriptive. However, as my central aim is to provide a synoptic overview, which stimulates further discussion and clarification among discourse theorists, rather than achieving a premature (and false) closure, these criticisms are wide of the mark. As the contributors to this volume demonstrate, reflections about method within discourse theory are already part of an ongoing and open-ended conversation, and my reflections are designed to accelerate this discussion within discourse theory and post-Marxism more generally.

In this spirit, I want to conclude by enumerating some areas that require further attention. Among the topics discussed in this essay, the use of rhetorical categories and the analysis of subjectivity call for greater theoretical elaboration. While there is a growing interest in these issues, theoretical reflections remain at a protean stage. Another area which is broached in the chapter, but not fully developed, is the role of comparative research. Recent studies have shown that this is a potentially fruitful mode of empirical research for discourse theorists to engage in. On a theoretical level, however, the strategy remains underdeveloped. Two further areas in need of more theorization are the role of content and narrative analysis in interpreting texts. Once again, while these topics have been addressed and utilized by some researchers in discourse theory, the numerous theoretical, philosophical, and practical issues concerning the precise function, if any, of quantitative methods, the role of sampling, and the representativeness of the documents examined, as well as the relationship between narrative theory and discourse theory, remain to be clarified. With respect to generating information, the role of focus groups as a means of obtaining data as text has barely been touched upon, but there is no obvious theoretical reason why they should be excluded. Finally, psychoanalytical categories and methods are also underexplored in this essay. Psychoanalysis can help us to understand the relationship between theorists and their objects of research, especially with respect to interviewing and ethnographic techniques, where the logic of transference is to the fore, as well as the use of psychoanalytical categories and techniques to analyse and interpret texts.

## Notes

1. I would like to thank Steven Griggs, Aletta Norval, and Albert Weale for their comments and criticisms on earlier versions of this chapter. Special thanks to Jason Glynos and Jacob Torfing for their close readings and helpful remarks.
2. As this chapter focuses primarily on explanatory issues, the normative dimensions of discourse theory are excluded. Suffice to say that, on a normative level, discourse

theory does not propose a general and determinate set of ethical values, principles, and norms, which can be derived from its ontological presumptions. However, these assumptions do rule out certain possibilities, whether they be essentialist or foundationalist conceptions of the good which are grounded on God, natural law, or Reason, as well as purely instrumentalist or consequentialist normative schemas. More positively, the assumptions of discourse theory lead to the affirmation of values such as democracy, pluralism, and contingency. It is beyond the scope of this chapter to address these important issues in any more depth.

3. Popper (1989, p. 47) tends to make problem-solving an ontological postulate, which is coextensive with evolution itself, while Oakeshott (1962) objects to the technocratic and instrumentalist overtones of the concept.
4. To some degree, this is acknowledged by Winch, as part of his approach is precisely to supplement deficient understandings by employing 'external' theoretical and descriptive languages. However, these alternative languages are generally too formal and in need of far more elaboration to be of use in such an enterprise.
5. This claim has its roots in Nietzsche's notorious suggestion that 'there are no facts, only interpretations' (cited in Danto, 1965), as well as Husserl's injunction that it is necessary to reduce 'facts' to their 'sense', and 'the given' to its 'conditions of possibility' (Laclau, 1990, p. 213). Nietzsche's claim has, of course, to be qualified, as it does not reduce all facts to subjective perspectives (see Nehamas, 1985, pp. 62–73). Similarly, with respect to Husserl, it should be stressed that discourse theorists would not accept that 'sense' or meaning is fixed by a 'transcendental subject'. Instead, in keeping with the assumptions of discourse theory, meaning is essentially historical and contingent.
6. For example, Foucault's archaeological and genealogical methods of analysis involve the making of explicit and implicit comparisons between discursive formations, orders of discourse and systems of power/knowledge. Similarly, Quentin Skinner and James Tully's rethinking of the history of ideas deliberately analyse the past so as to cast light and open up possibilities in the present, as do Peter Winch and Hans-Georg Gadamer's 'hermeneutics of recovery', when they use comparative case studies to contextualize and decentre our apparently universal forms of life. Not only do these thinkers and theorists furnish a variety of reasons for engaging in comparative research, they also elaborate a range of methods, devices, techniques, and therapies to capture the comparative ethos and further its ends.
7. This discussion brackets for the time being questions about the *status* of the interviewee. As it is argued in my examination of subjectivity below, the interviewee is not taken to be the originator of an authentic discourse, but as the articulator of statements from a particular position of enunciation.

## Bibliography


Althusser, L. (1990) *Philosophy and the Spontaneous Philosophy of the Scientists* (London, Verso).

Campbell, G. (1999) *The Road to Kosovo* (Boulder, Westview Press).

Cioffi, F. (1998) *Wittgenstein on Freud and Frazer* (Cambridge, Cambridge University Press).

Connolly, W. E. (1981) *Appearance and Reality in Politics* (Cambridge, Cambridge University Press).

Connolly, W. E. (1987) *Politics and Ambiguity* (Madison, University of Wisconsin Press).

Connolly, W. E. (1995) *The Ethos of Pluralization* (Minneapolis, University of Minnesota Press).
Cox, R. (1981) 'Social Forces, States, and World Orders', *Millennium*, 10 (2), pp. 126–55.
Danto, A. (1965) *Nietzsche as Philosopher* (London, Macmillan).
Derrida, J. (1976) *Of Grammatology* (Baltimore, John Hopkins University Press).
Derrida, J. (1982) *Margins of Philosophy* (Brighton, Harvester Press).
Dreyfus, H. (1986), 'Why Studies of Human Capacities Modelled on Ideal Natural Science Can Never Achieve Their Goal', in J. Margolis, M. Krausz, and R. M. Burian (eds), *Rationality, Relativism and the Human Sciences* (Dordrecht, Martinus Nijhoff).
Flyvbjerg, B. (2001) *Making Social Science Matter: Why Social Inquiry Fails and How it Can Succeed Again* (Cambridge, Cambridge University Press).
Foucault, M. (1977) *Discipline and Punish* (Harmondsworth, Penguin Books).
Foucault, M. (1985) *The Use of Pleasure* (New York, Pantheon).
Foucault, M. (1991) 'Politics and the Study of Discourse', in G. Burchell, C. Gordon, and P. H. Miller (eds), *The Foucault Effect* (London, Harvester Wheatsheaf).
Giddens, A. (1976) *New Rules of Sociological Method* (London, Hutchinson).
Griggs, S., and Howarth, D. (2002) 'An Alliance of Interest and Identity? Explaining the Campaign against Manchester Airport's Second Runway', *Mobilization*, 7 (1), pp. 43–58.
Habermas, J. (1987) *The Philosophical Discourse of Modernity* (Cambridge, Polity).
Heidegger, M. (1962) *Being and Time* (Oxford, Basil Blackwell).
Howarth, D. (1997) 'Complexities of Identity/Difference: the Ideology of Black Consciousness in South Africa', *Journal of Political Ideologies*, 2 (1), pp. 51–78.
Howarth, D. (2000a) *Discourse* (Buckingham, Open University Press).
Howarth, D. (2000b) 'The Difficult Emergence of a Democratic Imaginary: Black Consciousness and Non-racial Democracy in South Africa', in D. Howarth, A. J. Norval, and Y. Stavrakakis (eds), *Discourse Theory and Political Analysis: Identities, Hegemonies and Social Change* (Manchester, Manchester University Press).
Howarth, D. (2002) 'Ethnic and Racial Identities in a Changing South Africa: the Limits of Social Science Explanation', *South African Historical Journal*, 46, pp. 250–74.
Howarth, D. (2004) 'A Heideggerian Social Science? Heidegger, Kisiel and Wiener on the Limits of Anthropological Discourse', *Anthropological Theory*, 4 (2), pp. 229–47.
Howarth, D. (2005) 'Hegemony, Subjectivity and Radical Democracy', in S. Critchley and O. Marchant (eds), *Laclau: a Critical Reader* (London, Routledge).
Jaworski, A., and Coupland, N. (eds) (1999) *The Discourse Reader* (London, Routledge).
Kuhn, T. (1970) *The Structure of Scientific Revolutions*, 2nd edn (Chicago, Chicago University Press).
Lacan, J. (2002) *Ecrits* (New York, Norton and Company).
Laclau, E. (1990) *New Reflections on the Revolution of Our Time* (London, Verso).
Laclau, E. (2000) 'Constructing Universality', in J. Butler, E. Laclau, and S. Žižek, *Contingency, Hegemony, Universality* (London, Verso).
Landman, T. (2000) *Issues and Methods in Comparative Politics* (London, Routledge).
Marx, K. (1973) *Grundrisse* (Harmondsworth, Penguin).
Marx, K. (1976) *Capital: a Critique of Political Economy*, Vol. 1 (Harmondsworth, Penguin).
Mitchell, T. (1991) *Colonising Egypt* (Cambridge, Cambridge University Press).
Mulhall, S. (1996) *Heidegger and* Being and Time (London, Routledge).
Nehamas, A. (1985) *Nietzsche* (Cambridge, Harvard University Press).
Norval, A. J. (1996) *Deconstructing Apartheid Discourse* (London, Verso).

Norval, A. J. (2004) 'Hegemony after Deconstruction: the Consequences of Undecidability', *Journal of Political Ideologies*, 9 (2), pp. 139–57.
Oakeshott, M. (1962) *Rationalism in Politics and Other Essays* (London, Methuen).
Popper, K. (1989) *Conjectures and Refutations*, 5th edn (London, Routledge).
Robinson, J. (1996) *The Power of Apartheid: State, Power and Space in South African Cities* (Oxford, Butterworth-Heinemann).
Said, E. (1995) *Orientalism*, 2nd edn (Harmondsworth, Penguin Books).
Salecl, R. (1994) 'The Crisis of Identity and the Struggle for New Hegemony in the Former Yugoslavia', in E. Laclau (ed.), *The Making of Political Identities* (London, Verso).
Scott, J. (1985) *Weapons of the Weak* (New Haven, Yale University Press).
Scott, J. (1990) *Domination and the Arts of Resistance: Hidden Transcripts* (New Haven, Yale University Press).
Scott, J. (1998) *Seeing like a State* (New Haven, Yale University Press).
Shapiro, I. (2002) 'Problems, Methods, and Theories in the Study of Politics', *Political Theory*, 30(4), pp. 596–619.
Skinner, Q. (1969) 'Meaning and Understanding in the history of ideas', *History and Theory*, 8, pp. 3–53.
Skinner, Q. (2002) *Visions of Politics*, Vol. 1 (Cambridge, Cambridge University Press).
Smith, A. M. (1994) *New Right Discourse on Race and Sexuality: Britain 1968–1990* (Cambridge, Cambridge University Press).
South African Department of Information (1973) *Progress through Separate Development: South Africa in Peaceful Transition* (Pretoria, South African Government Printer).
Staten, H. (1984) *Wittgenstein and Derrida* (Lincoln, Nebraska, University of Nebraska Press).
Taylor, C. (1971), 'Interpretation and the Sciences of Man', *The Review of Metaphysics*, 25 (1), pp. 3–51.
Taylor, C. (1981) 'Understanding and Explanation in the *Geisteswissenchaften*', in S. H. Holtzman and C. M. Leich (eds), *Wittgenstein: to Follow a Rule* (London, Routledge and Kegan Paul).
Taylor, C. (1985) *Philosophy and the Human Sciences, Philosophical Papers 2* (Cambridge, Cambridge University Press).
Torfing, J. (1999) *New Theories of Discourse* (Oxford, Blackwell).
Tully, J. (1995) *Strange Multiplicity: Constitutionalism in an Age of Diversity* (Cambridge, Cambridge University Press).
van Dijk, T. (1997a) *Discourse as Structure and Process* (London, Sage).
van Dijk, T. (1997b) *Discourse as Social Interaction* (London, Sage).
Weber, M. (1949) *The Methodology of the Social Sciences* (New York, Free Press).
Winch, P. (1990) *The Idea of a Social Science and Its Relation to Philosophy*, 2nd edn (London, Routledge).
Wittgenstein, L. (1953) *Philosophical Investigations* (Oxford: Basil Blackwell).
Wittgenstein, L. (1977) *Remarks on Colour* (Oxford, Basil Blackwell).
Wittgenstein, L. (1979) 'Remarks on Frazer's *Golden Bough*', in C. G. Luckhardt (ed.), *Wittgenstein: Sources and Perspectives* (Sussex, Harvester).
Wodak, R., and Meyer, M. J. (2001) *Methods of Critical Discourse Analysis* (London, Sage).
Žižek, S. (1994) 'The Spectre of Ideology', in S. Žižek (ed.), *Mapping Ideology* (London, Verso).

# Index